Model Driven Engineering
and Ontology Development

T0140295

Dragan Gašević · Dragan Djurić · Vladan Devedžić

Model Driven Engineering and Ontology Development

Second Edition

Foreword to First Edition by Bran Selic
Foreword to Second Edition by Jean Bézivin

 Springer

Dr. Dragan Gašević
School of Computing and
   Information Systems
Athabasca University
1 University Drive
Athabasca, AB T9S 3A3
Canada
dgasevic@acm.org

Dr. Dragan Djurić
University of Belgrade
FON – School of Business
   Administration
Department of Information
   Systems and
Jove Ilica 154
11000 Belgrade
Serbia
dragandj@gmail.com

Prof. Vladan Devedžić
University of Belgrade
School of Business
   Administration
Dept. Information Systems &
   Technologies
Jove Ilica 154
11000 Belgrade
Serbia
devedzic@fon.rs

ISBN 978-3-642-10134-2   e-ISBN 978-3-642-00282-3
DOI 10.1007/978-3-642-00282-3
Springer Dordrecht Heidelberg London New York

Cover design: KuenkelLopka GmbH

Printed on acid-free paper

Springer is part of Springer Science+Business Media (www.springer.com)

To our families

Foreword to the 2nd Edition

In the young history of informatics, this book tells yet another story of connecting the world and the machine. Our discipline continuously attempts to create precise mathematical models of the world around us and of the basic mechanisms of our networked computer systems. These models have different properties that make them more or less appropriate to different goals. Their objective is not only to understand the word, but to help complement it and act on it. The main challenge is the alignment between the business system and the technical platform system. Many organizations struggle to meet their evolving business needs and goals in explicit and precise relation to their underlying technical information system. Shared abstract notations allow descriptions of both situations with common formalisms.

In the sixties and seventies, computer science pioneers proposed to bridge the problem space and the solution space through low-level constructs like procedures. Methods like top-down programming, or step-wise refinement, helped achieving this coupling. In the eighties, the object paradigm was found to be practical and efficient in describing the business side and the technical platform side at the same time. This has certainly triggered more work to study even richer abstractions based on different additional and combined paradigms like rules, relations, events, states, functions, services, and many more. Ways to accommodate multiparadigm systems have been investigated. Many tree-based notations have been proposed with XML technologies. The scope of this book, however, is that of graph-based notations like model-driven engineering or ontology engineering. One of the lessons it teaches is that there may not be a unique ideal abstraction to bridge the world problem space and the machine solution space. On the contrary, we may well have to live with different abstraction frameworks, different representation systems, and different technical or modeling spaces.

While there are some other books on similar subjects, this one is unique for several reasons. Instead of opposing different technologies or schools, it tries to understand them, to characterize them, to compare them, and finally to bridge them so that one may be able to use them in simultaneous or alternative ways when solving real problems. Technologies have to be agilely combined to contribute to solutions in a collaborative way. This book offers not only high-level conceptual presentations, but also implementation-level coverage of the presented technologies, and even hands-on guidance for their joint or separate applications to practical cases.

The authors take the reader through the entire presentation of the multiple facets of model-driven engineering and ontology engineering. They provide a wonderful pedagogical work that clearly and progressively introduces the main concepts, and their contribution may be recommended as an excellent introductory textbook on both technologies. They give an understanding of why and how these solutions may be concretely used in problem-solving and this itself is of tremendous interest to the researcher, the engineer, or the student that will read the book. Beyond these separate presentations, however, they relate them both conceptually and practically; and this is a complete originality of their contribution. The message is not about a silver bullet revealed, but instead about how different conceptual tools may be wisely selected and applied to achieve optimal solutions. New technologies are arriving on the market at a very rapid pace. It is hard to choose between them. Furthermore, as an organization accumulates assets in its information system, new technologies constantly emerge that seem to make previous ones obsolete. Technology interoperability must now be seriously considered. In this book, the authors have successfully performed a clever balancing act by producing a coherent and comprehensive guide on two technical spaces and a bridging framework that is well-grounded, both conceptually and practically. But the main message is that their method may also be generalized and applied to other technical spaces as well, and I am sure this will provide much inspiration for further work.

Finally, the reader will discover that the authors are presenting important variants of language engineering. Modeling languages and programming languages, general purpose languages, and domain-specific languages are becoming central to software engineering, to data engineering, and to system engineering. We know that the number of computer-based applications that will have to be built for various needs in upcoming decades is exponentially increasing. However, the number of professional computer scientists that will be available to produce these applications will follow a very slow linear progression. The only way out of this difficult situation is to mobilize computer scientists to not directly build the applications, but to provide the numerous domain languages that may guide end users to write precise and verifiable domain code themselves. At the end of this book, the reader will realize that she/he is now much more prepared to face these important new challenges of language engineering.

Nantes, France   *Jean Bézivin*
February 2009

Foreword to the 1st Edition

The first time I paid attention to the term "ontology" was in the late 1980s when I was part of an engineering team that was responsible for defining what we would now call a domain-specific modeling language. In our case, the domain was telecommunications software and the purpose of our language was to give system architects the ability to describe the high-level structure of their software in the most direct and most expressive manner possible.

The team members were all experienced designers with deep knowledge of the domain so that we had no trouble putting together the initial list of key language concepts. We knew that we needed to include standard architectural modeling constructs such as components, ports, connectors, and the like. We also wanted our language to be object-oriented, so notions such as class, objects, and inheritance were added to the list. However, soon after this very promising start, all progress ground to a halt. Somehow, the definition of the seemingly trivial fine-grain details of these constructs kept eluding us despite long, passionate, and occasionally acrimonious discussions that can only be compared to medieval theological debates.

It was our good fortune that at that point we met Professor Doug Skuce of the University of Ottawa. He had a method and a tool that helped us develop an explicit ontology for our domain. From that exercise we learned that our difficulties stemmed from the fact that, although we shared a general intuition for the chosen constructs of our language, there were numerous subtle and *unstated* differences in our individual conceptualizations that were a barrier to mutual understanding. Furthermore, we discovered that certain commonly used terms had multiple meanings—all equally valid—but which we had not differentiated adequately, leading to much confusion. Only after we had defined our ontology, which included semi-formal definitions of all key terms and their relationships, were we able to finish our task successfully.

Ever since, I've felt that defining a formal domain ontology is a useful and often necessary step in almost any software project. This is because software deals principally with ideas rather than physical artifacts. Whereas the nature of physical artifacts is generally self-evident, this is not the case with conceptual entities, which are products of the mind. As we all know, different minds see the same thing differently.

The definition and application of ontologies for developing software systems is a central theme of this book. However, the book is about much more than that. It explains, in a clear and didactic manner, how a variety of recent buzzword developments in software theory and practice (intelligent agents, Model Driven Architecture, metamodeling, etc.) can be combined, and brings us to the threshold of the next step in the evolution of the World Wide Web: the *Semantic Web*. Like the Internet before it, the Semantic Web promises to introduce a significant and qualitatively new phenomenon into our lives. This is because it endows the network of disparate information that is currently accessible on the Internet with *meaning*. Because this meaning can be gleaned and processed *automatically* by software, the Semantic Web opens up the exciting and awe-inducing possibility of a unified global intelligence accessible to all.

In the first half of the book, the authors navigate deftly through the prolific and highly confusing *gemüscht* of technologies, tools, and standards such as XML, RDF, OWL, MDA, and UML, and explain how they relate to each other in the context of the idea of the Semantic Web. They introduce the notion of *modeling spaces*, which provides a conceptually simple yet comprehensive framework for understanding and addressing issues within the domain considered. Using that framework, the second half of the book describes a practical strategy for realizing key elements of the Semantic Web based on existing industry standards.

The book is equally suited to those who merely want to be informed of the relevant technological landscape, to practitioners dealing with concrete problems, and to researchers seeking pointers to potentially fruitful areas of research. The writing is technical yet clear and accessible, and is illustrated throughout with useful and easily digestible examples.

I would also highly recommend this book to sociologists studying the interplay between society and technology. It clearly demonstrates that the core technologies required for constructing the Semantic Web are available and moving forward inexorably. Society must be prepared to deal with something so ripe with potential. We must understand not only how the Semantic Web can be useful but also what dangers lurk within it.

Ottawa, Canada   *Bran Selic*
December 2005

Preface

The idea of ontologies emerged in applied artificial intelligence some time ago as a means for sharing knowledge (Gruber 1993). Following the development of ontologies and related Web technologies (e.g., HTML and XML), Tim Berners-Lee, Jim Hendler, and Ora Lassila envisioned the next generation of the Web, called the Semantic Web (Berners-Lee et al. 2001). Being based on ontologies, the Semantic Web has the potential for semantically richer representations of things (e.g., Web pages, applications, and persons) and their relations on the Web, and thus should provide us with more intelligent services. That idea might have initially sounded very futuristic and too enthusiastic, but it has recruited a lot of important players from both academia and industry into very extensive and well-funded research efforts. Today, we have quite impressive results, manifested by standards that have been adopted (RDF and OWL), development frameworks (Jena), best-practice and deployment recommendations, and many applications (e.g., PiggyBank).

Of course, researchers are still facing many challenges in their efforts to realize the full vision of the Semantic Web. Probably the first and most important goal is to persuade many industrial developers and software engineers to use and develop ontologies in their everyday practice. However, ontologies rely on well-defined and semantically powerful concepts in artificial intelligence, such as description logics, reasoning, and rule-based systems. Since software engineers are largely unfamiliar with these concepts, ontologies have a price that must be paid for the benefits that they provide.

Trying to address the above problems, researchers have started exploring the potential of some widely adopted software engineering tools and methodologies for ontology development. Stephen Cranefield did the pioneering research by proposing that UML, a well-known software modeling language, should be used for ontology development (Cranefield 2001a). After him, several researchers have explored further the similarities, differences, and equivalences between UML and ontology languages, as well as the potential of the most recent software engineering initiative called the Model Driven Architecture (MDA), and its accompanying standards, the Meta-Object Facility (MOF) and XML Metadata Interchange (XMI), for ontology development (Baclawski et al. 2002a; Djurić et al. 2005a; Falkovych et al. 2003). This resulted in the initiation of a process for adopting an MDA-based ontology standard by the Object Management Group (OMG), a software engineering standardization consortium (OMG ODM RFP 2003).

In this book we try to fill the gap in the literature covering the subject of applications of the MDA for ontology development on the Semantic Web. Other books cover either the MDA initiative (Kleppe et al. 2003; Mellor et al. 2003b) or the Semantic Web (i.e., ontology development) only (Fensel 2004; Stuckenschmidt and van Harmelen 2005; Zhong et al. 2003). This book gives a comprehensive overview of both themes, with the main emphasis on how we can employ MDA-related standards to develop Semantic Web ontologies. The book is closely related to the recent OMG initiative for the ODM; it is the first description of that new language.

The book is based on our experience obtained from a series of tutorials entitled "MDA Standards for Ontology Development" that we have given at several international conferences on the Semantic Web (the International Semantic Web Conference, the European Semantic Web Conference, and the International World Wide Web Conference) and on software engineering (the International UML Conference and the International Conference of Web Engineering).

What Happened Since the First Edition?

Since the publication of the first edition of the book, there has been a lot of research done in the areas of the Semantic Web and the MDA. Here, we highlight a few of the most notable initiatives and results:

- The OMG adopted the final specification of the ODM document (OMG ODM 2007). While the ODM is not an official standard yet, the final adopted specification is an important sign signaling the end of the journey in achieving the initial goals set up in the OMG's ODM request for proposals (OMG ODM RFP 2003). Moreover, there have been first tools that implement the emerging standard.
- Several research groups started looking into the research challenges that are going beyond the scope of the ODM. These include exploration of the use of the ODM with software modeling languages; metamodeling of Semantic Web rule languages (e.g., Semantic Web Rule Language and Rule Interchange Format); transforming between rule and constraints used in software engineering and the Semantic Web; and developing ontology reasoners.

- Social technologies and their wide adoption made a significant impact on the research related to the Semantic Web. One of the most notable ones is related to knowledge capture through the use of mechanisms such as collaborative tagging, folksonomies, and social networking. This certainly opens new ways in which ontologies are developed, used, and evolved.
- The software modeling community came closer to the organization and definition of a new software engineering discipline. Model Driven Engineering (MDE) is now a widely adopted term that refers to the area of software modeling, model-driven language definitions (i.e., metamodeling), and model transformations. Looking from this MDE broader perspective, the MDA is just one metamodeling architecture along with the set of OMG standards. Similarly, there is the Eclipse Modeling Framework (EMF), which also provides its own set of languages similar to those of the OMG. As well, the MDE research community very much advanced the area of model transformations and their tooling support. Doubtless, this is also an important step toward the reconciliation of the MDE and Semantic Web paradigms.

Second Edition

The major goal of the second edition is to reflect the above changes and provide an up-to-date perspective on the state of the art in this area. Probably the most notable change is that of the book's title. As explained in the last bulleted point above, we felt that the earlier title *Model Driven Architecture and Ontology Development* does not reflect the scope of the book properly. Therefore, we renamed the book *Model Driven Engineering and Ontology Development*.

Besides these changes, let us also mention that the Semantic Web community has started working on the development of OWL 2, the next version of the Web Ontology Language (OWL). However, the state of the OWL development is still in the early stages at the time of writing this edition (December 2008). This is the reason why OWL 2 considerations and the OWL 2 metamodel definitions are not included in this edition. Knowing that the OWL 2 working documents are also using metamodeling, we are certain that future editions of this book will have a lot of exciting results to report on.

Organization, Structure, and Changes

The book is divided into three parts. Part I covers the basics of both the main topics—ontologies and the MDA. First, Chap. 1 gives a brief overview of the field of knowledge representation in artificial intelligence. Chapters 2 and 3 introduce the main concepts of ontologies, the Semantic Web, standards, applications, tools, and some open research questions. The major changes in Chap. 2 are related to the examples of ontologies for social networking, and explanation of the Social Web principles of knowledge capture. Chapter 4 has probably undergone the biggest changes, in order to broaden its initial focus only on the Model Driven Architecture, and its main standards (the MOF and XMI) and mechanisms (UML profiles). Now this chapter also introduces the basic principles of model driven engineering, discusses other metamodeling platforms, and defines model transformation and constraint languages. Part I is concluded by Chap. 5 with modeling spaces, a conceptual framework defined to provide an easier understanding of approaches to modeling, such as ontologies and MOF-defined modeling languages (UML and the ODM).

Part II is the central part of the book. It starts with Chap. 6, which presents a comprehensive review of several approaches and tools that aim to bridge the gap between ontology development and software engineering methodologies. This chapter also lists the relations between UML and ontology languages, and shows the research results on metamodeling of Semantic Web rule languages. Chapter 7 explains the motivation for the forthcoming OMG ontology development standard for the ODM, and the requirements the standard has to fulfill. Next, Chaps. 8 and 9 describe the current specifications of the OMD and the Ontology UML Profile, respectively. Finally, Chap. 10 analyzes the mappings between MDA-based languages (the ODM and the OUP) and Semantic Web ontology languages.

Part III is dedicated to applications that will support the practical use of languages that conform to the OMG ontology development standard, and to some practical aspects of how to develop ontologies using those MDA-based languages. First, Chap. 11 is a short tutorial showing how to develop ontologies using the OUP in two state-of-the-art UML tools (MagicDraw and Poseidon for UML). The new version of this chapter also introduces the Atlas Transformation Language (ATL) and provides basic information about its tooling support. Chapter 12 describes an implementation of an ontology-building platform called AIR, developed entirely following MDE principles. Chapter 13 discusses two examples of ontologies developed using the OUP and MDA standards. Finally, we added Chap. 14, which provides an insight into the research that goes beyond the scope of the ODM specification and metamodel-based definition of ontology language. It provides insights into model driven engineering of ontology development tools and reasoners as well as integration of Semantic Web rule languages with software modeling.

Throughout the book, we use many ontologies, UML and other MDA-based models, and transformations between them. In order to allow you to try them out and use them in practice, we have created a Web page containing supplementary resources. You can reach this Web page at http://www.modelingspaces.org. Besides the resources referred to in the book, this Web page contains the slide handouts of the tutorials that we have given at many international conferences.

Acknowledgments

Some of the content of this book has been previously published by organizations that are not part of the Springer group. We thank these organizations for their kind permission to use the material for this book; in particular:

- IEEE Press,
- Rinton Press,
- Journal of Educational Technology & Society, and
- Journal of Object Technology.

We are very grateful to Jelena Jovanović, Nenad Krdžavac, and Colin Knight for a huge amount of help in preparing the first edition of the book and for giving us many useful comments and suggestions. We very much appreciate the great help of Milan Milanović in preparting this second revision. We are also very thankful to Adrian Giurca, Sergey Lukichev, Marko Ribarić, and Gerd Wagner for great research collaboration that very much inspired changes made in this edition. We would also like to thank all the members of the GOOD OLD AI research group (http://goodoldai.org.yu) at the University of Belgrade, Serbia and Montenegro, for providing us with a great environment and many useful ideas that enormously improved the quality of the book. Dragan Gašević is very grateful to Tom Calvert, Marek Hatala, Kinshuk, Rory McGreal, and Griff Richards for their great support and understanding. In addition, Dragan Gašević is very grateful to the Natural Sciences and Engineering Research Council of Canada, the Alberta Ingenuity Fund, and Athabasca University, for their continuing research funding support.

We thank Bran Selic for agreeing to write the book's foreword. A special mention should be given to Ralf Gerstner of Springer, who invited us to write this book, motivated us to work on its revision, and had a lot of patience in working with us. We are very thankful to Evan Wallace, Elisa Kendall, Bob Colomb, Anna Gerber, Dan Chang, Lewis Hart, and other colleagues from the OMG's Ontology PSIG for giving us up-to-date information about the OMG's ODM standardization efforts in the last six years.

Vancouver, Canada   *Dragan Gašević*
Belgrade, Serbia   *Dragan Djurić*
Belgrade, Serbia   *Vladan Devedžić*
December 2008

Contents

Part II Model Driven Engineering and Ontologies

Part III Applications

Part I Basics

1 Knowledge Representation

Knowledge is understanding of a subject area (Durkin 1994). It includes concepts and facts about that subject area, as well as relations among them and mechanisms for how to combine them to solve problems in that area.

The branch of computer science that studies, among other things, the nature of human knowledge, understanding, and mental skills is artificial intelligence (AI). The goal of AI is to develop computer programs to do the things that humans usually call "intelligent."

There are dozens of definitions of AI in the literature, none of them being complete and all-encompassing. The reason for such incompleteness is the complexity of the phenomenon of intelligence. Still, the study of human knowledge and its representation in computers is so very central in AI that even some definitions of the discipline recognize that fact. For example:

> AI is the branch of computer science that attempts to approximate the results of human reasoning by organizing and manipulating factual and heuristic knowledge. (Bandwidth Market 2008)

> Artificial intelligence. The range of technologies that allow computer systems to perform complex functions mirroring the workings of the human mind. Gathering and structuring knowledge, problem solving, and processing a natural language are activities possible by an artificially intelligent system. (e-Learning Guru 2008)

It is said that AI aims at making programs that represent, encode, and process knowledge about problems—facts, rules, and structures—rather than the data of problems.

The objective of this chapter is to survey some of the most important concepts and principles of knowledge representation. The chapter takes a pragmatic approach—rather than providing a comprehensive study of all aspects of knowledge representation, it covers only those that lay the foundations for understanding the rest of the book.

D. Gašević et al., *Model Driven Engineering and Ontology Development*, 2nd edn.,
DOI 10.1007/978-3-642-00282-3_1, © Springer-Verlag Berlin Heidelberg 2009

1.1 Basic Concepts

In AI, *knowledge storing* is the process of putting knowledge, encoded in a suitable format, into computer memory. *Knowledge retrieval* is the inverse process—finding knowledge when it is needed. *Reasoning* means using knowledge and problem-solving strategies by means of an intelligent program to obtain conclusions, inferences, and explanations. An important prerequisite for these processes is *knowledge acquisition*—gathering, organizing, and structuring knowledge about a topic, a domain, or a problem area, in order to prepare it for putting into the system.

AI studies the above processes starting from observations of the human mind's intelligent activities. For example, a person who has never had an experience with handheld computers may happen to take one in his/her hand. The person may examine it for a while, learn how to "play" with it, and memorize the experience, as well as the handheld's features. Memorizing (knowledge storing) involves abstraction and modeling. The person's mind will somehow store all the essential features of the handheld computer, and will be able to retrieve that knowledge later when he/she takes the handheld computer to work with it again. Moreover, if he/she has had experience with desktop or laptop computers before, he/she will probably get along with the handheld more easily by reasoning about its possible features.

Unlike the human mind, computers do not have such a transparent mechanism for acquiring and representing knowledge internally, just by themselves (Arnold and Bowie 1985). They rely on humans to put the knowledge into their memories. It is then the task of humans to decide on how to represent knowledge inside computers.

So far, AI has come up with a number of different representations, or models of various *types of human knowledge* (see Sect. 1.3). Each one is associated with a method to structure and encode knowledge in an intelligent system, and a specific related data structure (such as a table, a tree, or a link). None of them is perfect or the best. Each representation and each data structure has some deficiencies that make it inadequate for representing all kinds of knowledge. Moreover, careful selection of a knowledge representation may simplify problem solving, whereas an unfortunate selection may lead to difficulties or even failure to find a solution. Complex problems require a combination of several different representations.

The above paragraphs raise the question: What is the theory behind knowledge representation? An incomplete and vague, but good approximate answer is: cognitive science. *Cognitive science* is the interdisciplinary study of mind and intelligence, embracing philosophy, psychology, artificial intelligence, neuroscience, linguistics, and anthropology (Stanford Encyclopedia of Philosophy 2008). One of the key issues in cognitive science is the study of human thinking in terms of representational structures in the mind, and computational procedures that operate on those structures (Hofstadter 1994). An important hypothesis is that the human mind has *mental representations* analogous to computer data structures. Moreover, cognitive science assumes that the computational procedures of the mind are similar to computational algorithms. There are a number of approaches in this field of study, and there is no consensus about the nature of the representations and computations that constitute thinking.

Different mental representations of the human mind, as proposed by cognitive theorists—such as logical propositions, rules, concepts, images, and analogies—constitute the basis of different *knowledge representation techniques* (e.g., rules, frames, and logic; see Sect. 1.4). Each technique has advantages and disadvantages for capturing particular types of human knowledge. This is so because each representation technique emphasizes certain information about a topic or a problem, while ignoring other information (Hofstadter 1994).

A special category of techniques is used to represent *inexact and uncertain knowledge* about the world. Human expressions such as "That's probably true" imply a certain *degree of belief* in a fact or event that is being talked about. In other words, much human knowledge is not absolutely certain; on the contrary, it is often inexact, imprecise, and incomplete. The techniques used to represent such knowledge are typically based on probability theory, the theory of evidence, and fuzzy-logic theory.

In order to be practical, every knowledge representation technique needs a *notation*. A formal notation often used for representing knowledge is *first-order predicate calculus*. Of course, it is not suitable for all types of knowledge. The notation of *description logics* has also proven expressive enough to represent knowledge formally. More recently, the trend has been to use XML syntax for representing knowledge structures.

Starting from various notations, AI researchers have developed a number of *knowledge representation languages* to support various representation techniques. Being artificial languages, knowledge representation languages usually have precisely defined grammars to help the parsing of expressions in these languages and ease the machine processing of the knowledge represented. However, ease of parsing sometimes comes at the expense of human readability.

Note that knowledge representation and intelligent reasoning are always intertwined, both in the human mind and in AI (Minsky 1985; Russell and Norvig 2002). The mind uses mental representations of the world and mental procedures such as deduction, search, matching, rotation, and retrieval to make inferences about the world. Likewise, AI reasoners use encoded knowledge and inference procedures to solve problems.

This intertwining makes it possible to answer the fundamental question: What is knowledge representation? Davis et al. (1993) answer this question by discussing five different roles of a knowledge representation.

The first role of a knowledge representation is to serve as a *surrogate*, i.e., a *substitute* for things from the real world inside an intelligent entity. Typically, things from the real world are external to the reasoner, whereas the corresponding representations are internal to it. Internal representations enable reasoning to substitute for direct interaction with the world. Operations on representations substitute for operations on real-world things. Being surrogates and only approximations/models of reality, all knowledge representations are inevitably imperfect in terms of completeness, which may lead to incorrect reasoning.

The second role of a knowledge representation is *making a set of ontological commitments* about the real world. By expressing only a part of the information about the world and ignoring the rest, knowledge representation also makes a kind of selection: it determines what the intelligent system can "see" in the world, and to what it remains "blind." In fact, it is the knowledge representation that brings in focus the aspects of the world that are believed to be relevant. For example, a representation of the human hand may include details of its anatomy, but omit completely any knowledge of its function. This representation may be encoded in various languages and using various notations; however, the essential part is not the form but the content.

This is not to say that the form is irrelevant to ontological commitment. On the contrary, the very selection of the representation used to encode a piece of knowledge implies commitments and constraints. Rules, logic, frames, etc., all embody a point of view about the kinds of things that are important in the world, i.e., commitments about what to see in it. Rules imply inference logic about object–attribute–value triplets, whereas frames bring objects and their interactions into view.

The third role of a representation is as a *fragmentary theory of intelligent reasoning*. Every representation indicates at least a partial belief about how people reason intelligently and what it means to reason intelligently. Furthermore, there is a set of conclusions that an intelligent system is permitted to draw for each particular representation; this set is usually very large and insufficiently constrained for practical purposes. On the other hand, there is also an indication of which inferences are appropriate to draw for each representation, i.e., the intelligent inferences. Finally, every representation typically incorporates only a part of the complex phenomenon of intelligent reasoning.

The fourth role of a knowledge representation is as a *medium for efficient computation*. That is to say, to use a representation a machine must compute with it, which makes computational efficiency a central issue in the notion of representation. To this end, it should be noted that every representation, by its nature, provides some guidance about how to organize knowledge in order for computation with it to be most efficient. For example, frames are suitable for taxonomic reasoning. Hence organizing them into taxonomic hierarchies increases the reasoning efficiency. Other representations may suggest different organizations of knowledge.

A knowledge representation is also a *medium for human expression*, which is its fifth role. Recall that, in the course of knowledge acquisition, humans (knowledge engineers) gather, organize, and store knowledge in the knowledge base of an intelligent system. To do so, humans have to create and communicate representations to machines and to each other. In that process, questions such as the following arise: How general is the representation used? How precise is it? How expressive? How suitable is it as a language for communication? How easy is it for humans to think or "talk" in that language? What kinds of things are easy to express in that language? And so on.

1.2 Cognitive Science

In brief, cognitive science studies the nature of the mind. More precisely, it studies cognition—mental states and processes such as thinking, reasoning, remembering, language understanding and generation, visual and auditory perception, learning, consciousness, and emotions (Clark 2001). In addition to the theoretical goal of understanding human thinking, cognitive science can have the practical goal of improving it, which requires normative reflection on what we want thinking to be (Stanford Encyclopedia of Philosophy 2008).

Historically, cognitive science and AI have developed in parallel. In the mid 1950s, experimental psychology was dominated by behaviorism, a view that psychology should restrict itself to examining the relation between observable stimuli and observable behavioral responses. Internal mental states and processes were completely neglected by behaviorists, which was a view that virtually denied the existence of the mind. Cognitive science appeared as a reaction to that position—its view was that mental states and processes actually mediate between input stimuli and output responses. It was suggested that information in the mind is encoded in *chunks*, mental representations that require mental procedures for encoding and decoding the information. From the very beginning, the mind–computer analogy became dominant in cognitive science:

> The mind is to the brain as software is to hardware. Mental states and processes are like computer programs implemented in brain states and processes. (Rapaport 2000)

The interdisciplinary nature of cognitive science is best reflected in its diverse research methodology. For cognitive psychologists, the primary method is *experimentation with human participants*. People (usually undergraduate students) are brought to the laboratory to study their mental processes (e.g., the mistakes they typically make in deductive reasoning, their performance when solving problems using analogies, the way they form and apply concepts, and so on) under controlled conditions. Another set of methods has been developed by researchers interested in *computational models* that simulate aspects of human performance: these researchers form and test models intended to be analogous to mental operations. The third kind of contribution to the rich methodology of cognitive science originated from linguists. Linguists are interested in *identifying grammatical principles* that provide the basic *structure of human languages*. They start from noticing subtle differences between grammatically correct and incorrect phrases. Neuroscientists' research is based on *observing what is happening in various parts of the brain* while people are doing various mental tasks. In their experiments with nonhuman subjects, neuroscientists can insert electrodes and record the firing of individual neurons. With humans, the methods are noninvasive and include various kinds of magnetic and positron-based scanning devices to observe what is happening in different parts of the brain while people are doing mental tasks such as mental imagery and word interpretation. Cognitive anthropologists examine human thinking to consider *how thought works in different cultural settings* (Stanford Encyclopedia of Philosophy 2008).

It should be stressed that the philosophy of the mind is also important to cognitive science, although it does not have a distinct method. Philosophy shares its theoretical work with that in other fields, and is also concerned with empirical results. It deals with questions such as the nature of representation and computation, the relation between mind and body, and the nature of explanations.

The best work in cognitive science comes from combining methods from different disciplines. For example, cognitive psychology and AI can be combined through computational models of how people behave in experiments.

The best way to grasp the complexity of human thinking is to use multiple methods, especially psychological and neurological experiments and computational models. Theoretically, the most fertile approach has been to understand the mind in terms of representation and computation. (Stanford Encyclopedia of Philosophy 2008)

Two of the most widely used computational paradigms for describing mental representations and the processes of the mind in cognitive science are the *symbolic* and *connectionist* paradigms. In the symbolic paradigm, the mind exists as a physically implemented "symbol system," i.e., an implementation of an effectively computable procedure (a universal machine). An important hypothesis here is that a physical system is capable of intelligent behavior if and only if it is a physical symbol system. In other words, intelligent systems can manipulate symbols through a variety of mental states and procedures; and, vice versa, physical symbol systems are capable of being intelligent systems.

The connectionist paradigm is inspired by physical neurons and their connections in the human brain. Physical neurons are modeled as specific interconnected data structures and processors—artificial neurons—and there are corresponding algorithms that model the firing of neurons and the spreading of activation in an *artificial neural network*. The aim is to propagate information along the links between the (large number of) neurons from the input to the output. The network can be trained to exhibit a desired intelligent behavior on the output, which is equivalent to the learning capability of the human brain. Technically, the learning of an artificial neural network is achieved by adjusting the weights associated with the links between the neurons. The point here is that intelligence is achieved without symbolic computation; it *emerges* over time, through the training procedure.

Combinations of the two major paradigms have also been explored, in two ways. One way is based on the fact that some cognitive processes are easy to implement symbolically (e.g., problem solving, reasoning, and game playing), whereas some others are more easily implemented using the connectionist approach (e.g., some aspects of visual perception and learning). The other way views connectionism as a lower level of cognitive processing, i.e., as a way of implementing symbolic processes (Rapaport 2000). For example, logical reasoning may be explained in terms of "connectivity patterns" that correspond precisely to symbolic representations.

All these paradigms suggest that there is no single computational model of the mind. It is actually the mind–brain–computation triad that requires further exploration, where each member of the triad may be used to suggest new ideas about the others. Most of today's computers are sequential processors, whereas the brain performs parallel processing of many operations at once.

Currently, there are six widely established cognitive theories about the nature of the representations and computations that can be used to explain how the mind works (Stanford Encyclopedia of Philosophy 2008): formal logic, rules, concepts, analogies, images, and neural connections.

- *Formal logic.* This theory hypothesizes that people make the inferences they do because they have mental representations similar to sentences in propositional and predicate logic, as well as deductive and inductive procedures that operate on those sentences. Many complex kinds of knowledge and many inferences can be understood in terms of applying deductive and inductive procedures to the sentences. For example, the rule of logic called *modus ponens* states that if A is true and "A implies B" is also known to be true, then B is true. Another example is the *resolution principle* of gathering specific information/evidence in order to determine the truth of an assertion or to prove some previously established goal. The assertion "P is true" holds if it can be shown that "$\neg P$ is true" cannot hold because it leads to a contradiction with the evidence. John Sowa (2000) generalizes the power of logic explicitly:

  Everything that can be stated clearly and precisely in any natural language can be expressed in logic. There may be aspects of love, poetry, and jokes that are too elusive to state clearly. But anything that can be implemented on a digital computer in any programming language can be specified in logic. (Sowa 2000)

- *Rules.* Much of human knowledge is naturally described in terms of rules of the form "IF . . . THEN. . . ." Moreover, much of human thinking and reasoning can be modeled by rule-based systems, because people have mental rules and procedures for using those rules to search a space of possible solutions. They also have procedures for generating new rules. Applying these kinds of procedures produces intelligent behavior.

- *Concepts.* In cognitive science, concepts are viewed as sets of typical features (slots). Concepts correspond partially to the words in spoken and written language. Schemas and scripts are more complex than concepts that correspond to words, but are also sets of features. Concepts usually belong to various kind-of and part-of hierarchies. Applying concepts in intelligent processing means obtaining an approximate match between concepts and things in the world, and using inheritance through kind-of hierarchies to infer about more general concepts.

- *Analogies.* People have verbal and visual representations of situations that can be used as cases or analogues in new situations. They also have retrieval, mapping, and adaptation processes that operate on those analogues and produce intelligent behavior. Computational models of analogical reasoning simulate how people retrieve, map, and apply source analogues to target situations.
- *Images.* People have visual images of objects, spaces, and situations, and are capable of processing and manipulating those images. An image is worth a thousand words, as the ancient Chinese said—images are often much more suitable in representations than lengthy verbal/textual descriptions. Computational image processing that supports human pictorial representations includes procedures such as scanning, rotation, focusing, zooming, and transformation.
- *Neural connections.* Some mental representations involve simple processing units of the brain—neurons—linked to each other by excitatory and inhibitory connections. Some human neurophysiological processes spread activation between these units via their connections; some others modify the connections. Applying these processes produces various kinds of intelligent behavior, such as vision, decision making, explanation selection, and meaning-making in language comprehension.

The central and appealing hypothesis of cognitive science, that the mind works by means of representations and computations, has been criticized as well. The critics complain that cognitive science neglects the importance of emotions, consciousness, and the physical environment in human thinking, as well as some social aspects of thought and the contribution of the body to thought and action. Some critics also doubt that the mind can be effectively described as a computational system in the standard sense, and suggest describing it as a dynamic system or system of quantum physics instead.

1.3 Types of Human Knowledge

Cognitive psychologists have identified a number of different types of knowledge that humans commonly use, and practical AI systems implement some of these types using corresponding knowledge representation techniques. The existence of multiple types of knowledge in human minds indicates the capability of humans to organize their knowledge in a structured way and to use that knowledge to solve problems efficiently.

Table 1.1 summarizes the categories and types of knowledge that most humans typically use; nowadays, AI systems implement many of these types.

- *Procedural knowledge* is about *how* to do something, for example, how a problem is solved. Some typical types of knowledge in this category are rules, problem-solving strategies, agendas, and procedures.
- *Declarative knowledge* describes what is known about a topic or about a problem. For example, some statements of declarative knowledge may describe details of concepts and objects. Some other statements may express facts that are either true or false.

Table 1.1 Commonly used types of human knowledge (adapted from Durkin 1994)

Category	Explanation/type
Procedural knowledge	Rules
	Strategies
	Agendas
	Procedures
Declarative knowledge	Concepts
	Objects
	Facts
Metaknowledge	Knowledge about other types of knowledge
	and how to use them
Heuristic knowledge	Rules of thumb
Structural knowledge	Rule sets
	Concept relationships
	Concept-to-object relationships
Inexact and uncertain knowledge	Probabilities
	Uncertain facts, rules, relationships, and evidence
	Fuzzy sets and logic
Commonsense knowledge	Default propositions
	Approximate concepts and theories
	General hierarchies and analogies
Ontological knowledge	Concepts
	Relationships between concepts
	Axioms
	Constraints

- *Metaknowledge* is knowledge about knowledge. It is used to decide what other knowledge is best suited for solving the problem at hand, what other knowledge is irrelevant to the problem and should therefore not be considered at all, and how to direct the problem-solving process into the most promising areas of the solution space.

- *Heuristic knowledge* includes those rules of thumb that guide the problem-solving process on the basis of previous experience in solving problems, individual intuition and skills, and a good understanding of the problem. However, heuristic knowledge is not strict. Also, problem solving based on heuristic knowledge is not guaranteed to be successful (i.e., it is not guaranteed to find a solution to the problem). Heuristic knowledge is usually compiled empirically from fundamental, deep knowledge about the problem, and is expressed as simple heuristics that help guide the processes of solving the problem and moving through the solution space.
- *Structural knowledge* describes mental models and the organization of problems, solutions, and their respective spaces. Typically, relationships between different pieces of knowledge from other categories (such as kind-of, part-of, grouping, and sets) are described by structural knowledge.
- *Inexact and uncertain knowledge* characterizes problems, topics, and situations in which information is inherently imprecise, unavailable, incomplete, random, or ambiguous. Inexact information and knowledge is often described in terms of a priori, a posteriori, and conditional probabilities of events. Uncertain knowledge is associated with expressions about a subjective belief in the validity of the knowledge, as well as with fuzzy linguistic terms (such as little, warm, or high) rather than precise quantitative measures, and degrees of membership of sets ranging between 0 and 1 rather than strict true or false membership.
- *Commonsense knowledge* is the term used to denote a vast amount of human knowledge about the world which cannot be put easily in the form of precise theories (McCarthy 1999). In many situations, humans rely on this kind of knowledge when facing an imprecise or incomplete characterization of the problem they are trying to solve, or when they simply lack more appropriate knowledge. It is always difficult to know in advance what part of commonsense knowledge will become relevant in solving a problem. Also, the consequences of applying that knowledge cannot be fully determined. Applying commonsense knowledge requires using defaults: approximate concepts (concepts without clear definitions) and approximate theories (theories involving approximate concepts), as well as general hierarchies and analogies.
- *Ontological knowledge* is an essential supplement to knowledge about a specific domain—it describes the categories of things in that domain and the terms that people use to talk about them (Sowa 2000). For example, the ontological knowledge about an object-oriented language contains the concept of a class, and the ontological knowledge about a

relational database includes tables and fields. Ontological knowledge also describes relations between such categories, and the axioms and constraints in the domain. Obviously, the types of ontological knowledge overlap with the types of the other categories of knowledge (declarative and structural knowledge). The important difference, however, is in the meanings of the various categories.

1.4 Knowledge Representation Techniques

There is no single "best" theory that explains all human knowledge organization. There is no single "best" technique for structuring data in all computer programs either. Likewise, there is no single ideal knowledge representation technique suitable for all applications. When building practical intelligent systems, developers should select the best knowledge representation technique to suit the application. To do this, they must have a good understanding of the various types of human knowledge and a palette of knowledge representation techniques to select from.

Note that the correspondence between the types of human knowledge discussed in the previous section and knowledge representation techniques is not necessarily one-to-one. Some techniques can be used to represent knowledge in two or more of the categories and types listed in Table 1.1. For example, rules of various forms, used as a knowledge representation technique, can represent parts of procedural knowledge, heuristic knowledge, metaknowledge, and inexact/uncertain knowledge. Likewise, facts, used as a declarative knowledge type, can be represented using several techniques—propositions, object–attribute–value triplets, multiple-valued facts, uncertain facts, etc.

The traditional AI techniques most frequently used to represent knowledge in practical intelligent systems include object–attribute–value triplets, uncertain facts, fuzzy facts, rules, semantic networks, and frames. Most of them are also important for understanding the rest of this book, and hence they are briefly surveyed in this section. More recently, ontologies have acquired major importance in knowledge representation as well. They are covered in detail from Chap. 2 onwards.

Simpler knowledge representation techniques can be used within more complex ones. For example, various techniques for representing facts can be used to describe parts of rules, frames, and semantic networks.

1.4.1 Object–Attribute–Value Triplets

Object–attribute–value (O–A–V) triplets are a technique used to represent facts about objects and their attributes. More precisely, an O–A–V triplet asserts an attribute value of an object. For example, the English phrase "The color of the ball is yellow" can be written in O–A–V form as "Ball–color–yellow" and represented graphically as in Fig. 1.1.

Fig. 1.1   An example of an O–A–V triplet

Objects usually have more than one attribute, so in a graphical representation there may be multiple arrows (denoting attributes) and boxes (denoting attribute values) for each oval (representing an object). Some attributes may be single-valued as in the above example, whereas others may be multiple-valued (e.g., "Travel–purpose–business, pleasure").

1.4.2 Uncertain Facts

A simple but frequently used extension of O–A–V triplets allows uncertainty of facts to be described. A *certainty factor* is a numeric value assigned to a statement that represents the degree of belief in the statement (Durkin 1994). Such numeric values are usually discrete and are taken from a previously specified interval (e.g., [0, 1], [−1, 1], [0–100], and the like). Discrete values usually have linguistic counterparts. For example, the certainty of a statement can be described using the following terms and their equivalent certainty factors: "definitely false" (−1.0), "probably false" (−0.5), "unknown" (0.0), "probably true" (0.5), and "definitely true" (1.0). The statement "The river is probably long" can be written as an uncertain O–A–V fact "River–length–long (CF = 0.5)," and its graphical representation may look as in Fig. 1.2.

Fig. 1.2   An uncertain fact

The continuous interval of possible certainty factor values can be divided into continuous subintervals and each subinterval can be assigned a discrete value. More fine-grained subintervals mean more variety in certainty factor values and more possibilities for expressing uncertainty precisely.

1.4.3 Fuzzy Facts

Fuzzy facts represent uncertainty using the imprecise and ambiguous terms commonly found in natural languages. For example, the statement "The person is old" may be interpreted differently by different people, who may have different understandings of the term "old." The *fuzzy set* representing old people may look as in Fig. 1.3 and is defined by a corresponding *membership function*. This function can be used to calculate the actual numerical value of a membership in the fuzzy set, on a scale from 0 to 1.

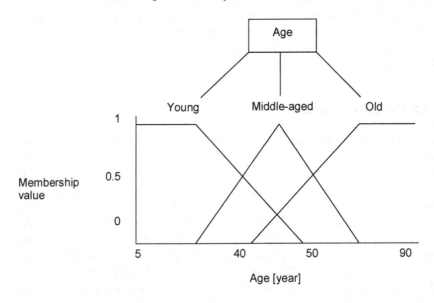

Fig. 1.3   Fuzzy sets on age

1.4.4 Rules

A rule is a knowledge representation technique and a structure that relates one or more *premises* (*conditions*, or *antecedents*), or a *situation*, to one or more *conclusions* (*consequents*), or *actions*. The premises are contained in the IF part of the rule, and the conclusions are contained in the THEN part, so that the conclusions may be inferred from the premises when the premises are true. For example:

IF	The time is after midnight
AND	I am hungry
THEN	I should not eat now

Premises are typically represented as facts, for example using O–A–V triplets. Actions can assert a new fact or can perform an operation (e.g., invoke a procedure).

Another interpretation of rules, premises, and conclusions is obtained from the state–transition view. There is a collection of states—situations that might occur in the application environment. A rule describes the logic of moving from a start state (a set of valid premises) to a goal state (described by the rule's conclusions).

Uncertain rules may include certainty factors, both in the premises and in the conclusions, and imply uncertain inferences. For example:

IF	The time is after midnight (CF = 0.5)
AND	I am hungry
THEN	I should not eat now (CF = –0.5)

In uncertain rules, omitting an explicit value for a certainty factor in a premise means "take the previously inferred CF value" or "take the default CF value." Conclusions made with uncertain premises cannot be absolutely true, but absolutely certain premises may lead to an uncertain conclusion.

Fuzzy rules contain fuzzy sets in their IF and THEN parts. They actually map fuzzy sets to one another:

IF	The meal is *hot*
THEN	I should wait a *little* before I eat it.

The knowledge of a practical intelligent system may be represented using a number of rules. In such a case, the rules are usually grouped into a hierarchy of *rule sets*, each set containing rules related to the same topic.

1.4.5 Semantic Networks

Semantic networks (or concept maps) are a knowledge representation technique that attempts to reflect cognition (Barr and Feigenbaum 1981; Rapaport 2000). Designed after the psychological model of the human associative memory, semantic networks are graphs made up of objects, concepts, and situations in some specific domain of knowledge (the nodes in the graph), connected by some type of relationship (the links/arcs). Figure 1.4 shows an example. The network represented expresses several interrelated facts: Billy *is a* Labrador, which is *a kind of* a dog. The other kinds of dogs shown are setters and bulldogs. A dog *has* legs, and the *number of* legs is 4.

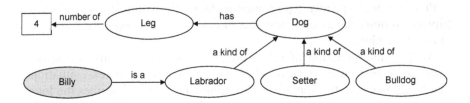

Fig. 1.4   A simple semantic network

Note that arcs can be labeled to denote an arbitrary relationship between concepts. However, kind-of, part-of, and is-a relationships are the most common. The graphical notation used to represent semantic networks is not standardized, but the things that can be typically represented in such networks are concepts (classes), their instances (objects), attributes of concepts, relationships between classes and objects, and values of attributes. As in object-oriented programming, objects/instances should normally have values for all attributes defined in the concept. There may be default values for some attributes (e.g., dogs normally have 4 legs). Kind-of relationships denote inheritance. Also, parts of semantic networks are easily recognized as O–A–V triplets (e.g., "Leg–number of–4").

It is easy to insert new nodes, relationships, and values into a semantic network. The technique has proven to be intuitively clear and easy to learn, and is widely used by AI specialists and psychologists alike. However, semantic networks are known to be weak in representing and handling exceptions to the knowledge they represent. In large networks, all nodes must be carefully examined for exceptions.

1.4.6 Frames

A frame is a technique and a data structure for representing stereotypical knowledge of some concept or object. Frames are similar to classes and objects in object-oriented programming. There are *class frames*, which represent common features of a set of similar objects (e.g., *dog*, *student*, or *movie*). *Instance frames* represent specific instances of a class frame (e.g., instances of the above three class frames may be the instance frames Billy, Joan, and *The Legends of the Fall*, respectively).

Each frame is easy to visualize as a form with various fields to be filled. The fields correspond to *slots* (or *properties*) of the frame. A typical slot of a frame is its *name*. Instance frames also typically have a corresponding *class* slot. The other slots depend on the nature of the frame itself.

Instance frames inherit all slots of the corresponding class frame. However, an instance frame may change the values of some slots or even add new slots (and their values). There can be many instance frames corresponding to one class frame.

In fact, frames are tightly related to semantic networks. An important difference between the two techniques is that, unlike semantic networks, frames include procedural knowledge as well, in the form of *facets*. Facets are typically attached to slots and contain procedures (methods, or demons) that are invoked automatically when the value of the slot is changed, or when it is needed (read). For example, an *if-changed* method may be invoked for each slot for which it is necessary to check the numeric value that is to be written into the slot. Likewise, an *if-needed* method may be called to supply the slot's value from a database or from a spreadsheet.

Another knowledge representation technique related to frames is that of *scripts*, which describe activities involving the corresponding knowledge, and also supply possible outcomes and scenarios.

1.5 Knowledge Representation Languages

The central component of any knowledge-based intelligent system is its *knowledge base*. The knowledge base contains a set of *sentences*—the units of the knowledge represented using one or more knowledge representation techniques, i.e., assertions about the world (Russell and Norvig 2002). The sentences are expressed in a knowledge representation language.

New sentences can be added to the knowledge base, in order for the information and solutions provided by the system to be both accurate and complete. Queries can be made to the knowledge base to obtain what the system currently knows about the world. Functions that implement these actions must rely on the details of the knowledge representation language.

Knowledge representation languages should be capable of both syntactic and semantic representation of entities, events, actions, processes, and time. However, not all of the existing knowledge representation languages have support for all of these things. Also, each existing language supports some, but not all, popular knowledge representation techniques. In addition, some knowledge representation languages are designed to provide support for knowledge communication and interchange between intelligent systems.

The dividing line between knowledge representation languages and programming languages is not strict. One may argue that traditional AI programming languages such as Lisp and Prolog support knowledge representation as well. Unlike popular programming languages such as C and Java, AI languages provide some built-in mechanisms for deriving facts from other facts, which is important for representing knowledge (as opposed to representing data). Others may argue that it is necessary for a knowledge representation language to have explicit support (in terms of data structures and language constructs) for knowledge representation techniques such as rules, frames, scripts, and semantic networks.

Ideally, a successful knowledge representation language should both be *expressive* enough to let the knowledge base developer structure and encode all the necessary knowledge easily, and make the represented knowledge *understandable* by humans. The language and the knowledge represented in it should cause a system using that knowledge to *behave* as if it knows it.

The subsections that follow briefly overview important design paradigms for knowledge representation languages, deliberately leaving out ontology representation languages, which are covered in the later chapters.

1.5.1 Logic-Based Representation Languages

Much knowledge representation can be done in a logic-based language (or "logic language" for simplicity). Moreover, many of the other frequently used knowledge representation paradigms are built on top of formal logics. Note the plural here—there are actually many formal logics. They partially overlap, but are also different in terms of how much they can express and in terms of notational and other details.

Both historically and pragmatically, logic-based languages are an important branch of AI.

1.5.1.1 Rationale, Pros and Cons

The popularity of formal logics as the basis for knowledge representation languages arises for practical reasons. They are all formally well founded and are suitable for machine implementation. Also, every formal logic has a clearly defined syntax that determines how sentences are built in the language, a semantics that determines the meanings of sentences, and an inference procedure that determines the sentences that can be derived from other sentences. Furthermore, most logic languages are designed to be precise and to avoid the incomplete and ambiguous expressions frequently found in natural languages. Even fuzzy logic has this property, in spite of the fact that it is suitable for representing ambiguity arising from linguistic terms.

On the other hand, all sentences in logics are assertions. Reasoning based on formal logics is limited to deriving truth values and proofs for such assertions. In formal logics, it is difficult to model interrogations and those kinds of human reasoning that involve assumption, likelihood, belief, disbelief, doubt, desires, etc. Also, designing a complete valid inference procedure is a very complex task for many logics.

Nevertheless, precise and formally clearly expressed assertions are a good starting point. It may be the case that the syntax and semantics of a logic are quite suitable for a certain application, and that only the reasoning needs to be specifically designed for that particular application. Some may complain that designing and developing a reasoner is not an easy task, but the alternatives (e.g., frame-based and rule-based languages) have proven not to be perfect either. Moreover, since logic-based roots can often be traced in many other formalisms, the shortcomings of logic cannot be eliminated easily. Using something completely different instead, such as neural networks, may only reverse the problem—things that are very easy to do with logic languages can be very hard to do with another formalism.

Note, however, that agreement to use a logic language does not solve other knowledge base development problems automatically. For example, setting up the vocabulary for building the sentences in the knowledge base can be a time-consuming task.

1.5.1.2 Propositional Logic

A proposition is a logical statement that is either true or false. For example, "The princess is in the palace." An O–A–V triplet is a more complex form of proposition, since it has three distinct parts.

Propositional logic is a form of symbolic reasoning. It assigns a symbolic variable to a proposition, for example:

A = The princess is in the palace

The truth value (*true* or *false*) of the variable represents the truth of the corresponding statement (the proposition). Propositions can be linked by logical operators (AND [∧], OR [∨], NOT [¬], IMPLIES [→ or ⇒], and EQUIVALENCE [⇔]) to form more complex statements and rules:

IF	The princess is in the palace	(A)
AND	The king is in the garden	(B)
THEN	The king cannot see the princess	(C)

The symbolic representation of the above rule in propositional logic is:

$$A \wedge B \rightarrow C$$

Thus, propositional logic allows formal and symbolic reasoning with rules, by deriving truth values of propositions using logical operators and variables. Finding the truth value of an arbitrary statement is a matter of examining the truth values of the variables and the truth tables of the logical operators in component parts of the statement. In fact, this procedure means checking the statement's validity or satisfiability—the proof theory of propositional logic. Deduction systems based on propositional logic are syntax-based (i.e., the actual meaning of the symbols is unimportant in the reasoning process; what matters is the formal proof). A deduction system for propositional logic is called a propositional calculus.

However, this simple form of reasoning may be inadequate or too mechanistic. In many situations, it is difficult to assign a variable to a whole statement. Also, the truth value of a statement can often be subjective and prone to interpretation, and is generally computationally exponential. First-order logic offers a more fine-grained approach, in which parts of statements can be represented and reasoned about logically (Durkin 1994; Russell and Norvig 2002; Sowa 2000).

1.5.1.3 First-Order Logic (First-Order Predicate Calculus)

First-order logic extends propositional logic by introducing the *universal quantifier*, $\forall$, and the *existential quantifier*, $\exists$ (see below for details). It also uses symbols to represent knowledge and logical operators to construct statements. Its symbols may represent constants, variables, predicates, and functions.

Constants are symbols that begin with a lowercase letter. *Variables* are symbols that begin with an uppercase letter. Propositions are represented using *arguments*—objects of propositions—and *predicates*—assertions about objects. For example, the proposition "The princess is in the palace" would be written in first-order logic as

in(princess, palace)

The predicate *in* can be used with variables to write more general propositions that capture various special cases (instantiations):

in(X, Y)

The previous statement can be instantiated by propositions such as "The princess is in the palace" and "The king is in the garden":

in(princess, palace)
in(king, garden)

A *function* is a mapping from entities of a set to a unique element of another set:

father(princess) = king

Using predicates, functions, and logical operators, it is possible to specify rules:

in(princess, palace) ∧ in(king, garden) → ¬see(king, princess)

The universal quantifier ∀ and the existential quantifier ∃, in first-order logic, denote the range or scope of variables in statements. The combination "∀x" is interpreted as "for each x" or "for all x." "∃x" means "there exists an x such that." For example:

∃X see(X, princess)   "Someone sees the princess"
∀X see (X, princess)   "Everyone sees the princess"

The range of quantifiers in first-order logic is restricted to simple, un-analyzable individuals, hence the name "first-order." In *higher-order logic*, function variables and predicate variables can be governed by quantifiers (Sowa 2000).

Knowledge represented with first-order logic is written in the form of predicates and rules. Reasoning with first-order logic is performed using predicates, rules, and general rules of inference (such as modus ponens and resolution) to derive conclusions.

First-order logic is simple—it is two-valued logic with just two quantifiers and the basic Boolean operators. However, used as a knowledge representation language, it forms a sound basis upon which many other AI languages are built (e.g., Prolog). It is like an assembly language for knowledge representation (Durkin 1994). Higher-order logic, modal logic, fuzzy logic, and even neural networks can all be defined in first-order logic. In other words, it can be used as a metalanguage for defining other kinds of logic, and even more:

> First-order logic has enough expressive power to define all of mathematics, every digital computer that has ever been built, and the semantics of every version of logic including itself. (Sowa 2000)

1.5.1.4 Knowledge Interchange Format (KIF)

KIF is a particular logic language based on first-order logic, specifically designed to make it useful as a mediator in the translation of other languages—an "interlingua" (Genesereth and Fikes 1992). The idea is to have translators from other languages to KIF and to other languages from KIF. If it is necessary to perform a translation from a representation described in a language A to an equivalent representation in another language B, it requires only A-to-KIF and KIF-to-B translators; KIF is used as an intermediate language.

The description of KIF includes specifications of both its syntax and its semantics. The semantics is similar to that of first-order logic. KIF uses the prefix notation of first-order logic with extensions to support nonmonotonic reasoning and definitions. The following simple examples illustrate the syntax of KIF:

(forall ((?x P)) (Q ?x))	;"All P are B"
(exist ((?x P)) (not (Q ?x))	;"Some P is not Q"
(president 802 thomas jefferson)	; a record in the database ;of presidents
(president 345 abraham lincoln)	; another record in the database of ; presidents

Another important extension of KIF with respect to first-order logic is the use of the backquote (') and comma (,) operators, which enable the encoding of knowledge about knowledge. For example,

(notes mary '(president ,?x ,?y ,?z))

The above sentence represents the knowledge that Mary notes the sentences about presidents. The backquote operator is applied to the inner sentence, which is a knowledge statement itself; the entire inner statement is used as an argument in the outer statement. The question marks denote variables, but the comma operator applied to the variables ?x, ?y, and ?z specifies that they should not be taken literally. In other words, the commas specify that Mary notes instances of the sentence (president ?x ?y ?z), not the sentence itself.

KIF can be also used to describe functions, sets, and many other concepts.

Conceptual Graphs (Sowa 2000) provide a suitable graphical notation for logic. They are based on existential graphs, augmented with features from linguistics and semantic networks. As a graphical notation, they are of interest for KIF because they have expressive power identical to that of KIF, and anything stated in one can be automatically translated to the other.

1.5.1.5 Description Logics

An entire group of languages for knowledge representation, based on description logics, is of particular interest in the context of ontology representation and development (Chap. 2 and onwards). The semantics of the underlying concepts of these languages identifies them as decidable fragments of first-order logic.

Developing a knowledge base using a description logic language means setting up a *terminology* (the vocabulary of the application domain) in a part of the knowledge base called the *TBox*, and *assertions* about named individuals (using the vocabulary from the TBox) in a part of the knowledge base called the *ABox*. The vocabulary consists of concepts and roles. *Concepts* denote sets of *individuals*. *Roles* are binary relationships between individuals. There are *atomic* concepts and roles (names of concepts and roles) and *complex* concepts and roles (terms for concepts and roles). The complex concepts are built using descriptions expressed in the corresponding description logic language and are assigned names in the TBox. For example, if *Person* and *Female* are atomic concepts and *hasChild* is an atomic role (a relation), part of a TBox defining complex concepts about family relationships may look like this (adapted from Baader et al. 2003):

Woman ≡ Person ⊓ Female

Man ≡ Person ⊓ ¬Woman

Mother ≡ Woman ⊓ ∃ hasChild.Person

Father ≡ Man ⊓ ∃ hasChild.Person

Parent ≡ Mother ⊔ Father

Grandmother ≡ Mother ⊓ ∃ hasChild.Parent

MotherWithManyChildren ≡ Mother ⊓ ≥3 hasChild

MotherWithoutDaughter ≡ Mother ⊓ ∀ hasChild.¬Woman

Wife ≡ Woman ⊓ ∃ hasHusband.Man

Husband ≡ Man ⊓ ∃ hasWife.Woman

In the above concept definitions, each symbol of the form $\exists R.C$ or $\forall R.C$ denotes the set of those individuals from the set corresponding to the concept C for which the relation (role) R holds. The symbols $\sqcap$ and $\sqcup$ denote intersection and union, respectively. ≥ 3 hasChild is a value restriction on the cardinality of the corresponding set (in this case, the minimum; the set includes all those instances of the atomic role hasChild in the domain of interpretation for which the value restriction holds).

In fact, the TBox defines (in a general way) semantic relationships between individuals introduced in the ABox and their properties. In other words, the ABox describes a specific state of affairs in the world in terms of the concepts and roles defined in the TBox. An ABox corresponding to the above TBox might be

MotherWithoutDaughter(JANE)
hasChild(JANE, CHARLES)
Father(ABRAHAM)
hasChild(ABRAHAM, ISAAC)

An intelligent system with a knowledge base structured as a TBox–ABox pair can reason about its terminology and assertions. It can determine whether a description in the TBox is *satisfiable* (i.e., noncontradictory), and whether there is a *subsumption* relationship between two descriptions (i.e., one is more general than the other). For example, in the above TBox *Person* subsumes *Woman*, and both *Parent* and *Woman* subsume *Mother*. Two important reasoning tasks about assertions in the ABox are to determine whether the assertions imply that a particular individual is an *instance* of a given concept description, and whether a set of assertions is *consistent* (whether it has a model). From a pragmatic point of view, consistency checks of sets of assertions and satisfiability checks of concept descriptions help to determine whether a knowledge base is meaningful at all. Subsumption tests help to organize the terminology into a meaningful hierarchy of concepts according to their generality. Each test can also be interpreted as a query about objects of interest; it retrieves the set of individuals that satisfies the test.

A subclass of description logic languages allows *rules* to be used in addition to the TBox and ABox to describe knowledge. The rules are of the operational form $C \Rightarrow D$ ("if an individual is an instance of C, then derive that it is also an instance of D"), or of the declarative form $\mathbf{K}C \sqsubseteq D$ (the *inclusion axiom* form; the operator $\mathbf{K}$ restricts the application of the axiom to those individuals that appear in the ABox and for which the ABox and TBox imply that they are instances of C). Such rules can be used to add assertions to the ABox in an operational environment (an intelligent system) containing a knowledge base. These rules can be interpreted logically. Alternatively, the environment may provide an application program interface (API) with appropriate functions through which programs can operate on the knowledge base in terms of adding, retracting, and modifying concepts, roles, and assertions.

1.5.2 Frame-Based Representation Languages

In all frame-based representation languages (or, for simplicity, "frame representation languages"), the central tenet is a notation based on the specification of frames (concepts and classes), their instances (objects and individuals), their properties, and their relationships to each other (Welty, 1996). This object-orientedness is human-centered. For this reason, frame-based languages are favored by many over logic languages as more appealing and more effective from a practical viewpoint (Baader et al. 2003).

In addition to object-orientedness, frame-based languages also provide for expressing generalization/specialization, i.e., organizing concepts into hierarchies. They also enable reasoning, by making it possible to state in a formal way that the existence of some piece of knowledge implies the existence of some other, previously unknown piece of knowledge. With frame-based languages, it is possible to make classifications—concepts are defined in an abstract way and objects can be tested to see whether they fit such abstract descriptions.

To get a feeling for the nature and syntax of frame-based languages, consider the following piece of code, in the KM language (Clark and Porter 2004):

```
(every Buy has
        (buyer ((a Agent)))
        (object ((a Thing)))
        (seller ((a Agent))))
```

The above code partially defines the class *Buy*, saying something like "All buy events have a buyer and a seller (both of type *Agent*), and an object (of type *Thing*) which is bought." In fact, it defines only the properties of the instances of the class, and not the properties of the class itself (things such as the parent class(es), the words or phrases used to denote objects of the class, and so forth). The latter may be defined as follows:

```
(Buy has
        (superclasses (Transaction))
        (terms ("buy" "purchase")))
```

In KM, both of the above code snippets are referred to as frames. A KM class typically needs two frames to describe it, one for the properties of the class, and another for the properties of the members of the class.

The traditional frame-based languages lacked precise characterization of their semantics. Moreover, discrimination between different types of knowledge embedded in a frame system was not clear. As a result, every frame-based system behaved differently from the others (which were developed using different frame-based languages), in many cases despite virtually identical-looking components and even identical relationship names (Baader et al. 2003). As a consequence, different systems could not interoperate and share knowledge. Later frame languages introduced more formal semantics, retaining the hierarchical concept structures and ease of representation and simultaneously improving the efficiency of reasoning and the representational rigor. For example, the KL-ONE system of Brachman and Schmoltze (1985) introduced description logic formalism into representing frames. KL-ONE not only greatly improved the representational rigor of frame-based languages, but also spawned an entire new class of frame systems. CLASSIC (Brachman et al. 1991) was one of them. The following example is the CLASSIC encoding of two concepts (*JAPANESE-CAR-MAKE* and *RICH-KID*) and one role (*thing-driven*):

```
define-concept[JAPANESE-CAR-MAKER,
              (ONE-OF Mazda Toyota Honda)];
define-role[thing-driven];
define-concept[RICH-KID,
              (AND STUDENT
                   (ALL thing-driven SPORTS-CAR)
                   (AT-LEAST 2 thing-driven))]
```

The first two definitions in the above example have obvious meanings. In the third one, the *ALL* construct is used to describe any object that is related by the *thing-driven* role solely to individuals that can be described by the concept *SPORTS-CAR* ("something all of whose *thing-driven* are *SPORTS-CARs*"). The third definition also uses the *AND* construct to make the composition of the three concept expressions that follow it. So, *RICH-KID* is defined to be "a *STUDENT* who drives *AT-LEAST* 2 things, *ALL* of which are *SPORTS-CARs*." The correspondence between CLASSIC constructs and operators and constructs from the underlying description logics is easy to notice (e.g., *AND* corresponds to ⊓, *ALL* to ∀, and *(ALL thing-driven SPORTS-CAR)* to ∀ thing-driven.SPORTS-CAR).

Note, however, that most frame languages are just a new syntax for parts of first-order logic (Welty 1996). This means that most of these languages do not offer anything new in expressiveness. For instance, the KM code shown in the example about buys, buyers, and sellers can be represented equivalently in KIF as

(forall (?b)

   (exists (?a) (=> (isa ?b Buy) (and (buyer ?b ?a) (isa ?a Agent)))))
(forall (?b)
   (exists (?a) (=> (isa ?b Buy) (and (object ?b ?a) (isa ?a Thing)))))
(forall (?b)
   (exists (?a) (=> (isa ?b Buy) (and (seller ?b ?a) (isa ?a Agent)))))

Frame-based languages are usually suitable for representing knowledge that does not change. Only very few of them are able to deal with non-monotonic changes in the knowledge being represented.

Another disadvantage of frame-based languages is the inadequate way in which they deal with procedural knowledge. The way they do this is usually to use some limited arithmetic, plus calling procedures and functions written in a procedural language and attached to slot facets. The procedural knowledge encoded in this other language is not represented in a frame-based way—it is hard-coded in the corresponding function/procedure. As a consequence, the resulting systems can only reason *with* that knowledge, but not *about* it.

1.5.3 Rule-Based Representation Languages

Rule-based representation languages (or, simply, "rule languages") are popular in commercial AI applications, such as expert systems (Durkin 1994). The rule-based paradigm is easy to understand, and there are a number of practical tools for building rule-based systems. Every rule-based language has an appropriate syntax for representing the If–Then structure of rules. On the other hand, there are considerable syntactic differences between different languages in terms of how they actually represent If–Then rules.

Vianu (1997) notes that there are two broad categories of rule-based languages: *declarative* (*model-theoretic*) languages, which attempt to provide declarative semantics for programs, and *production system* languages, which provide procedural semantics based on forward chaining of rules.

The criteria for other possible classifications of rule-based languages may be related to what is allowed in the rules. Some languages allow only the assertion of new facts in the knowledge base in the Then part of the rules. Other languages allow facts to be retracted from the knowledge base as an effect of rule firing. Yet another group of languages allows the embedding and/or invocation of procedural code (written in another, procedural language) in the rule syntax. Rule languages also differ in terms of the extent to which they control rule ordering during the inference process. Further classifications of rule languages are possible.

However, systems built using traditional rule languages have been shown to have two important limitations (Welty 1996):

- they are quite restrictive when applied to large problems (i.e., when the rule base is large), as there is no ordering of the rules;
- inferences cannot be limited to those dealing only with the objects of interest.

More recent rule languages combine rules with frame-based features that provide object orientation, better structuring of knowledge through generalization/specialization and concept hierarchies, and natural inference capabilities such as classification and inheritance. The synergy between rule-based languages and frame-based languages brings about an important advantage: information about a specific concept can be stored together with that concept, as opposed to rule-based systems where information about one concept may be scattered throughout the rule base. For example, a set of rules can be stored with a frame slot and activated through an if-needed demon whenever the slot value is read. Alternatively, a set of rules may be written to reason about a certain concept (frame) in detail.

As an example of a language that combines rules and frames, consider the following code, written in the native language of Jess, a popular expert-system development tool (Friedman-Hill 2003):

```
(deftemplate person (slot age))
. ..
(defrule check-age
        (person (age ?x))
        (test (> ?x 30))
=>
        (printout t ?x "is over 30!" crlf))
```

This example defines a frame (*person*) using the *deftemplate* construct, and a rule (*check-age*) using the *defrule* construct. The rule checks to see if an instance of the *person* frame has a value of the *age* slot greater than 30; if so, an appropriate print action is taken.

The rule-based representation formalism is recognized as an important topic not only in AI, but also in many other branches of computing. This is especially true for Web engineering. Rules are one of the core design issues for future Web development, and are considered central to the task of document generation from a central XML repository. Much of the interoperability between different applications in e-commerce also relies on rules and needs a Web interchange format. Rules can be also used for declarative specification of Web services.

In response to such practical demands from the world of the Web, the *Rule Markup Initiative* has taken steps towards defining *RuleML*, a shared *Rule Markup Language* (RuleML 2008). RuleML enables the encoding of various kinds of rules in XML for deduction, rewriting, and further inferential–transformational tasks. The Rule Markup Initiative's approach to rule categorization is more detailed, more fine-grained, and more practically oriented than the categorization by Vianu described above (RuleML 2008). The rule categories currently considered by the Rule Markup Initiative include (Wagner et al. 2003):

- production rules—the If–Then rules commonly found in numerous AI systems, such as expert systems;
- integrity rules (or integrity constraints)—assertions that must hold in all evolving states of a discrete dynamic system;
- reaction rules—rules that observe triggering events, check conditions in the forward direction in a natural fashion, perform an action only when and if all the necessary events/conditions are observed/met, and may also include an optional postcondition (in other words, rules specifying the reactive behavior of a system in response to triggering events);
- derivation rules—rules with one or more conditions and a conclusion, which imply using a procedure to derive the conclusion from the condition(s) (e.g., rules for defining derived concepts);
- transformation rules—transformation constructs that consist of a transformation invoker, a condition, and a transformation return (e.g., conditional directed equations or term-rewriting rules).

An example rule in English may state that "if someone likes music, then John likes that guy." Represented in RuleML, as an adaptation of a similar example from Boley et al. (2001), this rule may look like this:

```
<rulebase label="likesMusic">
    <imp>
            <_head><atom>
                    <rel>likes</rel>
                    <ind>John</ind>
                    <var>x</var>
            </atom></_head>
            <_body><atom>
                    <rel>likes</rel>
                    <var>x</var>
                    <ind>music</ind>
            </atom></_body>
    </imp>
</rulebase>
```

Without going into details of RuleML tagging, we recall that such an XML-based representation can be translated into another XML-based format using an appropriate XSL transformation (XSLT). For example, the above RuleML rule can be translated into an equivalent Jess rule using the RuleML-to-Jess XSLT:

```
(defrule likesMusic
    (likes ?x music)
=>
    (likes John ?x))
```

The Rule Markup Initiative now covers a number of new developments, including Java-based rule engines, an RDF-only version of RuleML, and MOF-RuleML (an abstract syntax of RuleML considered as a MOF model). See Chaps. 3 and 4 for a detailed explanation and discussion of RDF (Resource Description Framework) and MOF (Meta Object Facility).

1.5.4 Visual Languages for Knowledge Representation

The use of visual languages for knowledge representation is compelling for many reasons (Kremer 1998). The most obvious one is that the domain may require representation in a way that is not possible with purely textual or symbolic languages. Even if another formal knowledge representation language is available and suitable, in preliminary knowledge acquisition the appropriate formal structure for that language may not be apparent. Domain experts may have difficulties in communicating and articulating their domain knowledge in terms of formal knowledge structures; hence knowledge engineers may want to use visual representations for easier communication with the experts and for relaxation of formal discipline. Also, the syntax of logic, frame, and rule languages may often be complicated and may require knowledge of tiny details which may be quite unappealing even to knowledge engineers.

Visual languages for knowledge representation may be based on various kinds of graphs, forms (query by example), purely spatial relationships (iconic sentences), matrices (spreadsheets), and simple text layouts (outlining tools). Most of them facilitate knowledge representation by at least partially eliminating the need to use the rigorous syntax of symbolic or text-based languages. Under the surface, they often transform the represented knowledge into another language (such as first-order logic).

Note that many of the graphical user interfaces (GUIs) of knowledge acquisition and representation tools serve the purpose of collecting and transforming user input into the knowledge base. However, calling a GUI a visual language may provoke objections, especially in the context of visual languages for knowledge representation. In many cases, the GUI is there just to hide the details of the underlying representation language. On the other hand, this role of the GUI proves to be very useful in knowledge engineering. For example, JessGUI is a forms-based GUI that transforms a knowledge engineer's input into Jess syntax, thus making it possible for the knowledge engineer to avoid learning the Jess language (Jovanović et al. 2004).

In a more narrow sense of the term, visual languages rely on two- or three-dimensional graphics and always involve pictures of some sort, typically nodes and connecting arcs (Kremer 1998); text is involved as well, but for labeling and annotation purposes. However, more importantly, in order for visual languages to be interpreted reliably, it is necessary to specify their syntax and semantics formally. As with all other formal languages, such a specification involves precise definition of:

- terminal and nonterminal symbols;
- productions (derivation rules), i.e., the grammar;
- unambiguous semantics.

Specifying a visual language in this way must reflect its primary intent—to render knowledge into a form amenable to computational support, i.e., to straightforward, unambiguous interpretation by a computer program.

Myers (1990) has provided a comprehensive taxonomy of all visual languages, including those for knowledge representation. It includes several categories of visual languages for knowledge representation and shows that all of them can be subsumed by the general notion of *concept maps*, i.e., semantic networks. For example, visual languages such as Petri nets and flowcharts can also be interpreted as concept maps. The common feature of all categories of visual languages for knowledge representation is that they may be described in terms of relational grammars. As a consequence, all visual languages for knowledge representation used in practice fall into the category of concept maps, or have concept map languages which implement them.

All concept map languages provide graphical elements, used to represent typed *nodes* and typed *arcs*, as well as their labels. Other visual indicators may be used to distinguish between the nodes and arcs of different types (e.g., different shapes, colors, and line types). In fact, concept maps implement a simple graph theory. Frequently used extensions include the implementation of *partitions* or *contexts*, usually in the form of a box drawn around a subgraph.

Like frames, concept maps are object-oriented, human-centered, and easy to comprehend and use. The way they enable the structuring of a body of knowledge is much more salient than other forms of knowledge representation, such as pure text and logic (Kremer 1998). They can be used both at an informal level, such as for "brainstorming," and at a very formal level, such as for representing knowledge in the knowledge base of an intelligent system.

Well-known examples of visual languages for knowledge representation include KRS (Gaines 1991), which is the visual counterpart of the CLASSIC frame language, and Conceptual Graphs (Sowa 2000). Conceptual Graphs are more elaborate, more complex, more accurate, more expressive, more detailed, and more fine-grained than KRS. Although originally intended to represent natural-language expressions in a graphical form, they can actually represent many more forms of knowledge, including first-order logic (recall from Sect. 1.5.1 that Conceptual Graphs actually represent a visual counterpart of logic). It is of particular importance that Conceptual Graphs also have their "linear form," i.e., a pure text representation, evolved for ease of use by computer programs. For the sake of completeness, this feature of Conceptual Graphs should be noted here as an analogue of other graphical–text representation pairs, such as that in RDF, and that provided by the Unified Modeling Language (UML) tools that enable serialization of UML models to an XML representation using XML Metadata Interchange (XMI). Chapters 4 and 5 cover these topics in detail. In fact, much of this book argues that UML itself is an extremely suitable visual language for knowledge representation, even though it was originally developed as a software engineering tool.

1.5.5 Natural Languages and Knowledge Representation

Natural languages can express almost everything related to human experience, and hence they can be conceived of as knowledge representation languages as well. Natural languages are very expressive, and are also suitably declarative for knowledge representation. Moreover, they can be thought of as metalanguages for explaining both other natural and artificial languages (such as programming languages, other knowledge representation languages, and all other formal languages) and themselves (Sowa 2000).

However, the use of natural languages for knowledge representation in AI is very restricted, owing to the fact that they are extremely complex for machine processing. Parsing sentences in human languages successfully is one of the most difficult computing problems, and still remains a challenge. Even more important and more difficult is the problem of machine understanding of the meaning of natural languages.

On the other hand, there are several examples of research, experimentation, and practical developments in describing knowledge *about* natural languages using knowledge representation techniques. Such efforts are of high importance for ontological engineering (see Chap. 2 for a detailed explanation of ontological engineering). For example, DATR is a language designed for lexical knowledge representation, i.e., for representing knowledge about words taken from natural languages (Evans and Gazdar 1996). More precisely, DATR represents knowledge about *lexemes*, the fundamental units of the lexicon of a natural language; for instance, "bind," "binds," "bound," and "binding" are forms of the English lexeme "bind." In DATR, lexical knowledge is encoded in a rather "minimalist" semantic network of nodes, each node representing a word, a lexeme, or a class of lexemes. A set of attributes and their values is encoded with each node and represents the links. For example, the node describing the lexeme "bind" may be described by the following attribute–value pairs: *syntactic category—verb*; *syntactic type—main* (i.e., it is a main verb, not an auxiliary one); *syntactic form—present participle*; *morphological form—bind-ing*. In addition to such nodes and links, DATR has a number of constructs that are impossible to visualize in terms of simple inheritance hierarchies of semantic networks. Nevertheless, the semantics of DATR is defined in an explicit, mathematically rigorous way.

Another interesting approach is that of using *controlled languages* for knowledge representation (Pulman 1996). A controlled language is a restricted form of a natural language that can be systematically related to the underlying knowledge representation language of an intelligent system. The restrictions apply to both the vocabulary and the syntax of the natural language, and produce output that can be analyzed and processed both as a formal language and as a restricted natural language. The purpose of using a controlled language for knowledge representation is that it may be easier to represent human knowledge in computers in two steps, rather than trying to encode it in a formal symbolic language directly from its natural-language form. The first step is the transformation from a natural language to its appropriate controlled-language counterpart. In the second step, the controlled-language sentences are transformed into sentences of a more formal knowledge representation language (such as first-order logic, possibly augmented with some higher-order constructs).

For example, the English rule "If John has 30 dollars, and he likes going to restaurants, then he will go out for dinner" may be represented in a controlled English as follows:

CONDITION:
 P has Q dollars
 P likes going to restaurants
ACTION
 P will go out for dinner

It is comparatively easy even for people without knowledge-engineering skills to express their knowledge in this way, and it is then rather straightforward to translate it to, for example, first-order logic.

Note that controlled languages are different from canned text and macro-style templates such as "<person> has <number> dollars," which involve replacing the variable parts with specific words at run time. Unlike controlled languages, templates do not support the interactive knowledge refinement that some types of applications may require, and are rigid, overly simplistic, mechanistic, and also prone to representational infidelity during processing.

1.6 Knowledge Engineering

In order to develop practical knowledge bases, it is necessary to acquire human knowledge (from human experts or from other sources), to understand it properly, to transform it into a form suitable for applying various knowledge representation formalisms, to encode it in the knowledge base using appropriate representation techniques, languages, and tools, to verify and validate it by running the practical intelligent system that relies on it, and to maintain it over time. These activities are parts of the process called *knowledge engineering*, and the people who perform them are *knowledge engineers* (Barr and Feigenbaum 1981; Durkin 1994; Friedman-Hill 2003; Russell and Norvig 2002).

It is important to understand that knowledge-engineering activities never occur linearly, in sequence. On the contrary, they are all interwoven and require rigorous discipline. It is not uncommon for knowledge engineers to return many times to alternative knowledge representation techniques and tools if they realize that those they are currently using are not suitable. Unfortunately, it is not always easy to tell suitable from unsuitable techniques and tools before the knowledge has been at least partially encoded, i.e., before at least one cycle of the above time-consuming activities has been completed. Minimizing the number of cycles depends on many factors, including the structure of the problem, the skills and experience of the knowledge engineer(s), the representation formalisms and tools used, and, most importantly, how successful the communication is between the knowledge engineer(s) and the human expert(s) in the process of knowledge acquisition.

Knowledge acquisition from human experts is difficult for several reasons, some of which are:

- cognitive mismatch between the expert and the knowledge engineer—they often perceive, present, explain, and prioritize things differently;
- knowledge transformation problems—there are always difficulties in representing the knowledge that the expert has supplied with the available tools and techniques, no matter how proven and/or sophisticated they are;
- consistency maintenance—in order to maintain high quality and consistency in the knowledge represented, it is necessary to update the knowledge base whenever changes in the domain occur or new knowledge is revealed.

There is a whole range of techniques that knowledge engineers use in the acquisition of knowledge from human experts (Mitchell 1998). Direct techniques either rely on the expert's ability to articulate his/her knowledge directly, or collect the expert's behavior. In both cases, there is a more or less straightforward way to represent the acquired knowledge using some well-known knowledge representation technique(s). The direct methods include interviews, questionnaires, observation of task performance, protocol analysis (asking the expert to "think aloud" while performing a task), interruption analysis (asking the expert to work without thinking aloud, and interrupting him/her when the knowledge engineer can no longer understand what the expert is doing), drawing closed curves, and inferential flow analysis (with various weights assigned to the links between concepts and processes). The indirect techniques make various assumptions about how experts represent their knowledge. Results from psychology and cognitive science show that experts recognize old patterns in new problems more effectively than do nonexperts, and that they use a variety of knowledge structures (tables, lists, hierarchies, networks, flow diagrams, and many more). Examples of indirect techniques include various kinds of concept grouping (clustering, sorting, and constructing hierarchies) that the expert is asked to perform explicitly, the use of case-based analysis, and repertory grids (where the expert is asked to evaluate various cases of solving a problem along a number of different "dimensions," i.e., features). After collecting data using an indirect technique, the knowledge engineer is supposed to work on it with the expert and formulate the underlying knowledge explicitly using appropriate knowledge representation techniques.

Over the years, efforts in the field of knowledge engineering have resulted in the development of various structured methodologies. The best-known example is CommonKADS (Schreiber et al. 1994). This advocates developing multiple models of the domain knowledge (such as a conceptual model, organizational model, application model, and task model) to cover various aspects of the domain knowledge and help cope with the complexities of building the knowledge base. Furthermore, Common-KADS suggests modeling four categories of knowledge—domain knowledge, task knowledge, inference knowledge, and strategic knowledge—as well as modeling with knowledge reuse in mind. The latter often involves building partial models that are then reused with appropriate refinement in each particular case. CommonKADS insists on strong correspondence between the knowledge models and their implementations—the resulting knowledge bases should clearly and explicitly reflect the models they rely on.

A number of graphical software tools have been developed to support various activities in the process of knowledge engineering, including visual knowledge representation languages. Some of these are covered in the subsequent chapters.

1.7 Open Knowledge Base Connectivity (OKBC)

Developers of intelligent systems use various techniques, languages, and tools to represent, manipulate, and process knowledge in the knowledge bases of their systems. A particular technique, language, or tool may be favored by a knowledge engineer for a number of reasons (e.g., suitability for the particular problem, ease of representation, processing efficiency, or previous experience with the underlying formalism(s)). If the resulting system is developed to operate as a stand-alone one, such preferences may prevail and it may not be necessary to worry about other issues.

However, the resulting system may need to interoperate with other systems and applications, both intelligent and conventional. The other systems and applications will then typically demand services from the intelligent system and access to its knowledge, which implies communication between them. Owing to the potential variety of the underlying knowledge representation formalisms, providing communication interfaces and ensuring reliable interoperability may be difficult. Implementation of full-scale communication and interoperation may be time-consuming and may become quite cumbersome. Even worse, supporting all the idiosyncrasies of the underlying knowledge representation formalisms for each particular application may turn out to mean an enormous multiplication of effort.

OKBC (Chaudhri et al. 1998) is a protocol for accessing knowledge bases stored in *knowledge representation systems* (intelligent systems based on knowledge representation techniques and languages described in Sect. 1.5), and in systems that can be viewed externally as knowledge representation systems (such as object-oriented database systems). It specifies a set of generic operations for access to knowledge bases from various applications. These operations serve as an interface to the knowledge bases. To the external applications demanding services, this interface layer provides some independence from the software and tools that implement and manipulate the knowledge base. Moreover, it enables the development of tools (e.g., graphical browsers, frame editors, analysis tools, and inference tools) that operate on many knowledge representation systems. It also supports knowledge base reuse and composition from multiple individual systems. Version changes of the underlying knowledge representation systems and even transitions to other knowledge representation systems should be transparent to the external applications that access knowledge bases through OKBC.

Just like application programming interfaces for database systems (e.g., Java Data Base Connectivity (JDBC)), OKBC is an application programming interface for knowledge representation systems. Figure 1.5 illustrates this idea. Each generic OKBC operation is invoked from the application using a method implemented in the appropriate programming language for the application. In turn, each knowledge representation system implements the protocol in its own way. Hence each knowledge base manipulated by the protocol is serviced directly by the underlying knowledge representation system. OKBC specifies its generic operations in a language-independent way, but also provides appropriate language bindings for

Java, Lisp, and C to facilitate the use of generic operations from some of the most popular programming languages. The bindings establish language-specific conventions for naming, passing arguments, returning values, etc.

Fig. 1.5   OKBC as an application programming interface

Note that OKBC is a knowledge communication protocol, not a knowledge representation language. In fact, OKBC complements knowledge representation languages in that it specifies generic operations to *access* and *manipulate* knowledge, whereas representation languages *describe* the knowledge declaratively. The OKBC operations are those typically supported by knowledge representation systems, in terms of reasoning and knowledge manipulation (e.g., checking slot values, assessing predicates for truth values, and inheritance).

Since OKBC evolved from an earlier protocol (called the Generic Frame Protocol) that focused only on frame representation systems, many of its operations reflect frame-based representation and reasoning (e.g., *create-class*, *create-individual*, *enumerate-frame-slots*, *get-slot-facets*, and *get-kb-roots*). Other operations serve the pragmatics of using the protocol (e.g., *open-kb*, and *establish-connection*).

The underlying *OKBC Knowledge Model* is object-oriented and is precisely specified in terms of constants, frames, slots, facets, classes, individuals, and knowledge bases. This implies that the knowledge obtained from or provided to a knowledge representation system using OKBC is expressed in a way specified by the OKBC operations and the OKBC Knowledge Model. In other words, the OKBC Knowledge Model serves as an implicit interlingua that knowledge representation systems and external applications that use OKBC translate knowledge into and out of. Implementing the translation from the knowledge representation system side may raise some minor initial problems of ambiguity and confusion due to terminological inconsistencies—in practice, different systems often use the same term to mean different things, or use different terms to mean the same thing. The translation from the application side is much easier to implement, since the majority of applications in which one may want to use

OKBC to communicate with knowledge bases are nowadays object-oriented anyway, just like the OKBC Knowledge Model.

OKBC assumes a client–server architecture for application development and supports standard network protocols such as TCP/IP. A client application may access multiple OKBC servers, which in turn can access multiple knowledge representation systems. Each communication with an OKBC server requires establishing a connection with it first, finding out about the available knowledge representation systems available on the server, and opening a specific knowledge base. All of these operations are directly supported by the appropriate OKBC operations.

1.8 The Knowledge Level

The notion of the *knowledge level* was introduced by Allen Newell (1982) to better distinguish between different important views (levels of abstraction) associated with intelligent systems, their organization, the knowledge represented in their knowledge bases, and their operation. It was also used by Newell to discuss the nature of knowledge and the important distinction between knowledge and its representation. As Newell points out, there are three levels/views from the most concrete to the most abstract: the implementation level (originally, Newell called this level the logic level), the logical level (originally, the symbol level), and the knowledge level (epistemological level). The new names for the three levels and the adapted view of the levels presented here have been taken from Russell and Norvig (2002) and are more appropriate for the coverage in this book.

- *Implementation level.* This is the level of the knowledge base of an operational intelligent system. At this level, knowledge representation means all of the *data structures* deployed to hold the domain knowledge and other knowledge necessary to solve the current problem, as well as those deployed to hold the current problem description. When it is necessary to make a clear distinction between the former and the latter (e.g., in expert systems), then the term *working memory* is used to denote the latter. In any case, at the implementation level, both the knowledge and the problem description are represented as data structures. Taking the process view, the implementation level consists of the read/write operations and various internal computations of the system that access and update the knowledge at that level.
- *Logical level.* All data structures in the knowledge base represent something, and hence an interpreter is needed to process them in a way

consistent with the representation. In other words, the logical level is the level of knowledge representation. It includes the underlying knowledge representation paradigms, formalisms, techniques, and languages that are used to represent the system's knowledge, implemented using the corresponding data structures at the implementation level, as well as the processes (interpretations) used by the system to reason and make inferences and derivations with that knowledge. At this level, the knowledge is encoded into sentences.

- *Knowledge level.* This is a distinct computer systems level, above the logical level, characterized by knowledge as the medium and by the principle of rationality as the law of behavior (Newell 1982). It is tightly coupled to the notions of competence and rationality. At the knowledge level, an intelligent system is described in terms of what it knows (the *content*), what its goals are, and what actions it is capable of taking in order to pursue those goals. The system's body of knowledge, described at the knowledge level, is largely unstructured, in terms of both capacity and structural constraints. The system is intelligent if it is capable of rational behavior; i.e., if it knows that one of its actions will lead to one of its goals, it will select and perform that action.

As an illustration of the three different levels/views and the kinds of information associated with them, consider again the example of the king and the princess in Sect. 1.5.1. At the knowledge level, an intelligent system may be said to know that the king cannot see the princess from the garden, because she is in the palace. The system can also be said to use abstract procedures and functions that add new knowledge to the knowledge base and query the knowledge base. For example, an abstract procedure may add the knowledge that the prince is also in the palace; an abstract function enquiring who is in the palace will then return the princess, the prince, and possibly some other people. This knowledge and the abstract update/query processes assume nothing about the actual knowledge representation within the system. At the logical level, predicates such as in(princess, palace) and in(king, garden) may be the sentences that represent/encode the knowledge contained in the knowledge body. These predicates are now processed by logical inference procedures to assess their truth values and derive new knowledge (facts), such as ¬see(king, princess). Still, it is up to the implementation to encode the sentences into suitable data structures. The logical sentence in(princess, palace) may be encoded as the string "in(princess, palace)." Or it may be an entry in a table defined by a relation in(Who, Where) and indexed by persons and locations. Or it may be implemented as something else.

As another illustration, consider an OKBC operation such as *copy-frame* (Fig. 1.5). At the knowledge level, an external system may be said to know how to use OKBC to replicate frames. At the logical level, it has to invoke the OKBC *copy-frame* operation and pass it appropriate arguments as required by its specification. However, the external system is not concerned with how the *copy-frame* operation is implemented by the knowledge representation system, nor how the frames are implemented by that system.

Newell originally included computer hardware in his discussion of the implementation (logic) level. True, it is the hardware—the logic circuits and the registers—that performs all the low-level operations upon data structures. It is not necessary, though, for the purpose of this brief overview, to go to that level of detail concerning the implementation of knowledge representation inside a computer. However, it must be stressed that the way the data structures and the related interpreter procedures are designed and implemented is certainly very relevant for the performance of the system (and hardware does matter here). Nevertheless, it is irrelevant to the logical (symbol) level and the knowledge level.

As another illustration, consider an OKBC operation such as copy-frame (Fig. 1.5). At the knowledge level, an external system may be said to know how to use OKBC to replicate frames. At the logical level, it has to invoke the OKBC copy-frame operation and pass it appropriate arguments as required by its specification. However, the external system is not concerned with how the copy-frame operation is implemented by the Knowledge Representation System, nor how the frames are implemented by that system.

Newell originally included computer hardware in his discussion of the implementation (logic) level. True, it is the hardware—the logic circuits and the registers—that performs all the low-level operations mentioned in this text. It is not necessary, though, for the purpose of this text's overview, to go to that level of detail concerning the implementation of knowledge representation inside a computer. However, it must be stressed that the data structures and the relative interpreter routines are designed and implemented separately. Any relevant for the performance of the system, and hardware does enhance both. Nevertheless, it is irrelevant to the logical (symbol) level and the knowledge level.

2 Ontologies

The word "ontology" comes from the Greek *ontos,* for "being," and *logos,* for "word." In philosophy, it refers to the subject of existence, i.e., the study of being as such. More precisely, it is the study of the *categories* of things that exist or may exist in some domain (Sowa 2000). A domain ontology explains the types of things in that domain.

Informally, the ontology of a certain domain is about its terminology (domain vocabulary), all essential concepts in the domain, their classification, their taxonomy, their relations (including all important hierarchies and constraints), and domain axioms. More formally, to someone who wants to discuss topics in a domain D using a language $L,$ an ontology provides a catalog of the types of things assumed to exist in $D;$ the types in the ontology are represented in terms of the concepts, relations, and predicates of $L.$

Both formally and informally, the ontology is an extremely important part of the knowledge about any domain. Moreover, the ontology is the fundamental part of the knowledge, and all other knowledge should rely on it and refer to it.

This chapter covers ontologies from the perspectives of computing and knowledge representation. It takes a pragmatic approach, explaining the benefits of developing and applying ontologies, the tools and languages used for the development and implementation of ontologies, and the methodologies that bring discipline and rigor to the process of building ontologies. It also shows some examples of ontologies and briefly discusses some applications.

Ontologies have become a very popular topic, not only in AI but also in other disciplines of computing. There are also efforts focused on developing ontologies in many other branches of science and technology. Hence ontologies are growing fast into a distinct scientific field with its own theories, formalisms, and approaches. For a more comprehensive coverage of the field, see Staab and Studer (2004).

D. Gašević et al., *Model Driven Engineering and Ontology Development,* 2nd edn., DOI 10.1007/978-3-642-00282-3_2, © Springer-Verlag Berlin Heidelberg 2009

2.1 Basic Concepts

In AI, the term "ontology" has largely come to mean one of two related things (Chandrasekaran et al. 1999):

- a representation vocabulary, often specialized to some domain or subject matter;
- a body of knowledge describing some particular domain, using a representation vocabulary.

In both cases, there is always an associated underlying data structure that represents the ontology.

A number of fields of AI and computing use ontologies: knowledge representation, knowledge engineering, qualitative modeling, language engineering, database design, information retrieval and extraction, and knowledge management and organization (McGuinness 2002).

2.1.1 Definitions

There are many definitions of the concept of ontology in AI and in computing in general. The most widely cited one is:

Ontology is a specification of a conceptualization. (Gruber 1993)

This definition is certainly the most concise one, and requires some further clarification. *Conceptualization* means an abstract, simplified view of the world. If the knowledge base of an intelligent system is to represent the world for some purpose, then it must be committed to some conceptualization, explicitly or implicitly. That is, every body of formally represented knowledge is based on a conceptualization. Every conceptualization is based on the concepts, objects, and other entities that are assumed to exist in an area of interest, and the relationships that exist among them. This also clarifies the meaning of the term "world"—in practice, "world" actually refers to some phenomenon in the world, or to some topic (or topics), or to some subject area.

The other part of the above definition—*specification*—means a formal and declarative representation. In the data structure representing the ontology, the type of concepts used and the constraints on their use are stated declaratively, explicitly, and using a formal language. The formal representation implies that an ontology should be *machine-readable*. However, an ontology is not "active;" it cannot be run as a program. It represents declaratively some knowledge to be used by programs.

> Ontology . . . can be seen as the study of the organization and the nature of the world independently of the form of our knowledge about it. (Guarino 1995)

Guarino augments the above definition with the notion of a *formal ontology,* the theory of a priori distinctions between the entities of the world (physical objects, events, regions, quantities of matter, ...), as well as between the meta-level categories used to model the world (concepts, properties, qualities, states, roles, parts, ...). Fundamental roles are played in formal ontology by the theory of part–whole relations and topology (the theory of the connection relation).

> Ontology is a set of knowledge terms, including the vocabulary, the semantic interconnections, and some simple rules of inference and logic for some particular topic. (Hendler 2001)

The important parts in Hendler's definition are the *semantic interconnections* and *inference and logic.* The former says that an ontology specifies the meaning of relations between the concepts used. Also, it may be interpreted as a suggestion that ontologies themselves are interconnected as well; for example, the ontologies of "hand" and "arm" may be built so as to be logically, semantically, and formally interconnected. The latter part means that ontologies enable some forms of reasoning. For example, the ontology of "musician" may include instruments and how to play them, as well as albums and how to record them.

Swartout and Tate offer an informal and metaphorical but extremely useful definition for understanding the essentials of an ontology:

> Ontology is the basic structure or armature around which a knowledge base can be built. (Swartout and Tate 1999)

Figure 2.1 illustrates this idea. Like an armature in concrete, an ontology should provide a firm and stable "knowledge skeleton" to which all other knowledge should stick. Another important issue here is the distinction between ontological knowledge and all other types of knowledge, illustrated in Table 1.1. An ontology represents the fundamental knowledge about a topic of interest; it is possible for much of the other knowledge about the same topic to grow around the ontology, referring to it, but representing a whole in itself.

Fig. 2.1   Illustration of Swartout and Tate's definition of an ontology

Kalfoglou stresses yet another important issue related to ontologies:

An ontology is an explicit representation of a shared understanding of the important concepts in some domain of interest. (Kalfoglou 2001)

The word *shared* here indicates that an ontology captures some *consensual* knowledge. It is not supposed to represent the subjective knowledge of some individual, but the knowledge accepted by a group or a community. All individual knowledge is subjective; an ontology implements an explicit cognitive structure that helps to present objectivity as an agreement about subjectivity. Hence an ontology conveys a shared understanding of a domain that is agreed between a number of individuals or agents. Such an agreement facilitates accurate and effective communication of meaning. This, in turn, opens up the possibility for knowledge sharing and reuse, which enables semantic interoperability between intelligent agents and applications.

2.1.2 What Do Ontologies Look Like?

The answer to the above question depends on the level of abstraction. When implemented in a computer, they typically look like XML-based files. Alternatively, they can be represented in a computer using a logic language, such as KIF (Genesereth and Fikes 1992). Since ontologies are always about concepts and their relations, they can be represented graphically using a visual language. Graphical tools for building ontologies always support conversion from a graphical format to XML and other text-based formats (see Sect. 2.2.1).

Humans can express ontologies as sets of declarative statements in a natural language. However, natural-language statements are difficult to process in a computer. Recall also from the definitions that representing ontologies in a computer requires a formal language.

As an example of the representation of ontologies at different levels of abstraction, consider again the concept of a musician. For the sake of

simplicity, assume that the concepts used to describe the essential knowledge about the notion of a musician are *musician, instrument,* some products of his/her work, namely *albums* the musician has recorded and music
events (e.g., concerts) in which he/she has participated, and devoted *admirers* (fans), who maintain his/her fame as an artist. Also, assume that the
variety and multitude of relations among these concepts that can be considered may be reduced to just a few of the most essential ones, such as the
facts that each musician *plays* some instrument, that when giving concerts
he/she *plays at* that concert, that the admirers come to *attend* such events,
and that the musician also *records* music albums. We deliberately avoid in
this simple example the numerous kind-of and part-of relations to other
concepts associated with musicians and their work.

These natural-language statements represent the conceptualization of the
Musician ontology. At a high level of abstraction, this ontology can be informally diagrammed as the semantic network shown in Fig. 2.2.

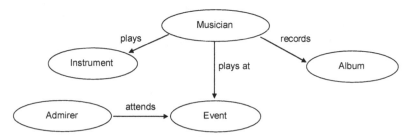

Fig. 2.2   Musician ontology visualized as a semantic network

Obviously, the representation in Fig. 2.2 suffers from many deficiencies. It is not a formal specification, i.e., it is not expressed in any formal
language. It does not show any details, such as the properties of the concepts shown or the characteristics of the relations between them. For example, musicians have names, and albums have titles, durations, and
years when they were recorded. Likewise, nothing in this semantic network shows explicitly that the musician is the *author* of an album that
he/she records (note that recording engineers in music studios can also be
said to record albums, but they are usually not the authors). Nevertheless,
the semantic network in Fig. 2.2 does show some initial ideas about the
Musician ontology.

For more detail and for a formal graphical representation, consider the
UML model in Fig. 2.3. This represents the same world as does the semantic network in Fig. 2.2, but allows the properties of all the concepts used to
be specified unambiguously, as well as the roles of concepts in their relations.

Another important detail in this representation is an explicit specification of the cardinalities of all concepts.

Figure 2.4 shows part of the Musician ontology in an equivalent XML-based format. The OWL language (Smith et al. 2004) used in this representation is described in more detail in Chap. 3. It is not necessary to go into all the details of this representation, since in practice the representation is always generated automatically, starting from a graphical ontology editor (see Sect. 2.2.1). However, note that it is exactly *this* representation of ontologies that is nowadays most widely used at the implementation level.

Fig. 2.3   UML model of the Musician ontology

2.1.3 Why Ontologies?

Ontologies provide a number of useful features for intelligent systems, as well as for knowledge representation in general and for the knowledge engineering process. This subsection summarizes the most important of these features, and is based on the treatments in Chandrasekaran et al. (1999), Gruber (1993), Guarino (1995), McGuinness (2002), and Schreiber et al. (1994).

```
<owl:Class rdf:ID="Event"/>
<owl:Class rdf:ID="Album"/>
<owl:Class rdf:ID="Instrument"/>
<owl:Class rdf:ID="Musician"/>
<owl:Class rdf:ID="Admirer"/>
<owl:ObjectProperty rdf:ID="author">
        <owl:inverseOf>
               <owl:ObjectProperty rdf:ID="opus"/>
        </owl:inverseOf>
        <rdfs:domain rdf:resource="#Album"/>
        <rdfs:range rdf:resource="#Musician"/>
</owl:ObjectProperty>
<owl:ObjectProperty rdf:ID="player">
        <rdfs:range rdf:resource="#Musician"/>
        <rdfs:domain rdf:resource="#Instrument"/>
</owl:ObjectProperty>
<owl:ObjectProperty rdf:ID="loudness">
        <rdf:type
rdf:resource="http://www.w3.org/2002/07/owl#FunctionalProperty"/>
        <rdfs:domain rdf:resource="#Instrument"/>
</owl:ObjectProperty>
...
```

Fig. 2.4   The Musician ontology represented in OWL (excerpt)

2.1.3.1 Vocabulary

An ontology provides a *vocabulary* (or the names) for referring to the terms in a subject area.

In real life, there is a whole spectrum of different kinds of vocabularies. A *controlled vocabulary,* such as a catalog, provides a finite list of terms together with an unambiguous interpretation of those terms. Every use of a term from a controlled vocabulary (e.g., "musician") will denote exactly the same identifier (say, 1). A *glossary* provides a list of terms and their meanings, but the meanings are specified in natural language and may often be interpreted differently by different people. Hence they are not unambiguous and thus are not suitable for machine processing. A *thesaurus* provides some additional semantics in the form of synonym relationships between terms, which drastically reduces ambiguity. However, thesauri do not provide explicit term hierarchies (McGuinness 2002).

Ontologies are different from such human-oriented vocabularies in that they provide *logical statements* that describe what the terms are, how they are related to each other, and how they can or cannot be related to each other. They also specify *rules* for combining the terms and their relations to define extensions to the vocabulary. As Chandrasekaran et al. (1999)

note carefully, it is not the vocabulary as such that qualifies as an ontology, but the conceptualizations that the terms in the vocabulary are intended to capture. An ontology specifies terms with *unambiguous meanings*, with semantics independent of reader and context. Translating the terms in an ontology from one language to another does not change the ontology conceptually. Thus an ontology provides a vocabulary, *and* a machine-processable *common understanding* of the topics that the terms denote. The *meanings* of the terms in an ontology can be communicated between users and applications.

2.1.3.2 Taxonomy

A *taxonomy* (or *concept hierarchy*) is a hierarchical categorization or classification of entities within a domain. It is also a clustering of entities based on common ontological characteristics. The classification/clustering is organized according to a predetermined system. A good taxonomy should separate its corresponding entities into mutually exclusive, unambiguous groups and subgroups that, taken together, include all possibilities. It should also be simple, easy to remember, and easy to use. A good example of a taxonomy is a Web site's taxonomy; it is the way the site organizes its data into categories and subcategories, sometimes displayed in a site map.

Every ontology provides a taxonomy in a machine-readable and machine-processable form. However, an ontology is more than its corresponding taxonomy—it is a full specification of a domain. The vocabulary and the taxonomy of an ontology together provide a *conceptual framework* for discussion, analysis, or information retrieval in a domain. Note that simple taxonomies such as those of Web sites may not necessarily include complete generalization/specialization hierarchies (i.e., subclassing and is-a relations) for the concepts. With ontologies, the subclassing is strict, is formally specified, includes formal instance relationships, and ensures consistency in deductive uses of the ontology.

2.1.3.3 Content Theory

Since ontologies identify classes of objects, their relations, and concept hierarchies that exist in some domain, they are quintessentially *content theories* (Chandrasekaran et al. 1999). Ontologies not only identify those classes, relations, and taxonomies, but also specify them in an elaborate way, using specific *ontology representation languages* (see Sect. 2.2.1 and Chap. 3). Classes are specified using frame-based representation principles, i.e., their properties, property values, and possible value restrictions

(restrictions on what can fill a property) are specified as well. In some ontology representation languages, the value of one property may be expressed as a mathematical equation using values of other properties. Also, some languages allow developers to specify first-order-logic constraints between terms and more detailed relationships such as disjoint classes, disjoint coverings, inverse relationships, and part–whole relationships, etc. (McGuinness 2002). Thus ontologies represent knowledge in a very structured way.

Well-structured and well-developed ontologies enable various kinds of *consistency checking* from applications (e.g., type and value checking for ontologies that include class properties and restrictions). They also enable and/or enhance *interoperability* between different applications. For example, we may want to expand the Musician ontology illustrated in Figs. 2.2, 2.3, and 2.4 to include the concept of a *street musician,* to denote a musician who entertains people in the street. One way to do this is to define a *performsIn* property in the Musician class and include in the ontology a definition stating that a street musician is a Musician whose *performsIn* property has the value "Street." This definition may be used to expand the term "StreetMusician" in an application that does not understand that term, but does understand the terms "Musician," "performsIn," and "Street." If that application is asked by another application if a certain person is a street musician, it will "understand" the question and may be able to answer by querying a database of musicians to see if it contains an entry with the appropriate values of the *name* and *performsIn* fields.

Being content theories, ontologies clarify the structure of domain knowledge. Developing an ontology requires an effective *ontological analysis* of the domain whose content the ontology is intended to represent. Ontological analysis reveals the concepts of the domain knowledge, their taxonomies, and the underlying organization. Without such analysis, no knowledge representation for the domain can be well founded. Through ontological analysis, the entire process of knowledge engineering acquires a strong flavor of modeling. The resulting knowledge base does not merely transfer the knowledge extracted from a human expert, but also models the problem domain in the form of the observed behavior of an intelligent agent embedded in its environment (Gaines 1991; Gruber 1993; Guarino 1995; Schreiber et al. 1994).

2.1.3.4 Knowledge Sharing and Reuse

The major purpose of ontologies is not to serve as vocabularies and taxonomies; it is *knowledge sharing* and *knowledge reuse* by applications. The point is that every ontology provides a description of the concepts and relationships that can exist in a domain and that can be shared and reused among intelligent agents and applications (recall that the description looks like a formal specification of a program; see Figs. 2.3 and 2.4). Moreover, working agents and applications should be able to communicate such ontological knowledge. Shared ontologies let us build specific knowledge bases that describe specific situations but clearly rely on the same underlying knowledge structure and organization.

As Neches et al. note, there are many senses in which the work that went into creating a knowledge-based system can be shared and reused (Neches et al. 1991); for example:

- through the inclusion of source specifications—the content of one module is copied into another one at design time, is then possibly extended and revised, and is finally compiled into a new component;
- through the runtime invocation of external modules or services—one module invokes another, either as a method from a class library or through a Web service, and the like;
- through communication between agents—the messages that intelligent agents send to and receive from each other can have various kinds of knowledge as their content;
- through the exchange of techniques—sharing and reusing not the content, but the approach behind it (in a manner that facilitates reimplementation of the content itself).

These modes of sharing and reuse require shared understanding of the intended interpretations of domain terms, compatibility of the domain models used by different agents and applications, and compliance with the kinds of requests that the external modules/services are prepared to accept. All of it is facilitated by shared ontologies. Shared ontologies ameliorate the problems of heterogeneous representations in the knowledge bases of different systems (even those developed using the same representational paradigm), dialects within language families, varieties in communication conventions, and model mismatches at the knowledge level (often caused by a lack of a shared vocabulary and domain terminology).

As an example of facilitating knowledge sharing and reuse by means of ontologies, suppose that someone has conducted a thorough ontological analysis of the topic of musicians, and has developed a much more elaborated Musician ontology than that shown in Figs. 2.2, 2.3, and 2.4. This ontology would include domain-specific terms such as *musician* and *musical event,* some general terms such as *profession, location,* and *attendance,* and terms that describe behavior, such as *playing* and *recording.* An ontology captures the intrinsic conceptual structure of the domain (Chandrasekaran et al. 1999), and can be used as a basis for developing a rich domain-specific knowledge representation language for building knowledge bases in that domain. In the present case, the language would provide a syntax for encoding knowledge about musicians in terms of the vocabulary, concepts, and relations in the ontology. Anyone who wanted to build a knowledge base related to musicians could use that content-rich knowledge representation language and thus eliminate the need to perform the time-consuming knowledge analysis task again—the language would already have a large number of terms that embodied the complex content theory of the domain. In this way, the Musician ontology could be shared among different developers, and reused as the "armature" knowledge in a number of knowledge bases and applications.

Make no mistake, though—in practice, knowledge sharing and reuse is still not easy, even if an ontology is readily available for a given purpose. To name but a few reasons, note that there are several different languages for representing ontologies, and knowledge base development tools may not support the language used to develop the ontology. There are also competing approaches and working groups, creating different technologies, traditions, and cultures. There may be several different ontologies that have been developed to describe the same topic or domain. Selecting any one of them may not satisfy all the requirements that the knowledge engineer must fulfill. Combining them may be anything but easy, because subtle differences between them may require a lot of manual adjustment, and the resulting ontology may still be inadequate. On top of all that, there is the problem of knowledge maintenance, since all parts of knowledge (including ontological knowledge) evolve over time.

2.1.4 Key Application Areas

There are many potential applications of ontologies, but Fikes (1998) has offered a high-level list of key application areas: collaboration, interoperation, education, and modeling.

Collaboration. Different people may have different views of the same problem area when working on a team project. This is particularly true for interdisciplinary teams, with specialists from different branches of science, technology, and development having different foci of interests and expertise. For such specialists, ontologies provide a unifying knowledge skeleton that can be used as a common, shared reference for further development and participation—these people can simply talk more easily to each other when they have such a stable, consensual knowledge armature to rely on.

Perhaps even more importantly, ontologies play the same role in collaboration between intelligent agents in terms of agent-to-agent communication. When an agent sends a message to another agent that it is communicating with, the other agent must have the same world model (i.e., the same ontology) in order to interpret the message correctly. Knowledge exchange between agents is much more feasible when the agents are aware of the ontologies that the other agents are using as world models.

Interoperation. Ontologies enable the integration of information from different and disparate sources. End users typically do not show much interest in how they get their information; they are much more interested in getting the information they need, and getting all of it. Distributed applications may need to access several different knowledge sources in order to obtain all the information available, and those different sources may supply information in different formats and in different levels of detail. However, if all the sources recognize the same ontology, data conversion and information integration are easier to do automatically and in a more natural way.

Education. Ontologies are also a good publication medium and source of reference. Since they presumably always result from a wide consensus about the underlying structure of the domain they represent, they can provide reliable and objective information to those who want to learn more about the domain. Simultaneously, domain experts can use ontologies to share their understanding of the conceptualization and structure of the domain.

Modeling. In modeling intelligent, knowledge-based applications, ontologies represent important reusable building blocks, which many specific applications should include as predeveloped knowledge modules. For example, the Musician ontology defines knowledge that can be used as is in both a recommender system that suggests to users what new music CDs they should buy, and a Web-based intelligent educational system that learners may use to find out more about famous instrumentalists of the twentieth century.

Fikes' classification can be seen from a more pragmatic perspective as well. In fact, many consider e-commerce to be *the* application domain for ontologies. Ontologies can enable machine-based communication between buyers and sellers, can help in customer-profiling tasks, can support vertical integration of markets, and can describe reuse between different marketplaces. In e-commerce, ontologies can be applied in terms of all of the four categories (roles) that Fikes suggested.

Another extremely demanding general application area provides very fertile soil for applying ontologies—search engines. Ontologies can support structured, comparative, and customized searches (McGuinness

2002). Concepts and taxonomies from ontologies can be used to find pages with syntactically different but semantically similar content, simultaneously eliminating many irrelevant hits. For example, if a user searches the Web for special offers on music CDs of individual performers and gets too many hits, an intelligent search engine can consult an ontology such as the Musician ontology to obtain relevant properties that can help to refine the search. On the basis of the properties retrieved, the user may be presented with a special-purpose form to fill in, so that he/she can provide a detailed set of specifications for the CDs of interest (such as the preferred instrument, and live or studio recordings). The ontology may also offer refinements using its generalization/specialization relations; so, in the case of individual performers, the user may also be automatically asked to select between instrumentalists and singers, and, further on, to select between guitarists, pianists, and so on. While waiting for user input, the search engine could proactively perform a less refined search in the background and possibly cache information for further (more refined) searches.

2.1.5 Examples

The following brief descriptions of some existing ontologies are intended to show the variety of ontologies and their potential uses. Some of the examples have been selected by starting from ontology libraries available on the Web (DAML Ontology Library 2008; OWL Ontology Library 2008; Protégé Ontologies Library 2005). The others have been selected taking into account their popularity.

2.1.5.1 Example 1: The Gene Ontology Project (http://www.geneontology.org/)

This project provides a controlled vocabulary to describe gene and gene product attributes for any organism. The ontology has three organizing principles: molecular function, biological process, and cellular component. A gene product has one or more molecular functions. Also, a gene product is used in one or more biological processes, and might be associated with one or more cellular components. This ontology is frequently updated and is available for download in various formats.

2.1.5.2 Example 2: The Learner Ontology

One of the results achieved in the ELENA project (http://www.elena-project.org/en/index.asp?p=8–1) was an ontology of learners in Semantic Web eLearning applications (integrated standard-based learner profile for

Semantic Web eLearning publications, http://www.elena-project.org/images/ other/learner.rdfs). The ontology pertains to learner modeling in open P2P environments, where learner profiles are distributed and, also, fragments of learner profiles are distributed. It covers various features of learners, several types of security access, various levels of the learner profile, and so on.

2.1.5.3 Example 3: The Object-Oriented Software Design Ontology (ODOL)

The objectives of the Web of Patterns project (http://www-ist.massey. ac.nz/wop/) are to create an ontology to describe the design of object-oriented software, to represent software design patterns (Gamma et al. 1995) and related ideas using the concepts developed in that ontology, and to provide a flexible framework that can be used by the software engineering community to share knowledge about software design. The ODOL-based descriptions of patterns are OWL documents that can be imported by popular ontology development editors such as Protégé (see Sect. 2.2.1 for a more detailed description of Protégé).

2.1.5.4 Example 4: The Friend Of A Friend Ontology (FOAF)

Currently one of the most popular ontologies, FOAF "makes it easier to share and use information about people and their activities (e.g., photos, calendars, weblogs), to transfer information between Web sites, and to automatically extend, merge and re-use it online" (Brickley and Miller 2007). It is the evolving result of the FOAF project (http:// www.foaf-project.org/), which is creating a Web of machine-readable pages describing people.

The ontology itself (http://xmlns.com/foaf/spec/index.rdf) defines an RDF vocabulary (see Sect. 3.2.2 for more details on the RDF language) for expressing metadata about people and their interests, relationships, and activities. Typically, one uses the terms (metadata) defined in the ontology to create her/his FOAF file. It is a machine-readable RDF file describing a person in terms of her/his personal data, what she/he creates and does, and who she/he knows. Alternatively, people can use the FOAF vocabulary to annotate their personal Web pages.

The project also provides tools that help users create their FOAF files without too much worrying about the low-level idiosyncrasies of RDF.

2.1.5.5 Example 5: Ontology of Online Communities

The SIOC (Semantically-Interlinked Online Communities) Core Ontology provides the main concepts and properties required to describe information from online communities (e.g., message boards, wikis, blogs, etc.) (Bojārs and Breslin 2008). Developers can use this ontology to express information contained within community sites. The major concepts defined in the ontology include community, container (e.g., forum, blog), item, post, role, site, space, thread, user, and user group. For instance, using the SIOC ontology concepts one can describe a blog post semantically (who wrote it, more information about the author, what is the title, what is the topic, were there replies or not (and if there were, who wrote them), and the like). In addition, SIOC documents may use other existing ontologies to enrich the information described.

2.2 Ontological Engineering

To develop a really useful ontology requires a lot of engineering effort, discipline, and rigor. *Ontological engineering* denotes a set of design principles, development processes and activities, supporting technologies, and systematic methodologies that facilitate ontology development and use throughout its life cycle—design, implementation, evaluation, validation, maintenance, deployment, mapping, integration, sharing, and reuse. Ontological engineering provides a design rationale for the development of knowledge bases and enables systematization of knowledge about the world of interest and accumulation of knowledge (Mizoguchi and Kitamura 2001).

Knowledge engineering for an intelligent system should always include ontological engineering, which implies using specific development tools and methodologies.

2.2.1 Ontology Development Tools

The standard tool set of an ontology engineer includes ontology representation languages and graphical ontology development environments. More recently, ontology-learning tools have also started to appear, in order to partially automate the development process and help in the evolution, updating, and maintenance of ontologies. Other tools are also required in the context of developing ontologies for deployment on the Semantic Web (see Chap. 3).

2.2.1.1 Ontology Representation Languages

There are a number of ontology representation languages around. Some of them were developed at the beginning of the 1990s within the AI community. Others appeared in the late 1990s and later, resulting from the efforts of AI specialists and the World Wide Web Consortium (W3C). Roughly speaking, the early ontology representation languages belong to the pre-XML era, whereas the later ones are XML-based. Also, most of the later ones were developed to support ontology representation on the Semantic Web, and hence they are also called *"Semantic Web languages."* Other common names for them are *"Web-based ontology languages"* and *"ontology markup languages"* (Gómez-Pérez and Corcho 2002).

Some of the best-known examples of the early ontology representation languages are:

- KIF (Genesereth and Fikes 1992), which is based on first-order logic;
- Ontolingua (Gruber 1992), which is built on top of KIF but includes frame-based representation;
- Loom (MacGregor 1991), based on description logics.

Among the widely used Web-based ontology languages are:

- SHOE (Luke and Heflin 2000), built as an extension of HTML;
- XOL (Karp et al. 1999), developed by the AI center of SRI International as an XML-ization of a small subset of primitives from the OKBC protocol called OKBC-Lite;
- RDF (Manola and Miller 2004), developed by the W3C as a semantic-network-based language to describe Web resources;
- RDF Schema (Brickley and Guha 2004), also developed by the W3C, is an extension of RDF with frame-based primitives; the combination of both RDF and RDF Schema is known as RDF(S);
- OIL (Fensel et al. 2001), which is based on description logics and includes frame-based representation primitives;
- DAML+OIL (Horrocks and van Harmelen 2002) is the latest release of the earlier DAML (DARPA Agent Markup Language), created as the result of a joint effort of DAML and OIL developers to combine the expressiveness of the two languages;
- OWL, or Web Ontology Language (Smith et al. 2004), developed under the auspices of the W3C and evolved from DAML+OIL; OWL is currently the most popular ontology representation language.

Some of these Web-based ontology languages are described in detail in Chap. 3. For more comprehensive information and comparative studies of all of them, see the sources cited above, and also Corcho et al. (2002) and Gómez-Pérez and Corcho (2002).

The ontological-engineering reality of having a number of ontology representation languages is best expressed in the following quotation:

> Ideally, we would like a universal shared knowledge-representation language to support the Semantic Web, but for a variety of pragmatic and technological reasons, this is unachievable in practice. Instead, we will have to live with a multitude of metadata representations. (Decker et al. 2000)

There are a number of implications of that multitude. For example, an application may already use another ontology, developed in a language other than that which the developers have chosen for building a new ontology. Experience shows that combining ontologies developed using different languages can require a lot of effort—two languages coming from different branches of the ontology-language research communities may not be compatible, and may require painful manual adaptation in order to provide interoperability at a satisfactory level. However, sometimes the developers may be constrained by the fact that the development tools support only a few languages. The situation is even worse if there are other applications that already use an ontology that the new application needs to consult as well, but design considerations show that another language would be much more appropriate for the new application. On the other hand, an appropriate ontology representation language may facilitate the integration of an ontology into a new application. Moreover, a newer ontology representation language may simply be more expressive than the other languages of choice, and translators to and from those other languages may already exist as well. Note that the ontology community has already developed a number of such translators, although many of them suffer from partial loss of knowledge in the translation process.

2.2.1.2 Ontology Development Environments

No matter what ontology representation language is used, there is usually a graphical *ontology editor* to help the developer organize the overall conceptual structure of the ontology; add concepts, properties, relations, and constraints; and, possibly, reconcile syntactic, logical, and semantic inconsistencies among the elements of the ontology. In addition to ontology editors, there are also other tools that help to manage different versions of ontologies, convert them into other formats and languages, map and link between ontologies from heterogeneous sources, compare them, reconcile and validate them, and merge them. Yet other tools can help acquire, organize, and visualize the domain knowledge before and during the building of a formal ontology (Denny 2002).

Graphical *ontology development environments* integrate an ontology editor with other tools and usually support multiple ontology representation languages. They are aimed at providing support for the entire ontology development process and for the subsequent use of the ontology (Corcho et al. 2002).

Protégé. Currently the leading ontology development editor and environment, Protégé was developed at Stanford University and has already been through a number of versions and modifications (Protégé 2005). It facilitates the defining of concepts (classes) in an ontology, properties, taxonomies, and various restrictions, as well as class instances (the actual data in the knowledge base). Furthermore, its uniform GUI (Fig. 2.5) has a tab for the creation of a knowledge acquisition tool for collecting knowledge into a knowledge base conforming to the ontology. Customizable forms determine how instance information is presented and entered. The knowledge base can then be used with a problem-solving method to perform various inference tasks.

Protégé conforms to the OKBC protocol for accessing knowledge bases stored in knowledge representation systems. Applications built on top of such systems can be executed within the integrated Protégé environment.

Protégé supports several ontology representation languages, including OWL and RDF(S). Some forms of reasoning over ontologies developed with Protégé are also facilitated; for example, since OWL is based on description logics, inferences such as satisfiability and subsumption tests are automatically enabled.

Protégé's plug-in-based extensible architecture allows integration with a number of other tools, applications, knowledge bases, and storage formats. For example, there are plug-ins for the ezOWL (Visual OWL) editor, for the OWL-S editor (enabling loading, creating, management, and visualization of OWL-S services), and for Jess (which allows the use of Jess and Protégé knowledge bases together), as well as storage back ends for UML (for storing Protégé knowledge bases in UML), XML Metadata Interchange (XMI; for storing Protégé knowledge bases as XMI files), DAML+OIL (for creating and editing DAML+OIL ontologies), and many more formats.

Fig. 2.5 A screen from Protégé

Initially, Protégé was used to develop ontologies in application domains such as clinical medicine and the biomedical sciences. Over the years, its user community has grown rapidly and it is now used in a number of other application domains. More information can be found in Noy et al. (2001).

Other environments. Although Protégé is currently the most widely used ontology development environment, there are literally dozens of other tools and environments. A relatively recent comparative survey (Denny 2004) discovered the fact that there is a lot of room for improvement in all such environments. For example, a number of users suggested an enhancement in the form of a higher-level abstraction of ontology language constructs to allow more intuitive and more powerful knowledge-modeling expressions. Many users also would like friendlier visual/spatial navigation among concept trees/graphs and linking relations, more options for using reasoning facilities to help explore, compose, and check ontologies, more features for aligning ontologies with one another, and tools that would help integrate ontologies with other data resources such as enterprise databases. The desirable improvements also include support for natural-language processing and collaborative development.

The overall sentiment expressed by users of the various ontology development environments clearly reflects the need for facilitating the use of such tools by domain experts rather than by ontologists. Likewise, there is a strong need for the integration of ontology development environments with existing domain and core ontologies and libraries, as well as with standard vocabularies. Another, more contemporary, focus is emerging as well—ontology development in concert with trends in enterprise application integration and development trends.

2.2.1.3 Ontology-Learning Tools

Ontology development is hard work. Even with the most advanced ontology development languages, environments, and methodologies, a major problem in ontological engineering still remains in the area of knowledge acquisition and maintenance—the collection of concepts and relations in a domain, achieving consensus on them among the domain experts and other interested parties, and frequent updates due to the dynamics of the knowledge structure of the domain and its unpredictable changes over time.

This fact has created the idea of *ontology learning*, with the objective of partially automating the processes of ontology development and maintenance by developing tools and frameworks to help extract, annotate, and integrate new information with old information in an ontology. The typical sources of information are Web documents, which reflect sufficiently well the dynamics of change in most domains. A typical prerequisite for enabling (semi)automated information extraction from Web documents is the use of natural-language-processing and text-processing technologies.

To this end, Maedche and Staab (2001) have proposed an ontology-learning framework and developed an ontology-learning environment called the Text-To-Onto workbench. The framework and tool are based on an architecture that combines knowledge acquisition with machine learning from Web documents. The framework recognizes the fact that traditional machine learning techniques rely on data from structured knowledge bases or databases, and hence are not applicable to documents and other sources of information on the Web, which are at best partially structured or semistructured. Instead, the framework relies on natural-language-processing, data-mining, and text-mining technologies. The specific techniques that it applies are ontology learning from free text, dictionaries, and legacy ontologies; reverse engineering of ontologies from database schemata; and learning from XML documents.

The framework suggests several steps in the ontology-learning process:

- importing and reusing existing ontologies by merging their structures or defining mapping rules between those structures;
- modeling major parts of the target ontology using ontology extraction from Web documents with support from machine learning;
- outlining the target ontology to fit it to its primary purpose;
- refining the ontology at a fine granularity (in contrast to extraction);
- validating the resulting ontology by use of the target application;
- repeating the above steps to include new domains in the constructed ontology, to fine-tune it, or to maintain and update its scope.

Note that much of this process is semiautomated, i.e., the ontology engineer is supposed to interactively select and run a number of techniques from a graphical environment. He/she first has to select the potential sources of ontological information from the Web, such as HTML and XML documents, databases, or existing ontologies, and then drive the discovery process to exploit them further. This may include indexing various documents, so as to transform semistructured documents such as online dictionaries into a predefined relational structure. The process also assumes access to a natural-language-processing system that enables lexical analysis, tokenization, named-entity recognition, and other operations over a free-form natural-language text. The Text-To-Onto ontology-learning workbench integrates an ontology editor and all of the above other tools and techniques. A modified, generalized association-rule learning algorithm known from the field of data mining is used to discover relations between concepts in a given class hierarchy. The relations discovered are collected in a database, which can also be visualized to help analyze the relations more effectively.

A similar idea has been exploited by Navigli et al. in their OntoLearn architecture, which uses the Ariosto language processor (Navigli et al. 2003). OntoLearn extracts terminology from appropriate Web sites, warehouses, and documents exchanged among members of a virtual community, filters it using natural-language processing and statistical techniques, and interprets it semantically using the WordNet lexical knowledge base (WordNet 2008). The extracted terminology and concepts are then related semantically according to taxonomic (kind-of) and other semantic relations obtained from WordNet and a rule-based inductive-learning method. The initial ontology is then edited, validated, enriched, and updated interactively, again with the aid of WordNet, which ensures correct use of various synonyms, hypernyms, homonyms, and the like for semantic disambiguation between terms in the ontology.

All approaches to ontology learning such as the above two are promising, but are still very much in the research phase and have not been integrated into common ontology development environments such as Protégé.

2.2.2 Ontology Development Methodologies

An ontology development methodology comprises a set of established principles, processes, practices, methods, and activities used to design, construct, evaluate, and deploy ontologies. Several such methodologies have been reported in the literature. From surveys such as those in Corcho et al. (2002) and Staab and Studer (2004), as well as from some more recent developments in the area of Web technologies, we can conclude that:

- most ontology development methodologies that have been proposed focus on *building* ontologies;
- some other methodologies also include methods for *merging, reengineering, maintaining,* and *evolving* ontologies;
- yet other methodologies build on general software development processes and practices and apply them to ontology development;
- there are also methodologies that exploit the idea of *reusing existing ontological knowledge* in building new ontologies;
- some of the more recently proposed methodologies are based on the idea of using *publicly available community-based knowledge* to simplify and speed-up development of ontologies.

There is no one best methodology, because there is no one "correct" way to model a domain. Also, ontology development is necessarily an iterative process.

Of the methodologies in the first of the above five categories, some are fairly general and merely suggest steps to be followed in the ontology development process. An example is the simple methodology proposed by Noy and McGuinness (2001). Others advise specific ontology development processes (such as the one proposed by van der Vet and Mars (1998) for bottom-up construction of ontologies). As an illustration, consider the steps in the ontology-building process suggested in Noy and McGuinness (2001):

- Determine the domain and scope of the ontology—this should help create a clear vision of the ontology's coverage, its intended use, the types of questions the information in the ontology should provide answers to, and maintenance guidelines.

- Consider reusing existing ontologies—since ontology development is hard work, it is always a good idea to check if someone else has already done the work and made the result publicly available, so that it can be refined and extended to suit a particular domain or task. Language conversion, interoperability, and tool support issues are important here as well.
- Enumerate important terms in the ontology—this is where building the terminology starts.
- Define the classes and the class hierarchy—this step, closely intertwined with the next one, can be performed top-down (identifying the most general concepts and classes first), bottom-up (identifying the most specific ones first), middle-out (starting from some important middle-layer concepts and expanding the hierarchy in both directions), or using a combination of these approaches.
- Define the properties (slots) of classes—describe the internal structure of concepts by explicating their extrinsic properties (e.g., *name, duration,* and *use*), intrinsic properties (e.g., *weight*), parts, and relations to other classes and individuals in those classes.
- Define the facets of the slots—these are things such as the slot value type, the allowed values (domain and range), the number of values (cardinality), and other features of the values that the slot can take.
- Create instances—this includes filling in the slot values for each instance created.

Again, the process outlined above is much more complicated in practice. It requires one to consider a lot of conflicting issues and a number of fine-grained details. After multiple, usually time-consuming, iterations, at least a minimum consensus about the final ontology should be achieved.

An example of a more comprehensive methodology is the *Methontology framework* (Fernández-López et al. 1999). Methontology's starting point is that ontological engineering requires the definition and standardization of the entire ontology life cycle—from the specification of requirements to maintenance—as well as methodologies and techniques that drive ontology development through the life cycle. So, the Methontology framework includes:

- identification of the ontology development process;
- a life cycle based on evolving prototypes;
- the methodology itself, which specifies the steps for performing each activity, the techniques used, the products of each activity, and an ontology evaluation procedure.

The ontology development process in Methontology comprises the following phases:

- *specification*—identification of the ontology's terminology, primary objective, purpose, granularity level, and scope;
- *conceptualization*—organizing and structuring in a semiformal way the knowledge acquired during the specification phase, using a set of intermediate representations that both domain experts and ontologists can understand (thus bridging the gap between their mindsets);
- *implementation*—using an ontology development environment to formally represent and implement the products of the above two phases, namely concepts, hierarchies, relations, and models.

In addition to the above major stages of ontology development, Methontology covers processes that run in parallel throughout the ontology life cycle, i.e., along with the processes taking place in the above three major stages: quality assurance, integration, evaluation, maintenance, documentation, and configuration management. It also identifies interdependencies between the life cycle of the ontology being developed and the life cycles of other, related ontologies. Furthermore, Methontology specifies in detail the techniques used in each activity, the products that each activity outputs, and how they have to be evaluated.

Methontology also recognizes the importance of knowledge acquisition. In this framework, knowledge acquisition is the long process of working with domain experts, and its activities are intertwined with activities from the specification and conceptualization phases. It comprises the use of various knowledge acquisition techniques (see Sect. 1.6) to create a preliminary version of the ontology specification document, as well as all of the intermediate representations resulting from the conceptualization phase.

Note that Methondology is suitable for building ontologies either from scratch or by reusing other ontologies as they are, or by a process of reengineering them.

An example of the third category of ontology development methodologies and processes—those that rely on general software engineering principles—can be found in Devedžić (2002). It proposes an ontology development methodology analogous to that of object-oriented software analysis and design. The rationale is as follows. Ontologies represent concepts, their properties, the values of those properties, events and their causes and effects, processes, and time (Chandrasekaran et al. 1999). Also, ontologies always include some kind of hierarchy, and most ontologies represent and support generalization, inheritance, aggregation (part-of), and instantiation relationships among their concepts. Nearly all of these issues are relevant to an object-oriented analysis and design for a problem domain. Moreover, the processes that ontological engineers use in ontology development (see above) almost coincide with established processes of object-oriented analysis and design (see e.g., Larman 2001). In both cases, it is important to assemble the domain vocabulary at the beginning, often starting from the domain's generic nouns, verbs, and adjectives. The result of an object-oriented analysis is actually a draft of the domain ontology relevant to the application. True, software analysts do not call this result an ontology. Object-oriented analysis stresses different aspects from those that ontological analysis does, but the parallels are obvious. In the next phase, object-oriented designers define classes, objects, hierarchies, interface functions, and the system's behavior, while ontological engineers use various intermediate representations to design ontologies in detail. Both kinds of specialists commonly use various templates for specifying details of their products. Some classes become merged and some refined, and so do some ontologies. Class libraries and previous design specifications often provide the possibility of reuse in object-oriented design, and so do previously encoded and publicly available ontologies in ontological engineering.

A similar methodology described in Devedžić (1999) is built on the idea of using *design patterns* as simple and elegant solutions to specific problems in object-oriented software design (Gamma et al. 1995). Design patterns provide a common vocabulary for designers to communicate, document, and explore software design alternatives. They contain the knowledge and experience that underlie many redesign and recoding efforts of developers who have struggled to achieve greater reuse and flexibility in their software. Although design patterns and ontologies are not the same, they overlap to some extent. First, both of them are about vocabularies, about knowledge, and about "architectural armatures." Both concepts also describe things at the knowledge level. Ontologies are more common-sense-oriented; design patterns are more concrete. Next, it is possible to draw an analogy between libraries of ontologies and catalogs of design patterns. Although catalogs of design patterns do not provide ready-to-use building blocks like ontologies from libraries, some attempts are being made to make ready-to-use blocks available from them (see e.g., Staab and Studer 2004). Also, it does not take a hard mental shift to view ontologies as abstract patterns or as knowledge skeletons of domains. Likewise, it is not too hard to understand design pattern templates as knowledge of what the ontologies of design patterns may look like. All of these similarities support the possibility of developing ontologies in much the same way as software systems are developed using design patterns.

Given the efforts required by ontology building, reuse and reusability are very important issues for cost-effective and high-quality ontology engineering. *Ontology reuse* is the process in which existing (ontological) knowledge is used as input to generate new ontologies (Paslaru Bontas and Mochol 2005). Depending on the content of the knowledge sources and their overlapping, one can distinguish between ontology merging and integration.

An example of ontology reuse methodology presented in Paslaru Bontas and Mochol (2005) suggests developing a new ontology incrementally, starting from input knowledge sources, and going through two major phases. In the first phase, developers concentrate just on the concepts represented in the input sources; additional information comes later. The point of this first phase is to incrementally define a common vocabulary of terms and concepts in the input sources (merging). This vocabulary contains several lists of potential ontological primitives (concept names, properties, axioms). This incremental process includes computing syntactical similarities between concept names belonging to different source ontologies, word stemming, stop-word elimination, concept ranking, and other linguistic refinement techniques. Note that this first phase can be largely automated.

In the second phase, the user selects the relevant relationships, which can be added incrementally to the ontology until a certain level of complexity has been achieved.

Although relatively straightforward when simplified, this methodology has proved to be very useful and cost-saving. In addition, it allows reusing heterogenic input sources when developing a new ontology.

Recently, Web 2.0 technologies (O'Reilly 2005) have gained popularity in attempts to develop methodologies that reduce the time needed to develop ontologies. The idea here is to use *folksonomies* as the basis for ontology development. Folksonomies emerge from *collaborative tagging* as relatively fuzzy *categorizations* of data and information, as opposed to more strict and precise *classifications* of information specified by ontologies.

Note that an ontology is essentially a highly structured *taxonomy* (and much more!), i.e., a relatively rigid hierarchical classification of concepts. It requires a great deal of detail and consensus among domain experts and developers. Once developed (after a considerable effort), it is relatively difficult to modify. Still, it enables us to express precise constraints such as "Every jaguar is a cat with exactly four legs" (Halpin and Shepard 2006).

On the other hand, folksonomies result from the collaborative tagging efforts of a community of users and emerge more-or-less spontaneously, creating a specific ecosystem in which dynamics and change are always promptly reflected. On the other hand, folksonomies alone cannot be used efficiently and effectively for classification and knowledge sharing across the boundaries of the corresponding community, simply because they lack structure—they are just collections of terms that give insight into collective attention (Gruber 2005). They are also undisambiguated, and only statistically (but not semantically!) aligned (Hendler 2007).

Ontology development methodologies that start from folksonomies use the metaphor of "letting wanderers create paths through use, and then paving the emerging walkways" (Halpin and Shepard 2006). Once a folksonomy stabilizes enough through collaborative tagging, the tags can be used as the (partial) list of terms in the corresponding ontology. Heuristics for getting to concept hierarchies from these tag-terms are as follows:

* Tags that co-occur with other tags often represent more general concepts than more specific tags that co-occur with other tags less often. For example, "musician" co-occurs with both "pianist" and "guitar player," and as such often represents a superclass of both.
* On the other hand, "pianist" usually does not co-occur with more tags than "musician." Likewise, "pianist" typically co-occurs with "music" and so it likely is a subclass.
* Co-occurring tags can also suggest the semantics of O-A-V triplets (e.g., "Eric Clapton," "author," "song") or A-V pairs ("Eric Clapton," "Layla").
* Detecting synonyms in tags can be difficult, but it is likely for a community that within the tagging ecosystem, synonyms will merge over time.

Of course, these steps are not easy to automate. Likewise, there is no guarantee that the ontology one needs to develop will already have its readily available and stabilized folksonomy counterpart.

In addition, not all of the relationships among the concepts in an ontology can be easily and accurately derived from the corresponding folksonomy. At best, developers can hope the folksonomy will help them create a related *lightweight ontology*. Such an ontology typically provides just a taxonomy of related concepts and terms, with very few cross-taxonomical links (properties), very few logical relations between the concepts, and very few axioms and constraints imposed on the concepts. Unlike formal *heavyweight ontologies* that are difficult to create because they include a number of properties, axioms, and constraints, lightweight ontologies are easy to create. On the other hand, once developed, heavyweight ontologies are relatively easy to deploy; lightweight ontologies are not.

Still, there are estimates from authoritative sources that "the majority of the ontologies on the Semantic Web [are expected] to be lightweight. [. . .]

Our experiences to date in a variety of . . . applications (knowledge management, document retrieval, communities of practice, data integration) all point to lightweight ontologies as the most commonly occurring type" (Davies et al. 2002). For this reason, an ontology development methodology has been suggested that focuses on developing lightweight ontologies, while simultaneously capturing the strengths of heavyweight formal ontologies (Zhu and Madnick 2006). In this methodology, the high level concepts included in the lightweight ontology are complemented by subtle differences in the interpretation of the concepts captured as *context descriptions* outside the ontology. These context descriptions enable a scalable solution to semantic interoperability among disparate data sources and contexts. Since context descriptions are represented formally, there is an automated way to make data conversions from one context to another. This way, the lightweight ontology remains the skeleton of semantic interoperability between contexts and applications, while largely automated updates to the context descriptions and conversions reflect the dynamics and scalability of contexts and semantics.

Two important observations come out of this brief survey of ontology development methodologies. First, there are many common points in the various methodologies. Steps in different processes may be named differently, may also be of different granularity, or may only partially overlap; but the processes are still very much alike. Second, many of the principles and practices of ontology development are analogous to those of software engineering. The major topic of this book—applying the principles and standards of the MDA modeling and development approach, taken from software engineering, to ontology development—is completely in line with these observations.

2.3 Applications

Ontologies have become a major conceptual backbone for a broad spectrum of applications (Staab and Studer 2004). There is an increasing awareness among researchers and developers that ontologies are not just for knowledge-based systems, but for all software systems—all software needs models of the world, and hence can make use of ontologies at design time (Chandrasekaran et al. 1999). The major application fields for ontologies nowadays include knowledge management, e-learning, e-commerce, and integration of Web resources, intranet documents, and databases. They also include cooperation of Web services with enterprise applications, natural-language processing, intelligent information retrieval (especially from the Internet), virtual organizations, and simulation and modeling. The following examples from a broad spectrum of ontology application scenarios are but a few typical illustrations.

2.3.1 Magpie

Magpie is a tool that supports semantic interpretation of Web pages, thus enabling intelligent Web browsing (Domingue et al. 2004). It automatically associates an ontology-based semantic layer with Web resources, which enables the invocation of relevant services within a standard Web browser. In other words, ontologies make it possible to associate meaning with information on a Web page and then, on the basis of the identified meaning, to offer the user appropriate functionalities. In fact, Magpie offers complementary knowledge sources relevant to a Web resource, thus facilitating quick access to the underlying background knowledge and helping the user to make sense of content and contextual information on Web pages the user may be unfamiliar with.

Magpie works as a plug-in to standard Web browsers and appears as an additional toolbar in the browser. It relies on the availability of ontologies that represent various domains of discourse. The user can select an ontology for Magpie to work with, and the buttons that will appear in the Magpie toolbar will correspond to the concepts in the ontology. He/she can then use the Magpie toolbar to toggle highlighting of specific concepts of interest to him/her for the browsing session. The underlying ontology selected must be populated by instances, possibly automatically mined from relevant Web pages. The browser, when showing a Web page, will then highlight information related to the types of entities in the ontology that the user has selected from the Magpie toolbar. For example, if the ontology selected is the Musician ontology, and the highlighted concepts in the Magpie toolbar are Instrument and Album, in the home page of, say, a rock and roll star shown in the browser, words such as "guitar" and "keyboards" will be highlighted, and so will the titles of the star's albums.

Magpie detects patterns in the browsing session by tracking interesting items in the browsing log with the aid of an ontology-based filter. When a pattern is detected, Magpie activates an appropriate context-dependent trigger service. In the case of the Musician ontology and Web pages related to musicians and their activities, Magpie may use one panel to show the names of the musicians that it has semantically recognized from the Web pages in the browsing log, and another panel to show the titles of all of the albums related to those names in one way or another. In yet another panel, it may show musicians and albums not explicitly mentioned on the pages accessed in that session, but obtained from the populated ontology. This reveals explicitly to the user the information semantically related to the context of the browsing session. By right-clicking on any of the highlighted concepts on the page shown, the user can access from a popup menu any of the context-dependent (i.e., ontology-dependent) semantic services. In the case of musicians, these might be related to their concerts and tours, colleagues, managers, and so forth.

2.3.2 Briefing Associate

Knowledge sharing and reuse through automatic exchange of Web documents among applications and agents is possible only if the documents contain ontologically encoded information, often called semantic markup or semantic annotation, that software agents and tools can interpret accurately and reliably. Current annotation technology is covered in more detail in Chap. 3, but it suffices for this overview of Briefing Associate to note that annotation is usually performed manually (using annotation tools), which is a tedious and error-prone process. Briefing Associate deploys ontological knowledge to encode document annotation automatically as authors produce documents (Tallis et al. 2002).

The approach used in Briefing Associate can be described in simple terms as extending a commercial, frequently used document editor with ontology-based additional tools that the targeted category of authors will be highly motivated to use. Whenever such an author applies any of the additional tools, an appropriate annotation is automatically created and inserted into the document. Thus annotation comes at virtually no extra cost, as a by-product of activities that the author would perform anyway. The prerequisites include the existence of domain ontologies that authors creating documents can rely on, and easy creation of specific widgets to represent the ontology-based additional editing tools.

To this end, Briefing Associate has been implemented as an extension of Microsoft's PowerPoint in much the same way as Magpie extends standard Web browsers (see above)—it appears in PowerPoint's native GUI as a toolbar for adding graphics that represent a particular ontology's classes and properties. The graphical symbols on the toolbar are obtained from a special-purpose tool that lets graphic designers create such symbols to visually annotate ontologies. In a hypothetical example, the Musician ontology might be visualized with that tool, and various graphical symbols might be created to represent musical events, instruments, and the other concepts in the ontology. These symbols would then be inserted into the toolbar to represent the domain ontology (Musician) in PowerPoint.

To the domain author, the native PowerPoint GUI is still there, the editing process continues normally, and the resulting slide show looks as if the ontology was not used in the editing of the presentation. However, using any graphical symbol from the additional toolbar in the presentation document results in inserting a transparent annotation into the slides, which is saved with the document. PowerPoint installations not extended with Briefing Associate ignore such transparent annotations. However, the point is that the annotation can be used by Briefing Associate internally to produce various metadata (such as the document title, the author, and a reference to the ontology used), and additional XML-based documents that can be published on the Web so that other agents and applications can locate the main document more easily and automatically interpret its content in terms of the concepts in the ontology.

2.3.3 Quickstep and Foxtrot

Quickstep and Foxtrot are ontology-based recommender systems that recommend online academic research papers (Middleton et al. 2004). Although they both focus on a relatively small target group of Web users, the principles built into these two systems can be translated to other target groups as well.

In general, recommender systems unobtrusively watch user behavior and recommend new items that correlate with a user's profile. A typical example of such recommendation can be found on Amazon.com, where users obtain suggestions about what books, CDs, and other items to buy according to their observed shopping behavior and a previously created set of user profiles. Recommender systems usually create user profiles on the basis of user ratings of specific items and the content of items; however, in many cases, this may be insufficient and can lead to inconsistent recommendations.

Quickstep and Foxtrot rely on ontology-based user profiling. They use a research-paper topic ontology to represent user interests in ontological terms. True, some of the fine-grained information held in the raw examples of interest is lost in this way. However, the ontology allows inference to assist user profiling through is-a relationships in the topic classification. Moreover, communication with other, external ontologies is enabled, and so is visualization of user profiles in terms of the topic ontology. Both systems provide a set of labeled example papers for each concept in the ontology to assist the creation of initial user profiles. The users themselves can add papers of interest to such sets in order to fine-tune their profiles and to reflect their changing needs. Through profile visualization, the users can better understand what the recommenders "think" about their interests and adjust their profiles interactively.

2.4 Advanced Topics

Being shared world models, content theories, representational artifacts of essential knowledge about topics and domains, and reusable building blocks of knowledge-based systems, ontologies are also tightly coupled to other concepts related to domain/world modeling, such as metadata and metamodeling. Being simultaneously concept hierarchies, ontologies also raise the question of how far the generalization/specialization in the hierarchies can extend.

2.4.1 Metadata, Metamodeling, and Ontologies

The prefix "meta" means one level of description higher. *Metadata* are data about data, and a *metamodel* is a model used to describe other models. Metadata are descriptions of data, and metamodels are descriptions used to characterize models.

From a more practical point of view, metadata most often represent some description of digital resources, especially on the Web. Such a description is a mechanism for expressing the semantics of the resource as a means to facilitate seeking, retrieval, understanding, and use of information. The nature and purpose of metadata are referential, that is, metadata express something about some resource. For example, Web documents, considered as a class of resources, are described in terms of their *authors, titles, URIs,* etc. A specific Web document is described by a metadata record containing metadata (characterizing all Web documents) and their specific values (characterizing that specific document only), i.e., by a set of attribute–value pairs (metadata–value pairs) such as "*author*–Denny, M.," and "*title*–Ontology building: a survey of editing tools."

Metadata can be expressed in various forms. For example, the *title* element of an HTML page represents embedded metadata. A *metadata language* is a shared description system that can be used to encode metadata.

One view of ontology representation languages is that they can be used as metadata languages—ontologies engineered with such languages can provide vocabularies for metadata to facilitate the management, discovery, and retrieval of resources on the Web. However, some consistency must be ensured in using terms defined in these ontologies as metadata. To an extent, this has been provided by standardization initiatives such as the

Dublin Core Metadata Initiative (DC Metadata Schema 2008), which promotes the widespread adoption of interoperable metadata standards and is developing specialized metadata vocabularies for describing various electronic resources. The purpose of such standards is to support both machine interoperability (information exchange) and targeted resource discovery by human users of the Web.

A metamodel is an explicit model of the constructs and rules needed to build specific models within a domain of interest. This characterizes a valid metamodel as an ontology, since such constructs and rules represent entities in a domain and their relationships, i.e., a set of building blocks used to build domain models. In other words, a metamodel is an ontology used by modelers. For example, when software developers use UML to construct models of software systems, they actually use an ontology implemented in it. This ontology defines concepts such as objects, classes, and relations. However, not all ontologies are modeled explicitly as metamodels.

2.4.2 Standard Upper Ontology

Imagine that someone wants to extend the simple Musician ontology shown in Figs. 2.2, 2.3, and 2.4 and has included concepts such as *street musician, professional musician,* and *occasional musician* using a direct *is-a* link (relation) to the higher-level concept of *musician.* In the case of the Musician ontology, *musician* is also one of the top-level concepts. However, an obvious question might be: Is there an even higher-level, more general concept than *musician* that we can use as a generalization of the concept of *musician* through another direct *is-a* link? In other words, what concept extends the Musician ontology upwards, starting from the concept of *musician?*

Apart from the obvious dilemma of selecting the right concept to suit one's purpose (is that concept *Performer, Profession,* or something else?), another problem quickly becomes apparent when one starts thinking about such extensions—how far up is it possible to go in this way? The problem can be reformulated as a series of questions such as:

- Is there a highest, root concept, and if so, what is it?
- What does the hierarchy of higher, i.e., upper-level, concepts look like?
- Who is responsible for those upper-level concepts?

The first question is easy to answer, but only technically—just as Java defines the *Object* class as the topmost class, it is possible to define such a root concept to model all of the upper-level concepts in a single upper-level ontology. In fact, there are examples of such technical approaches and even implementations of the concept of "topmost;" for instance, Protégé internally implements the concept of *Thing* as the root concept of all hierarchies and ontologies.

However, the problem is far more complex than a simple technical implementation, because it concerns a number of scientific and technical disciplines. Today, researchers in the fields of computer science, artificial intelligence, philosophy, library science, and linguistics are making attempts to formulate a comprehensive, formal, upper-level ontology to provide definitions for general-purpose terms and act as a foundation for more specific domain ontologies. However, workers in none of these fields have been able, on their own, to construct a *standard* upper-level ontology (Niles and Pease 2001).

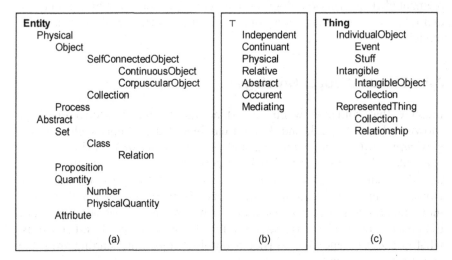

Fig. 2.6   Top levels of various concept hierarchies for the upper-level ontology: (**a**) according to Niles and Pease (2001); (**b**) according to Sowa (2000); (**c**) according to Lenat and Guha (1990) and Lenat (1995)

It is intuitively clear that such an endeavor must be a collaborative effort of specialists from different fields, but that fact creates a consensus problem—philosophers themselves have not yet reached a consensus on what the upper-level concept hierarchy should look like, let alone the question of a consensus among experts from other disciplines. Figure 2.6 shows some of the proposed hierarchies (root concepts shown in bold face), but the second of the questions listed above is still open. Although the hierarchies represented may appear to be trees, in many approaches they are actually more complex structures, i.e., lattices. In Fig. 2.6c, for example, a lattice is implicitly present in the fact that the Collection concept appears in two different branches, which, in terms of frame-based languages, implies multiple inheritance. For the sake of simplicity, the representation in Fig. 2.6b is not shown here in its expanded version, which is actually also a complex lattice (Sowa 2000). Its root concept, ⊤, was originally defined as *universal type* that subsumes all other concepts.

It is clear from Fig. 2.6 that a consensus is so lacking that even the term used for the root concept is different in different representations. The lack of a consensus arises for an obvious reason: it is extremely difficult to conceive such a very large, wide-coverage ontology, in spite of the fact that there is a need for one and that there already exist the necessary formal ontology representation languages.

Going back to practice, the need for a standard upper-level ontology was the driving force that caused the IEEE to organize the Standard Upper Ontology Working Group (SUO WG) to develop such a standard ontology under its project P1600.1 (SUO WG 2008). This is, at least at the moment, an answer to the third of the questions listed above. The *standard upper ontology* (SUO) that will result from this project is limited to metaconcepts and generic, abstract, and philosophical concepts, which therefore are general enough to address (at a high level) a broad range of domain areas. It is intended to provide a structure and a set of general concepts upon which domain ontologies (e.g., medical, financial, or engineering) could be constructed. The collaborators in the SUO WG come from various fields of engineering, philosophy, and information science. The group has started from several upper-level ontologies suggested in the literature so far, e.g., SUMO (Suggested Upper Merged Ontology, Niles and Pease 2001); the CYC ontology (Lenat and Guha 1990; Lenat 1995); the upper-level ontology described by Russell and Norvig (2002); and John Sowa's upper-level ontology (Sowa 2000), and is trying to accommodate most of their concepts and relations under the same umbrella. It is estimated that the SUO will eventually contain between 1000 and 2500 terms and roughly ten definitional statements for each term. Currently, the representation language used for the SUO is a somewhat simplified version of KIF, called SUO-KIF.

When completed, the SUO is envisioned to have a variety of purposes, such as the design of new knowledge bases and databases, re-use/integration of legacy databases (by mapping their data elements to a common ontology), and integration of domain-specific ontologies. Since the SUO is an IEEE-sponsored open-source standards effort, it is hoped that it will eventually be embraced by a large class of users. Also, the SUO is based on very pragmatic principles and any distinctions of strictly philosophical interest have been removed from it (Niles and

Pease 2001); because of this, it should be simpler to use than some of the other upper-level ontologies that the working group started from.

The point is that the SUO will contribute to the goal of enhancing application interoperability by providing a common framework for the integration and sharing of different databases, knowledge bases, and domain ontologies, by virtue of shared terms and definitions. An important implication is that all other SUO-compliant ontologies that may exist under such a common ontological framework will be interconnected in some way.

2.4.3 Ontological Level

Recalling Allen Newell's idea of describing knowledge representation in terms of the implementation, logical, and knowledge levels (Sect. 1.8), one may ask a simple question: Where do ontologies fit in this three-layer scheme? They do have a formal representation and structure, and thus might be thought of as parts of the logical level. On the other hand, they also represent the essential concepts and relations in a domain, and all of the other domain knowledge relies on them, which may qualify them as parts of the knowledge level.

The dilemma was resolved by Guarino (1995), who proposed the notion of the *ontological level* and placed it as an intermediate level in between the logical and knowledge levels. The purpose of the ontological level is to constrain and to make explicit the intended model of the knowledge representation language, i.e., the intended meaning of the primitives of the knowledge representation formalisms used.

As an example, consider the following expression at the logical level: $\exists x.\ Musician(x) \wedge Beginner(x)$. At the knowledge level, this expression may be intended to mean that *Musician* is a concept and that *Beginner* is the value (filler) of the property *Level*. However, it is also perfectly valid in the real world to think of *Beginner* as a concept as well. If the modeler wants to make sure that the system interprets *Beginner* as the value of the property *Level,* and not as another concept, then it is actually the ontology that must clearly state so, thus explicitly constraining the possible interpretations.

3 The Semantic Web

The Semantic Web is the new-generation Web that tries to represent information so that it can be used by machines not just for display purposes, but for automation, integration, and reuse across applications (Boley et al. 2001). It has been one of the hottest R&D topics in recent years in the AI community, as well as in the Internet community—the Semantic Web[1] is an important W3C activity (SW Activity 2008).

> Semantic Web is about making the Web more understandable by machines (Heflin and Hendler 2001). It is also about building an appropriate infrastructure for intelligent agents to run around the Web performing complex actions for their users (Hendler 2001). In order to do that, agents must retrieve and manipulate pertinent information, which requires seamless agent integration with the Web and taking full advantage of the existing infrastructure (such as message sending, security, authentication, directory services, and application service frameworks) (Scott Cost et al. 2002). Furthermore, Semantic Web is about explicitly declaring the knowledge embedded in many Web-based applications, integrating information in an intelligent way, providing semantic-based access to the Internet, and extracting information from texts (Gómez-Pérez and Corcho 2002). Ultimately, Semantic Web is about how to implement reliable, large-scale interoperation of Web services, to make such services computer interpretable—to create a Web of machine-understandable and interoperable services that

---

[1] The Semantic Web is sometimes referred to as Web 3.0, in order to make a difference between its technologies and the technologies like blogging, social bookmarking (tagging), social networking, and the like, known collectively as Web 2.0 (or Social Web). Within the broad spectrum of Web technologies, Semantic Web and Web 2.0 technologies can be seen as complementing rather than competing with each other. Both are useful and exciting. Although tackling different sets of problems, these two sets of technologies can be combined to produce interesting results.

D. Gašević et al., *Model Driven Engineering and Ontology Development*, 2nd edn.,
DOI 10.1007/978-3-642-00282-3_3, © Springer-Verlag Berlin Heidelberg 2009

intelligent agents can discover, execute, and compose automatically. (McIlraith et al. 2001; Devedžić 2004a)[2]

3.1 Rationale[3]

Why do we need all that? Isn't the Web an immense, practically unlimited source of information and knowledge that everyone can use?

The problem is that the Web is huge, but not smart enough to easily integrate all of those numerous pieces of information that a user really needs. Such integration at a high, user-oriented level is desirable in nearly all uses of the Web. Today, most Web information is represented in natural-language; however, our computers cannot understand and interpret its meaning. Humans themselves can process only a tiny fraction of information available on the Web, and would benefit enormously if they could turn to machines for help in processing and analyzing the Web contents (Noy et al. 2001). Unfortunately, the Web was built for human consumption, not for machine consumption—although everything on the Web is *machine-readable,* it is not *machine-understandable* (Lassila 1998). We need the Semantic Web to express information in a precise, machine-interpretable form, ready for software agents to process, share, and reuse it, as well as to understand what the terms describing the data mean. That would enable Web-based applications to interoperate both on the syntactic and the semantic level.

Note that it is Tim Berners-Lee himself who pushes the idea of the Semantic Web forward. The father of the Web first envisioned a Semantic Web that provides automated information access based on machine-processable semantics of data and heuristics that use these metadata (Berners-Lee et al. 1999, 2001). The explicit representation of the semantics of data, accompanied with domain theories (that is, ontologies), will enable a Web that provides a qualitatively new level of service—for example, intelligent search engines, information brokers, and information filters (Decker et al. 2000; Fensel and Musen 2001).

People from W3C have already developed new technologies for Web-friendly data description. Moreover, AI people have already developed

---

[2] Paragraph reprinted (with minor adjustments to citation formatting of Devedžić [2004a]) with permission from IOS Press.

[3] Section reprinted (with minor adjustments to citation formatting) from Devedžić [2004a]) with permission from IOS Press.

some useful applications and tools for the Semantic Web (Noy et al. 2001; Scott Cost et al. 2002).

There are a number of important issues related to the Semantic Web. Roughly speaking, they belong to the following categories: languages for the Semantic Web, ontologies, semantic markup (semantic annotation) of pages on the Semantic Web, development frameworks, reasoning, and services that the Semantic Web is supposed to provide.

The current state of Semantic Web developments is such that the first two of the above categories are well supported by appropriate technologies, whereas the other four need further development. In other words, the focus is currently on *data* on the Web and on representing semantic interconnections of data. W3C Semantic Web Activity is very specific about it (SW Activity 2008):

> The Semantic Web provides a common framework that allows data to be shared and reused across application, enterprise, and community boundaries. . . . It is based on the Resource Description Framework (RDF).

> The Semantic Web is a *web of data*. There is lots of data we all use every day, and it is not part of the Web. I can see my bank statements on the Web, and my photographs, and I can see my appointments in a calendar. But can I see my photos in a calendar to see what I was doing when I took them? Can I see bank statement lines in a calendar?

> Why not? Because we don't have a web of data. Because data is controlled by applications, and each application keeps it to itself.

> The Semantic Web is about two things. It is about common formats for integration and combination of data drawn from diverse sources, whereas the original Web mainly concentrated on the interchange of documents. It is also about language for recording how the data relates to real world objects. That allows a person, or a machine, to start off in one database, and then move through an unending set of databases which are connected not by wires but by being about the same thing.

3.2 Semantic Web Languages

In the literature, the Web-based ontology languages listed in Chap. 2 are usually called Semantic Web languages as well. However, W3C is more specific about this (SW Activity 2008):

The Semantic Web Activity . . . develops open specifications for those technologies that are ready for large scale deployment, and identifies, through open source advanced development, the infrastructure components that will be necessary to scale in the Web in the future.

The principal technologies of the Semantic Web fit into a set of layered specifications. The current components are the Resource Description Framework (RDF) Core Model, the RDF Schema language, and the Web Ontology language (OWL). Building on these core components is a standardized query language for RDF, SPARQL (pronounced "sparkle"), enabling the "joining" of decentralized collections of RDF data. The GRDDL Recommendation and the work on RDFa aims at creating bridges between the RDF model and various XML formats, like XHTML. The POWDER Working group develops technologies to find resource descriptions for specific resources on the Web; descriptions which can be "joined" to other RDF data. Finally, SKOS is a model and an RDF vocabulary for expressing the basic structure and content of concept schemes such as thesauri, classification schemes, subject heading lists, taxonomies, "folksonomies," other types of controlled vocabulary, and also concept schemes embedded in glossaries and terminologies.

The above statement is a rough textual equivalent of the major part of Tim Berners-Lee's vision of Web development, aptly nicknamed the "Semantic Web layer-cake" Fig. 3.1 (Berners-Lee et al. 1999, 2001). Note that in the Semantic Web layer-cake, higher-level languages use the syntax and semantics of the lower levels. All Semantic Web languages use XML syntax; in fact, XML is a metalanguage for representing other Semantic Web languages. For example, XML Schema defines a class of XML documents using the XML syntax. RDF provides a framework for representing metadata about Web resources, and is XML-based as well. RDF Schema, OWL, and other ontology languages also use the XML syntax.

The following subsections discuss the Semantic Web layer-cake in more detail and depict the genesis of the current state of the art in the domain of Semantic Web languages. Note, however, that the Semantic Web layer-cake has a number of versions. As the Semantic Web technologies evolve, the Semantic Web layer-cake gets modified accordingly, more details are introduced, and the focus can shift from one point to another. For the latest version of the Semantic Web layer-cake, see http://www.w3.org/2007/03/layerCake.svg.

Fig. 3.1   Tim Berners-Lee's Semantic web layer-cake

3.2.1 XML and XML Schema

It is important for Semantic Web developers to agree on the data's syntax and semantics before hard-coding them into their applications, since changes to syntax and semantics necessitate expensive modifications of applications (Wuwongse et al. 2002).

Current Semantic Web languages rely on an XML-based syntax (Klein 2001; XML 2005). Generally, XML (eXtensible Markup Language) enables the specification and markup of computer-readable documents. It looks very much like HTML in that special sequences of characters—tags—are used to mark up the document content, and that XML data is stored as ordinary text. Unlike HTML, however, XML can be used to annotate documents of arbitrary structure, and there is no fixed tag vocabulary. Typically, XML tags contain information indicating the human interpretation of pieces of the document's content, such as *<name>*, *<musician>*, and *<record>*. Thus XML lets people *meaningfully* annotate documents by adding context to and indicating the meaning of the data. People can define their own custom tags to represent data logically, making XML documents self-describing (because the tags describe the information the documents contain).

Figure 3.2 shows an example of how the same piece of information can be represented in HTML and in XML. Obviously, HTML is layout-oriented, whereas XML is more structure-oriented.

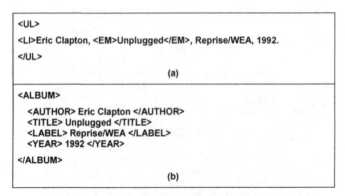

```
<UL>
<LI>Eric Clapton, <EM>Unplugged</EM>, Reprise/WEA, 1992.
</UL>
```
(a)

```
<ALBUM>
    <AUTHOR> Eric Clapton </AUTHOR>
    <TITLE> Unplugged </TITLE>
    <LABEL> Reprise/WEA </LABEL>
    <YEAR> 1992 </YEAR>
</ALBUM>
```
(b)

Fig. 3.2   (**a**) A piece of HTML code (**b**) The same information in XML code

However, XML does not itself imply a specific machine interpretation of the data. In the piece of XML in Fig. 3.2b, the meaning is not formally specified. The information is only encoded in an unambiguous syntax, but its use and the semantics are not specified. In other words, XML is aimed only at the structure of a document, not at a common machine interpretation of it. It provides only a data format for structured documents, without specifying a vocabulary.

On the other hand, owing to the standardized data format and structure of XML documents, programs and scripts can dynamically access and update the content, structure, and style of such documents (DOM 2005). Appropriate parsers and other processing tools for XML documents are readily available. Moreover, XML is extensible in a standardized way, and hence enables customized markup languages to be defined for unlimited types of documents.

Using XML for document and data exchange among applications requires prior agreement on the vocabulary, its use, and the meaning of its terms. Such agreement can be partly achieved by using XML schemas, which provide a mechanism to specify the structure of XML documents. Every XML schema provides the necessary framework for creating a category of XML documents (XML Schema 2008). The schema describes the various tags, elements, and attributes of an XML document of that specific category, the valid document structure, the constraints, and the custom data types (these are based on built-in types, such as integer and string). The XML Schema language also provides some limited support for specifying the number of occurrences of child elements, default values, choice groups, etc. The encoding syntax of the XML Schema language is XML, and just like XML itself, XML Schema documents use *namespaces* that are declared using the *xmlns* attribute. The example schema in Fig. 3.3 declares the *xsd* namespace and uses it throughout its element definitions.

Namespaces define contexts within which the corresponding tags and names apply. The schema shown corresponds to a category of XML documents such as that shown in Fig. 3.2b.

```
<xsd:schema xmlns:xsd="http://www.w3.org/1999/XMLSchema">
<xsd:element name="ALBUM" type="ALBUMTYPE"/>
<xsd:complexType name="ALBUMTYPE" >
  <xsd:element name="AUTHOR" type="xsd:string"
    minOccurs="1" maxOccurs="unbounded"/>
  <xsd:element name="TITLE" type="xsd:string"/>
  . . .
  <xsd:element name="YEAR" type="xsd:integer"/>
</xsd:complexType>
</xsd:schema>
```

Fig. 3.3   An example of an XML schema

3.2.2 RDF and RDF Schema

XML provides an easy-to-use syntax for encoding all of the kinds of data that are exchanged between computers, by using XML schemas to prescribe the data structure. However, since it does not provide any interpretation of the data beforehand, it does not contribute much to the semantic aspect of the Semantic Web. To provide machine interpretation of Web data, a standard model is needed to describe facts about Web resources. Such a standard model can be specified by use of RDF and RDF Schema.

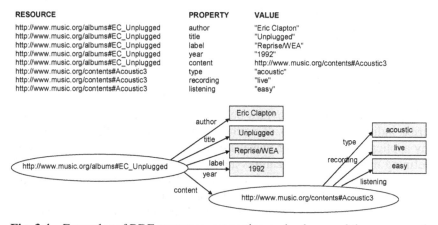

RESOURCE	PROPERTY	VALUE
http://www.music.org/albums#EC_Unplugged	author	"Eric Clapton"
http://www.music.org/albums#EC_Unplugged	title	"Unplugged"
http://www.music.org/albums#EC_Unplugged	label	"Reprise/WEA"
http://www.music.org/albums#EC_Unplugged	year	"1992"
http://www.music.org/albums#EC_Unplugged	content	http://www.music.org/contents#Acoustic3
http://www.music.org/contents#Acoustic3	type	"acoustic"
http://www.music.org/contents#Acoustic3	recording	"live"
http://www.music.org/contents#Acoustic3	listening	"easy"

Fig. 3.4   Examples of RDF resources, properties, and values, and the corresponding graph

RDF's model for representing data about "things on the Web" (resources) is that of O–A–V triplets and semantic networks. A resource description in RDF is a list of *statements* (triplets), each expressed in terms of a Web *resource* (an object), one of its *properties* (attributes), and the *value* of the property (Manola and Miller 2004). The value can be a literal (text), or another resource. Every RDF description can be also represented as a directed labeled graph (a semantic network), parts of which are equivalent to RDF statements. Figure 3.4 shows several such triplets and the corresponding graph. These can be represented in an RDF encoding (which also uses XML syntax), as in Fig. 3.5.

The fact that the value of a property in an RDF encoding can be either a literal value or another resource creates a *stripping pattern* in the RDF encoding format (Fig. 3.6). This makes it easy to check the overall consistency of an RDF-encoded document. It also makes RDF a suitable format for visual knowledge representation languages based on semantic networks.

```
<Album rdf:ID="EC_Unplugged"
        xmlns:rdf="http://www.w3.org/1999/02/22-rdf-syntax-ns#"
        xmlns="http://www.music.org/albums#"
        xml:base="http://www.music.org/albums">
    <author>Eric Clapton</author>
    <title>Unplugged</title>
    <label>Reprise/WEA</label>
    <year>1992</year>
    <content>
        <Content rdf:ID="Acoustic3"
                xmlns="http://www.music.org/contents#">
            <type>acoustic</type>
            <listening>easy</listening>
            <recording>live</recording>
        </Content>
    </content>
</Album>
```

Fig. 3.5   RDF encoding of the resources shown in Fig. 3.4

An RDF model itself provides only a domain-neutral mechanism to describe individual resources. It neither defines (a priori) the semantics of any application domain, nor makes assumptions about a particular domain. Defining domain-specific features and their semantics, i.e., ontologies, requires additional facilities. RDF itself is used to describe instances of ontologies, whereas RDF Schema encodes ontologies.

RDF Schema (RDFS) provides an XML-based vocabulary to specify classes and their relationships, to define properties and associate them with classes, and to enable the creation of taxonomies (Brickley and Guha 2004). To do all this, RDFS uses frame-based modeling primitives such as

Class, subClassOf, Property, and *subPropertyOf.* The *Resource* concept occurs in the root of all hierarchies and taxonomies. Figure 3.7 shows an example of an RDFS encoding.

```
<?xml version="1.0"?>
<Resource-A>
  <property-A>
    <Resource-B>
      <property-B>
        <Resource-C>
          <property-C>
            Value-C
          </property-C>
        </Resource-C>
      </property-B>
    </Resource-B>
  </property-A>
</Resource-A>
```

Fig. 3.6   The stripping pattern of an RDF model

```
<rdf:RDF        xmlns:rdf="http://www.w3.org/1999/02/22-rdf-syntax-ns#"
                xmlns:rdfs="http://www.w3.org/2000/01/rdf-schema#"
                xml:base="http://www.music.org/albums">

  <rdfs:Class rdf:ID="Album">
     <rdfs:subClassOf rdf:resource="http://www.w3.org/2000/01/rdf-schema#Resource"/>
  </rdfs:Class>

  <rdfs:Class rdf:ID="Content">
     <rdfs:subClassOf rdf:resource="http://www.w3.org/2000/01/rdf-schema#Resource"/>
  </rdfs:Class>

  ...

  <rdf:Property rdf:ID="author">
     <rdfs:domain rdf:resource="#Album"/>
     <rdfs:range rdf:resource="#Musician"/>
  </rdf:Property>

  ...

  <rdf:Property rdf:ID="year">
     <rdfs:domain rdf:resource="#Album"/>
     <rdfs:range rdf:resource="http://www.w3.org/2000/01/rdf-schema#Literal"/>
  </rdf:Property>

  ...

</rdf:RDF>
```

Fig. 3.7   RDFS encoding of albums (excerpt)

There is an important departure in RDFS from the classical frame-based paradigm: properties are defined separately from classes. An implication is that anyone, anywhere, anytime can create a property and state that it is usable with a class, or with multiple classes. Each property is typically described by *rdfs:domain* and *rdfs:range,* which restrict the possible combinations of properties and classes. For example, in Fig. 3.7 the domain of the property *year* is restricted to the class *Album,* which means that this property is used only with that class. On the other hand, a property may be defined so as to feature multiple classes. As in the classical case, in class hierarchies classes inherit properties from their ancestors.

RDF(S) provides a standard model to describe facts about Web resources, but modelers often need even richer and more expressive primitives to specify the formal semantics of Web resources. RDFS is quite simple compared with full-fledged knowledge representation languages. For example, one cannot state in RDFS that "this class is equivalent to this other class," and cannot specify cardinality constraints.

3.2.3 DAML+OIL

DAML+OIL has evolved from two other languages, DAML-ONT (Hendler and McGuinness 2000) and OIL (Fensel et al. 2001), both of which were heavily influenced by RDF(S). In the context of the Semantic Web layer-cake (Fig. 3.1), RDF(S) defines a simple model for representing semantics and basic ontological-modeling primitives, whereas DAML-ONT, OIL, and DAML+OIL all aim at providing a more expressive ontology development vocabulary. They offer richer ways to define concepts and attributes, and a more intuitive choice of some of the modeling primitives (widely used modeling primitives from logic-based and frame-based languages).

DAML-ONT (Hendler and McGuinness 2000) was part of the DARPA Agent Markup Language (DAML) initiative, aimed at supporting the development of the Semantic Web. As an ontology language, it covered the capturing of definitions of terms—classes, subclasses, and their properties, as well as their restrictions and individual object descriptions. Another part of the DAML language (called DAML-LOGIC) addressed the issue of encoding inference and general logical implications. DAML-ONT stressed the role of ontological markup of Web resources to facilitate intercommunication between agents.

OIL (Ontology Inference Layer) originated from a European initiative; its formal semantics was based on description logics and it had a set of customized editors and inference engines to support working with it (Fensel et al. 2001).

```
<rdf:RDF
 xmlns:rdf ="http://www.w3.org/1999/02/22-rdf-syntax-ns#"
 xmlns:rdfs="http://www.w3.org/2000/01/rdf-schema#"
 xmlns:daml="http://www.daml.org/2001/03/daml+oil#"
 xmlns    ="http://www.daml.org/2001/03/daml+oil-ex#"
>

<daml:Ontology rdf:about="">
 <rdfs:comment>
  An example simple DAML+OIL ontology.
 </rdfs:comment>
 <daml:imports rdf:resource="http://www.daml.org/2001/03/daml+oil"/>
</daml:Ontology>

<daml:Class rdf:ID="Musician">
 <rdfs:label>Musician</rdfs:label>
 <rdfs:comment>
  This class assumes just two disjoint kinds of musicians - instrumentalists and singers.
 </rdfs:comment>
</daml:Class>

<daml:Class rdf:ID="Album">
 <rdfs:label>Album</rdfs:label>
 <rdfs:comment>
  The class describing recorded albums.
 </rdfs:comment>
</daml:Class>

<daml:Class rdf:ID="Instrumentalist">
 <rdfs:subClassOf rdf:resource="#Musician"/>
</daml:Class>

<daml:Class rdf:ID="Singer">
 <rdfs:subClassOf rdf:resource="#Musician"/>
 <daml:disjointWith rdf:resource="#Instrumentalist"/>
</daml:Class>

...

</rdf:RDF>
```

Fig. 3.8   An example DAML+OIL ontology—header and classes (excerpt)

One of OIL's important emphases was on a layered approach to ontology language specification. *Core OIL* largely coincides with RDFS. This means that even simple RDFS agents can process Core OIL ontologies and understand their semantics, and that an OIL processor can understand RDFS. *Standard OIL* captures semantics and makes complete inference viable by means of the necessary mainstream modeling primitives, such as *Class-def* (equivalent to *rdfs:Class*), *Subclass-of* (*rdfs:subClassOf*), *Slot constraint* (*oil:hasSlotConstraint* and *oil:SlotConstraint*), *AND* (*oil:and*), *NOT* (*oil:not*), and *Has-value* (*oil:hasValue*). Furthermore, *Instance OIL* provides thorough integration of individuals through a full-fledged database capability, and *Heavy OIL* opens the language to the possibility of including even higher-level representational and reasoning needs, such as various rule languages and metaclasses.

DAML+OIL (Horrocks and van Harmelen 2002; Scott Cost et al. 2002) has merged the principles and advantages of DAML and OIL, in an effort to develop a universal Semantic Web language that can enable machines to read data and interpret and draw inferences from it. As a result, and in addition to providing rules and definitions similar to those of RDF(S), DAML+OIL also enables further constraints and relationships among resources to be specified, including cardinality, domain and range restrictions, and union, disjunction, inverse, and transitive rules.

```
<rdf:RDF
...
>

...

<daml:ObjectProperty rdf:ID="isAuthorOf">
 <rdfs:domain rdf:resource="#Musician"/>
 <rdfs:range rdf:resource="#Album"/>
</daml:ObjectProperty>

...

<daml:DatatypeProperty rdf:ID="year">
 <rdfs:comment>
  year is a DatatypeProperty whose range is xsd: nonNegativeInteger.
  year is also a UniqueProperty (there is only one year when an album is recorded)
 </rdfs:comment>
 <rdf:type rdf:resource="http://www.daml.org/2001/03/daml+oil#UniqueProperty"/>
 <rdfs:range rdf:resource="http://www.w3.org/2000/10/XMLSchema#nonNegativeInteger"/>
</daml:DatatypeProperty>

...

<Musician rdf:ID="Eric Clapton">
 <rdfs:label>Eric Clapton</rdfs:label>
 <rdfs:comment> Eric Clapton is a musician.</rdfs:comment>
 <name><xsd:string rdf:value="Eric Clapton"/></name>
 ...
</Musician>

...

</rdf:RDF>
```

Fig. 3.9   An example DAML+OIL ontology—properties and individuals (excerpt)

DAML+OIL divides the universe into two disjoint parts—the *datatype domain* (the values that belong to XML Schema datatypes), and the *object domain* (individual objects, considered to be members of classes described within DAML+OIL or RDF). Likewise, there are generally two sorts of DAML+OIL properties—those that relate objects to other objects (specified by *daml:ObjectProperty*), and those that relate objects to datatype values (specified by *daml:DatatypeProperty*). The syntax for classes and properties is similar to that of DAML and OIL (Figs. 3.8 and 3.9); instances of classes and properties are written in RDF(S) syntax (Fig. 3.9).

3.2.4 OWL

OWL (Smith et al. 2004; Bao et al. 2008) is a successor to DAML+OIL (see Fig. 3.10). Like its predecessors, the OWL vocabulary includes a set of XML elements and attributes, with well-defined meanings. These are used to describe domain terms and their relationships in an ontology. In fact, the OWL vocabulary is built on top of the RDF(S) vocabulary. Things such as *Class* and *subClassOf* exist in OWL as well, and so do *ObjectProperty, DatatypeProperty,* and many more, as a heritage from DAML+OIL (see Fig. 3.11).

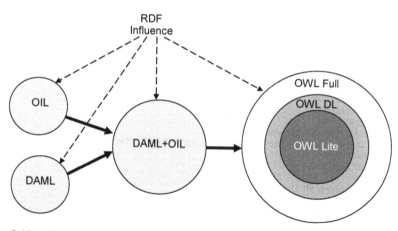

Fig. 3.10   The genesis of OWL

An important feature of the OWL vocabulary is its extreme richness for describing relations among classes, properties, and individuals. For example, we can specify in OWL that a property is *Symmetric,* the *InverseOf* another one, an *equivalentProperty* of another one, and *Transitive;* that a certain property has some specific *cardinality,* or *minCardinality,* or *maxCardinality;* and that a class is defined to be an *intersectionOf* or a *unionOf* some other classes, and that it is a *complementOf* another class. Similarly, a class instance can be the *sameIndividualAs* another instance, or it can be required to be *differentFrom* some other instance. For example, using the *equivalentProperty* relation, the object properties *author* and *artist* are specified to be equivalent in Fig. 3.11. Thus, if an instance of Album specifies its *artist,* and an application "knowing" that an album must have an *author* consults the ontology to "understand" what the instance is about, it will infer that the *artist* specified in the instance is actually the *author* of the album. A nice consequence is that reasoning can be performed in spite of such terminological differences.

```
<?xml version="1.0"?>
<rdf:RDF
   xmlns="http://www.music.org/musicians.owl#"
   xmlns:rdf="http://www.w3.org/1999/02/22-rdf-syntax-ns#"
   xmlns:xsd="http://www.w3.org/2001/XMLSchema#"
   xmlns:rdfs="http://www.w3.org/2000/01/rdf-schema#"
   xmlns:owl="http://www.w3.org/2002/07/owl#"
xml:base="http://www.music.org/musicians.owl">
<owl:Ontology rdf:about="Musician"/>
<owl:Class rdf:ID="Musician"/>
<owl:Class rdf:ID="musician_Class_13">
   <rdfs:subClassOf rdf:resource="#Musician"/>
</owl:Class>
<owl:Class rdf:ID="Instrument"/>
<owl:Class rdf:ID="Album">
   <rdfs:subClassOf rdf:resource="http://www.w3.org/2002/07/owl#Thing"/>
   <rdfs:subClassOf>
    <owl:Restriction>
     <owl:onProperty rdf:resource="#title"/>
     <owl:cardinality rdf:datatype="http://www.w3.org/2001/XMLSchema#int">1</owl:cardinality>
    </owl:Restriction>
   </rdfs:subClassOf>
   <rdfs:subClassOf>
    <owl:Restriction>
     <owl:onProperty rdf:resource="#year"/>
     <owl:cardinality rdf:datatype="http://www.w3.org/2001/XMLSchema#int">1</owl:cardinality>
    </owl:Restriction>
   </rdfs:subClassOf>
</owl:Class>
<owl:ObjectProperty rdf:ID="author">
   <owl:equivalentProperty rdf:resource="#artist"/>
   <rdfs:domain rdf:resource="#Album"/>
   <rdfs:range rdf:resource="#Musician"/>
</owl:ObjectProperty>
<owl:ObjectProperty rdf:about="#artist">
   <rdfs:range rdf:resource="#Musician"/>
   <rdfs:domain rdf:resource="#Album"/>
</owl:ObjectProperty>
   ...
```

Fig. 3.11   Excerpt from the Musician ontology developed in Protégé

Another important DAML+OIL heritage is OWL's layered structure, also indicated in Fig. 3.10. In fact, OWL is not a closed language; it is, rather, a combination of three increasingly expressive sublanguages building on top of each other, designed to suit different communities of implementers and users. *OWL Lite* is intended to support the building of simple classification hierarchies and simple constraints. To this end, the ability to specify constraints in OWL Lite is rather restricted; for example, the only cardinality values permitted in OWL Lite are 0 and 1. *OWL DL* reflects the description-logic foundation of its predecessor, DAML+OIL. OWL DL provides the maximum expressiveness, but also guarantees that all conclusions are computable and will finish in a finite time. It includes all OWL language constructs, although it imposes certain restrictions on using them. *OWL Full* supports users who want maximum expressiveness and the syntactic freedom of RDF, but does not guarantee computational completeness and decidability. OWL Full can be viewed as an extension of RDF, whereas OWL Lite and OWL DL can be viewed as extensions of a restricted view of RDF (see Smith et al. 2004 for details).

This brief description of OWL is based on the W3C Recommendation from 2004. The current version of the language is OWL 2 (Bao et al. 2008), which is still under development and which still needs to be standardized. Detailed description of the new features implemented in OWL 2 are beyond the scope of this book; it is sufficient to mention here that they include extra syntactic sugar, additional property and qualified cardinality constructors, extended datatype support, simple metamodeling, and extended annotations.

3.2.5 SPARQL

Unlike OWL and RDF(S), SPARQL is not intended for ontology and resource representation, but for querying Web data; precisely, it is a query language for RDF (Prud'hommeaux and Seaborne 2008).

To understand SPARQL, the view of RDF resources as semantic networks (set of triplets; see Fig. 3.4) helps. SPARQL can be used to:

- extract information from RDF graphs in the form of URIs, bNodes, and plain and typed literals;
- extract RDF subgraphs;
- construct new RDF graphs based on information in queried graphs.

SPARQL queries match graph patterns against the target graph of the query. The patterns are like RDF graphs, but may contain named variables in place of some of the nodes (resources) or links/predicates (i.e., properties). The simplest graph pattern is like a single RDF triplet (resource–property–value triplet, or O–A–V triplet). For example, consider the two RDF triplets in Fig. 3.12. Clearly, they both match the simple triplet pattern shown in Fig. 3.13. A *binding* is a mapping from a variable in a query to terms. Each triplet in Fig. 3.12 is a *pattern solution* (a set of correct bindings) for the pattern in Fig. 3.13. *Query results* in SPARQL are sets of pattern solutions. The results of the query represented by the pattern in Fig. 3.13 are the following pattern solutions:

album	**author**
http://www.music.org/albums#EC_Unplugged	Eric Clapton
http://www.music.org/albums#PG_UP	Peter Gabriel

Fig. 3.12   Simple RDF triplets

Fig. 3.13   A simple RDF triplet pattern

Simple graph patterns can be combined into more complicated graph patterns using various operators. For example, the graph in Fig. 3.14 matches the more complex pattern shown in Fig. 3.15, and the pattern solution is

album	http://www.music.org/albums#EC_Unplugged
content	http://www.music.org/contents#Acoustic3
recording	live

Syntactically, SPARQL queries are of the form presented in Fig. 3.16. Obviously, the syntax closely resembles that of database query languages such as SQL. The SELECT clause contains variables, beginning with "?" or "$." The WHERE clause contains a pattern. Prefixes are used as an abbreviation mechanism for URIs and apply to the whole query.

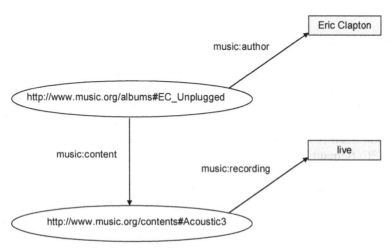

Fig. 3.14   A more complex RDF graph

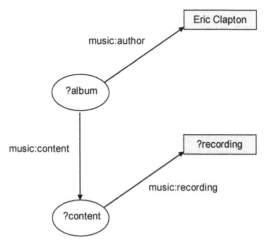

Fig. 3.15   A more complex SPARQL pattern

```
SELECT      ?author
WHERE       { <http://www.music.org/albums#EC_Unplugged> <http://www.music.org/elements/auhor> ?author }

PREFIX      music: <http://www.music.org/elements/>
SELECT      ?author
WHERE       { <http://www.music.org/albums#EC_Unplugged> music:author ?author }

PREFIX      music: <http://www.music.org/elements/>
PREFIX      : <http://www.music.org/albums>
SELECT      $author
WHERE       { :EC_Unplugged  music:author  $author }
```

Fig. 3.16   Examples of SPARQL queries

3.2.6 GRDDL

GRDDL is a mechanism for **G**leaning **R**esource **D**escriptions from **D**ialects of Languages (Davis 2006). In other words, it is a technique for obtaining RDF data from XML documents and in particular XHTML pages. In fact, GRDDL has much to do with semantic markup (annotation), presented in Sect. 3.4, but is covered here in order to make the explanation of the W3C Semantic Web Activity statement (quoted in the beginning of Sect. 3.2) complete.

The idea is as follows. The same information can be described in different XML dialects. For example, Fig. 3.17 shows the fact that Patti Smith, a musician and a poet, is the author of the album *Twelve,* specified in two different XML formats. In addition to these two formats, there exist several other XML languages for representing the same information.

```
iTunes Music Library

        <key>Artist</key>
          <string>Patti Smith</string>
        <key>Album</key>
          <string>Twelve</string>

Audioscrobbler

        <album>
            <artist mbid="">Patti Smith</artist>
            <name>Twelve</name>
        ...
        </album>
```

Fig. 3.17   Two different XML representations of the same information

In order to be Semantic Web ready, the same information can be represented in RDF as well, as in Fig. 3.18.

```
<rdf:RDF
    xmlns:foaf="http://xmlns.com/foaf/0.1/"
    xmlns:rdf="http://www.w3.org/1999/02/22-rdf-syntax-
ns#"
    xmlns:dc="http://purl.org/dc/elements/1.1/">

  <rdf:Description rdf:about=
"http://musicbrainz.org/mm-2.1/album/7d454abc-84d2-321e-
a23d-bcbc76d3fdd1">
    <dc:title>Twelve</dc:title>
    <foaf:maker>
      <foaf:Agent rdf:about=
  "http://musicbrainz.org/mm-2.1/artist/33a4c423-733f-
347c-d9b4-af7c7b111cc9">
        <foaf:name>Patti Smith</foaf:name>
      </foaf:Agent>
    </foaf:maker>

  </rdf:Description>
</rdf:RDF>
```

Fig. 3.18 RDF version of information shown in Fig. 3.17

GRDDL can be used to generate RDF content such as that shown in Fig. 3.18, starting from various uniform XML representations such as those shown in Fig. 3.17. Such representations can be embedded in (X)HTML files as microformats, or they can come from XML files directly. The result is quite intriguing: structured content is used to extract its authoritative meaning (semantics), and the two pieces of information are separated. GRDDL enables this by associating transformations with an individual (X)HTML or XML document. The associations are made either through direct inclusion of references, or indirectly through profile documents. Content authors can develop (or reuse) the transformations for producing RDF from their content and use GRDDL to refer to them. The transformations are commonly expressed using the XSLT 1.0 transformation language.

GRDDL provides a number of ways for transformations to be associated with content, each of which is appropriate in different situations (Davis 2006). The simplest method for authors of (X)HTML content is to embed a reference to the transformations using a link element in the head element of the document, as in Fig. 3.19 (a similar, namespace-qualified attribute is used in XML documents instead). The link element contains the token `transformation` in the `rel` attribute and the URI (in this example, a hypothetical one) of the instructions for extracting RDF in the `href` attribute. The `profile` attribute of the `head` element denotes that the document contains GRDDL metadata, i.e., that it can be processed by GRDDL to extract RDF content. (When displaying such a GRDDL annotated page, browsers will simply ignore this additional annotation.)

```
<!DOCTYPE html PUBLIC "-//W3C//DTD XHTML 1.1//EN"
"http://www.w3.org/TR/xhtml11/DTD/xhtml11.dtd"><html
xmlns="http://www.w3.org/1999/xhtml" xml:lang="en"
lang="en">
<html>
  <head profile="http://www.w3.org/2003/g/data-view">
    <title>The Greatest Albums in 2007</title>
    <link rel="transformation"
href="http://music.org/2005/10/albums.xsl"/>
  </head>
  <body>
  ...
  </body>
<html>
```

Fig. 3.19 The simplest method for associating transformations with content in HTML pages

This way, GRDDL provides a standardized way of getting (RDF) data *out* of (X)HTML or XML documents—portions of information in the original document get rendered to RDF. Note that microformats only enable putting data *into* (X)HTML code, but not to get them out. In addition, GRDDL shifts the content author's burden from representing data in RDF to creating XSLT for a specific dialect of XML.

3.2.7 RDFa

Like GRDDL, RDFa (RDF in attributes) is also a language related to semantic annotation. It enables authors of Web pages (written in (X)HTML) to encode structured data inherently present in the pages more completely and more explicitly (Adida and Birbeck 2008). This way, the authors actually mark up human-readable data with machine-readable indicators for browsers and other programs to interpret. This semantic interpretation would provide cases for application interoperation such as:

- importing information about Patti Smith's concert in London, UK, directly into the user's desktop calendar;

- detecting a license on a Web document and informing the user of details of her rights automatically;
- publishing information about media (photos, audio, video) along with the media files; this additional information may include the creator's name, the topic, and other relevant information to enable structured search and sharing.

True, these cases can be partially covered by using microformats as well. The advantages of RDFa over microformats are its consistent syntax, the use of RDF-based markup, better scale-up, and the use of namespace-qualified elements to resolve syntactic conflicts (e.g., `foaf:name` and `prod:name`).

Figure 3.20 illustrates RDFa markup. There are two basic attributes that RDFa uses when annotating (X)HTML pages: `rel` and `property`. The `rel` attribute is used in hypertext link elements to specify the kind of *relationship* between the current page and the linked one. In the lower half of Fig. 3.20, the `<a rel="foaf:homepage."` `..>` element specifies that the relationship between the current page and the linked page is `foaf:homepage`. Assuming that the current page is `http://devedzic.fon.rs`, this means that the `<a rel="foaf:homepage."` `..>` element establishes the O-A-V triplet:

```
(http://devedzic.fon.rs,
foaf:homepage,
http://www.goodoldai.org.yu)
```

similar to the RDF triplets shown in Fig. 3.12. This triplet specifies that the corresponding hypertext link element links a homepage to the current page, and the homepage is `http://www.goodoldai.org.yu`.

The `property` attribute is used to augment existing text within the page with semantic information. For example, the `property="contact:title"` attribute specified in Fig. 3.20 effectively creates the O-A-V triplet:

```
("Vladan Devedzic,"
contact:title,
"Professor of Computer Science")
```

with the obvious meaning.

All such `rel` and `property` information can be extracted from annotated pages to create a set of RDF triplets (an RDF graph) that represent(s) the content of the page semantically. Tools are available on the Web that can generate the corresponding RDF triplets from an (X)HTML+RDFa file in various RDF serialization formats (e.g., see RDFa Distiller at http://www.w3.org/2007/08/pyRdfa/).

```
<html xmlns="http://www.w3.org/1999/xhtml"
      xmlns:contact="http://www.w3.org/2001/vcard-
rdf/3.0#"
      xmlns:foaf="http://xmlns.com/foaf/0.1/"
      xmlns:dc="http://purl.org/dc/elements/1.1/">
...
<span about="http://fon.fon.rs/foaf.rdf#devedzic">
  <p><span property="foaf:name">Vladan Devedzic</span>is a
  <span property="contact:title">
    Professor of Computer Science
  </span> with the
  <span property="contact:org">
    Department of Software Engineering,
    FON - School of Business Administration,
    University of Belgrade
  </span>.
  <p>His long-term professional goal is to bring close
      together the ideas from the broad fields of
      intelligent systems and software engineering.
      His current professional and research interests
      include
  <span property="foaf:interest"   con-
tent="http://en.wikipedia.org/wiki/Knowledge_modeling">kno
wledge modeling</span> and
  <span property="foaf:interest"
    content="http://www-ksl.stanford.edu/kst/what-is-an-
ontology.html">ontologies
  </span>.
  <p>He is the founder and the chair of the
    <span property="foaf:member">
      <span about="http://www.goodoldai.org.yu"
            typeof="foaf:Group">
        <a rel="foaf:homepage"
            href="http://goodoldai.org.yu/"
            target="_blank">
          <span property="dc:title"
            xmlns:dc="http://purl.org/dc/elements/1.1/">
              GOOD OLD AI
          </span>
        </a> research group.
      </span>
    </span>
</span>
...
</html>
```

Fig. 3.20   An excerpt from an RDFa annotated XHTML page

As with GRDDL, current browsers ignore this additional RDFa markup when displaying the page.

3.2.8 SKOS

The term *knowledge organization systems* is used by W3C to denote different types of *controlled vocabularies* or *concept schemes,* such as thesauri, classification schemes, subject heading lists, taxonomies, terminologies, glossaries, and so on.

The Semantic Web Interest Group of W3C mediates the development of specifications and standards to support the use of knowledge organization systems within the framework of the Semantic Web. Their work is called *SKOS (Simple Knowledge Organization Systems)*, and is currently focused on the development of the following specifications (Miles and Brickley 2005):

- SKOS Core Vocabulary—a set of RDFS classes and RDF properties that can be used to express the content and structure of a concept scheme in a machine-understandable way, as an RDF graph;
- SKOS Core Guide—a guide for using SKOS Core Vocabulary for development and publishing content schemes on the Semantic Web;
- Quick Guide to Publishing a Thesaurus on the Semantic Web— directions for expressing the content and structure of a thesaurus, and metadata about a thesaurus, in RDF;
- SKOS API—a Web service API for interacting with a knowledge organization system data source.

In addition to the above specifications, the SKOS efforts also include the development of an RDF vocabulary for describing mappings between concept schemes (called SKOS Mapping), and an RDF vocabulary containing extensions to the SKOS Core Vocabulary Specification useful for specialized applications (called SKOS Extensions).

Table 3.1 shows some of the classes (beginning with an upper-case letter) and properties (beginning with a lower-case letter) defined in the SKOS Core Vocabulary. The prefix (namespace) `skos:` is defined as `xmlns:skos="http://www.w3.org/2004/02/skos/core#"`.

The way these terms are used in practice is illustrated in Fig. 3.21. As in any RDF graph, ovals in the figure denote domain concepts, arrows indicate concept properties, and boxes represent the literal values of the corresponding properties (in this case, the concept labels expressed in natural language). Since SKOS Core Vocabulary is intended for representing concept schemes in a machine-understandable way, Jovanović (2005) used it to specify the vocabulary for the ontology of Intelligent Information Systems (IIS). The ontology is related to the course on IIS that she teaches. The course includes selected topics from the broad field of IIS, and the Semantic Web is one of them. Each domain concept from the IIS ontology (indicated by the `iis:` namespace prefix) is represented as an instance of the `skos:Concept` class (via the `rdf:type` property). The IIS concept scheme is represented as an instance of the `skos:ConceptScheme` class. Note also the use of alternative labels for the concept `iis:semweb` (middle right in Fig. 3.21), and its associations with the related concepts of Ontologies and Semantic Web Tools (`iis:knowrep002` and `iis:appl01`, middle left). The IIS concept scheme includes several top-level concepts in its hierarchy (e.g., the Semantic Web and intelligent agents). These are included in the concept scheme using the `skos:inScheme` and `skos:hasTopConcept` properties (middle upper).

Table 3.1 Some terms from the SKOS core vocabulary (after Miles and Brickley 2005)

Term	Explanation
skos:Concept	An abstract idea or notion; a unit of thought
skos:ConceptScheme	A set of concepts, optionally including statements about semantic relationships between those concepts (e.g., a thesaurus)
skos:Collection	A meaningful collection of concepts
skos:prefLabel	The preferred lexical label for a resource, in a given language
skos:altLabel	An alternative lexical label for a resource
skos:hiddenLabel	A lexical label for a resource that should be hidden when generating visual displays of the resource, but should still be accessible to free text search operations
skos:broader	A concept that is more general in meaning
skos:narrower	A concept that is more specific in meaning
skos:hasTopConcept	A top level concept in the concept scheme
skos:inScheme	A concept scheme in which the concept is included
skos:isSubjectOf	A resource for which the concept is a subject
skos:related	A concept with which there is an associative semantic relationship

There is an OWL DL-compatible binding of the SKOS Core ontology, developed at the University of Saskatchewan, Canada; it is available from http://ai.usask.ca/mums/schemas/2005/01/27/skos-core-dl.owl. An example of a SKOS Vocabulary that uses this OWL-DL–compatible binding is applied in Gašević and Hatala (2006) to improve learning resource searches. The ACM Computing Classification System is an example presented in OWL-DL compatible SKOS.

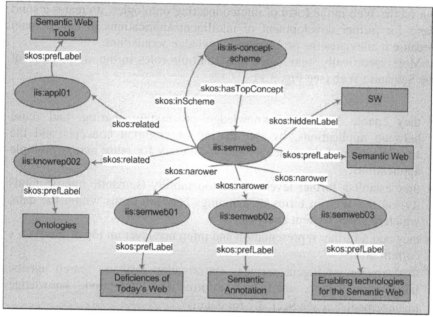

Fig. 3.21 A segment of the IIS domain ontology describing concepts of the Semantic Web (after Jovanović 2005)

3.3 The Role of Ontologies

Another direct answer to the question "Why ontologies?" asked in Chap. 2 is "Because they are essential building blocks in the infrastructure of the Semantic Web, or currently in the web of data." Semantic-level interoperation among Web applications is possible only if the semantics of Web data is explicitly represented on the Web as well, in the form of machine-understandable domain and content theories—ontologies. Through automatic use and machine interpretation of ontologies, computers themselves can offer enhanced support and automation in accessing and processing Web information. This is qualitatively different from the established practices of using the Web, in terms of extracting and interpreting information—instead of putting the main burden on the user, the Semantic Web should do much of that job itself (Fensel and Musen 2001).

Ontologies enable access to a huge network of machine-understandable and machine-processable human knowledge (Fig. 3.22), encoded in XML-based formats. Once the essential knowledge of a certain domain has been put on the Web in the form of interconnecting ontologies, it creates a solid basis for further development of intelligent applications in that domain because it alleviates the problem of knowledge acquisition.

More specifically, ontologies play multiple roles in the architecture of the Semantic Web (see Fig. 3.1):

- they enable Web-based knowledge processing, sharing, and reuse between applications, by the sharing of common concepts and the specialization of the concepts and vocabulary for reuse across multiple applications;
- they establish further levels of interoperability (semantic interoperability) on the Web in terms of mappings between terms within the data, which requires content analysis;
- they add a further representation and inference layer on top of the Web's current layers;
- they enable intelligent services (information brokers, search agents, information filters, intelligent information integration, knowledge management, …; see Sect. 3.7 for details).

Note, however, that the prerequisites for all of the above roles include not only an initial effort by the interested communities to create ontologies, but also considerable discipline in annotating the relevant applications and Web resources to get them interconnected with the ontologies (see Sect. 3.4). Also, supporting tools are needed for those millions of developers of Web pages and applications who weave their domain knowledge into the Web daily. Using knowledge representation techniques in such tools becomes increasingly important. Last but not least, an all-encompassing framework for developing the network of ontologies and interconnecting them across domains is also highly desirable. Efforts are under way to provide such a framework in the form of a standard upper ontology, as discussed in Sect. 2.4.2.

With ontologies, the Semantic Web provides a qualitatively new level of service, as it becomes an extremely large system with various specialized reasoning services. Ontologies provide an infrastructure for transforming the Web of information and data into the Web of knowledge—the Semantic Web.

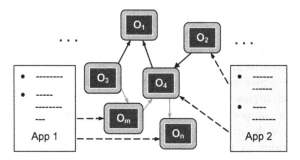

Fig. 3.22   Interconnecting ontologies and applications on the Semantic Web

3.4 Semantic Markup

Ontologies serve merely to standardize and provide interpretations for Web content. To make content machine-understandable, Web resources must contain *semantic markup*, or *semantic annotation*—descriptions which use the terminology that one or more ontologies define (Heflin and Hendler 2001). Such ontologically annotated Web resources enable reasoning about their content and advanced query-answering services. They also support ontology creation and maintenance, and help map between different ontologies.

Through the process of semantic markup of Web resources, information is added to the resources without changing the originals. The added information may serve human users in much the same way as highlighted text does in paper-based documents, or, more importantly, may enhance the semantic analysis and processing of Web resources by computers. For example, semantic annotation may help intelligent agents discover Web resources more easily, or it may indicate that the content of different resources is semantically similar. Also, adequate metadata about the semantic markup added to a resource might help search engines locate the right information.

There are several levels of sophistication in annotating Web resources and making applications use the markup. The simplest approach is to use annotation tools to mark up downloaded Web pages manually and save the annotation together with the pages locally. Typically, such annotation is in the form of highlighted text, new elements inserted into the document, and hyperlinks. For example, much of the GRDDL and RDFa markup described in Sects. 3.2.6 and 3.2.7 are done using this approach. However, Web servers do not normally allow annotated Web resources to be uploaded back. A more sophisticated approach is to save the markup in a separate document (locally or on a remote server) and load it in a browser along with the document. The next step up in sophistication is provided by collaborative Wiki sites that let their users insert and share their comments and other annotations along with Web pages.

None of the above cases necessarily has to be supported by explicitly represented ontologies. As a consequence, such approaches have been aimed mainly at supporting human users. On the other hand, if ontologies are used to drive the markup creation, then machine consumers can make use of annotations as well. Ontology-based annotation tools enable unstructured and semistructured information sources to be linked with ontologies.

There are numerous approaches to ontology-based markup (Handschuh and Staab 2003a). As an illustration, consider how semantic markup is done according to the CREAM framework (Handschuh and Staab 2002, 2003b). This framework is suitable for both annotation of existing Web pages and annotation of content while authoring a Web page. The key concept in the CREAM framework is *relational metadata,* i.e., metadata that instantiate interrelated definitions of classes in a domain ontology. More precisely, for various instantiations of classes and properties in an ontology, there may exist several semantic relationships; relational metadata are annotations that contain relationship instances. The annotations are represented as an XML serialization of RDF facts and are attached to HTML pages as in the hypothetical, simplified example shown in Fig. 3.23. Assume that a Web page at the hypothetical URL http://www.guitar.org/legendaryrecordings contains information about the album *Unplugged* by Eric Clapton, whose homepage is at http://www.ericclapton.com/. Assume also that the Musician ontology sketched in Fig. 2.2 is implemented in OWL and used to annotate these two Web pages. Furthermore, let two namespaces be defined as follows:

xmlns:musician="http://www.music.org/musicians#"
xmlns:album="http://www.music.org/albums#"

Obviously, the markup attached to the Web pages uses the terminology defined in the ontology. The musician:records part of the markup attached to the musician's home page points to the Web page about the album, thus making a semantic connection between the two pages. The annotation itself may be created using a user-friendly graphical tool such as Ont-O-Mat, which is a specific implementation of the CREAM framework that Handschuh and Staab used (Handschuh and Staab 2002, 2003b). In Ont-O-Mat, an author can design a new Web page or can load and display an existing one to be annotated. In either case, while editing the

Web page the author can also load an ontology to be used for markup, and display its term hierarchies and concept/attribute descriptions graphically. By selecting parts of the content of the Web page being edited and connecting them with the terms in the ontology by simple mouse clicks and drag-and-drop operations, the author can produce the markup almost for free—not much additional effort is needed to insert the annotations with such a graphical tool. When the author saves the Web page at the end of the process, the markup is saved as well.

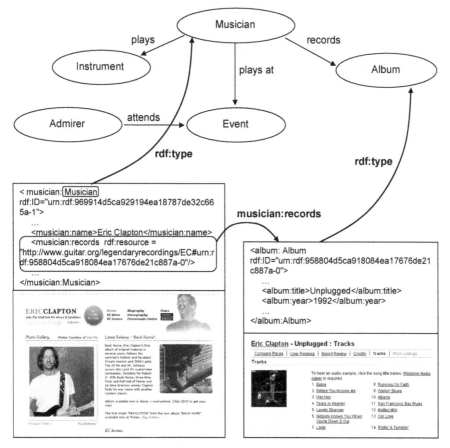

Fig. 3.23   A simplified example of the application of the principles of semantic annotation in the CREAM framework, after an idea from Handschuh and Staab (2002); the namespaces and URIs shown are hypothetical

The CREAM framework has evolved over the years (Handschuh et al. 2003a, b) to enable querying a Web site semantically about the resources it publishes. The resources are typically kept in a database on a server, and the site developer may annotate the database model (i.e., the entities and their relationships) and publish the annotation in RDF. The annotation will describe the structure of all the tables involved in a query of the site, thus acting as an API that hides the intricacies of access to the database on the server side. A suitable place for publishing the annotation is the header part of the site's main Web page. A client may wish to use a specific ontology to put semantic queries to the server. To do this, the client must first create rules for mapping between the terms in his/her ontology and the terms that are used in the database model on the server side and published there as a set of RDF annotations. The tool called OntoEdit can be used to create and publish the mapping rules. The user (or a third party) can then load both the ontology and the mapping rules to query the database, for example through a Web-service API.

We can conclude from the above example and from Heflin and Hendler (2001) and Hendler (2001) that in order for annotation of Web pages with ontological information to be effective:

- nonexperts in ontological engineering must be able to perform this task, starting from existing ontologies, transparently, through normal computer use;
- most Web page developers need not even know that ontologies exist, but should still be able to do (almost) free markup;
- ontology-driven authoring tools should support both authoring and annotation processes by enabling class hierarchies based on a number of underlying ontologies to drive the creation of Web pages;
- the content of the pages being designed and developed should be presented, modified, and mixed consistently, using ontologies linked to libraries of terms, and interlinked in order to reuse or change terms;
- tool developers should enable libraries of ontologies to be accessed from the tools that they develop, in order to support appropriate markup of pages in a wide range of domains.

3.5 Development Frameworks

Web application developers who care about the semantics of data their applications use, as well as about using that semantics in an innovative way, typically ask a question like: "How do I use all this Semantic Web stuff in Java?"

Jena Semantic Web Toolkit (McCarthy 2004) enables developers to exploit RDF data models (RDF graphs like those in Fig. 3.14) in their Java applications. It is an open source Java framework and API for representing, persisting, and querying RDF models.

In Jena, an RDF model is represented by the `Model` interface, each resource is represented using the `Resource` interface, and each property is represented using the `Property` interface. A special type of `Model` is `OntModel`, which is used to create, characterize, and manipulate OWL ontologies and their properties; see Sect. 3.6 and Fig. 3.27 for more details. The `ModelFactory` class can be used to create an empty model first, and then resources can be added to the model and properties can be added to the resources. For example, the simple Java code in Fig. 3.24 shows how to represent the following RDF triplet in Jena:

```
("http://somewhere/PattiSmith,"
vcard:FN,
"Patti Smith")
```

```
// some definitions
static String musicianURI   = "http://somewhere/PattiSmith";
static String fullName      = "Patti Smith";

// create an empty Model
Model model = ModelFactory.createDefaultModel();

// create the resource
Resource pattiSmith = model.createResource(musicianURI);

// add the property
pattiSmith.addProperty(VCARD.FN, fullName);
```

Fig. 3.24   Creating a simple RDF model with Jena

Jena often uses "constant" classes such as the VCARD class in Fig. 3.24. Such classes hold objects representing all the definition's well-known schemas, such as VCARD, Dublin Core, and the like.

In addition, Java code using Jena API often defines `String` constants that represent URIs of specific lightweight ontologies, called *RDF vocabularies*. An RDF vocabulary is a defined set of predicates (an ontology) that can be used in an application. A data type, domain, and range are also defined for each predicate in the vocabulary, and so are the relationships, if any, of one predicate to another. For example, `http://purl.org/vocab/relationship/` is the URI of the RELATIONSHIP vocabulary for describing relationships between people (it defines predicates such as `siblingOf`, `parentOf`, `childOf`, and the like). Such URI `String` constants are then typically used as prefixes for URIs of model properties created in the Java code; for example:

```
Property childOf =
model.createProperty(relationshipUri,"childOf");
```

Each call to addProperty() such as the one in Fig. 3.24 essentially adds another triplet or *statement* to the RDF model. The Jena Model interface defines a listStatements() method, Fig. 3.25, for inspecting an RDF model. This method returns an StmtIterator, a subtype of Java's Iterator over all the statements in a Model; these can be represented by Jena's Statement interface. Statement provides accessor methods to the subject, predicate, and object of a statement. The getResource() and getProperty() methods are useful for retrieving resources from a model and inspecting them in more detail.

```
// list the statements in the Model
StmtIterator iter = model.listStatements();

// get the predicate, subject and object of each statement
while (iter.hasNext()) {
    Statement stmt = iter.nextStatement();  // get next statement
    Resource subject = stmt.getSubject();     // get the subject
    Property predicate = stmt.getPredicate();// get the predicate
    RDFNode object = stmt.getObject();        // get the object
    ...
}
```

Fig. 3.25   Inspecting an RDF model with Jena

Jena also has methods for reading and writing RDF models in the XML format from/to files, as well as for persisting RDF models on a filesystem or in a relational database (PostgreSQL, Oracle, and MySQL). Likewise, the models can be queried. The core Jena API supports only a limited query primitive. However, Jena's com.hp.hpl.jena.rdql package contains all of the classes and interfaces needed to create and execute more powerful *RDQL* queries on an RDF model from Java code. RDQL stands for RDF Query Language, and is an SQL-like W3C-defined language for querying RDF models (Seaborne 2004).

Another Java framework for working with RDF data is *Sesame* (Leigh 2008). A high-level architectural view of Sesame reveals its several layers of components/APIs. Together, they provide:

- interfaces and implementation for all basic RDF entities (URI, blank node, literal, and statement);
- a set of parsers (used to translate RDF files to sets of statements) and writers (used for reverse translations) for various RDF file formats;

- support for various types of RDF manipulation, storage, and reasoning;
- client-server communication with a Sesame server over HTTP.

A *Sesame repository* is an RDF data store. Sesame supports main memory repositories, native (disk files) repositories, relational database repositories, as well as (remote) Sesame server repositories. The first action to be taken when working with Sesame is to create an appropriate repository using the `Repository` interface; for example:

```
Repository repository =
        new SailRepository(new MemoryStore());
repository.initialize();
```

To interact with the repository, a `RepositoryConnection` must be created using the `Repository.getConnection()` method:

```
RepositoryConnection con =
        repository.getConnection();
```

Using the connection, data (files or individual statements) can be uploaded and retrieved. Figure 3.26 shows an example of adding statements to the repository. The code is self-explanatory.

In Sesame, RDF statements are created and treated in a *context*. A context describes where the statements originated from, and is often represented by a URI (just like subjects and predicates of RDF statements).

RDF models in Sesame are queried and inspected using SPARQL.

3.6 Reasoning

Reasoning is a process of using known facts and/or assumptions in order to derive a conclusion or make an inference (NumberNut.com 2008). It is a complex process involving a number of abilities, including association, categorization, cause and effect, problem solving, organization, generalization, and judgment of safety (Community Transitions 2008). It engages the mental processes that endow our imagination, perceptions, thoughts, and feelings with intelligibility (Phillweb 2008). In other words, it is the cognitive process of looking for reasons to justify beliefs, conclusions, actions, or feelings.

Reasoning also refers, more specifically, to the act or process of using one's reason to derive one statement or assertion (the conclusion) from a prior group of statements or assertions (the premises) by means of a given method (Phillweb 2008). This interpretation is close to what Semantic Web researchers and developers try to achieve in their applications. To achieve reasoning in Semantic Web applications, they must deploy an inference engine that can derive additional statements which the knowledge represented in their knowledge bases (as well as in the associated ontologies) does not express explicitly. The inference engine can invoke query answering; inference explanation; common set-theory operations of union, intersection, and difference; predicate logics inferencing; description logics checking for satisfiability, subsumption, consistency, and instance-of relationships; etc.

```
ValueFactory f = repository.getValueFactory();

// create resources and literals to make statements out of
URI pattiSmith =
          f.createURI("http://music.org/people/pattiSmith");
URI bruceSpringsteen =
          f.createURI("http://music.org/people/bruceSpringsteen");
URI name = f.createURI("http://music.org/ontology/name");
URI person = f.createURI("http://music.org/ontology/Person");
Literal pattisName = f.createLiteral("Patti Smith");
Literal brucesName = f.createLiteral("Bruce Springsteen");

try {
   RepositoryConnection con = myRepository.getConnection();

   try {
      // Patti Smith is a person
      con.add(pattiSmith, RDF.TYPE, person);
      // Patti's name is "Patti Smith"
      con.add(pattiSmith, name, pattisName);

      // Bruce Springsteen is a person
      con.add(bruceSpringsteen, RDF.TYPE, person);
      // Bruce's name is "Bruce Springsteen"
      con.add(bruceSpringsteen, name, brucesName);
   } finally {
      con.close();
   }
} catch (OpenRDFException e) {
   // handle exception
}
```

Fig. 3.26 Adding individual RDF statements to a Sesame repository

Several reasoning and consistency checking tools for the Semantic Web have already been developed and are being constantly improved. Well-known examples include OWL reasoning tools such as FaCT (Horrocks 2004), RACER (Haarslev and Moller 2001), and Pellet (Sirin et al. 2007) specifically developed for the decidable description logic. Given an OWL ontology, they can classify the ontology (perform subsumption reasoning) so as to reduce redundancy and detect any inconsistency within it. To an extent, they can also perform instance-level reasoning. However, these tools are still far from perfect. They can only flag an OWL class as inconsistent, but they cannot explain their decision. They do not provide any debugging support, and datatype support is very limited (such as integer and string).

Alternative reasoners that complement FaCT and RACER in some way have been developed as well. An example is Alloy Analyzer (Wang et al. 2006; Li 2007), that works not only with OWL, but also with the SWRL (Horrocks et al. 2004) and SWRL-FOL (Patel-Schneider et al. 2004) languages. Alloy Analyzer analyzes models written in Alloy, a structural modeling language based on first-order logic, for expressing complex structural and behavioral constraints. Alloy treats relations as first class citizens. It can also combine various structured entities by using relational composition. Alloy models can be transformed to OWL/SWRL/SWRL-FOL models and vice versa.

Another Semantic Web reasoner, called LoRD (Krdžavac et al. 2006), designed using principles of model-driven engineering, is described in Chap. 14.

Current support for reasoning provided by development frameworks like Jena and Sesame is illustrated in GRDDL. The figure shows an example of using Jena's classes and interfaces to create and deploy a reasoner to derive additional statements (that the model does not express explicitly), given an ontology and an RDF model (McCarthy 2004).

The example uses an OWL ontology created from WordNet, a large lexical database for the English language (Miller et al. 2006). WordNet is essentially a large network of meaningfully related words and concepts that can be navigated with a specific browser. Within the network, nouns, verbs, adjectives, and adverbs are grouped into sets of *cognitive synonyms* (*synsets*), each expressing a distinct concept. Synsets are interlinked by means of conceptual-semantic and lexical relations. RDF representations of WordNet are available (Graves 2006; van Assem et al. 2006), and Jena enables using them.

In Fig. 3.27, an OWL ontology is used with the WordNet model in order to query WordNet about music. Hence an `OWLReasoner` is created; Jena itself provides several `Reasoner` types to work with different types of ontology. The OWL WordNet ontology thus created is then bound to the WordNet model itself to create an inference model (Jena's `InfModel` interface). Note that `ReasonerRegistry.getOWLReasoner()` returns an OWL reasoner in its default configuration; to create an inference model needed to work with WordNet, it is necessary to bind it to the WordNet ontology first (using the `Reasoner#bindSchema()` method). Queries can then be created as RDQL strings and executed using the inference model created.

```
// Make a new model to act as an OWL ontology for WordNet
OntModel wnOntology = ModelFactory.createOntologyModel();
...
// Get a reference to the WordNet plants model
ModelMaker maker = ModelFactory.createModelRDBMaker(connection);
Model model = maker.openModel("wordnet-music",true);

// Create an OWL reasoner
Reasoner owlReasoner = ReasonerRegistry.getOWLReasoner();

// Bind the reasoner to the WordNet ontology model
Reasoner wnReasoner = owlReasoner.bindSchema(wnOntology);

// Use the reasoner to create an inference model
InfModel infModel =
        ModelFactory.createInfModel(wnReasoner, model);
...
// Create a new query
// passing a String containing the RDQL to execute
Query query = new Query(queryString);

// Set the inference model as the source of the query
query.setSource(infModel);
```

Fig. 3.27   An example of reasoning with Jena (after McCarthy 2004)

3.7 Semantic Web Services

Roughly speaking, *Web services* are activities that allow both end users and, under appropriate circumstances, software agents to invoke them directly (Preece and Decker 2002). In the traditional Web model, users follow hypertext links manually. In the Web services model, they invoke tasks that facilitate some useful activity (e.g., meaningful content-based discovery of resources, fusion of similar content from multiple sites, or commercial activities such as course advertising and registration for distance learning) (Devedžić 2004b).

Technically, Web services are autonomous, platform-independent computational elements that can be described, published, discovered, orchestrated, and programmed using XML artifacts for the purpose of developing massively distributed interoperable applications. The platform-neutral and self-describing nature of Web services and, particularly, their ability to automate collaboration between Web applications make them more than just software components. In the *service-oriented architecture* (Vinoski 2002; Fig. 3.28), Web services advertise themselves in a registry, allowing client applications to query the registry for details of the service and interact with the service using those details.

The service-oriented architecture shown in Fig. 3.28 can greatly enhance the traditional development process in the case of the development of Web applications, since the client-side system can be built on the basis of Web services, even if those services are not yet available or are not known by the developers. This is because every Web service is described through a service description language, dynamically discovered by applications that need to use it, and invoked through the communication protocol defined in its interface (Vinoski 2002). The central component in Fig. 3.28—the service directory—is a dynamically organized, but highly structured (e.g., as a tree, or as a table/database) information pool pertaining to various services. The underlying assumption is that at every point in time the directory lists those services that are ready to be invoked by the user; these services are assumed to advertise their readiness and availability to the directory. Hence an agent can find out about the available services by looking up the directory. Then it can decide whether to automatically invoke a suitable service on the user's behalf, or merely suggest that the user interact with the service directly.

Fig. 3.28   Service-oriented architecture

There is a lot of supporting technology for developing, publishing, and using Web services, such as WSDL (Web Services Description Language), WSFL (Web Services Flow Language), UDDI (Universal Description, Discovery, and Integration), and SOAP (Simple Object Access Protocol). See Preece and Decker (2002) for starting points on the use of these technologies.

Note, however, that in the Semantic Web the idea is to employ *intelligent* Web services to go beyond the XML/RDF infrastructure of Web pages, i.e., to explore Web services that intelligent-systems technology can make possible. Intelligent Web services may turn the Web into a collection of different resources, each with a well-defined interface for invoking its services (Vinoski 2002). In other words, intelligent Web services deploy intelligent-systems techniques to perform useful, reusable tasks for Web users. This view of Web services implies that the properties, capabilities, interfaces, and effects of Web services must be encoded in an unambiguous, machine-understandable form, and properly marked up to make the services computer-interpretable, with a use that is apparent, and agent-ready (McIlraith et al. 2001). Such requirements, in turn, imply the need for ontologies of Web services, to be used as machine-readable descriptions of services (as to how they run), including the consequences of using those services. Each such ontology should explicitly represent the logic of the services and the terms needed to describe the invocation of those services. Web service ontologies bring intelligence to Web services, because they enable integration of agents and ontologies in some exciting ways. For example, an agent performing a keyword-based Web search may invoke services such as controlled vocabularies that enable fuzzy-terms-based searches and inexact matches; if the requested keyword is not in the dictionary, the service can come up immediately with a more general concept suggested in the ontology.

The difference between conventional and intelligent Web services is best understood through the pragmatics of their use. In the conventional case, the user has to discover the desired service first (using a search engine). In most cases, this involves a lot of reading of the Web pages discovered. Alternatively, the user may execute a service to see whether it satisfies his/her request; this, in turn, means filling in the forms of the service manually and composing manually the sequence of services required to complete a complex task.

On the other hand, intelligent Web services enable automatic service discovery, using preprovided semantic markup of Web pages and ontology-enhanced search engines. Intelligent agents can execute such services on behalf of their users automatically, since the semantic markup of a service provides a declarative API that tells the agent what input is necessary for automatic invocation, what information will be returned, and how to execute and, potentially, interact with the service automatically. Automatic service composition and interoperation are also provided, since the semantic markup of services provides all the necessary information to select, compose, and respond to services. The markup is encoded and stored at the sites of the services, and appropriate software tools manipulate the markup together with specifications of the service task's objectives.

Obviously, the real power of intelligent Web services results not from their individual use, but from combining them in a variety of ways (Preece and Decker 2002). This creates the need for standard models of interaction between services (McIlraith et al. 2001). Such models should be implemented as declarative, machine-processable descriptions of how to combine intelligent Web services to achieve more sophisticated tasks. The descriptions can be encoded in Web service composition languages such as WSFL or OWL-S (see below), and contain the knowledge about how to perform the sophisticated real-life tasks that the services perform (Preece and Decker 2002). The point is that implementing these composition descriptions on the Web makes them downloadable, understandable, and executable for everyone, not only humans but also automated agents.

Recently, the idea of intelligent Web services has evolved slightly into the concept of *Semantic Web services* (Payne and Lassila 2004), in the form of an augmentation of Web Service descriptions through Semantic Web annotation to facilitate higher-level automation of service discovery, composition, invocation, and monitoring in an open, unregulated, and often chaotic environment (that is, the Web). The objective of Semantic Web services is to provide a ubiquitous infrastructure for deploying intelligent multiagent systems on the Web.

The Semantic Web community has already developed *OWL-S*, an OWL-based ontology of Web services and a core set of markup language constructs for describing the properties and capabilities of Web services in unambiguous, computer-interpretable form (Martin et al. 2004). OWL-S comes with supporting tools and agent technology to enable automation of services on the Semantic Web, including automated Web service discovery, execution, interoperation, composition, and execution monitoring.

Conceptually, the top level of the OWL-S ontology appears as in Fig. 3.29 (Martin et al. 2004). The *ServiceProfile* describes what a service does. It specifies the service's input and output types, preconditions, and effects. The *ProcessModel* describes how the service works; each service is either an *AtomicProcess* that executes directly, or a *CompositeProcess,* i.e., a composition that combines subprocesses (Fig. 3.30). The *ServiceGrounding* contains the details of how an agent can access the service. This grounding specifies a communications protocol, the parameters to be used in the protocol, and the serialization techniques to be employed for communication. Such a rich description of services greatly supports automation of their discovery and composition.

OWL-S service descriptions are structured as OWL documents, so developers can build them using all of OWL's domain-modeling features, as well as concepts from other ontologies (Sirin et al. 2004). Also, some aspects of the derivation of OWL-S descriptions directly from WSDL descriptions can be partially automated.

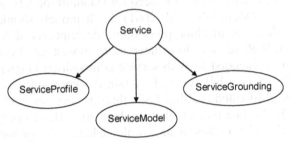

Fig. 3.29   Top level of the OWL-S ontology (after Martin et al. 2004)

```
<owl:Class rdf:ID="CompositeProcess">
    <rdfs:subClassOf rdf:resource="#Process"/>
    <owl:disjointWith rdf:resource="#AtomicProcess"/>
    <owl:disjointWith rdf:resource="#SimpleProcess"/>
    <rdfs:comment>
        A CompositeProcess must have exactly 1 composedOf property.
    </rdfs:comment>
    <owl:intersectionOf rdf:parseType="Collection">
        <owl:Class rdf:about="#Process"/>
        <owl:Restriction>
            <owl:onProperty rdf:resource="#composedOf"/>
            <owl:cardinality rdf:datatype="&xsd;#nonNegativeInteger">
                1</owl:cardinality>
        </owl:Restriction>
    </owl:intersectionOf>
</owl:Class>
```

Fig. 3.30   An excerpt from the OWL-S ontology defined in Martin et al. (2004)

The tricky part in building Semantic Web service descriptions using OWL-S is combining different services from different providers—these services might assume different ontologies (Payne and Lassila 2004). Thus mapping of concepts between different ontologies and composition of new concepts from multiple ontologies is necessary. One way around this problem is to have agents and service requesters translate service descriptions into a familiar ontology to formulate valid requests. This translation can be done by employing a set of "bridging axioms." Sirin et al. have proposed an alternative approach—generating service compositions that satisfy users' requirements through an interactive metaphor (Sirin et al. 2004). This approach assumes knowledge-based indexing and retrieval of services by both agent brokers and humans, as well as automated reasoning about the services, but is essentially semiautomated, since the user is involved in the composition of the services as well. Nevertheless, the supporting tool that Sirin et al. have developed uses contextual information to locate semantically interoperable services that it can present to the user at each stage of

the composition framework. Built on top of OWL-S, this tool enables semantic discovery and filtering to determine a meaningful set of candidate
services on the basis of advertised Semantic Web service descriptions. The
user's involvement here is reduced to a necessary minimum—it is the user
who has the final word about selecting a particular service (for the next
step in composition) after the automatic filtering of candidate services. The
next step in automation might be creating an intelligent agent to do this selection on behalf of the user. However, owing to the huge variety of possible services, and of the respective domain ontologies and their representations, as well as variations in the composition, such an agent (or even a
multiagent system) may not be easy to build.

3.8 Open Issues

While the Semantic Web is certainly gaining momentum, it is important to
realize that some still unresolved problems and factors hold back its more
rapid development. Critics of the Semantic Web frequently complain that
there is no "killer app" for the Semantic Web yet, which they interpret as a
sign of a poorly grounded field and poorly envisioned future development.

In spite of the fast-growing representational and technological support,
the development of ontologies is still hard work. Tools such as Protégé are
easy to use; but, nevertheless, someone always has to transfer human
knowledge about a topic or subject to the ontological representation. Given
that a domain ontology is supposed to represent the essential concepts in a
domain and their relationships, the process always requires knowledge acquisition in which human experts are involved to a large extent. Building
and representing ontologies in computers is not so much a technical matter
as a matter of obtaining and organizing high-quality human knowledge
about the domain of interest. True, partial automation of this process is
possible by applying machine learning techniques or starting from folksonomies, but such approaches are largely still under development.

Moreover, domain knowledge is seldom static—it evolves over time;
much information that was once relevant may easily become obsolete, and
new, important information may be discovered after the ontology has been
built and represented on the Web explicitly. That raises the important issue
of knowledge maintenance.

As already mentioned in Sect. 2.1, the term "ontology" is sometimes
used to refer to a body of knowledge describing a domain, typically a domain of commonsense knowledge, using a representation vocabulary
(Chandrasekaran et al. 1999). However, commonsense ontologies are still

not widely available, and efforts to create a standard upper ontology are still under way (see Sect. 2.4.2). The Austin-based company Cycorp has devoted many years to creating CYC, a huge ontology of commonsense knowledge that has been used in a wide range of applications (Lenat and Guha 1990; Lenat 1995). The CYC ontology is extremely impressive, but Cycorp retains proprietary rights to the vast bulk of it and has released only a small part of it (called OpenCYC) to the public (Niles and Pease 2001; SUO WG 2008). The contents of CYC have not been subject to extensive peer review, and thus using it as a standard would be problematic.

On the other hand, Cycorp's philosophy is grounded in the fact that spontaneous development of domain-specific ontologies for the Semantic Web may lead to a Web rich in semantics, but poor in ontological consistency. Interrelating many heterogeneous ontologies in a useful way is anything but easy if they are richly specified (which takes a lot of effort in itself). However, if developers were to create a number of lightweight ontologies just to get started, they might want to use CYC to elaborate their ontologies, by employing it to describe more precisely the intended meanings of the terms they have used. In this case, CYC could serve as a global point of integration for many domain-specific ontologies through a large corpus of encoded commonsense knowledge.

To the same end, researchers have recently initiated a series of workshops called VoCamps, dedicated to initial development of RDF vocabularies (VoCamp 2008). The idea is best reflected in the following quotation from the VoCamp Web site:

> VoCamp is a series of informal events where people can spend some dedicated time creating lightweight vocabularies/ontologies for the Semantic Web/Web of Data. The emphasis of the events is not on creating the perfect ontology in a particular domain, but on creating vocabs that are good enough for people to start using for publishing data on the Web. The intention is to follow a "paper first, laptops second" format, where the modelling is done initially on paper and only later committed to code. (VoCamp 2008)

Note another reference to the idea of the Web of Data as a lightweight version of the Semantic Web vision, and as the current trend: develop a number of vocabulary-level ontologies first (rather than putting too much effort into developing highly specified, semantically rich and consistent ontologies), and then use them as the foundation for implementing the Semantic Web vision further. This is completely in line with the reasoning that further growth of the Web of Data/Semantic Web is heavily dependent on the availability of vocabularies/ontologies that can be used to publish data. Although a number of key vocabularies/ontologies are in widespread use, there are also many areas with little or no vocabulary coverage, hindering the ability to publish data in these domains.

Automation is a key issue for many aspects of the Semantic Web, including annotation/markup. In practice, much of the semantic markup of Web resources has been done more or less manually. For example, RDFa annotation is still largely done by editing XHTML pages manually, and GRDDL is largely dependent on manual XSLT development. This is not only time-consuming and error-prone—it is tedious. Moreover, even high-level tools for manual annotation of XHTML pages using the terms from published ontologies are still lacking. Without them, any manual semantic annotation is similar to text-editor-based assembly language programming instead of using integrated Java development environments.

Furthermore, any markup is good only as long as the resource remains unchanged; what if the resource is modified and the markup is no longer valid?

Note that creating semantic markup will be one of the key factors for the success of the Semantic Web, but it is certainly not the ultimate goal. It is therefore necessary to enable easy annotation and automate the process as much as possible, as well as to achieve effortless updating of markup in the ever-changing environment of the Web. Automated annotation is a hot research topic, and there are several approaches.

Some also argue that the success of the Semantic Web will depend largely on the integration of Semantic Web technology with commercial software products. A good example of technology designed for this purpose is Briefing Associate (Tallis et al. 2002), discussed in Sect. 2.3. Its integration with MS PowerPoint, a tool used very widely for creating presentations, indicates a way to achieve the mass annotation of certain categories of documents without the authors having to care about it. Efforts are underway to enable such "semantic markup as a side effect" for different categories of Web resources, as well as to provide multiple annotations of the same resource to facilitate its reuse by multiple applications.

Semantic Web services represent an important step toward the full-blown vision of the Semantic Web, in terms of utilizing, managing, and creating semantic markup (Payne and Lassila 2004). Note that Semantic Web services nicely complement ontologies—services tackle behavioral issues of the Semantic Web (e.g., interactions between intelligent agents), whereas ontologies implement the Semantic Web's original objective of creating representational and logical frameworks to allow increasing automation in processing Web-based information and in improving the interoperability of Web-based applications.

Still, as Preece and Decker carefully note (2002), there is a trade-off between the functionality of Semantic Web services and the cost of developing the underlying markup and computational processes. The greater the functionality, the greater the cost. A more detailed study of the real needs of users may indicate a way to reduce this trade-off. This issue is closely related to another one—the trust that users will put in automated Semantic Web services. As Semantic Web services become more common, users will want to know about their quality before they delegate their hands-on browsing to hands-off "black box" services. This creates a need for a set of objective and subjective metrics for the quality of Semantic Web services, such as how well the service has "understood" the user's needs, how good it was in fulfilling those needs, and how accurate and complete the result was.

3.9 Quotations

The Semantic Web is a universal space for anything which can be expressed in classical logic. In the world of knowledge representation there are many different systems, and the following is an attempt to generalize.... Exposing rules as classic logic facts strips the (pragmatically useful) hint information which controls the actual sequence of operation of a local inference engine. When the facts corresponding to all the rules of all the inference engines are put onto the Web, then the great thing is that all the knowledge is represented in the same space. The drawback is that there is no one inference engine which can answer arbitrary queries. But that is not a design goal of the Semantic Web. The goal is to unify everything which can be expressed in classical logic (including more mathematics when we get to it) without further constraint. We must be able to describe the world, and our hopes and needs and terms and conditions. A system which tries to constrain the expressive power cannot be universal.... The choice of classical logic for the Semantic Web is not an arbitrary choice among equals. Classical logic is the only way that inference can scale across the Web. (Berners-Lee 1997–2004)

Instead of trying to rebuild some aspects of a human brain, we are going to build a brain of and for humankind. (Fensel and Musen 2001)

4 Model Driven Engineering

A relevant initiative from the software engineering community called Model Driven Engineering (MDE) is being developed in parallel with the Semantic Web (Mellor et al. 2003a). The MDE approach to software development suggests that one should first develop a model of the system under study, which is then transformed into the real thing (i.e., an executable software entity). The most important research initiative in this area is the Model Driven Architecture (MDA), which is being developed under the umbrella of the Object Management Group (OMG). This chapter describes the basic concepts of this software engineering effort.

4.1 Models and Metamodels

The idea of MDE stems from software engineering, and more specifically, from the recent research in software development. MDE evolved as a paradigm shift from the object-oriented technology, in which the main principle is that *everything is an object;* into the model engineering paradigm, based on the principle that *everything is a model* (Bézivin 2005). The object-oriented technology is about classes and objects, and the main relations are *instantiation* (an object is an instance of a class) and *inheritance* (a class inherits from another class). MDE is about models, but it is also about relations between a model and the system under study (which can be a software artifact or a real-world domain), metamodels, and model transformations. Similar to the object-oriented technology, MDE can be characterized by two main relations, namely, *representation* (a model represents a software artifact or real-world domain) and *conformance* (a model conforms to a metamodel). According to Jean-Marie Favre, MDE is a field of system engineering in which the process heavily relies on the use of models and model engineering (Favre 2004a). In that context, model engineering is considered the disciplined and rationalized production of models (Favre 2004a).

D. Gašević et al., *Model Driven Engineering and Ontology Development*, 2nd edn., DOI 10.1007/978-3-642-00282-3_4, © Springer-Verlag Berlin Heidelberg 2009

4.1.1 Models in General

Models play a major role in MDE. The most general definition says that a model is a simplified view of reality (Selic 2003); or, more formally, a model is a set of statements about a system under study (Seidewitz 2003). In fact, one can say that a model is a clear set of formal elements that describes something being developed for a specific purpose and that can be analyzed using various methods (Mellor et al. 2003a). In addition to what is specified by the definition of a model, an engineering model must possess, to a sufficient degree, the following five key characteristics (Selic 2003):

- *Abstraction.* A model is always a reduced rendering of the system that it represents.
- *Understandability.* It is not sufficient just to abstract away detail; we must also present what remains in a form (e.g., a notation) that most directly appeals to our intuition.
- *Accuracy.* A model must provide a true-to-life representation of the modeled system's features of interest.
- *Predictiveness.* We should be able to use a model to correctly predict the modeled system's interesting but nonobvious properties, either through experimentation (such as by executing a model on a computer) or through some type of formal analysis.
- *Inexpensiveness.* A model must be significantly cheaper to construct and analyze than the modeled system.

For MDE to be popularized and accepted by the software engineering community, the theory behind it should be precise and easy to grasp. Therefore, providing separate definitions of models is useful, but it needs to be done through a consistent theoretical framework. This implies a development of the MDE theory that must be comprehensive enough to address all the phenomena related to the languages and metamodels used in MDE (e.g., OWL, XML, and UML). It makes the study of MDE's theory critical. Modeling, as the spirit of MDE, is arguably the best method to study the theory of MDE, especially because of its natural ability in simplifying the specification and description of the intended goal (Bézivin 2001).

4.1.2 Model-Driven Engineering Theory

Here, we explain the model and metamodel phenomena by following Favre's notion of *megamodel* as a way to formally define the theory of

MDE (Favre 2004a).[1] The term megamodel is selected to avoid confusion with the basic meanings of the terms *model* and *metamodel*. Defining the formal theory in the form of a model which represents the basic MDE concepts and their relations helps us infer new facts about MDE that are not explicitly represented in the megamodel. From this perspective the megamodel can also be regarded as an ontology of MDE.

4.1.2.1 Megamodel Definition

Figure 4.1 shows an excerpt of Favre's extended megamodel (Gašević et al. 2007) represented in the form of a UML class diagram. The diagram defines the most abstract concept of discourse in MDE: *System*. The (incomplete) classification of systems shown in Fig. 4.1 distinguishes between physical systems, digital systems, and abstract systems. PhysicalSystem represents things from reality, such as a "travel agency." AbstractSystem is an abstraction in human minds that can be processed by human brains; for example, concepts and their relations from the biological domain. Finally, DigitalSystem is a digital representation that can be processed by computers, such as an XML document with an OWL representation of biological classes and their properties.

Fig. 4.1 The megamodel: classification of systems

The concept *Set,* was originally used in Favre's megamodel as an abstract system, the extensional meaning of a model (e.g., a set of all instances of an OWL class); and thus this extensional meaning is an abstract system as well. Moreover, the intensional meaning of a concept can be considered an abstract system under study (i.e., the idea being modeled). Finally, a model (e.g., OWL class) is itself an abstract system composed of the intensional and extensional systems.

---

[1] Portions reprinted with changes from Gašević et al. (2007).

In constructing the megamodel, the following definition of models is used: *A model is a set of statements about some system under study* (Seidewitz 2003). This definition introduces the notions of a model, a system under study, and their relations. The fact that being a model or a system under study (also called "subject" (Kühne 2005, 2006)) is a relative notion, not an intrinsic property of an artifact, is represented by the *non-transitive* relation *RepresentationOf* (or simply μ) between different systems. This means that one system can be a model of another system, and this can be represented by *RepresentationOf*. For example, an ontology of the biological domain (abstract system) is a representation of the conceptualization used by a biologist. A file in an OWL XML format (digital system) is a representation of the ontology of the biological domain. The same ontology can also be represented in an XML format of UML (i.e., UML XML Metadata Interchange, XMI).

Having in mind the purpose of metamodels as means for defining modeling languages, Favre suggests analyzing metamodels in terms of the language theory that is based on sets (Favre 2004b). The language theory allows us to formally represent relations between models and metamodels, so that one can reason about modeling languages, and thus deduce facts about modeling languages and their characteristics that are not explicitly asserted. In a very broad definition borrowed from the language theory in which *a language is a set of systems (or a set of sentences)*, it is emphasized that a language itself is an abstract system without any materialization.

4.1.2.2 Classification of Metamodels

A general definition of metamodels is given in the OMG's MOF specification (OMG MOF 2002; OMG MOF2 2006): *A metamodel is a model that defines the language for expressing a model.* This definition emphasizes the linguistic nature of metamodeling, in which metamodeling is used for defining modeling languages. Seidewitz gives the most commonly used definition of metamodels in MDE (Seidewitz 2003): *A metamodel is a specification model for a class of systems under study where each system under study in the class is itself a valid model expressed in a certain modeling language.* In fact, a metamodel is a specification model, which leads us to the conclusion that metamodels should be used to validate models represented in a specific language. That is, a metamodel makes statements about what can be expressed in the valid models of a certain modeling language.

Generally, a metamodel is any language specification written in English, such as the W3C's OWL language specification (Bechhofer et al. 2004) or the OMG's UML specification (OMG UML 2007a, 2007b). However, in order to automatically check the validity of models with respect to their metamodels, we need to formalize the definition of the metamodel. In the scope of the MDA's pile of standards, the MOF is defined as a metamodeling language for defining other languages (see Miller and Mukerji [2003] for further details about the MDA). In the common understanding of the MDA, metamodels and models are connected by the *instanceOf* relation, meaning that a metamodel element (e.g., the Class metaclass from the UML metamodel) is instantiated in the model level (e.g., a UML class Collie).

Earlier research in MDE recognized two different types of instantiation relations in various metamodeling architectures (Bézivin and Lemesle 1998): (i) instantiation of elements residing at different modeling layers; and (ii) instantiation of elements residing at the same modeling layer. This is further explored in Atkinson and Kühne (2003) where the example shown in Fig. 4.2 is used. We can say that *linguistic metamodeling* is equivalent to the definitions cited above (Seidewitz 2003; OMG MOF2 2006). In fact, linguistic metamodeling is a way of defining modeling languages and their primitives (e.g., Object, Class, MetaClass) on the layer of a metamodel (L2 in Fig. 4.2 or M2 in terms of the MDA). These language concepts are *linguistically* instantiated on the layer of models (L1 in Fig. 4.2 or M1 in terms of the MDA).

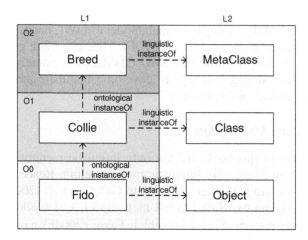

Fig. 4.2 Two types of metamodeling (Atkinson and Kühne 2003): ontological and linguistic

Ontological metamodeling is concerned with domain definition and uses ontological instantiation. For example, a UML object (Fido) is an ontological instance of a UML class (Collie). It is important to say that a UML class and a UML object are on different ontological layers (O0 and O1, respectively), but still they are on the same linguistic metamodeling layer (L1 or M1 in terms of the MDA). We can go further and provide more abstract domain types or domain metaclasses (Breed) on higher ontological layers (O2) without the need to leave the model layer L1.

This distinction of metamodeling types has two important implications for the MDA:

1. The existence of the M0 layer in the classical four-layer MDA architecture has been discarded, as there is no need to separate the M0 and M1 layers. In fact, the M0 layer comprising UML objects which are instances of UML classes is now a part of the M1 layer, but UML objects and UML classes are still on different ontological layers (O0 and O1).
2. The UML2 specification enables designing domain concepts whose instances can be both classes and objects.

Looking at the OWL language, we can identify both types of metamodeling. The OWL specification (Bechhofer et al. 2004) can be regarded as a model of the OWL modeling language, thus it is a linguistic metamodel. To allow for the automatic checking of ontology validity, this linguistic metamodel of OWL has to be specified by using a metamodeling language. Indeed, this is the role of the RDF schema of the OWL language that is a part of the official OWL specification. This schema can be regarded as a linguistic metamodel of the OWL language. To bring OWL ontologies to the MDA, a linguistic metamodel of OWL needs to be represented by an MDA language (i.e., the MOF). This, at a more general level, is the goal of the ODM initiative (OMG ODM 2007); namely, to use the MOF as a metamodeling language to develop a linguistic metamodel for representing ontological languages.

4.1.2.3 Linguistic Metamodels

Since in the rest of this book, we use only linguistic metamodeling, here we will define precisely only linguistic metamodeling. Readers interested in ontological metamodeling are referred to Gašević et al. (2007). We will define metamodeling by using Favre's megamodel, which allowed for the discovery of the pattern (Fig. 4.3a) which Favre (2004b) named the μεμ pattern. This pattern defines the notion of metamodel, where a metamodel is *a model of a set of models*. From this pattern, one can clearly see the difference between the notions of metamodel and modeling language. While the language per se is a set of sentences that can be used in a modeling language, a metamodel is a model of that set. This is very important, since metamodels are used as abstract syntax for modeling languages. That is, metamodels specify rules for structuring sentences in modeling languages. This is why there is a need for extension of the μεμ pattern—the conformance pattern shown in Fig. 4.3b. This implies that each model needs to be conformant to the metamodel of the modeling language in which the model is specified.

Fig. 4.3   The μεμ (**a**) and conformant (**b**) patterns

From this pattern we also explain metamodeling architectures, such as the well-known MDA. The number of times we apply this pattern (i.e., the number of metasteps) determines whether we are dealing with a model, a metamodel, a meta-metamodel, etc. For example, repeating this pattern two times leads us to the notion of a meta-metamodel. This is how the MOF is defined in the MDA architecture: the MOF is a model of a meta-modeling language, i.e., a language for defining modeling languages.

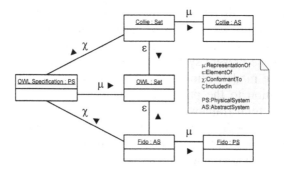

Fig. 4.4   Relations between models, metamodels, and modeling languages

To illustrate the above definition of the metamodel and the notion of the conformance pattern, let us further explore our example shown in Fig. 4.2. In Fig. 4.4, the individual Fido:AS and the class Collie:Set are elements of (ε) the OWL language (i.e., OWL:Set). Furthermore, we can say that a *modeling language* (in this case OWL:Set) *is a set of models*. Since a set is an abstract system, we need to represent (μ) a modeling language by a physical system in order to develop tools for checking the validity of expressions in that language. In fact, such a representation of (μ) a modeling language (OWL:Set) in the form of a physical system (OWL Specification:PS) is actually *a model of a modeling language*, i.e., a *metamodel*. As well, OWL individuals (Fido:AS) and classes (Collie:Set) must be conformant to the abstract syntax of the OWL language.

4.2 Types of Software Models

Ideally, developers should see an information system as an *independent* world during its development, without any artificial constraints such as the operating system, hardware, network performance, or application incompatibility.

One possible solution that can enable such an approach is to execute every information system on the same hardware platform, operating system, architecture, etc. Even though this may not sound very realistic, one may notice that this approach is already being applied to the Windows operating system and other related software technologies by the companies that produce them. However, even if all of the components were to be under the same development control, the field of information systems is so heterogeneous and prone to so many revisions that the constant need for improved versions of software would cause this approach to collapse.

Since there have already been many different platforms and too many conflicting requirements, it is very hard for developers to agree to one common solution. Accordingly, a more realistic scenario is to enable the coexistence of the present systems by representing them with models and by transforming models into other models. The MDA indeed attempts to provide a solution to the problem of such an integration. Although the OMG's architectural framework is constantly being changed, the primary goals of achieving both interoperability and portability are still unchanged.

The MDA defines three viewpoints (levels of abstraction) for analyzing systems. Given a viewpoint, we can define a representation of a system under study, that is to say a model of the system seen from that viewpoint. In fact, for each viewpoint there is a corresponding model, namely:

- the computational-independent model (CIM);
- the platform-independent model (PIM);
- the platform-specific model (PSM).

The CIM does not show details of the structure of the system. In software engineering, it is well known as a domain model specified by domain experts. This is very similar to the concept of an ontology.

The PIM is a computation-dependent model, but it does not consider the characteristics of specific computer platforms. In other words, the PIM is a model assumed to be executed on a technologically independent virtual machine.

The PSM finalizes the specification of a whole computer system. The main goal is to shift developers' focus from the PSM to both the PIM and the CIM. In this way, platform-specific details should be generated using various tools for automatic generation of those details (e.g., code). These tools should transform the PIM into the PSM (see Fig. 4.5). More details of these abstraction levels and their corresponding models can be found in Frankel (2003), Kleppe et al. (2003), and Mellor et al. (2003b).

Fig. 4.5 Transforming a platform-independent model (PIM) into platform-specific model (PSM) using transformation tools

4.3 The Model Driven Architecture

As already mentioned in Sect. 4.1.2, the MDA is a metamodeling architecture that consists of two metasteps, namely, those between models and metamodels and those between metamodels and meta-metamodels. In fact, the MDE offers a few complementary standards (see Fig. 4.6):

- the Meta-Object Facility (MOF);
- the Unified Modeling Language (UML);
- the MOF2 Query/View/Transformation (MOF 2 QVT, or simply QVT);
- the Object Constraint Language (OCL);
- the XML Metadata Interchange (XMI).

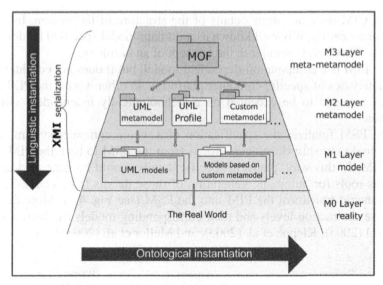

Fig. 4.6   The four-layer Model Driven Architecture and its orthogonal instance-of relations: linguistic and ontological

The topmost level of this architecture is the meta-metamodel, that is to say, the MOF. It is an abstract, self-defined language and framework for specifying, constructing, and managing technologically independent metamodels. It is a basis for defining any modeling language, such as UML or the MOF itself. The MOF also defines a backbone for the implementation of a metadata (i.e., model) repository described by metamodels (OMG MOF 2002; OMG MOF2 2006). The rationale for having these four levels with one common meta-metamodel is to enable both the use and the generic managing of many models and metamodels, and to support their extensibility and integration.

All metamodels, standard and custom (user-defined), that are defined in the MOF are placed in the M2 MDA level. One of these metamodels is UML, which stands as a language for specifying, visualizing, and documenting software systems. The basic concepts of UML (e.g., Class and Association) can be extended in UML profiles in order to adapt UML to specific needs. Models of the real world, which are represented by concepts from a metamodel belonging to the M2 level, are in the M1 level of the MDA four-level architecture. In the M0 level, are things from the real world that are modeled in the M1 level. For example, the MOF Class concept (from the M3 level) can be used for defining the UML Class concept

(M2), which, in turn, defines the Person concept (M1). The Person concept is an abstraction of the real thing *person*. We provide a more detailed discussion of modeling architectures and their mutual relations in the next chapter. Similarly, the metamodels of the OCL and QVT languages are defined in the M2 level of the MDA.

The bottommost layer is the instance layer (M0). There are two different approaches to describing this layer:

1. The instance layer contains instances of the concepts defined in the model layer (M1), for example, objects in programming languages.
2. The instance layer contains things from our reality, both concrete (e.g., Mark is an instance of the class Person, and Lassie is an instance of the class Dog) and abstract (e.g., UML classes—Dog, Person, etc.) (Atkinson and Kühne 2003).

In this book, we advocate the second approach, but we need to give more detail about its impact on UML. In UML, both classes and objects are in the same layer (the model layer) in the MDA four-layer architecture. The MDA layers are called linguistic layers. On the other hand, concepts from the same linguistic layer can be in different ontological layers. Hence, UML classes and objects are in different ontological layers, but in the same linguistic layer.

In addition to the aforementioned standards, the MDA is based on XMI, a standard that defines mappings of MDA-based meta-metamodels, metamodels, and models onto XML documents and XML schemas. Since XML is widely supported by many software tools, it empowers XMI to enable better exchange of meta-metamodels, models, and models.

4.4 Metamodeling Languages

In this section, we define two major metamodeling languages. The first one is the Meta-Object Facility defined in the scope of the OMG's standards dedicated to the MDA. The second one is the Ecore language that is defined in the scope of the Eclipse Modeling Framework (EMF) (Budinsky et al. 2009). Given that in the rest of the book we use only the MOF, here we provide only a basic high level introduction of the Ecore language.

4.4.1 The Meta-Object Facility

The MOF (OMG MOF2 2006) originated as an adaptation of the UML core, which had already gained popularity among software modelers, to the needs of the MDA. The MOF is, essentially, a minimal set of concepts which can be used to define other modeling languages. It is similar (but not identical) to the part of UML which is used in the modeling of structure. In the latest version (2.0), the concepts of the MOF and of the UML superstructure are derived from the concepts of the UML infrastructure.

Essentially, there is an OMG standard called the UML infrastructure (OMG UML 2007a), which contains basic concepts that are intended to be used in other metamodels. Figure 4.7 shows the dependency of some widely used metamodels based on the UML core package.

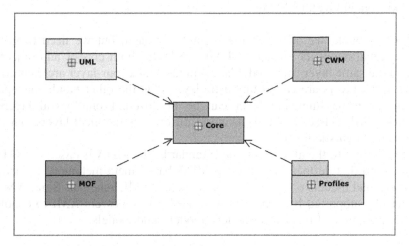

Fig. 4.7   The UML core package considered as a mutual kernel

The UML core package precisely defines the basic concepts that are frequently used in modeling. A notable difference with respect to the older version is that every concept in the new version is narrowly focused on some small aspect. This enables these concepts to be easily combined in various metamodels, avoiding usage of those aspects that are not required.

In version 2.0 of the MOF standard, there are two meta-metamodels to choose from:

- Essential MOF (EMOF);
- Complete MOF (CMOF).

EMOF is a compromise that favors simplicity of implementation over expressiveness, while CMOF is more expressive, but more complicated and harder to implement. Figure 4.8 shows EMOF and CMOF and their dependencies.

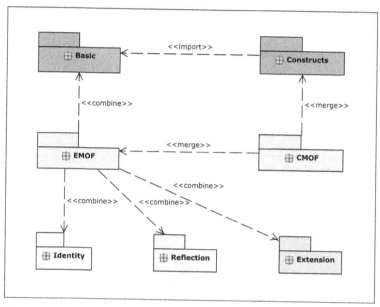

Fig. 4.8   EMOF and CMOF and their dependencies

From Fig. 4.8, we can see that EMOF is derived mostly from the Basic package of the UML infrastructure, whereas CMOF expands EMOF using concepts from the Constructs package (which is a part of the UML infrastructure).

Basically, the four main modeling concepts in the MOF are:

- Class—this models MOF metaobjects, concepts which are entities in metamodels (i.e., UML Class, Attribute, and Association, ODM Class, Property, etc., and even MOF concepts such as Class or Property);
- Association—this models binary relationships (UML or MOF superclasses and types, or ODM superproperties, for example);
- DataType—this models primitive types (String, Integer, etc.);
- Package—this modularizes other concepts; for example, it groups similar concepts.

Of course, there are many more such concepts, but these are the most important and most frequently used. For details, see the MOF specification

(OMG MOF2 2006). Figure 4.9 should give a feeling of what some meta-models look like. It shows part of the MOF definition of a metamodel.

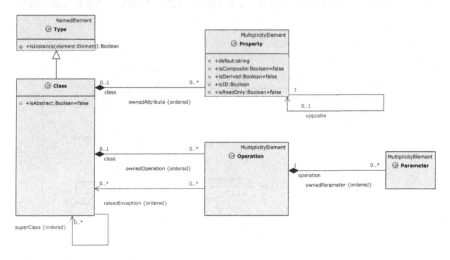

Fig. 4.9 The definition of part of a metamodel (in this case, EMOF is defined within itself)

Do not be confused by the fact that MOF Class is defined using MOF Class. This is like defining words in a dictionary: one word is defined by some other words, but all words are defined by words from the same dictionary. For example, the definition of "or" in a dictionary may include the following statement: "restating or clarifying the first item mentioned." So, the definition of "or" includes the word that it defines! Regarding other metamodels defined in EMOF, there is a part of the UML infrastructure that defines the UML Class concept, and that diagram is very similar to the diagram shown in Fig. 4.9. In this book, you will find a large part of the definition of the Ontology Definition Metamodel—it is defined in EMOF.

4.4.2 Ecore Metamodeling Language

The EMF is a conceptual modeling framework for the Eclipse extensible development platform (Budinsky et al. 2009). Being developed in parallel with the OMG's MDA, the EMF provides a similar set of languages for metamodeling and model interchange. The major difference is in the M3 level, where the EMF defines the Ecore metamodeling language instead of the MOF. Ecore is also defined by itself. In Fig. 4.10, the Ecore model (i.e., the EMF's meta-metamodel) with its core elements (attributes, relations, and operations) is shown. Ecore has a similar origin to that of the

MOF (i.e., UML); it is then obvious that the major concepts are defined in
a similar way.

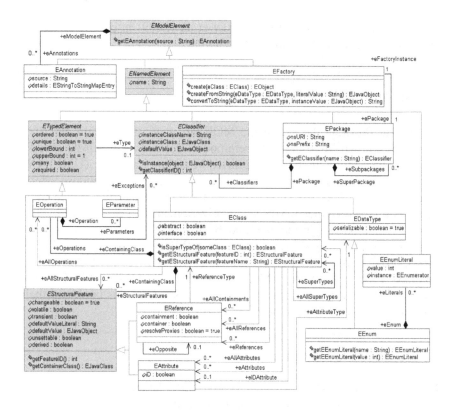

Fig. 4.10   The core element of the Ecore definition: The Ecore meta-metamodel
(the Ecore model as per its official definition given at
http://download.eclipse.org/modeling/emf/emf/javadoc?org/eclipse/emf/ecore/
package-summary.html#details)

From the above diagram, we can see that there are four basic ECore
constructs that are necessary to represent a model of a modeling language:

1. EClass—used for representing a modeled class. It has a name, zero or
   more attributes, and zero or more references.
2. EAttribute—used for representing a modeled attribute. Attributes
   have a name and a type.
3. EReference—used for representing an association between classes.

4. EDataType—used for representing attribute types, which can be either primitive (int or float) or object types (e.g., java.util.Date).

We refer interested readers to Budinsky et al. (2009) in order to find further details about the EMF and Ecore language.

4.5 Standardized MDA Metamodels

In order to illustrate the use of the MOF language, this section describes three well-known MOF-defined metamodels defined in the OMG specifications. This section includes the Unified Modeling Language (UML), Ontology Definition Metamodel (ODM), and Common Warehouse Metamodel (CWM). This list should not be taken as exhaustive, since there have been several other OMG standardization initiatives defined by following metamodeling principles and by using the MOF. Examples are: Semantics for Business Vocabularies and Rules (SBVR) (OMG SBVR 2008); Production Rule Representation (PRR) (OMG PRR 2007); and Business Process Definition Metamodel (BPDM) (OMG BPDM 2008). However, these specifications are beyond the scope of this book and their definitions are not discussed here.

4.5.1 Unified Modeling Language

The Unified Modeling Language (UML) is a language for specifying, visualizing, and documenting software systems, as well as for modeling business and other nonsoftware systems. UML is a result of the best practice in engineering modeling and has been successfully proven in modeling many big and complex systems.

As we have already mentioned, the UML core is the same as that of the MOF. Accordingly, we shall not discuss its elements; a comprehensive overview can be found in the UML language specification (OMG UML 2007a). UML is often identified as a graphical notation, which was true for its initial versions. Recently, UML has been recognized more as a language independent of any graphical notation rather than as a graphical notation itself.

However, UML is also very important as a language for the graphical representation of models of software systems. The point of view from which a problem under study is examined determines crucially which elements of that problem will be stressed in the final model. UML has features for emphasizing specific views of a model by using graphical representations of models, namely UML diagrams. In this way, we can abstract models; we may otherwise not be able to analyze and solve complex systems. Evolving from UML 1.x versions, UML2 consists of 13 diagrams:

- Structure Diagrams:
  - Class Diagram
  - Composite Structure Diagram
  - Component Diagram
  - Deployment Diagram
  - Object Diagram
  - Package Diagram
- Behavior Diagrams:
  - Activity Diagram
  - State Machine Diagram
  - Use Case Diagram
  - Interaction Diagrams:
    - Sequence Diagram
    - Communication Diagram
    - Interaction Overview Diagram
    - Timing Diagram

These diagrams provide developers with various perspectives on the system under study or development. A model which captures a whole system and is graphically represented by diagrams just integrates all these perspectives into one common entity, comprising the union of all modeled details of that system.

Probably the best overview of the use of the UML language is given in Fowler (2003); more details about the first versions of the language can be found in Booch et al. (1998) and Rumbaugh et al. (2004); and up-to-date information about the UML2 language can be found in its specification (OMG UML 2007a, 2007b).

4.5.2 Common Warehouse Metamodel (CWM)

The great complexity and diversity of the fields described by metamodels means that many different metamodels are constantly evolving. Even when those metamodels are based on the same meta-metamodel, their interoperation requires a number of bridges (i.e., transformations). This problem is emphasized in the field of data warehousing, where one aims to manipulate and integrate data based on a large number of different metamodels.

The Common Warehouse Metamodel (CWM) is an OMG open industrial standard for integrating tools for data warehousing and business
analysis. It is based on using common metadata (Poole 2002). CWM is an
example of an approach to model-based metadata integration. It is not one
monolithic metamodel, but actually comprises many different but related
models. Each model is an information subdomain in a business chain. Figure 4.11 shows a block diagram of the organization of CWM, namely the
metamodels contained in CWM.

CWM comprises several metamodels organized into the following layers: Object Model, Foundation, Resource, Analysis, and Management.
Metamodels located in the higher layers rely on metamodels from the
lower layers. The basic layer (Object Model) is based on UML, which is
actually a superset of it. In Fig. 4.11, we have emphasized metamodels that
are more relevant for designing metamodels of intelligent information systems, even though it is not very sensible to exclude any metamodel a priori. For example, the Data Mining metamodel belongs to the group of
metamodels of intelligent information systems.

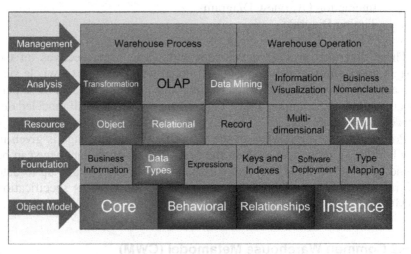

Fig. 4.11   The structure of Common Warehouse Metamodel (CWM)

CWM may have a big influence on the integration of metamodels for intelligent information systems. It can be used as either an extensible basis or
a template for building new metamodels.

4.5.3 Ontology Definition Metamodel

The MDA and its four-layer architecture provide a solid basis for defining the metamodels of any modeling language, and thus a language for modeling ontologies based on the MOF. Such a language can employ MDA tool support for modeling, model management, and interoperability with other MOF-based metamodels. The current software tools do not implement many of the fundamental MDA concepts. However, we can expect that most of these tools, which are presently oriented towards UML and the modeling layer (M1), will be improved and equipped with MDA support in the coming years.

Currently, there is a final specification for ODM adopted by the OMG (OMG ODM 2007). Originally, there was an RFP (Request for Proposal) within the OMG that was aimed at defining a suitable language for modeling Semantic Web ontology languages in the context of the MDA (OMG ODM RFP 2003). This RFP was the result of extensive previous research in the fields of MDA and ontologies (Baclawski et al. 2002a, 2002b; Brockmans et al. 2004; Cranefield 2001a; Djurić et al. 2005a; Falkovych et al. 2003; Kendall et al. 2002). In Chaps. 7, 8, and 9, we give a detailed overview of the OMG's ODM specification because of its high importance for this book.

4.6 UML Profiles

The UML profile is a concept used for adapting the basic UML constructs to a specific purpose. Essentially, this means introducing new kinds of modeling elements by extending the basic ones, and adding them to the modeler's repertoire of tools. In addition, free-form information can be attached to the new modeling elements.

4.6.1 Basics of UML Profiles

The basic UML constructs (model elements) can be customized and extended with new semantics by using four UML extension mechanisms defined in the UML specification (OMG UML 2007b): stereotypes, tag definitions, tagged values, and constraints.

Stereotypes enable one to define virtual subclasses of UML metaclasses, by assigning them additional semantics. For example, we may want to define the «OntClass» stereotype (see Fig. 4.12) by extending the UML Class «metaclass» to denote modeling elements used to represent ontological classes (and not other kinds of concepts).

Tag definitions can be attached to model elements. They allow one to introduce new kinds of properties that the model elements may have, and are analogous to meta-attribute definitions. Each tag definition specifies the actual values of the properties of individual model elements; these values are called tagged values. Tag definitions can be attached to a stereotype to define its virtual meta-attributes. For example, the «OntClass» stereotype in Fig. 4.12 has a tag definition specifying four tagged values (for enumeration, intersection, etc.).

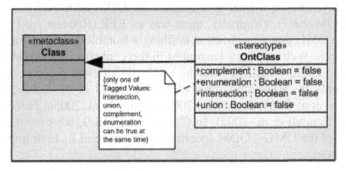

Fig. 4.12   A definition of a new stereotype

Constraints make it possible additionally to refine the semantics of the modeling element that they are attached to. They can be attached to a stereotype using OCL (Object Constraint Language) or the English language (i.e., spoken language) in order to precisely define the stereotype's semantics (see the example in Fig. 4.12). More details of UML extension mechanisms can be found in (OMG UML 2007b; Rumbaugh et al. 1998).

A coherent set of extensions of the basic UML model elements, defined for specific purposes or for a specific modeling domain, constitutes a UML profile. A UML profile definition in the context of the MDA four-layer metamodeling architecture means extending UML in the level of the metamodel layer (M2). One can understand such extensions as a new language, but can also understand UML as a family of languages (Duddy 2002). Each of these languages uses the UML notation with the four UML extension mechanisms. The recent UML specifications enable graphical notation to be used for specifying stereotypes and tagged definitions (Kobryn 2001). Thus, all of the stereotypes and tagged values used in this chapter have been defined in this way.

4.6.2 Examples of UML Profiles

Many important UML profiles have now been developed. Some UML profiles have been adopted by the OMG, such as the UML Profile for CORBA (OMG CORBA 2002) and the UML Profile for Enterprise Application Integration (OMG EAI 2004). Besides these formal specifications, several well-known UML profiles have been widely accepted by software engineers. One of the most popular ones is the UML profile for building Web applications developed by Jim Conallen (Conallen 2002). Recognizing the lack of UML primitives for modeling Web applications (e.g., links, Web forms, and Web pages), Conallen extended some UML model elements (e.g., Class and Attribute) with primitives relevant to Web applications (e.g., server page, client page, and form). Figure 4.13 shows a UML diagram of a Web application modeled using Conallen's UML profile. The diagram contains UML representations of server pages (e.g., spUnbounded), a form, and buttons on the form (e.g., Simulate). This example shows the feature of UML whereby one can develop a specific icon for each primitive developed in a UML profile. In Fig. 4.13, we have used the graphical features of the Rational Rose UML tool for modeling Web applications using this UML profile. Of course, the use and definition of graphical icons is optional. In fact, the same semantic meaning of an extended UML model element (e.g., Class) would be obtained if we used a graphical representation of standard model elements together with the standard way of representing stereotypes (e.g., the Simulate *button* in the "form" class).

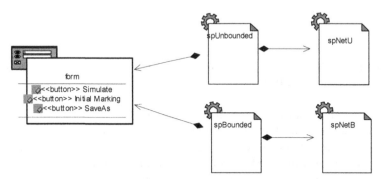

Fig. 4.13 UML diagram of a Web application modeled using a UML profile for modeling Web applications

Another important UML profile is that for modeling XML Schema developed by David Carlson (2001). Understanding the needs of developers of business applications to use a rich set of XML Schema features, Carlson found that the resulting schemas were difficult to share with wider audiences of users and business partners. In fact, other forms of representation and presentation of models are more effective than XML Schema when specifying new vocabularies or sharing definitions with users. Carlson proposed the use of UML as a standard for system specification and design. Figure 4.14 shows the Musician ontology represented in Carlson's UML profile for modeling XML Schema. It is important to note that each class and attribute has a corresponding stereotype (i.e., XSDcomplexType and XSDattribute). In this way, one can map this model onto an XML Schema definition using tools (e.g., an XSLT that transforms an XMI representation of a UML model into an XML Schema definition). Besides the stereotypes shown in Fig. 4.14, the UML Profile contains all other primitives required for defining XML Schemas.

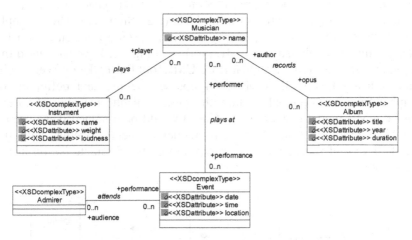

Fig. 4.14 A UML diagram of the Musician ontology, represented with the UML profile for modeling XML Schema

Note, finally, that there are many other important UML profiles apart from the ones that we have illustrated in this book. Some examples are the UML profile for database design (Naiburg and Maksimchuk 2001) and the UML profile for framework architectures. Taking into account the fact that the main goal of this book is to illustrate the use of MDA standards for developing ontologies, we shall explain the Ontology UML Profile in detail.

4.7 Model Transformations

In the MDA, model transformations are sequentially applied over models until the system's code is generated. In this section, we describe model transformations and transformation languages in more detail.[2]

4.7.1 Definitions

The MDA Guide (Miller and Mukerji 2003) gives a definition of model transformation: "Model transformation is the process of converting one model to another model of the same system." (Kleppe et al. 2003) defines model transformation as "automatic generation of the target model from a source model, which conforms to the transformation definition." Kurtev uses the following definition (2005): "A model transformation is a process of automatic generation of a target model from a source model, according to a transformation definition, which is expressed in a model transformation language."

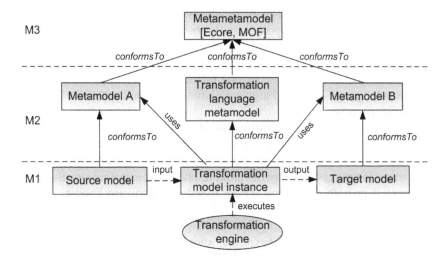

Fig. 4.15 Model transformations

In fact, a model transformation means converting an input model (or a set of input models) which conforms to one metamodel, to another

[2] This section was written with the great help of Mr. Milan Milanović (University of Belgrade in Serbia). We are very greatful for his kind help and permission to adapt parts of his work previously published in Milanović (2007).

model(s), which conforms to another metamodel (see Fig. 4.15). This conversion is done by defining rules that match and/or navigate elements of source models resulting in the production of elements of the target model. The transformation itself is a model, which conforms to some transformation metamodel (Bézivin et al. 2006).

4.7.2 Classification of Model Transformation Languages

Model transformation languages are characterized by many different features. Various research studies explored this area in order to allow for systematic analysis and classification of model transformation languages, and thus provide developers with a systematic approach to selecting the most suitable languages for their problems at hand. In this section, we describe some classifications of transformation languages based on various criteria defined in Gardner et al. (2003), Czarnecki and Helsen (2006), and Mens and van Gorp (2006).

A transformation language is *declarative* if transformation definitions written in that language specify relationships between the elements in the source and target models, without dealing with execution order. Relationships may be specified in terms of functions or inference rules. A declarative transformation engine applies an algorithm to the relationships to produce a result. In contrast, an *imperative* transformation language specifies an explicit sequence of steps to be executed in order to produce the result. An intermediate category may also be introduced, known as *hybrid* transformation languages. These languages have a mix of declarative and imperative constructs.

Some languages allow specification of transformation definitions that can be applied only in one direction: from a source model to a target model. These transformations are known as *unidirectional* transformations. Some other languages (usually declarative ones) allow definitions that may be executed in both directions. These transformations are known as *bidirectional* transformations. This capability is useful when two models must be synchronized. If a transformation language does not support definitions of bidirectional transformations, then two separate definitions may be used: one for each direction.

A typical transformation scenario takes one model as input and produces one model as output (*1-to-1* transformation). Generally, there are three other cases: *1-to-N*, *N-to-1*, and *M-to-N*. In many cases, multiple models are produced from a single source model (*1-to-N* transformation). For example, a single model may be used to generate some Java code and an XML schema used for data exchange. A model composition in which several models are integrated into a single one is an example of an *N-to-1* transformation. In a general case, support for *M-to-N* transformations ensures availability of the other three cases.

Finally, Brown et al. identify three types of model transformations (2005). *Refactoring transformations* deal with the reorganization of a model based on some well-defined criteria. In this case, the output is a revision of the original model, called the refactored model. *Model-to-model transformations* convert information from one model (or a set of models) into another model (or set of models). Typically, the flow of information is across abstraction boundaries. *Model-to-text transformations*[3] convert a model element into a text-based definition fragment. Here, we extend this classification with another transformation type—*text-to-model*. This transformation type allows for reverse engineering of software models from the low level software artifacts originally defined in the textual representation format.

4.7.3 Model Transformation Languages

In November 2005, the OMG published the final specification of the MOF2 Query View Transformation (QVT) standard (OMG QVT 2008). MOF2 QVT is defined by a MOF-based metamodel, and thus QVT is located in the M2 layer of the MDA.

The QVT architecture is shown in Fig. 4.16. The QVT metamodel comprises the three Domain Specific Languages (DSLs) for model transformations: *Relations, Core,* and *Operational Mappings*. These three languages form a hybrid transformation language: Relations and Core are declarative languages at two different levels of abstraction, with a normative mapping between them. The Relations language has a graphical concrete syntax and it specifies a transformation as a set of relations between models. The Operational Mapping language is an imperative language that extends both Relations and Core. The syntax of the Operational Mapping language provides constructs commonly found in imperative languages (e.g., loops and conditions). QVT has a mechanism called *BlackBox* for invoking transformation facilities expressed in other languages (e.g., XSLT and

---

[3] In the original work presented in Brown et al. (2005), this transformation type is called model-to-code transformation. However, we believe that model-to-text transformation has a more general meaning. In fact, we do not need to say explicitly that mode-to-text transformations are limited to object-oriented languages or to other programming languages. In fact, software artifacts such as ontology, configuration, deployment, data definitions, and message can also be generated from software models.

XQuery), which is also an important part of the specification. It is especially useful for integrating existing non-QVT libraries.

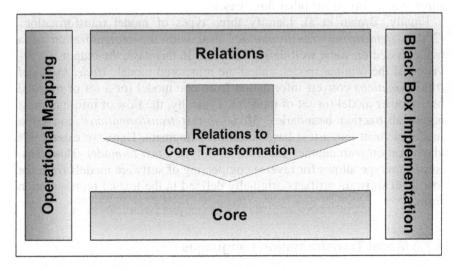

Fig. 4.16   The QVT architecture

The OMG's QVT only includes *model-to-model* transformations, in which models need to be conformant to the MOF 2.0 metamodel. The *model-to-text* and *text-to-model* transformation types are not included in the OMG's QVT standard.

4.7.4 Model Transformation Tools and Implementations

It is of course very important to use appropriate tooling support that allows for representing and transforming models. While the OMG adopted the QVT specification, the QVT language has not been fully implemented by one comprehensive tool. Let us just mention two of them. Borland Together Architect 2006[4] is a commercial QVT-like transformation tool, which is very close to the OMG's QVT standard. Its implementation is based on the Eclipse platform. It uses Ecore for model representation instead of the MOF. It supports operational transformations for mode-to-model transformations. SmartQVT[5] is an open source transformation tool implementation of the QVT Operational standard. It is also implemented on the Eclipse platform and supports the use of Ecore models.

---

[4] http://www.borland.com/together
[5] http://smartqvt.elibel.tm.fr

In addition, several research groups are creating their own model transformation tools and languages. In fact, these languages initiated the current QVT standard, and many of them are even today very commonly used in the MDE community. Most of these tools are available in the form of Eclipse plug-ins and are based on EMF (Eclipse Modeling Framework) for model manipulation. Some of them are commercial, while some of them are not. The discussion about the details of many different model transformation tools goes beyond the scope of this book and here we just list some of them: IBM MTF, UMLAUT NG, Kermeta, YATL, BOTL, FUUT-je, MTL, UMT, Mod-Transf, Tefkat, ModelMorf, GReAT, and VIATRA 2. In this book, we explain the details of only the Atlas Transformation Language (ATL) and its supporting tooling. The ATL language is a standard solution to model-to-model transformations in Eclipse,[6] while we provide details about ATL in Chap. 11.

4.8 Object Constraint Language

The Object Constraint Language (OCL) (OMG OCL2 2006), currently in version 2, is defined as an addition to the UML 2.0 and MOF 2.0 specifications.[7] It provides a way for expressing constraints and logic in models and metamodels. Initially, OCL was first introduced in UML, version 1.4. However, from UML version 2.0, OCL is defined by using the MOF. OCL is used for expressing: different pre- and post-conditions, invariants, constraint conditions, and results of model execution. OCL constraints can be defined on both models of MOF-defined modeling languages and MOF-defined metamodels. When an OCL expression is evaluated, the result is temporary. This means that the associated class, i.e., its concrete instances (objects), cannot change its condition during the expression evaluation.

For example, we can define the following constraint on a class `Person` shown in Fig. 4.17: a brother of a person's father is the person's uncle. In Chap. 14, we further discuss how OCL can be used together with the Semantic Web languages.

---

[6] http://www.eclipse.org/m2m/

[7] This section was written with the great help of Mr. Milan Milanović (University of Belgrade in Serbia). We are very greatful for his kind help and permission to adapt parts of his work previously published in Milanović (2007).

Fig. 4.17   Example of an OCL invariant

4.9 An XML for Sharing MDA Artifacts

XML Metadata Interchange (XMI) is an XML-based standard for sharing
MDA metadata (OMG XMI 2002). Although this standard sounds as if it
ought to be very well known, most practitioners are confused by this term.
We shall try to explain XMI using Fig. 4.18. The confusion comes from
the presence of several different XML schemas, and all of them are called
XMI. We usually encounter two kinds of XMI documents, or, more precisely, the two XML schemas defining XMI:

- the XML schema for MOF metamodels;
- the XML schema for UML models.

The first of these defines the syntax for sharing both MOF-based metamodels and the definition of the MOF itself. So, we use one schema in two
different MDA layers, M3 and M2, for sharing both meta-metamodels and
metamodels. For instance, the MOF is defined by itself, so we use the
MOF XML schema to describe the XMI document comprising the MOF
specification, and this document is also a part of the MOF standard.

Similarly, there is the document that describes the XMI standard containing the UML metamodel. However, UML is a modeling language that
developers use for various different models. It is obvious that there is a
need for an XML schema for exchanging UML models. In fact, there is the
standardized one called the UML XMI Schema. UML tools such as
IBM/Rational Rose, Poseidon for UML, and Together support this schema,
but some researchers report that we always lose some information when
sharing UML models between two UML tools (Uhl and Ambler, 2003).

Furthermore, it is well known to developers that we never employ
the UML XML Schema as an XML language in domain applications.
We always define a domain XML language, i.e., a domain XML

schema. Accordingly, there is a set of rules for mapping UML models into XML schemas (Grose et al. 2002). Thus, one can generate an XML schema for any UML model, while instances of models (i.e., objects) are shared in accordance with those schemas. In view of the presumption that both UML objects and UML classes are in the same MDA layer (the M1 layer), we regard the generated XML schemas and their instance XML documents as being placed in the M1 layer.

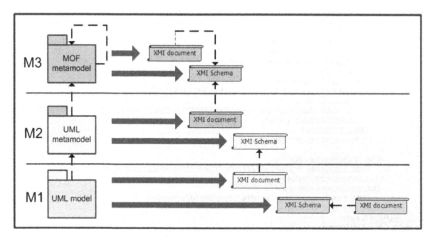

Fig. 4.18   Mapping MDA meta-metamodels, metamodels, and models to XMI

Since we have a set of rules for generating XML schemas from UML models, we can apply the same principle to the upper MDA layers (M2 and M3), and so we can produce an XML schema for each MOF-based metamodel. Using that principle, we have generated XML schemas for various metamodels (e.g., ODM [Djurić et al. 2005a]). For example, the developers of Protégé have produced an XML schema for a MOF-compatible metamodel of the Protégé ontology editor (Protégé 2005).

Summarizing the story about XMI, we can say that XMI is:

- a set of rules for the serialization of an object;
- a set of rules for the generation of schema.

Accordingly, the OMG has specified several documents related to XMI:

- the XML schema for MOF metamodels;
- the XMI document for the MOF metamodel;
- the XMI document for the UML metamodel; and
- the XMI schema for UML models.

In order to illustrate the aforementioned XMI documents and schemas, we show in Fig. 4.19 an excerpt from an XMI document representing the Musician UML class defined in the previous chapters. The document shown has been written in accordance with the standardized XMI schema for UML models. This document is in the bottommost level (M1) in Fig. 4.18, and is an instance of the XML schema defined in the level M2 in Fig. 4.18.

```
<UML:Class xmi.id="lm19247250m106c9d71d66m24d0" name="Musician"
   visibility="public" isSpecification="false" isRoot="true" isLeaf="true" isAbstract="false" isActive="false">
   <UML:Classifier.feature>
      <UML:Attribute xmi.id="lm19247250m106c9d71d66m24d1"
      name="name" visibility="private" isSpecification="false"
      ownerScope="instance" changeability="changeable"
      targetScope="instance">
         <UML:StructuralFeature.multiplicity>
            <UML:Multiplicity xmi.id="lm19247250m106c9d71d66m250c">
               <UML:Multiplicity.range>
                  <UML:MultiplicityRange xmi.id="lm19247250m106c9d71d66m250d" lower="1" upper="1"/>
               </UML:Multiplicity.range>
            </UML:Multiplicity>
         </UML:StructuralFeature.multiplicity>
         <!--   -->
         <UML:Attribute.initialValue>
            <UML:Expression xmi.id="lm19247250m106c9d71d66m24d2" language="java" body=""/>
         </UML:Attribute.initialValue>
         <UML:StructuralFeature.type>
            <UML:DataType xmi.idref="lm19247250m106c9d71d66m24d3"/>
         </UML:StructuralFeature.type>
      </UML:Attribute>
   </UML:Classifier.feature>
</UML:Class>
```

Fig. 4.19 An excerpt from a UML XMI document representing the Musician UML class

4.10 The Need for Modeling Spaces

After reading the previous section, readers can be expected to be confused by the use of many XML documents to represent models from different MDA levels. The main reason for doing this is that we are trying to represent one modeling paradigm (i.e., the MDA) in terms of another one (i.e., XML). One of the critical issues is that a metamodel can be represented using an XML document, but at the same time we generate an XML schema based on this same metamodel. Furthermore, we use both XML documents and MDA models to represent things taken from reality, but at the same time we represent MDA models using XML. So, are MDA models things from the real word? An additional question is whether instantiation relations between XML schemas and XML documents are the same as instantiation relations between MDA metamodels and models. Similar problems can be expected in understanding the differences and similarities between MDA models and ontologies. Since an understanding of the relations between these two modeling spaces is very important for the purpose of this book, the next chapter defines the concept of modeling spaces (Djurić et al. 2006).

5 Modeling Spaces

It is well known from software project management practice that developers' familiarity with the principles of several different modeling approaches can be beneficial for the development team. Changing the modeling and design aspects from time to time during the system development, e.g., from OO to relational, from relational to functional, and the like, often helps prevent schedule overruns (Zahniser 1993).

In practice, developers commonly use one or more integrated, complex tools that involve multiple modeling approaches. Remember your last round-trip with UML (OMG UML 2007b), Java/C# code, specialized technologies such as J2EE, database schemas, XML files, etc.? You do not always need to think about the relationships between these; sometimes it is a matter of choosing the right option from the menu of your favorite integrated development environment. However, you might find that, even when the tool you use supports changes from one modeling aspect to another, getting the big picture is a rather complex task. Things get even more complex in situations when the support provided by tools is not straightforward and you need a lot of effort to figure out how to transform one model to another.

Using a number of modeling approaches greatly increases the developers' ability to better describe the problem using the right approach, but is also more complex to comprehend in its entirety. Moreover, it can be difficult for software developers to adopt the practice of using a wide spectrum of modeling approaches because such approaches may seem too different and too unrelated to each other. In order to save time and effort when working under tight development schedules, practitioners tend to focus on individual aspects of modeling (Seidewitz 2003). For all these reasons, a common view of various modeling approaches is highly desirable.

We have defined a formal encompassing framework for studying many modeling problems in a more comprehensive way. We call this framework "modeling spaces." Its development was motivated by a desire to provide a better understanding of the vast diversity of things that can be modeled, and a clear rationale for using and combining different software modeling technologies. It has direct implications for software engineering processes

D. Gašević et al., *Model Driven Engineering and Ontology Development*, 2nd edn.,
DOI 10.1007/978-3-642-00282-3_5, © Springer-Verlag Berlin Heidelberg 2009

and activities, since it allows systematic change of modeling and design
views throughout the system development cycle.

5.1 Modeling the Real World

If we search a dictionary for the word "model," we find several definitions—most of them just referring to the special cases of models most often used; for instance: a replica of an item, a person wearing clothes at a
fashion show, or a drawing of a building. Few of these definitions are generally applicable. Fortunately, there is a simple and general definition—a
model is a simplified abstraction of reality (Hagget and Chorley 1967). Using that definition, we can explain why these special cases are models. A
person wearing clothes at a fashion show does not represent her-
self/himself, but the appearance of any person wearing those clothes; thus
that is a model. A drawing of a building is not just a sheet of paper with
lines; it is also a simplified abstraction of a building containing only data
that is important in a given context.

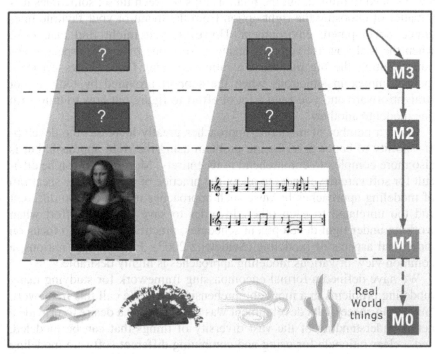

Fig. 5.1   A few common models put into an MDA-inspired layered architecture

Figure 5.1 shows some common examples of models put into a layered architecture conceptually inspired by the MDA—a famous painting (the Mona Lisa, also known as La Gioconda, painted by Leonardo da Vinci in the 16th century), and part of a music score (of the song "Smoke on the Water"). A noble Renaissance woman and a rock song are things from the real world, in the M0 layer. A painting and a sheet of music are obviously abstractions of real-world things. Therefore, they are models and can be put in the M1 (model) layer. Metamodels are used to define these models. In the case of a music score, which is a written interpretation of a song, the metamodel (M2) is a set of concepts—stave, note, etc.—and rules that define what each note means and how we can arrange them on a stave. In this context, the meta-metamodel (M3) includes self-defined concepts that also define a stave, note, etc. Although this architecture is imprecise and definitely not perfect from the perspective of music theory, at least it captures a formal interpretation of music.

Things get harder in the case of the painting. Is it possible to specify a metamodel that can define such a complex and ambiguous model as a masterpiece painting? A simplistic view based on physical appearance only might lead to a definition of this metamodel in terms of concepts such as line, circle, and color. The meta-metamodel would then be a set of concepts used to define line, circle, color, and their meanings. However, this painting, like any other work of art, is much more than just lines and colors. It has much to do with human psychology and experience and can be interpreted in many ways. It is much more difficult, if not impossible, to define a formal metamodel or meta-metamodel in this case. We may anticipate that they exist, but they will be extremely complex and implicit.

Another important issue is that, although the Mona Lisa and written notes are models, they are also things in the real world. We can hold them in our hands (if the guards let us do this, in the case of the Mona Lisa) and they can be items entered in an information system that stores information about art.

5.2 The Real World, Models, and Metamodels

The previous analysis leads to two important conclusions. First, something can be taken as a model if it is an abstraction of things in the real world, but it is simultaneously a thing in the real world. Whether we take it as a model or as a real-world thing depends on the context, i.e., on our point of view. Second, models can be defined using metamodeling concepts formally or implicitly. Since implicit metamodels, as in the case of works of art, cannot be precisely defined using formalisms, we shall analyze only formal models in the rest of this discussion. Nevertheless, many of the conclusions can also be applied to implicit metamodels.

Figure 5.2B shows a general modeling architecture that was inspired by the MDA, and is in fact a generalization of it. In such a modeling architecture, the M0 layer is the real world, as in Atkinson and Kühne (2003) and Bézivin (2004). It includes all possible things that we try to represent using models (the M1 layer). This representation may be more or less abstract and simplified, depending on how rich our models are. Models are defined using concepts defined in metamodels (M2), and so each metamodel determines how expressive its models can be. The metamodels are also defined using concepts. These concepts belong to meta-metamodels (M3). We could continue this layering to infinity, but it makes much more sense to stop at some point. The topmost layer contains the super-metamodel (Mn), which is metacircular (defined by its own concepts). Between Mn and M1, there are n-2 layers. This architecture is said to be n-layered, where n is the actual number of layers above M0.

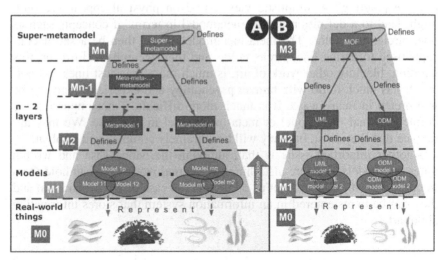

Fig. 5.2   (A) General four-layer modeling architecture (B) MDA

We use the term "represents" to denote that a model takes the place of a real-world thing, acting on its behalf in some specific context. Models' concepts "conformTo" the metaconcepts that define them, in the sense that metaconcepts determine their nature, specify their precise meaning and form, and identify essential qualities. These terms can be defined more precisely in specific contexts and modeling systems. In the context of art, the Mona Lisa represents the ideal of beauty. In a different way, a specification of an information system represents the actual programs in some other context. In yet another way, these programs represent the real business problem in a third context. Moreover, the abstraction is not absolute, but context-dependent; a real-world thing and its model could switch places when the context is changed.

The most widely known example of an n-layered architecture today is the Model Driven Architecture (MDA), based on three layers (Fig. 5.2B). The MDA's meta-metamodel, the Meta-Object Facility (MOF), is the super-metamodel (because M3 is the topmost layer here). The MOF standard defines an abstract language and a framework for specifying, constructing, and managing technology-neutral metamodels. In essence, the MOF is an object-oriented metamodeling language extracted from the UML core. Well-known examples of MOF-defined metamodels include UML and CWM (Common Warehouse Metamodel). In the MDA, the XML Metadata Interchange standard (XMI) is used to define a mapping from MOF-defined metamodels to XML documents and schemas, thus enabling sharing of meta-metamodels, metamodels, and models.

We shall not ask the question "How many layers are optimal?" here. In the original two-layered UML-based architecture, UML was the super-metamodel and the only metamodel. This solution was not able to support other metamodels, so another layer based on the MOF was added to support different kinds of models. We shall show later that most of today's popular modeling architectures can be considered as three-layered, and thus the following discussion will use three layers for the sake of simplicity.

5.3 The Essentials of Modeling Spaces

A modeling space (MS) is a modeling architecture based on a particular super-metamodel. Models in the M1 layer represent the real world in the context of a separate universe, organized in a hierarchy. Every layer above M0 in this hierarchy conforms to the higher layer, finally reaching the top layer containing the self-defined super-metamodel. If the super-metamodel was defined by some other concepts, it would not be a super-metamodel— it would exist at some lower layer in some other modeling space.

Figure 5.3 shows a few examples of well-known modeling spaces. The most straightforward example from this picture is the MOF MS. It is defined by the MOF meta-metamodel (MOF is the super-metamodel here), which in turn is defined by itself. It defines various metamodels, for instance UML (OMG UML 2007b) or ODM (Ontology Definition

Metamodel—a metamodel for ontology modeling in MDA) (Djurić et al. 2005a), that are used to describe models that represent things in the real world. The same reality is described in the context of other modeling spaces, such as EBNF and RDFS spaces. Resource Description Framework Schema (RDFS) is a language that defines classes of defined resources and their properties in a machine-processable way. Many software engineers would associate terms such as "model" and "modeling" exclusively with the UML "aristocracy," considering EBNF-based models (Java, C#, C++ code) as more technical, flattened artifacts and "ignoble citizens." However, Java code (and also C++ and other code) is a model, since it represents an abstraction of reality. The same applies to XML code, databases, books, etc.—they are all models, but modeled in terms of different modeling spaces, determined by different super-metamodels.

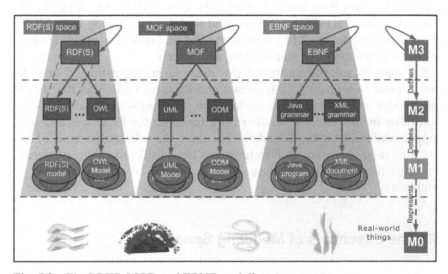

Fig. 5.3   The RDFS, MOF, and EBNF modeling spaces

If we model the real world in a particular modeling space, we shall use certain models. If we model the same reality in another modeling space, we shall describe it with different kinds of models, highlighting other characteristics when abstracting from reality. The models in the first modeling space will be a part of reality that we can model using the models in the second modeling space.

Figure 5.4 clarifies this duality with an example of the same thing being simultaneously a model and a real-world thing. Along the vertical axis, the world is modeled in the MOF modeling space. Along the horizontal axis is the EBNF space hierarchy, which is a real-world thing in the MOF space. An interesting observation here is that any modeling space, such as the

EBNF space or even the MOF space itself, is a part of the real world from the MOF-space point of view. In general, the way we model a business system or other "real" domain is very much the same as the way we model meta-metamodels, metamodels, or models from another modeling space. Of course, these models involve a certain level of abstraction, so there is a possibility of losing some information.

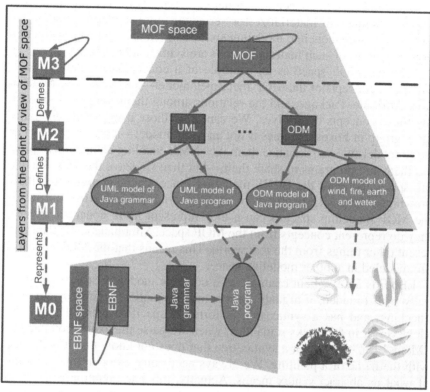

Fig. 5.4 The MOF MS sees EBNF MS as a set of things from the real world

For many software engineers, this duality is complicated to understand at first. Try a couple of analogies. Ghosts do not really exist (well, we hope not!), but they are things from the real world. Some people believe that there is life outside of the solar system, and some claim it is pure fiction; but life outside the solar system is a thing from the real world. Otherwise, we would not be able to model it using movies, literature, video games, etc. The fact that the M1–M3 layers are fiction and above the M0 layer does not mean that meta-metamodels, metamodels, and models are things outside of reality. Everything is in the real world; we just use a convention to put some things into layers, depending on the context.

5.4 Modeling Spaces Illuminated

Modeling spaces can be defined in a more or less abstract manner. Some modeling spaces are focused on conceptual (abstract or semantic) things, such as models, ontologies, and mathematical logics. These spaces are not aimed at in techniques for representation or for sharing their abstractions. We call such spaces conceptual modeling spaces. However, we must have some techniques to materialize (or serialize) those modeling spaces. We can do this using concrete modeling spaces, which are equipped with notation. Examples of such materializations are syntax and databases.

Take the MOF space as an example of a conceptual modeling space. The basic concepts of the MOF meta-metamodel—such as Class, Association, Attribute, Package, and the relations among them—are expressed using those concepts themselves. We can draw those using UML diagrams, but a group of boxes and lines is not an MOF model—it is a drawing of an MOF model. We can serialize them into XMI, enabling computers to process them and programs to share them—but then we leave the MOF modeling space and enter the EBNF modeling space. One can argue that these drawings, i.e., UML diagrams, or models serialized into XMI, are inside the MOF modeling space because they represent MOF concepts. Indeed, they do represent concepts from the MOF space. Simultaneously, they represent other things from the real world. This means that the MOF concepts are modeled in another modeling space.

EBNF is an excellent example of a concrete modeling space. Theoretically well founded, it arguably has some "semantics," primarily for type checking, and has a syntax that is formally specified using a grammar. However, it in fact lacks semantics; when we parse the expression name = "Mona Lisa," we obtain a syntax tree that does not know that it is dealing with the name of a painting. We always need some external interpretation of what its abstract syntax means. Actually, this interpretation is given in corresponding models from other technical spaces that have been serialized into the BNF form.

Being able to represent only bare syntax, concrete modeling spaces need some means to express the semantics, i.e., the meaning of the data they carry. Conceptual modeling spaces, on the other hand, are able to represent semantics, but need a means to represent their information physically. It is obvious that they should complement each other's representation abilities to create models that have both semantics and syntax. One of the most interesting examples of this symbiosis of various modeling spaces can be found in the OMG Model Driven Architecture.

We can find similar "modeling patterns" in spoken languages, where people of different nationalities use different languages to express the same meaning. Regardless of the fact that they have the same things in mind (i.e., the same semantics), they need some rules to share the meanings. Spoken languages have their own syntax for sharing semantics. Just as we can model the same semantics in different modeling spaces, we can talk about the same thing using different spoken languages. Similarly, definitions of mathematical languages (i.e., logics) include two parts: syntax and semantics.

Fig. 5.5   Orthogonal and parallel spaces

There are two types of scenarios in which more than one modeling space is used, both shown in Fig. 5.5:

- Parallel spaces—one modeling space models the same set of real-world things as another modeling space, but in another way. In this case, the relation between these modeling spaces is oriented towards pure transformation, bridging from one space to another. Examples of such parallel modeling spaces are the MOF and ECore (ECore is a meta-metamodel very similar to, but also different from, the MOF; although ECore is a little simpler than the MOF, they are both based on similar object-oriented concepts). As another example, the RDF(S) MS and the MOF MS can also be used as parallel spaces.

- Orthogonal spaces—one modeling space models concepts from another modeling space, taking them as real-world things, i.e., one MS is represented in another MS. This relation is often used in round-trip engineering to facilitate various stages of modeling a system. For example, in order to make a Java program, we could first use a Java UML profile to create classes and method bodies, then transform this UML model into Java code, and complete the Java program using a Java Integrated Development Environment. Orthogonal modeling spaces are also used when a conceptual modeling space is implemented using a concrete modeling space—for example, when one is developing an MOF-based repository to run in a Java virtual machine. If we use the MOF to define an RDFS or OWL metamodel, the MOF and RDFS spaces are orthogonal.

The MOF modeling space is the shining star of the MDA. Its meta-metamodel, the MOF, defines the core concepts used to specify all the metamodels that the MDA is based on (UML, CWM, and the MOF itself), and many other domain-specific metamodels. Software engineers are often confused about how these concepts are represented. The MDA includes a standard for representation (or serialization) of MOF-based models using XMI (which is an XML-based representation of objects), so when software engineers see XMI they often think it is UML (or the MOF).

The truth is a little different. The XMI document that they are looking at is an XML document that models concepts from the MOF modeling space in the XML modeling space using XML concepts such as "element" and "node." XML is then modeled with concrete XML syntax in the EBNF space. The same applies to the Java Metadata Interface (JMI) standard (Dirckze 2002); it models MOF concepts using Java constructs that enable the implementation of MOF-based repositories. Both the MOF XMI and the JMI standards are in fact standards for modeling MOF space models in other, concrete modeling spaces.

In Fig. 5.5A we can see several modeling spaces included in the MDA and their orthogonal, representation-oriented relations that, depending on the context, may form a "modeling circle" that can often be confusing. The Mona Lisa, the painting, is modeled in the MOF space using the concept of Object. This concept exists only as an idea—the MOF space is a conceptual modeling space, and hence it needs some kind of syntax for representation. Concrete modeling spaces such as those based on EBNF (Java and

XML) can be used to represent the MOF concepts. This is the second stage of the representation in Fig. 5.5—the object monaLisa in the MOF space is modeled in the EBNF space as the RefObject monaLisa (RefObject is a part of the JMI specification).

Such concrete concepts from XMI and JMI can be (and often are) also modeled using their corresponding MOF-based metamodels or UML profiles, bringing them back to the MOF modeling space. In Fig. 5.5, the monaLisaRefObject is an instance of the corresponding concept in the MOF-based Java metamodel in the MOF modeling space. The MOF space is involved two times in this "chain" of representations. First the model in the MOF space (monaLisa:modeldomain.Object) is in the M1 layer, but later it descends to the M0 layer in the hierarchy, although the other MOF model is used in the M1 layer.

However, the MDA is not the only standard for model-driven architectures—there is also EMF. Figure 5.5B shows the same real-world concept, the Mona Lisa painting, modeled in two different modeling spaces in parallel. It is often necessary to move completely from one modeling space to another by means of bridges; there is less room for confusion, because one modeling space is translated into another without changing the modeling layers. In this case, metamodels from the MOF modeling space (UML, ODM, etc.) translated into the corresponding ECore-based metamodels will still be in the M1 layer.

5.5 Modeling Spaces Applied

We are going to use Modeling Spaces as an aid in understanding many ideas we present in this book; so it is a good idea to show you an application from everyday software engineering life right away. Figure 5.6 shows a simplified example of different relationships between some modeling spaces included in a typical development process.

Typically, a development process starts with the extraction of requirements in the form of a Use Case (A): a text story written in natural language that represents the modeled business process. Based on that, we create more formal conceptualizations, called domain models, usually using UML (B). Our goal is to create working software; for example, in Java (C). During the process, we represent the same thing (a business process) using three kinds of models. We use one kind of model as a basis for creating some other kind, doing the manual or machine-aided transformation. These models have nothing to do with each other, except that they aid us in describing the same reality in a useful way at some point of development: from human-friendly to more machine-friendly. So we say that A, B, and C are parallel modeling spaces.

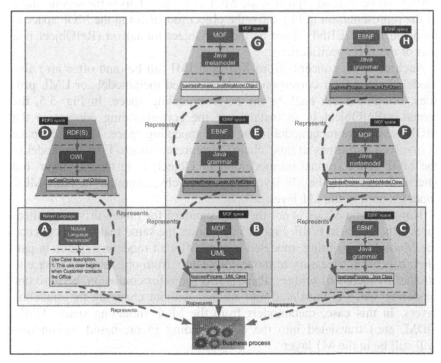

Fig. 5.6   A typical development process seen from different perspectives

In Fig. 5.6, some spaces are orthogonal to others: E to B, G to E, F to C, and H to F. Let us look at space B. The real-world thing (the business process) is modeled in MOF space using the concept of Class. This concept exists only as an idea—the MOF MS is conceptual, hence it needs some kind of syntax for representation. Concrete modeling spaces like those based on EBNF (Java, XML) can be used to represent the MOF concepts (E). The class businessProcess from the MOF space is represented in the EBNF space using Java syntax as the RefObject businessProcess (JMI-based implementation of UML in Java). These concrete concepts from XMI and JMI can be (and often are) also modeled using their corresponding MOF-based metamodels or UML profiles (G), bringing them back to the MOF MS. businessProcess concepts in E and G have nothing to do with the real-world business process directly. You can notice that the same modeling space can take on a role on many levels: so the model from a modeling space (B) can be a system under study in the same space (G)!

You may think: "Fine, but E and G are interesting only to developers of tools." Think about this example: a common confusion among many developers is to distinguish UML domain models (B) from UML models of their code (F). This is a matter of separating the conceptual perspective (or Platform Independent Model) from the software perspective (or Platform Specific Model). Mixing them up in diagrams and models (or in your head), which is a common mistake, makes the models more difficult to develop, understand, and maintain. Other common confusions include mistaking different serializations of UML (XMI, etc.) for UML, or the difficulties in distinguishing UML diagrams and UML models.

And this is only a simplified example, with only a couple of different modeling technologies involved. The value of modeling spaces increases in the case of more complex processes with many modeling approaches involved. And consider an agile process, in which you would not just sequentially change different approaches, but would use them almost in parallel—it is easy to get lost in the clutter. Just to make the example spicier in that sense, we added an OWL ontology created in one of the Semantic Web modeling spaces, RDFS (D).

5.6 A Touch of RDF(S) and MOF Modeling Spaces

The usage scenarios for parallel spaces most often pertain to conceptual MSs that model the same reality using different concepts. Each of these MSs is implemented in some other, more concrete MS, as a represented reality. In order to exchange models between conceptual MSs, it is necessary to provide transformations from one space to another. These transformations are also models (Bézivin et al. 2003), and should be developed in an MS that can represent both the source and the target MS. Moreover, the transformation also has to be represented in some concrete MS orthogonal to the source and target MSs, which leads from the conceptual model of the transformation to its implementation.

Figure 5.7 shows two parallel conceptual MSs, the RDF(S) MS and the MOF MS, and the space that represents them orthogonally, EBNF MS. MOF and RDF(S) model the real world in parallel, using modeling languages (UML, ODM, OWL, or another language) that are defined using different meta-metaconcepts. At the conceptual level, we could establish a transformation from one language to another, for example from the UML to the ODM and vice versa, in the same MS. An example of a transformation modeling language for such purposes in the MOF is Query-View-Transformation (QVT) (OMG QVT 2008). RDF and RDF Schema, and three different dialects of OWL, namely OWL Full, OWL DL, and OWL Lite, are examples of languages in the M2 layer of RDF(S) MS. There are a few initiatives to develop query and transformation languages in the RDF(S) MS (e.g., Triple, RQL [Haase et al. 2004]). The W3C have recommended such a language—SPARQL (Prud'hommeaux and Seaborne 2008).

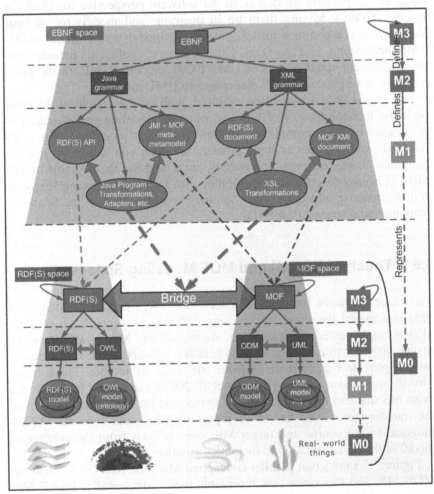

Fig. 5.7   Transformations between the RDF(S) MS and the MOF MS

We can also establish a transformation between the MSs, a bridge that transforms RDF(S) concepts to MOF concepts in the M3 layer. Using that bridge, we can transform any metamodel (language) defined in RDF(S) into its corresponding metamodel defined in the MOF (both are in the M2 layer). Of course, we can expect an information loss depending on how similar the meta-metaconcepts (M3) are. RDF(S) concepts, rdfs:Class, and rdf:Property are similar to, but not the same as the MOF Class, Association, and Attribute.

Both the MOF and the RDF(S) spaces can be represented in other, more concrete MSs. They can be implemented using repositories, serialized into XML, etc., which involves many MSs. For the sake of simplicity, we have skipped a few steps and have shown the spaces as Java program code and XML documents in the EBNF space. Models from the MOF space are modeled in Java code according to the JMI standard, and in XML according to the MOF XMI standard. For languages from RDF(S), XML is the natural method of representation. They can also be modeled using Java APIs (Jena, etc.).

Because the RDF(S)-MOF bridge is also a model, it can also be represented in a concrete MS representing meta-metamodels that should be bridged. Examples include an XSLT that transforms an MOF XMI document into an RDF(S) XML document and vice versa, a set of Java classes that adapt JMI interfaces to RDF(S) API interfaces, and a Java program that does a batch transformation from a JMI-based code to an RDF(S) API-based one.

As Fig. 5.7 shows explicitly, a single bridge models a transformation between two MSs in the M3 layer, between RDF(S) and MOF meta-metamodels. Transformations between metamodels situated in a single MS in the M2 layer are internal to that MS. However, they can be implemented through concrete MSs (e.g., EBNF for XSLT).

5.7 A Touch of the Semantic Web and MDA Technical Spaces

Modeling Spaces are an idea inspired by the concept of a technical space (TS), which is defined as a working context with a set of additional concepts, body of knowledge, tools, required skills, and possibilities (Kurtev et al. 2002). Fortunately, we can use MSs to enhance this fuzzy definition of TSs.

A technical space is a working context that includes various related MSs. Most often the TS is built around some MS, whereas the role of other MSs is supportive (e.g., implementation), or implicit (literature, know-how). For example, the MOF MS is at the center of the MDA TS. However, the MDA TS also partially includes other MSs: XML and EBNF in the area of XMI representation, EBNF in the area of repository implementation (JMI), an implicit MS that includes literature, etc. Transformations, for example to plain Java, C++, or VB code, are also models belonging to one or several MSs that are included to some extent in the MDA TS.

Figure 5.8 shows the overlap between the MDA TS and the Semantic Web TS in some MSs (most of the MSs belonging to these TSs have been omitted for the sake of simplicity). The MDA TS is built around the MOF MS, which resides completely in the MDA TS. The MDA TS also includes OWL ontologies that model MOF-based concepts or contain knowledge about the MDA, and which are parts of the RDF(S) MS. On the other hand, the Semantic Web TS includes the RDF(S) MS. In addition, it includes parts of the MOF MS related to the ODM metamodel and the Ontology UML Profile, and two-way transformations from these MOF-based models to OWL. These transformations are also part of the MDA TS. Recall that those transformations are also modeled, so they belong to some MSs as well. Some researchers are trying to identify a way to enable transformations between different MSs in the M3 layer using just one two-way transformation for all three layers (Bézivin et al. 2005).

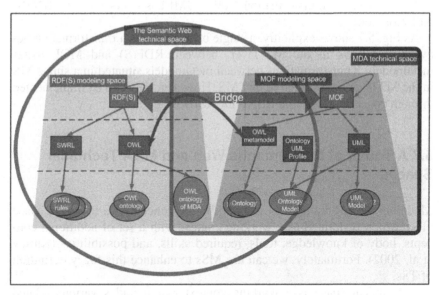

Fig. 5.8   The Semantic Web and Model Driven Architecture technical spaces

It follows from the above discussion that one technical space includes one or more modeling spaces and that every modeling space is a part of one or more technical spaces; a technical space is a means for grouping modeling spaces that have something in common or simply need to interact. A bridge connecting two modeling spaces is also a means for connecting the surrounding technical spaces.

5.8 Instead of Conclusions

Modeling spaces abstract and generalize a vast number of diverse modeling approaches, and can help engineers see the big picture of what underlies the software that they make or use. They also clarify the structures of different modeling approaches: their similarities and dissimilarities, their mutual relations, and how they work together. By making a clear distinction between conceptual and concrete, and parallel and orthogonal modeling spaces, developers can successfully select mechanisms to automate the transfer and sharing of information, knowledge, and even other modeling spaces between different projects and applications. Likewise, understanding specific modeling spaces helps one to select suitable modeling and development tools for a specific project.

In this book, we focus on a few modeling spaces, most notably the RDF(S) MS, the MOF MS and XML, and a few technical spaces, namely the Semantic Web TS, the Model Driven Architecture TS and the XML TS. The above discussion helps you to visualize what is going on.

5.8 Instead of Conclusions

Modeling spaces abstract and generalize a vast number of diverse model-ing approaches, and can help engineers see the big picture of what under-lies the software that they make or use. They also clarify the structures of different modeling approaches, their similarities and dissimilarities, their mutual relations, and how they work together. By making a clear distinc-tion between conceptual and concrete, and parallel and orthogonal model-ing spaces, developers can successfully select mechanisms to automate the transfer and sharing of information, knowledge, and even other modeling spaces between different projects and applications. Likewise, understand-ing the modeling spaces helps one to select suitable modeling and de-velopment solutions for a specific project.

In this book, we focus on a few modeling spaces – most notably the MDA MS, the MOF MS, and XML, among a few technical spaces, such as the relational, web DB, the World Editor, or the engineering and the XML technical spaces. I hope you to visualize what is going on.

Part II Model Driven Engineering and Ontologies

6 Software Engineering Approaches to Ontology Development

Ontologies, as formal representations of domain knowledge, enable knowledge sharing between different knowledge-based applications. Diverse techniques originating from the field of artificial intelligence are aimed at facilitating ontology development. However, these techniques, although well known to AI experts, are typically unknown to a large population of software engineers. In order to overcome the gap between the knowledge of software engineering practitioners and AI techniques, a few proposals have been made suggesting the use of well-known software engineering techniques, such as UML, for ontology development (Cranefield 2001a). However, software engineering approaches themselves do not enable the representation of ontology concepts derived from description logics, and such concepts are included in modern Semantic Web ontology languages (e.g., RDF, RDF Schema, and OWL).

6.1 A Brief History of Ontology Modeling

In this section we describe the existing efforts to enable the use of UML, as well as MDA-based standards, for ontological engineering. We explain the formal background of each approach and its relation to ontology languages. The idea is to recognize all similarities and differences between the two modeling spaces, and thus get a clearer picture about all issues that should be considered when bridging them.

6.1.1 Networked Knowledge Representation and Exchange Using UML and RDF

The idea of using UML in ontological engineering was first suggested by Cranefield (2001a). Cranefield found connections between the standard concepts of UML and those of ontologies: classes, relations, properties,

D. Gašević et al., *Model Driven Engineering and Ontology Development*, 2nd edn.,
DOI 10.1007/978-3-642-00282-3_6, © Springer-Verlag Berlin Heidelberg 2009

inheritance, etc. However, he also observed certain dissimilarities between them. The most important difference is related to the concept of a property—in UML, an attribute's scope is the class that defines it, whereas in an ontology a property is a first-class concept that can exist independently of a class. Here are the main presumptions of Cranefield's proposal for UML-based ontology development:

- UML class diagrams provide a static modeling capability that is well suited to representing ontologies, that is to say, modeling the taxonomy of the ontology's concepts and the relations between those concepts (i.e., the schema level of the ontology). For an example, see Fig. 6.1.
- UML object diagrams can be interpreted as declarative representations of knowledge, that is to say, they can be used for modeling instances of an ontology (i.e., body of knowledge) (Chandrasekaran et al. 1999). For an example, see Fig. 6.2.
- Object Constraint Language (OCL) can be used for specifying constraints on an ontology.
- The same paradigm can be used for modeling both ontologies and knowledge, which can be rather useful for software developers.

However, Cranefield recognized one significant current shortcoming of UML: the lack of a formal definition (Cranefield 2001b). The semantics of UML are defined by a metamodel, some additional constraints expressed in a semiformal language (i.e., OCL), and descriptions of the various elements of the language in plain English. Cranefield argued that the use of the basic features of class and object diagrams for representing ontologies and knowledge seems no more prone to misinterpretation than does the use of the Resource Description Framework—a language which underlies the Semantic Web but also lacks official formal semantics. Thus, he proposed an approach for integrating UML and RDF(S).

Cranefield's approach is founded on the following set of standards, which he recognized as important technological requirements for UML representations of ontologies and knowledge:

- XML Model Interchange (XMI), which stands for an XML-based standard for serializing UML models;
- well-known UML tools (e.g., IBM Rational Rose, Poseidon for UML, and MagicDraw) that can export the present UML artifacts in the UML XMI format;

- the Resource Description Framework (RDF) and RDF Schema (RDFS)—together often referred to as RDF(S), which is a W3C XML-based standard for sharing ontologies on the Semantic Web;
- eXtensible Stylesheet Language Transformations (XSLTs), which Cranefield used to transform UML XMI into:
  - a set of Java classes and interfaces corresponding to those in the ontology; and
  - RDF(S) (actually UML classes are transformed into RDFS, and UML objects into RDF statements).

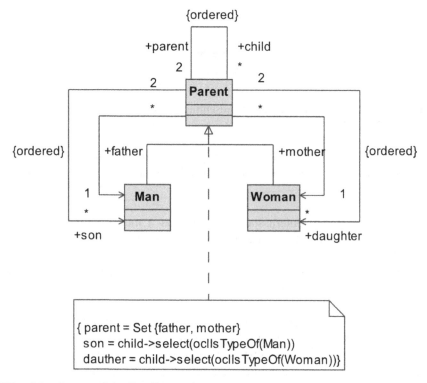

Fig. 6.1 A part of the Family ontology represented in the form of a UML class diagram, developed by Stephen Cranefield

The main problem that Cranefield had to deal with when generating an RDF schema that corresponds to a UML model is that RDF properties are first-class objects and are not constrained to the context of a particular class. This can lead to conflicting domain declarations if two (or more) different classes have equally named field attributes. He decided to prefix the name of each such field with the name of the class that it belongs to (e.g., `Person.name`). However, the disadvantage of this solution becomes obvious in the presence of inheritance, when fields of one class may be represented by properties with different prefixes, some referring to the class itself and others to the parent class.

Fig. 6.2 A UML object diagram representing instances of the ontology classes shown in Fig. 6.1

Besides the problem of transforming UML attributes and associations into RDF properties, Cranefield solved additional problems such as the following:

- When a UML attribute/association end has a multiplicity upper limit greater than a specific value, the XSLT used transforms that into an RDFS bag.
- When association ends have a UML "ordered" constraint, the XSLT transforms them into RDFS sequences.

Finally, note that Cranefield needed to extend the RDFS definition generated by the XSLT. He did this because there is no mechanism in RDFS to parameterize a collection type (such as `rdf:Bag`) with the type of elements that it may contain. Therefore, a nonstandard property `rdfsx:collectionElementType` was introduced to represent this information. Figure 6.3 presents the RDFS document generated by applying Cranefield's XSLT to the UML classes shown in Fig. 6.1.

Concluding this overview of the first and most cited UML-based approach to ontology development, we need to emphasize some of its limitations as well (especially since they propagate to the generated languages):

- One cannot deduce whether the same property has been attached to more than one class in the case of property inheritance.
- A hierarchy of properties cannot be created, even though this is allowed in RDFS.
- Standard UML cannot express advanced features of ontologies (e.g., OWL restrictions).
- The target RDFS ontology description does not have advanced restriction concepts (e.g., multiplicity).

```xml
<?xml version="1.0" encoding="UTF-8"?>
<rdf:RDF xml:lang="en"
    xmlns:rdfsx="http://nzdis.otago.ac.nz/2000/01/rdf-schema-extensions#"
    xmlns:rdfs="http://www.w3.org/2000/01/rdf-schema#"
    xmlns:rdf="http://www.w3.org/1999/02/22-rdf-syntax-ns#">
    <rdfs:Class rdf:ID="http://nzdis.otago.ac.nz/0_1/family#Person"/>
    <rdf:Property ID="http://nzdis.otago.ac.nz/0_1/family#Person.name">
        <rdfs:domain rdf:resource="http://nzdis.otago.ac.nz/0_1/family#Person"/>
        <rdfs:range rdf:resource="rdfs:Literal"/>
    </rdf:Property>
    <rdf:Property ID="http://nzdis.otago.ac.nz/0_1/family#Person.parent">
        <rdfs:domain rdf:resource="http://nzdis.otago.ac.nz/0_1/family#Person"/>
        <rdfs:range rdf:resource="rdf:Bag"/>
        <rdfsx:containerElementType rdf:resource="http://nzdis.otago.ac.nz/0_1/family#Person"/>
    </rdf:Property>
    <rdf:Property ID="http://nzdis.otago.ac.nz/0_1/family#Person.child">
        <rdfs:domain rdf:resource="http://nzdis.otago.ac.nz/0_1/family#Person"/>
        <rdfs:range rdf:resource="rdf:Seq"/>
        <rdfsx:containerElementType rdf:resource="http://nzdis.otago.ac.nz/0_1/family#Person"/>
    </rdf:Property>
    <rdf:Property ID="http://nzdis.otago.ac.nz/0_1/family#Person.father">
        <rdfs:domain rdf:resource="http://nzdis.otago.ac.nz/0_1/family#Person"/>
        <rdfs:range rdf:resource="http://nzdis.otago.ac.nz/0_1/family#Man"/>
    </rdf:Property>
    <rdf:Property ID="http://nzdis.otago.ac.nz/0_1/family#Person.son">
        <rdfs:domain rdf:resource="http://nzdis.otago.ac.nz/0_1/family#Person"/>
        <rdfs:range rdf:resource="rdf:Seq"/>
        <rdfsx:containerElementType rdf:resource="http://nzdis.otago.ac.nz/0_1/family#Man"/>
    </rdf:Property>
    <rdf:Property ID="http://nzdis.otago.ac.nz/0_1/family#Person.mother">
        <rdfs:domain rdf:resource="http://nzdis.otago.ac.nz/0_1/family#Person"/>
        <rdfs:range rdf:resource="http://nzdis.otago.ac.nz/0_1/family#Woman"/>
    </rdf:Property>
    <rdf:Property ID="http://nzdis.otago.ac.nz/0_1/family#Person.daughter">
        <rdfs:domain rdf:resource="http://nzdis.otago.ac.nz/0_1/family#Person"/>
        <rdfs:range rdf:resource="rdf:Seq"/>
        <rdfsx:containerElementType rdf:resource="http://nzdis.otago.ac.nz/0_1/family#Woman"/>
    </rdf:Property>
    <rdfs:Class rdf:ID="http://nzdis.otago.ac.nz/0_1/family#Man">
        <rdfs:subClassOf rdf:resource="http://nzdis.otago.ac.nz/0_1/family#Person"/>
    </rdfs:Class>
    <rdfs:Class rdf:ID="http://nzdis.otago.ac.nz/0_1/family#Woman">
        <rdfs:subClassOf rdf:resource="http://nzdis.otago.ac.nz/0_1/family#Person"/>
    </rdfs:Class>
</rdf:RDF>
```

Fig. 6.3   An RDF schema generated from the UML model shown in Fig. 6.1 using the XSLT that Cranefield developed

Regardless of all the aforementioned constraints of this approach, however, it is a quite useful solution and can be considered as a kind of agile UML-based approach to ontology development that bridges two different modeling spaces.

6.1.2 Extending the Unified Modeling Language for Ontology Development

Cranefield's pioneering work on using software engineering techniques for ontology development inspired other authors, and soon more advanced solutions to this problem started to emerge. Baclawski and colleagues have stressed that many mature UML tools and models and much expertise already exist and can be applied to knowledge representation systems, not only for visualizing complex ontologies but also for managing the ontology development process. They have introduced two UML-based approaches to ontology development (Baclawski et al. 2002a, b). This and the next subsection describe both of these solutions.

In their first proposal, Baclawski extended the UML metamodel with the constructs of the RDFS and DAML+OIL languages. Though their solution focuses only on the similarities and differences between the UML and DAML+OIL languages, they stated that it can be applied to other knowledge representation languages, such as:

- logical languages that express knowledge as logical statements (e.g., KIF);
- frame-based languages that are similar to object-oriented database languages;
- graph-based languages that include semantic networks and conceptual graphs.

Baclawski et al. tried to solve the problem of using UML for developing ontologies by defining appropriate mappings between the two modeling languages. Therefore they defined general-level mappings between UML and DAML+OIL (see Table 6.1). Additionally, they went into a profound theoretical discussion of the similarities and differences of these languages. Here we list only some of their most important findings (for details see Baclawski et al. 2002a):

- Knowledge representation languages do not have metalevel separation (e.g., an instance of a class may be a class).

- The concepts of classes and instances are common features of the two languages. This allows for consistent mappings of these concepts.
- Properties are a stand-alone concept, which is the main problem for transforming between the two languages.
- UML multiplicity constraints on associations can affect the membership of objects in classes related through an association. In DAML+OIL, constraints on properties are imposed somewhat indirectly by specifying that a class is a subtype of a class called "restriction."

Table 6.1 Rough overview of the relations between the concepts of the DAML+OIL and UML languages

DAML concept	Similar UML concept
Ontology	Package
Class	Class
As sets (union, intersection, etc.)	Not supported
Hierarchy	Class generalization relations
Property	Aspects of attributes, associations, and classes
Hierarchy	None for attributes, limited generalization for associations, class generalization for relations
Restriction	Constraints of association ends, including multiplicity and roles, implicitly as a class containing the attribute
Data types	Data types
Instances and values	Object instances and attribute values

- The semantics of the specialization/generalization relation are not equivalent:
  - UML's relation tends to provide behavioral reuse of modeled concepts. For example, in a graphical tool we would model the class Square so as to be the parent of the class Rectangle; the former class would have one attribute describing the dimensions of a graphical figure, while the latter class would have two attributes (width and height).
  - DAML+OIL's relation is set-theoretic (e.g., Rectangle is a parent of Square), which should closely reflect the relations between concepts in reality.
  - Finally, Baclawski et al. concluded that the mapping between these two relations is consistent, even though they are not semantically equivalent.

- RDF has a number of container notions: Bag, Seq, and Alt. The semantics of these notions are not very clear, and DAML+OIL has largely replaced them with the notion of a List. UML does have containers (in OCL), and it also has ordered associations which implicitly define a list within the context of an association.
- DAML+OIL has the ability to construct classes using boolean operations (union, intersection, and complement) and quantifiers.
- RDF allows one property to be a subproperty of another. UML has the ability to specify that one association is a specialization of another, although this construct is rarely used.
- Constructs in Semantic Web ontology languages are linked together either through the use of URIs or by using the hierarchical containment relationship of XML. UML uses names in a large number of namespaces. For example, each class has its own namespace for its attributes and associations. This is enriched by an ability to specify private, protected, and public scopes. Any mapping from UML to DAML+OIL or the reverse must have a mechanism for ensuring that names are properly distinguished.

Besides the aforementioned incompatibilities between UML and DAML+OIL, Baclawski and colleagues have stressed another important aspect. Ontology languages are monotonic, whereas UML and object-oriented languages are nonmonotonic. A system is monotonic if adding new facts can never cause previous facts to be negated. Such defined monotonicity is a necessity for realizing the goals of the Semantic Web. It supports representation of the diversities common to such a heterogeneous environment. Baclawski et al. considered modeling the concept of a *person* in order to depict this difference. They assumed that it has been specified that every person must have a name. Consider what would happen if a particular *person* object did not have a name. In UML, this situation would be considered as a violation of the requirement that every person must have a name, and a suitable error message would be generated. In a monotonic logic, on the other hand, one cannot draw such a conclusion. Baclawski et al. concluded that this distinction between UML and ontology languages makes it effectively impossible to define a mapping between these languages that would be able to preserve their semantics. However, it does not prevent one from defining a mapping that preserves semantic equivalence, and that is all that we are attempting to achieve.

A natural solution to bridging these two different languages is to extend UML with primitives that are equivalent to ones from DAML+OIL. However, solutions that use UML profiles, such as DUET, do not preserve semantics. Accordingly, Baclawski and colleagues made a specific recommendation for modifying the UML metamodel, thus enabling one to model using first-class properties, as well as to construct classifiers using boolean operations and quantifiers. In Fig. 6.4, we illustrate how MOF-based concepts of the UML metamodel (e.g., *Classifier* and *GeneralizableElement*) were extended with concepts from DAML+OIL (e.g., *DerivedClassifier, Restriction, Union, Intersection, Complement,* and *Property*) using the MOF's generalization/specialization relation. Figure 6.5 shows the associations among the newly added concepts in the UML metamodel.

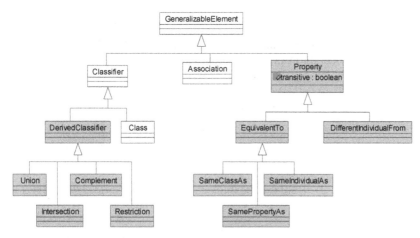

Fig. 6.4   The hierarchy of the metaclasses that are part of the extensions of the UML metamodel for DAML+OIL proposed in Baclawski et al. (2002a)

Since the development of a new tool able to support this extended UML metamodel would be expensive and time-consuming, Baclawski and colleagues proposed a UML profile based on their metamodel. Models based on that UML profile can be developed using tools for standard UML that are already available. In Fig. 6.6, we give an example of a UML diagram that Baclawski and colleagues developed in order to illustrate how to specify an association between the *Faculty* class and the *Organization* class. The *affiliation* association end belongs to the *location* property, which states that a *location* can be a *University,* a *School,* or an *Institute* that is not a *Company.*

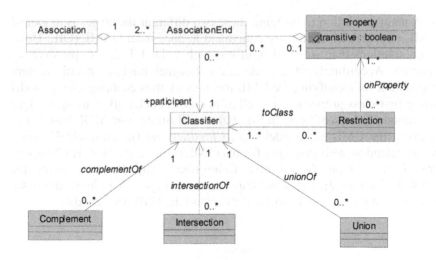

Fig. 6.5 The associations among metaclasses that are part of the extensions of the UML metamodel for DAML+OIL proposed in Baclawski et al. (2002a)

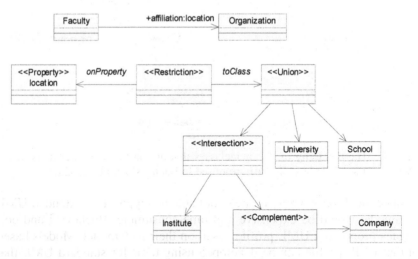

Fig. 6.6 An example of a UML model based on the UML extension for ontology development

Although this approach is the most comprehensive theoretical contribution to identifying relations between UML and DAML+OIL, it still has some shortcomings:

- DAML+OIL has evolved into OWL, which is the current W3C standard.
- Baclawski et al. did not develop any tool that would be able to map the extended UML into a Semantic Web language. Though standard UML tools could be used for developing ontologies, we still need a transformation tool for mapping models from one modeling language into another.
- An extended UML metamodel is not an optimal solution, as we do not need all UML concepts for ontology development. Actually, this issue was also recognized by Baclawski et al. themselves, and so they proposed an improved solution based on an independent ontology metamodel.

6.1.3 The Unified Ontology Language

Baclawski and colleagues realized that their initial solution was fairly awkward because it introduced some new concepts to the UML metamodel. Therefore, they have developed an independent ontology metamodel using the MOF; they have named it the Unified Ontology Language (UOL) (Baclawski et al. 2002b). This metamodel first appeared in public at an OMG meeting organized to initiate work on the Request for Proposals for specification of the Ontology Definition Metamodel (Baclawski et al. 2002b; OMG ODM RFP 2003). Although this metamodel was inspired by DAML+OIL, it also took the OWL language into account.

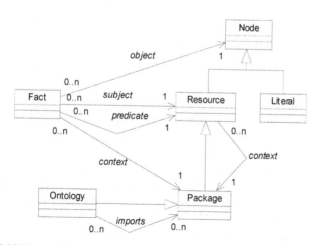

Fig. 6.7   MOF-compliant metamodel of the unified ontology language (UOL)

The proposed UOL should satisfy the following requirements:

- It must be an MOF-based modeling language (i.e., a metamodel).
- It must have a bounded two-way mapping between the core UML and the core UOL. The two-way mapping must preserve semantic equivalence on levels 0 and 1 of the MDA.
- The core UOL must include the same notions as the core UML, namely Package, Class, Binary association, Generalization, Attribute, and Multiplicity constraints.

Figure 6.7 gives a UML class diagram of an MOF-based metamodel for UOL which satisfies the aforementioned requirements. Although it seems rather small, it is a very high-level metamodel grounded on RDF and its triple-based paradigm. Furthermore, it is a solid starting point for a standard MOF-based ontology language. It is important to say that a similar solution has been used for defining the present ODM proposal.

6.1.4 UML for the Semantic Web: Transformation-Based Approach

Kateryna Falkovych and her colleagues (Falkovych et al. 2003) have proposed a transformation approach to the semantic extraction of ontologies from UML models. Their initial presumption is that UML and ontologies complement each other. That is to say, UML is designed for building models by human experts, while OWL is designed to be used at run time by intelligent processing methods. However, Falkovych et al. report that the process of translation is less than trivial, owing to the differences between the two languages.

With the above presumptions Falkovych and colleagues have proposed a transformation of UML diagrams into DAML+OIL ontologies which enables the semantics of UML concepts to be preserved. The main motivation for developing such a transformation is the existence of large sources of ontological knowledge already available in the UML design documents of existing applications. Furthermore, one can reason about UML models transformed into ontologies.

Taking into account the theoretical discussion in Baclawski et al. (2002a), Falkovych and her associates developed rules for transforming UML models into DAML+OIL ontologies. They also stresseded differences between properties in an ontology and UML associations/attributes. Since association is unique in UML, it is mapped into daml:ObjectProperty with a unique identifier for the property name. A UML attribute is mapped into daml:DatatypeProperty with a unique identifier attached. The rationale for mapping an attribute only to daml:DatatypeProperty and not to daml:ObjectProperty is that usually the type (range) of an attribute is a data type. Additionally, Falkovych et al. developed a taxonomy of association types in order to preserve semantics of UML associations and to distinguish association ends (see Fig. 6.8). Their taxonomy distinguishes between four subtypes of association: binary association, unidirectional association, aggregation, and composition, which are decomposed further into specific subtypes introduced for the purpose of mapping. This taxonomy is encoded as a separate DAML+OIL ontology, so that one can refer to it from the UML models transformed into DAML+OIL ontologies. Note also that all association types at the lowest level of decomposition (not shown in Fig. 6.8) can either have a name or be unnamed and can have role names attached to association ends.

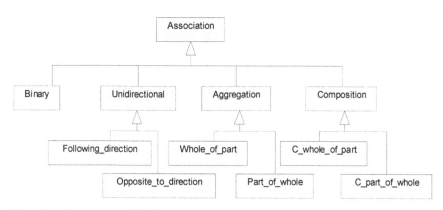

Fig. 6.8   Taxonomy of UML association types

Figs. 6.9 and 6.10 depict a UML binary unnamed association connecting two UML classes (*Boundary point* and *Boundary segment*) and its association ends (*has* and *form*). Note that the binary association is mapped into two daml:ObjectProperty elements. These two properties have the name of an association with a unique identifier attached to it, and they are distinguished by adding an underscore symbol (_) to one of them (i.e., *G.2* and *_G.2*). Furthermore, these two properties are inherited (using rdfs:subClassOf) from the corresponding class (*binary_unnamed*) in the taxonomy shown in Fig. 6.8. It is important to point out that association ends (*has* and *form*) are also mapped onto object properties, which are inherited from the properties representing the UML association (*G.2* and *_G.2*).

In fact, the original names of these two properties are extended by adding their UML unique identifiers, and thus their final names are *has_G.4* and *form_G.3*.

Fig. 6.9   DAML+OIL representation of the *Boundary point* UML class and its association and association end

Fig. 6.10   DAML+OIL representation of the *Boundary segment* UML class and its association and association end

Falkovych and her associates have implemented this mapping from UML models to DAML+OIL practically using XSLT. They found that XSLT was a quite cumbersome solution for more complex mappings, as well as very sensitive to the format of the input file.

Besides the very positive results of this approach, we have found that some limitations of this solution are the following:

- The lack of mechanisms for formal property specification in UML (e.g., for defining property inheritance or an *inverseOf* relation between properties). Hence one cannot express properties and other ontology primitives in UML, as was possible with the UML extension proposed by Baclawski and colleagues (Baclawski et al. 2002a). One might expect this limitation, as the primary goal of the solution was to map UML onto ontologies, and not in the opposite direction.
- The use of UML class diagrams, which contain only graphical artifacts of the real UML elements included in a model (e.g., all associations titled with the same name are assumed to represent the same property, although each association is a distinct model element in UML). Of course, this diagram problem can be partly overcome with XMI for UML 2.0, which supports diagram representation.

6.1.5 The AIFB OWL DL Metamodel

The next proposal that we analyze in this chapter is the one put forward by Saartje Brockmans and her colleagues (Brockmans et al. 2004). These researchers were inspired by the OMG ODM RFP and the initial submissions to that RFP, given in ODM DSTC (2003), ODM Gentleware (2003), ODM IBM (2003), and ODM Sandpiper&KSL (2003). Their basic idea was to enrich ODM with several separate metamodels, one for each knowledge representation (e.g., OWL DL), in order to achieve better readability and usability. Additionally, Brockmans et al. proposed the use of the OMG's OVT transformation language to perform mappings between different knowledge representations (OMG QVT 2008). They argued for such an approach rather than for having one core metamodel for knowledge representation languages that would be a common denominator of different knowledge representations and serve for mapping purposes. In fact, they are aware of the fact that their solution results in a higher number of mappings, but argue that each individual mapping is a lot more lightweight and easier to specify and maintain.

On the basis of the above ideas, Brockmans and colleagues developed a metamodel based on OWL DL using MOF2. This metamodel has a one-to-one mapping to the abstract syntax of OWL DL and thereby to the formal semantics of OWL DL. They also defined a UML profile on top of the metamodel. It is interesting to note that this UML profile contains graphical icons for ontology-specific primitives (e.g., restriction, union, and someValuesOf), similarly to the UML profile for developing Web applications described in Chap. 4 (Conallen 2002). One can use this UML profile to develop ontologies in most of the present UML tools (e.g., MagicDraw). However, to the best of our knowledge, the currently available tools do not provide support for transforming either the metamodel or the UML profile into any ontology language (e.g., OWL). Therefore, ontology developers are prevented from automatically employing ontologies developed using UML tools in Semantic Web ontology-based applications. More importantly, this initiative evolved into a bigger endeavor—the NeOn project.

6.1.6 NeOn Metamodels for the Semantic Web

NeOn[1] is an integrated project funded by the European Commission in the scope of Framework Program 6. The project investigates the lifecycle support for networked ontologies. Stemming from the work done by AIFB and collaborating with the OMG's group for ODM, the NeOn project developed a set of ontologies for networked ontologies. In particular, the project developed the metamodels for the following languages (Haase et al. 2007):

- OWL—metamodel based on the adopted ODM specification (OMG ODM 2007) with the support for the OWL 1.1 language (Motik et al. 2007). At the time of writing this book (December 2007), the project tries to integrate the support for the ongoing results in the development of the OWL 2 language (Bao et al. 2008).
- Rules—two metamodels that describe two important Semantic Web rule languages: SWRL and F-Logic. The SWRL metamodel originates from the previous work of AIFB on Rule Definition Metamodel described in (Brockmans et al. 2006).
- Mapping—metamodel that allows for mappings (e.g., equivalence, containment, and overlap) between concepts ontologies. This metamodel is defined by extending the OWL and SWRL metamodels.
- Modular ontologies—metamodel that provides support for developing modular ontologies in a very similar manner as software engineering supports modularization (e.g., partial import and encapsulation).

For each of the abovementioned metamodels, the NeOn project also developed corresponding UML profiles. The UML profiles are designed in the spirit of the previous work of AIFB (Brockmans et al. 2004, 2006).

---

[1] http://www.neon-project.org/

The OWL UML profile slightly diverges from the one proposed in the OMG's ODM specification though (OMG ODM 2007).

The important contribution of this work is the obvious impact on the future development of the OWL language in general by using MOF-based metamodeling in both OWL 1.1 and OWL 2 endeavors (Motik et al. 2007; Bao et al. 2008). It also indicates a high opportunity for the common future and coherent development of standards for the OWL language by both the OMG and W3C.

To the best of our knowledge, there has not been specific tool implementation that supports the use of the NeON metamodels and UML profiles. Bearing in mind the active involvement of this group in the OMG's ODM standardization effort, there is a significant contribution to the development of the QVT transformations (e.g., between OWL and UML) included in the ODM specification (OMG ODM 2007). However, it appears that the problem of bridging between different modeling and technical spaces still remains an issue to be solved. In Chap. 10, we discuss the importance of the consideration of different technical and modeling spaces while developing tooling support for ontology development in the MDE context.

6.1.7 The GOOD OLD AI ODM Proposal

Finally, the authors of this book have also proposed a solution to the OMG ODM RFP. This proposal provides a comprehensive response to the ODM RFP that defines a metamodel based on OWL Full (Djurić et al. 2005a), a corresponding ontology UML profile (see Chap. 9) (Djurić et al. 2005b), and the required transformations (see Chap. 10) (Gašević et al. 2005). On top of these definitions, an ontology editor called AIR (Djurić et al. 2007) has been developed (see Chap. 12). More details about this proposal, the tools developed, and their practical usage for developing ontologies are given later in this book.

6.2 Ontology Development Tools Based on Software Engineering Techniques

In describing the most relevant approaches to applying software engineering techniques to ontology development in the previous section, we aimed to reflect the most important issues differentiating the two modeling spaces used. In this section we outline some well-known tools that enable the development of ontologies using software engineering languages. In fact, this section discusses only UML-based tools, because of the wide acceptance of UML and its CASE tools by the software engineering community.

6.2.1 Protégé

Protégé is the leading ontological engineering tool (Noy et al. 2001). It has a complex software architecture, easily extensible through plug-ins. It is freely available (Protégé 2008). Many components providing interfaces to other knowledge-based tools (Jess, Argenon, OIL, PAL Constraint, etc.) have been implemented and integrated into Protégé. In the same manner, support is provided for various ontology languages and formats such as XML, DAML+OIL (back ends), and OIL (tab).

Formally speaking, Protégé has a MOF-compatible metamodel (see Fig. 6.11). The main reason for having a shared metamodel is that generic tools operating on any MOF-compliant model can be built (Protégé XMI 2008). The metamodel is designed as a MOF-compliant metamodel of Protégé ontologies that resides in the same metalevel as UML. While Protégé has basically been developed on top of an adapted version of the OKBC metamodel (see Sect. 1.7 for details of OKBC), until now there have been no attempts to map OKBC to the MOF. Since the MOF is the dominant standard in the object-oriented-software-technology community (and even more widely), one of the benefits of having a MOF-compliant representation of Protégé ontologies is improved interoperability with other MDA-based systems. Thus, the Protégé metamodel is a MOF-based definition of OKBC.

This metamodel is extensible and adaptable. This means that Protégé can be adapted to support a new ontology language by adding new meta-classes and metaslots to the Protégé ontology. The introduction of these new metamodeling concepts enables users to add the necessary ontology primitives (e.g., the Protégé class has different features from the OWL class). In this way it can, for instance, support RDFS (Noy et al. 2000) and OWL (Knublauch et al. 2004).

As a support for sharing MOF-compatible models, Protégé has two backends: UML (Protégé UML 2008) and XMI (Protégé XMI 2008). These two backends use the NetBeans MetaData Repository (MDR) (available from http://mdr.netbeans.org). NetBeans is an implementation of the Java Metadata Interface (JMI) specification (Dirckze 2002). JMI basically takes a MOF metamodel and generates Java interfaces that can be used to access model instances at run time. These interfaces provide an alternative mechanism to access and build Protégé metamodels. Using those interfaces, it would be possible to plug Protégé into other tools, such as

Java IDE NetBeans. Note also that the NetBeans MDR has features for exporting/importing XMI models, metamodels, and meta-metamodels.

The Protégé XMI backend uses an XMI schema (see Sect. 4.9) compliant with the Protégé MOF-defined metamodel shown in Fig. 6.11. In fact, this backend relies on features of the NetBeans MDR for importing and exporting XMI. One can find an example of a Protégé ontology represented in the Protégé XMI format in Protégé XMI (2008).

The Protégé UML backend exchanges UML v1.4 models (i.e., classes, and their relations), that is to say, models encoded in versions 1.1 and 1.2 of UML XMI. The backend uses the following rules to perform mapping between UML models and its own MOF-compatible metamodel (Protégé UML 2008):

- Each UML class is represented by one Protégé class of the same name, and with the same role (i.e., abstract or not abstract).
- The generated Protégé classes are arranged in an inheritance hierarchy as represented in the UML model (UML allows multiple inheritance). Since Protégé does not support concepts such as "interface," all UML interfaces are handled as classes.
- Each attribute of a UML class is represented by a slot of a suitable type. The new slot will have the name of the attribute, unless this name has already been taken by a different slot (from another UML class) with a different type. In this case, the slot will be renamed according to the format <attributeName>@<className>, which ensures unique slot names.
- The new Protégé slots obtain their multiplicity (which allows multiple values or not) and their minimum and maximum cardinalities from the UML model.
- During export of UML primitive slots (e.g., int, string, and symbol) are converted to simple attributes that are attached to all UML classes where the slot is used. Nonprimitive (instance) slots are translated into UML associations, whereby inverse slots are used to create bidirectional associations.
- Metaclasses are recognized by means of the <<metaclass>> stereotype for classes.

The developers of the Protégé UML backend also list a few limitations, namely:

- Instances (i.e., UML objects and ontology class instances—individuals) cannot be shared.

- UML associations of higher order (e.g., ternary relationships) have not been tested sufficiently.
- Inherited Protégé slots/UML attributes (defined for parent classes) are not recognized.
- Protégé does not provide real metamodel support for UML. Specifically, the Protégé metamodel (see Fig. 6.11) must be extended with specific concepts of UML, as has been done for various ontology languages (e.g., OWL and RDF) and knowledge representation languages (e.g., Jess and Algernon). For example, the *StandardClass* of the Protégé metamodel has been extended with the *UMLClass* in order to emphasize the differences between those two concepts. In fact, this is the same principle that Baclawski and colleagues (Baclawski et al. 2002a) applied when extending the UML metamodel to support the DAML+OIL language. Of course, here we have an opposite case, where the Protégé metamodel, which can be regarded as an ontology language, is extended with concepts from the UML metamodel. Actually, a Protégé profile is created (somewhat like a UML profile).

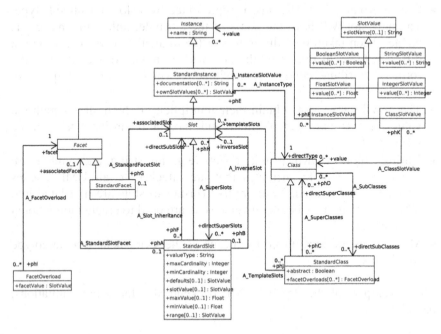

Fig. 6.11 Protégé MOF-compatible metamodel, based mainly on OKBC (Protégé XMI 2008)

It is obvious from the above discussion that one can transform UML models into many different ontology languages thanks to the abundance of Protégé plug-ins and backends. For instance, one can import a UML model represented in the UML XMI format into Protégé. Afterwards, one can either store that model in OWL or RDF(S) using the OWL plug-in, or transform it into a knowledge base format native to Jess (Java Expert System Shell; see http://herzberg.ca.sandia.gov/jess/), a rule-based engine, using JessTab (http://www.ida.liu.se/~her/JessTab/). The model can then be used in applications based on Semantic Web reasoners such as Jena (McBride 2002) or OWLJessKB (Kopena and Regli 2003). In fact, this model-sharing scenario reflects the future capacities of ontology-driven software development in the context of the Semantic Web (Knublauch 2004).

Regarding support for the present well-known UML tools, Protégé can share models directly with Poseidon for UML and MagicDraw, as they support versions 1.1 and 1.2 of UML. However, the IBM Rational Rose XMI add-in supports only XMI for UML v1.3, and thus direct model-sharing with Protégé is not possible. As a way around this problem, the developers of the Protégé UML backend recommend users to first import IBM Rational Rose UML XMI models into Poseidon for UML, and then export them into XMI models. XMI models created in such a way can be imported by the Protégé UML backend. In this chapter, we do not give detailed guidelines for sharing models between Protégé and UML tools, but detailed guidelines for Poseidon for UML and MagicDraw are provided in Chap. 12 in the form of a step-by-step procedure.

6.2.2 DUET (DAML UML Enhanced Tool)

A software tool called DUET (DUET 2008) enables the importing of DAML ontologies into IBM Rational Rose and ArgoUML and the exporting of UML models into the DAML ontology language. The tool is actually implemented as an add-in for IBM Rational Rose (see Fig. 6.12) and as a plug-in for ArgoUML. It is freely available.

This tool uses a quite simple UML profile that contains stereotypes for modeling ontologies (based on a UML package) and properties (based on a UML class). The mappings from the UML profile onto DAML shown in Table 6.2 are taken from DUET (2008). We advise readers to look also at the mappings from the DAML language to the DUET UML profile in DUET (2008). Note also that DUET uses an XSLT that transforms RDFS ontologies into equivalent DAML ontologies. In this way, an RDFS ontology can be imported into UML tools through the DAML language.

Fig. 6.12   A screen shot of the DUET IBM Rational Rose add-in

DUET is the first UML tool extension that enables sharing of ontologies between an ontology language (i.e., DAML) and a UML tool in both directions. However, since this tool uses a UML profile-based approach, it is not aware of the semantics of UML concepts, as would be the case if it had been based on a metamodel. Instead, DUET just provides a graphical notation. Furthermore, this is a specialized DAML language tool, which can lead to the loss of some semantic information when one is dealing with other languages such as OWL, an official W3C specification. To the best of our knowledge, this tool has not been updated in the last five years (at the time of writing, December 2008).

6.2.3 An Ontology Tool for IBM Rational Rose UML Models

Xp et al. is a freely available tool implemented in Java that transforms IBM Rational Rose models from the *mdl* format to RDF and RDFS ontologies (deVos and Rowbotham 2001; deVos et al. 2001). The tool has developed as a Java API that can be used from other applications or launched from a command prompt (see XP et al. 2002 for details). The target RDFS ontology is constructed according to the UML-to-RDF mappings in the OMG DAF specification (OMG DAF 2005). Figure 6.13 shows a simple UML model of Petri nets that we developed as a starting point for creating a Petri net ontology. After transforming the model from the *mdl* format into the RDFS format, we imported it into Protégé.

Table 6.2 Mappings from the DUET UML profile to the DAML language (DUET 2008)

UML	DAML	Discussion
<<DAMLontology>> Package	Ontology	Packages stereotyped <<DAMLontology>> become DAML ontologies. Package name becomes Ontology URI.
Class	Class	UML classes without stereotypes become DAML classes. UML class ownership of attributes and associations is not strongly represented in the DAML classes. No operation represented.
<<DAMLproperty>> Class	Property	A UML class stereotyped <<DAMLproperty>> becomes a DAML property or one of its subclasses; this subclass is determined by additional contextual information.
<<DAMLdatatype>> Class	Datatype	UML classes stereotyped <<DAMLdatatype>> become DAML datatypes.
Data type	XML Schema or DAML datatype	UML data types are generally mapped into XML Schema or user-defined DAML datatypes.
Associations and roles	Object property and restriction	UML associations and roles map to object properties and restrictions.
Attributes	Datatype property	Attributes map to datatype properties and restrictions. Attributes can only have datatypes as their range.
Generalization	subClassOf or subPropertyOf	The mapping of a UML generalization depends on the stereotype of the UML classes involved.
Import	Import	Package imports map directly to ontology imports.
Fully qualified names	Namespaces	Associations, roles, and classes from different packages are referenced using their fully qualified names; the package component of these names is mapped into XML namespaces and imported ontologies.

Comparing this tool with other related approaches discussed in this book, we have found that it has limitations similar to those that we mentioned when discussing Cranefield's software (XSLTs). Specifically, the tool uses only standard UML and does not provide a convenient solution for representing properties, their relations, advanced class restrictions, etc. In fact, the implementation of the tool is even more limited than that of Cranefield's software, since it is oriented exclusively toward IBM Rational Rose, whereas Cranefield's XSLT is applicable to any UML XMI document and is independent of UML tools.

Fig. 6.13 Using XP et al. to transform a UML model developed in IBM Rational Rose into an RDF Schema document that is then imported into Protégé

6.2.4 Visual Ontology Modeler (VOM)

The Visual Ontology Modeler (VOM) is the result of a collaborative work between Sandpiper Software Inc. and the Knowledge System Laboratory at Stanford University. To the best of our knowledge, this tool is not freely available. The tool extends IBM Rational Rose and enables ontology development with user-friendly wizards that automate the creation of a logical model and related diagrams (see Fig. 6.14).

The tool is based upon a UML profile for ontology development that is closely related to Protégé's metamodel for ontologies and to Gruber's Frame ontology (Gruber 1993). Apart from the use of well-known UML-based graphical notations for ontology development, VOM supports widely accepted Semantic Web ontology languages such as DAML+OIL and OWL.

Although this approach uses UML, we cannot say that it is a real MDA-based approach. Rather, it can be described as an MDA-compatible approach, since it is based not on an ontology metamodel, but on a UML profile. Compatibility with the MDA is achieved through support for this

UML profile and XMI. The transformations between UML models and the supported ontology languages are built into the programming logic of the IBM Rational Rose add-in, so that only IBM Rational Rose can perform them.

Fig. 6.14   The graphical user interface of the Visual Ontology Modeler (VOM), developed as an IBM Rational Rose add-in

6.3 Summary of Relations Between UML and Ontologies

In the course of various different approaches and tools for ontology development using software engineering techniques, we have tried to emphasize the state-of-the-art solutions to this problem. The goal of this section is to provide a concise summary of all the tools and approaches described in detail in the previous two sections. We also aim to indicate the most important differences between the two modeling approaches (ontologies and MDA) from the point of view of the most relevant languages (UML, OWL, and DAML+OIL).

6.3.1 Summary of Approaches and Tools for Software Engineering-Based Ontology Development

Table 6.3 summarizes the approaches analyzed in Sect. 6.1 and the tools presented in Sect 6.2. Specifically, this table reviews the MDA-based formal definitions (i.e., metamodels) of the approaches and tools discussed, the kinds of model interchange format that they use (e.g., UML XMI), the proposals for implementing the mappings (e.g., XSLT), and the target ontology languages (e.g., OWL). Table 6.3 also indicates how each specific approach and tool implements the transformation between MDA-based languages and ontology languages. This information is relevant because it reveals whether a certain solution (i.e., software component) can be reused across different applications independently of the tool it was originally implemented for. For example, XSLT-based solutions and XP et al. have potential for reuse. Finally, the table gives URLs for each approach or tool (if any exist) where one can find accompanying online resources.

6.3.2 Summary of Differences Between UML and Ontology Languages

Here we aim to summarize the most relevant incompatibilities between MDA-based approaches and ontology languages. As we have already mentioned, Baclawski and colleagues gave the most comprehensive list of incompatibilities (Baclawski et al. 2002a) when they proposed an extension of UML for the DAML language, and our summary mainly relies on that study. In Table 6.4, we present an outline of the incompatibilities between ontology languages and UML given in Baclawski et al. (2002a).

One additional aspect is also very important when comparing UML and ontology languages. Most of the authors cited here refer to UML as a graphical (diagramming) notation (Cranefield 2001b; Falkovych et al. 2003). This can be explained by the fact that UML was initially developed to serve as a graphical language for software modeling. However, the notion of UML models has evolved. UML models as defined in Seidewitz (2003) and Selic (2003) correspond semantically to the notion of ontologies defined in Hendler (2001). Therefore, one must have in mind this new concept of UML models when considering how to bridge gaps between ontologies and MDA modeling spaces. Of course, the UML graphical notation is still useful as a standardized and well-known syntax and can also be beneficial for the graphical representation of ontologies.

Table 6.3 An overview of the present UML- and MDA-based ontology development approaches and tools, and of the techniques that they apply to support transformation to Semantic Web languages

Approach	Metamodel	MDA sharing format	Transformation mechanism	Target language
Cranefield (Cranefield 2001a)	Standard UML	UML XMI	XSLT	RDFS, Java classes
Baclawski et al. (Baclawski et al. 2002a, b)	Standard UML, UML profile, and MOF-based metamodel	(not given— UML XMI and MOF XMI can be used)	–	DAML
Falkovych et al. (Falkovych et al. 2003)	Standard UML	UML XMI	XSLT	DAML+OIL
AIFB OWL DL (Brockmans et al. 2004)	MOF-based metamodel and UML profile	(not given— UML XMI and MOF XMI can be used)	–	OWL DL
GOOD OLD AI ODM (Djurić et al. 2005a, 2005b)	MOF-based metamodel and UML profile	ODM XMI UML XMI	XSLT	OWL
		http://www.sfu.ca/~dgasevic/projects/UMLtoOWL/		
Protégé	Protégé metamodel	Protégé XMI	Programmed (built-in component)	OWL, RDF(S), DAML+OIL, XML, UML XMI, Protégé XMI, ...
	Standard UML	UML XMI		
		http://protege.stanford.edu		
Visual Ontology Modeler (VOM) (Ceccaroni and Kendall 2003; Kendall et al. 2002)	UML profile	IBM Rational Rose	Programmed (built-in component)	OWL, DAML+OIL, RDFS
		http://www.sandsoft.com/products.html		
DUET	UML profile	IBM Rational Rose, ArgoUML	Programmed (built-in component)	DAML+OIL
		http://codip.grci.com/wwwlibrary/wwwlibrary/DUET_Docs/		
Xp et al.	Standard UML	IBM Rational Rose mdl files	Programmed (reusable component)	RDFS
		http://www.langdale.com.au/styler/xpetal/		

Table 6.4 Summary of incompatibles between UML and ontology languages, based mainly on Baclawski et al. (2002a)

Difference	Description
Monotonic and non-monotonic	Ontology languages are monotonic, whereas UML and object-oriented languages are nonmonotonic. A system is monotonic if adding new facts can never cause previous facts to be falsified.
Metalevels	Ontology languages do not have a rigid separation between metalevels. For example, in OWL Full, an instance of a class can be another class.
Specialization/ generalization	The UML generalization/specialization relation stimulates behavioral reuse, while the idea behind this relation in ontology languages is set-theoretical.
Modularity	Ontology languages do not have profiles, packages, or any other modularity mechanism supported by UML and object-oriented languages.
Containers and lists	UML packages are not at the same metalevel as RDF containers (Bag, Seq, and Alt), and the presentation features of packages also make them unsuitable for representing RDF containers.
Property	A property is a first-class (independent) modeling element in ontology languages, while the UML notion of an association/attribute is not a first-class concept.
Class constructors	Ontology languages have the ability to construct classes using boolean operations (union, intersection, and complement) and quantifiers. In UML, there is no corresponding primitive.
Cardinality constraints	This incompatibility originates form the first-class nature of ontology properties. In ontology languages one can specify a cardinality constraint for every domain of a property all at once, whereas in UML this must be specified separately for each association (end) belonging to the property.
Subproperties	Ontology languages allow one property to be a subproperty of another. UML has the ability to specify that one association is a specialization of another, although this construct is rarely used. However, UML does not allow inheritance of class attributes.
Namespaces	While Semantic Web ontology languages use URIs to relate their constructs, UML has various ways of connecting its constructs (e.g., each class is a namespace of its attributes, which can be specified further as having a private, protected, or public scope).

6.3.3 Future Development

Although the lessons learned from the approaches analyzed above are rather useful, none of them gives an ultimate solution to the problem of the use of the MDA for ontology development. Having realized this fact, the OMG had issued an RFP for adopting a standardized architecture called the Ontology Definition Metamodel (OMG ODM RFP 2003). This RFP specified that the new OMG standards have to contain the following elements:

- a formal description of a new MDA-based ontology language called the Ontology Definition Metamodel;
- a related UML profile called the Ontology UML Profile; and
- the necessary transformations between the Ontology Definition Metamodel and the Ontology UML Profile, as well as transformations to contemporary Semantic Web languages (i.e., OWL).

The existing experience overviewed in this chapter demonstrates that such a set of standards (promoting usage of all MDA concepts) can provide us with considerable benefits when defining a metamodeling architecture and can enable us to develop new MOF languages capable of expressing all concepts of ontology languages. Moreover, tooling support for such languages may benefit from the existing MDE development frameworks such as EMF. In the following chapters, we first describe in detail the present state of this OMG effort that resulted in the adopted specification (OMG ODM 2007). Next, we describe how MDE tooling can be leveraged to support the use of ontology languages developed by following the MDA standards.

7 The MDA-Based Ontology Infrastructure

Ontologies and the Model-Driven Architecture (MDA) are two modeling approaches that are being developed in parallel, but by different communities. They have common points and issues and can be brought closer together. Many authors have attempted to bridge the gaps and have proposed several solutions. The result of these efforts is the recent OMG's initiative for defining an ontology development platform.

7.1 Motivation

To be widely adopted by users and to succeed in real-world applications, knowledge engineering and ontology modeling must catch up with trends in mainstream software. It must provide good support in the form of software tools, and integration with existing and upcoming software tools and applications must be eased, which will add value on both sides. To be employed in common applications, knowledge management by software must be taken out of laboratories and isolated high-tech applications and put closer to ordinary developers. This issue has been addressed in more detail in Cranefield's papers (2001a, b).

With the development of the Semantic Web initiative, the importance of ontologies is increasing rapidly. Semantic Web researchers are trying to make ontology development and ontologies in general closer to software practitioners (Knublauch 2004). However, ontologies have more rigorous foundations closely related to well-known paradigms in AI (e.g., description logic, semantic networks, and frames). Thus, most of the current Semantic Web ontologies have been developed in AI laboratories. Accordingly, we need to answer some questions such as: How can we increase the number of ontology developers? How can we motivate software engineering practitioners to develop and use ontologies? Can we use software development tools to develop ontologies? Therefore, we need some ways to integrate software development and ontologies.

The integration of the ongoing software engineering efforts with the concept of the Semantic Web is not a new idea. Many researchers have

D. Gašević et al., *Model Driven Engineering and Ontology Development*, 2nd edn.,
DOI 10.1007/978-3-642-00282-3_7, © Springer-Verlag Berlin Heidelberg 2009

suggested using UML in order to solve this problem. However, UML is based upon an object-oriented paradigm, and has some limitations regarding ontology development. Hence, we can only use UML in the initial phases of ontology development. These limitations can be overcome using UML extensions (i.e., UML profiles; Duddy 2002), and other OMG standards, like the Model Driven Architecture. In addition, if we want to offer a solution consistent with the MDA proposals, we should also support the automatic generation of completely operational ontology definitions (e.g., in the OWL language) that are model driven (Selic 2003). Currently, the most important direction toward this goal is the one pursued by a dedicated research group within the OMG that is trying to achieve convergence of many different proposals for solutions to this problem (OMG ODM RFP 2003). The result of this effort is a standard language (i.e., a metamodel), the Ontology Definition Metamodel (ODM; OMG ODM 2007) based on the MDA standards (Miller and Mukerji 2003) and the W3C Web Ontology Language (OWL) recommendation (Bechhofer et al. 2004). OWL 1.1 (Patel-Schneider & Horrocks 2007) is almost here and OWL 2 is under development (Bao 2008). As the OWL development progresses it is expected that the ODM will follow with the appropriate adaptations.

7.2 Overview

MDA and its four-layer architecture provide a solid basis for defining metamodels of any modeling language, so it is a straightforward choice to define an ontology-modeling language in the MOF. Such a language can utilize the MDA's support in modeling tools, model management, and interoperability with other MOF-defined metamodels. The present software tools do not implement many of the concepts that are the basis of the MDA well enough. Most of these tools, which are usually oriented toward the UML and M1 layer, were expected to be enhanced in a few years after the release of UML 2 to support the MDA, but the advance is slower than promised. Large parts of these tools' functionality are still proprietary, but they can still offer an advanced tool support for many modeling purposes.

The effort to bridge the gap from OWL to MDA started with an RFP (Request for Proposal) within the OMG aimed at defining a suitable language for modeling Semantic Web ontology languages in the context of the MDA (OMG ODM RFP 2003). The idea of defining such an infrastructure in terms of Modeling Spaces is shown in Fig. 7.1. Two modeling spaces, RDF(S) and MOF, offer different benefits and tradeoffs in the scope of appropriate technological spaces. To use the best of both worlds, we need to find a way to bridge the gap and connect these spaces, and the first step is to define appropriate metamodels in the space that we are going to transfer to.

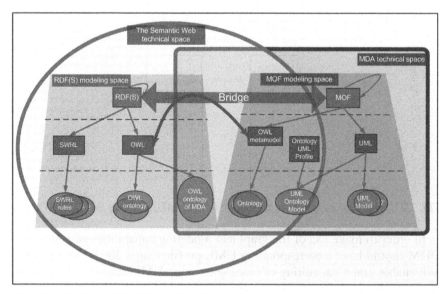

Fig. 7.1 Bridging RDF(S) and MOF modeling spaces

The authors of this book made a proposal for such architecture in accordance with this RFP. In this approach to ontology modeling within the scope of the MDA, shown in Fig. 7.2, several specifications needed to be defined:

- the Ontology Definition Metamodel (ODM);
- the Ontology UML Profile—a UML Profile that supports UML notation for ontology definition; and
- the two-way mappings between: OWL and the ODM, the ODM and other metamodels, the ODM and the Ontology UML Profile, and from the Ontology UML Profile to other UML profiles.

The Ontology Definition Metamodel (ODM) should be designed to include the common concepts of ontologies. A good starting point for the construction of the ODM is OWL, since that is the result of the evolution of existing ontology representation languages, and is a W3C recommendation. It is in the logical layer of the Semantic Web (Berners-Lee et al. 1999), on top of RDF Schema (in the schema layer).

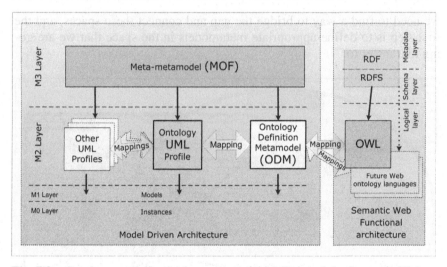

Fig. 7.2   Ontology modeling in the context of the MDA and the Semantic Web

In order to make use of the graphical modeling capabilities of UML, the ODM should have a corresponding UML profile (Sigel 2001). This profile will enable graphical editing of ontologies using UML diagrams, as well as provide other benefits of using mature UML CASE tools.

Both UML models and ODM models are serialized in XMI format, so the two-way transformation between them can be done using XSL transformation. OWL also has a representation in the XML format, so another pair of XSL Transformations should be provided for two-way mapping between the ODM and OWL. For mapping from the ODM into other meta-models or from the Ontology UML Profile into other, technology-specific UML Profiles, additional transformations can be added to support usage of ontologies in the design of other domains and vice versa.

Several official proposals followed the RFP (ODM DSTC 2003; ODM Gentleware 2003; ODM IBM 2003; ODM Sandpiper&KSL 2003); as well as unofficial proposals (Djurić et al. 2005a; Djurić 2004). The official proposals, proposed by IBM, Gentleware, etc., were joined together into a common submission (OMG ODM 2004). A revised joint submission followed in 2005 (OMG ODM RFP 2005). The discussion about the ODM in this book is based mainly on the most recent version of the OMG's ODM specification (OMG ODM 2007). The discussion about the UML profile in this book is based mostly on Djurić (2004) and Djurić et al. (2005c).

7.3 Bridging RDF(S) and MOF

Before we start on a more detailed description of the ODM, we must clarify the differences between metamodeling in the Semantic Web world, which is based on RDFS constructs, and in the object-oriented MDA, which is based on the MOF. Obviously, if we want to perform a transformation from the RDFS MS to MOF MS, we need to make transformation rules, which have to determine which target concept (defined in MOF) we should obtain from a source concept (defined in RDFS). The main task is to identify the most important differences and similarities between the main constructs in both spaces and decide how to overcome those differences. These concepts are briefly compared in Table 7.1, which groups the most similar concepts from both spaces.

Both good and bad news can be derived from this comparison. The good news is that there is a significant similarity: they are both a sort of entity-relationship–based world. In RDFS, rdfs:Class is a sort of entity, while rdf:Property is a sort of relation. In the MOF, Classifier represents an entity that is related to other entities via associations or attributes. Basically, a concept (at level M2 in the RDFS MS) that is modeled as an rdfs:Class (at level M3 in the RDFS space) becomes a concept (at level M2 in MOF space) that is an MOF Class (at level M3 in MOF space); a concept modeled as an rdfs:Property becomes an MOF Association or an MOF Attribute; and so on. For example, owl:Class (M2) is defined as an rdfs:Class (M3) in RDFS. In the MOF, it will be an OWLClass; an MOF Class. rdf:Property is also an rdfs:Class, so in the MOF MS it becomes an MOF Class RDFProperty. An example of an rdf:Property is rdfs:subclassOf; it should be transformed to an MOF Association RDFSsubClassOf.

The bad news is that corresponding concepts (rdfs:Class and Classifier and rdf:Property and Association or Attribute) have different natures. The concept of Class in RDFS (rdfs:Class) is not completely identical to the concept of Class that is defined in UML and the MOF. Every rdfs:Class is a set of resources, called a class extension. These resources are instances of that class. Two classes can have the same class extension but still be different classes. Classes in RDFS are set-theoretic, while traditional object-oriented classes are more behavioral. Unlike an object-oriented class, an rdfs:Class does not directly define attributes or relations to other resources, and there is no concept similar to that of methods. Attributes and relations are defined as properties.

Table 7.1   A brief description of the basic MOF and RDF(S) metamodeling concepts

MOF element	Short description	RDF(S) element	Short description
Element	Element classifies the elementary, atomic constructs of models. It is the root element within the MOF Model.	rdfs:Resource	Represents all things described by RDF. The root construct of the majority of RDF constructs.
DataType	Models primitive data, external types, etc.	rdfs:Datatype	Mechanism for grouping primitive data.
Class	Defines a classification over a set of object instances by defining the state and behavior they exhibit.	rdfs:Class	Provides an abstraction mechanism for grouping similar resources. In RDF(S), rdfs:Class also has a function that is similar to the MOF concept of Classifier.
Classifier	An abstract concept that defines classification. It is specialized by Class, DataType, etc.		
Association	Expresses relationships in the metamodel between pairs of instances of Classes.	rdf:Property	Defines a relation between subject resources and object resources.
Attribute	Defines a notional slot or value holder, typically in each instance of its Class.		
TypedElement	A TypedElement is an element that requires a type as part of its definition. A TypedElement does not itself define a type, but is associated with a Classifier. Examples are object instances, data values, etc.		In RDF(S), any rdfs:Resource can be typed (via the rdf:type property) by some rdfs:Class

In RDF, a property is a concept that represents a relation between a subject resource and an object resource. Therefore, it might look similar to the concept of attribute or association in the traditional, object-oriented sense. However, the important difference is that rdf:Property is a stand-alone concept; it does not depend on any class or resource, because the associations or attributes are in the MOF. In ontology languages, a property can be defined even with no classes associated with it. That is why a property cannot be represented as an ordinary association or attribute, its closest object-oriented relatives.

7.4 Design Rationale for the Ontology UML Profile

In order to customize UML for modeling ontologies, a UML profile for ontology representation, called the Ontology UML Profile, must be defined.

In developing our Ontology UML Profile we used the experience of other UML profile designers (e.g., see Juerjens 2003). Applying this experience to our case, we wanted our Ontology UML Profile to:

- offer stereotypes and tags for all recurring ontology design elements, such as classes, individuals, properties, complements, unions, and the like;
- make specific ontology-modeling and design elements easy to represent in UML diagrams produced by standard CASE tools, thus keeping track of ontological information in UML models;
- enable ontological knowledge to be encapsulated in an easy-to-read format and offer it to software engineers;
- make it possible to evaluate UML diagrams of ontologies and indicate possible inconsistencies; and
- support the Ontology Definition Metamodel, in order to be able to represent all ODM concepts.

Currently, several different approaches to ontology representation in UML have been proposed. We note two major trends among them:

- Extending UML with new constructs to support specific concepts of ontologies (Property, for example; Baclawski et al. 2002a). This approach is outdated.

- Using standard UML and defining a UML profile for ontology representation (Baclawski et al. 2002a). This approach is followed in all recently proposed solutions.

We believe that ontology representation in UML can be achieved without nonstandard UML extensions, and hence our approach belongs to the latter of the above two trends. In the Ontology UML Profile presented in this book, specific concepts of ontologies are annotated using the standard UML extension mechanisms described above. Models created with such a UML profile are supported by standard UML tools, since they do not add nonstandard concepts to UML, and thus they are UML models. This is also the approach that has prevailed in recent years, so it is safe to continue the discussion based on this approach.

The definition of a UML profile in the context of the MDA four-layer metamodeling architecture means extending UML at the metamodel layer (M2). One can understand these extensions as a new language, but also understand UML as a family of languages (Duddy 2002). Each of these languages uses UML notation with the four UML extension mechanisms. Recent UML specifications enable the use of graphical notation for specifying stereotypes and tagged definitions (Kobryn 2001). Thus, all stereotypes and tagged values that are defined in this book can be shown in this way.

The notation used for creation of a stereotype in an Ontology UML Profile («OWLClass» stereotype) accommodates UML's Class («metaclass»). Having this graphical notation for the UML extension mechanism can be useful for explaining certain relations between UML constructs and new stereotypes, and also between stereotypes themselves.

Since stereotypes are the principal UML extension mechanism, one might be tempted to think that defining an Ontology UML Profile is a matter of specifying a few stereotypes and using them carefully in a coherent manner. In reality, however, it is much more complicated than that. The reason is that there are a number of fine details to take care of, as well as the existence of some conceptual inconsistencies between the MDA and UML that may call for alternative design decisions.

8 The Ontology Definition Metamodel (ODM)

There were four separate proposals for the ODM in response to the OMG's ODM RFP (2003) submitted by the following OMG members: IBM (ODM IBM 2003), Gentleware (ODM Gentleware 2003), DSTC (ODM DSTC 2003), and Sandpiper Software Inc and KSL (ODM Sandpiper&KSL 2003). However, none of those submissions made a comprehensive proposal. For example, none of them proposed XMI bindings for the ODM, none of them proposed mappings between the ODM and OWL, and only IBM (ODM IBM 2003) and Gentleware (ODM Gentleware 2003) proposed an Ontology UML profile. Accordingly, the OMG partners decided to join their efforts, and the current result of their efforts together, is the ODM joint submission (OMG ODM 2004). A revised joint submission followed in August 2005 (OMG ODM RFP 2005). In this chapter we introduce the main concepts of the most current document in the time of writing, which is an OMG Adopted Specification (OMG ODM 2007). This is a beta version, so we do not expect any changes to be relevant to the level of discussion in this book.

8.1 ODM Metamodels

To create a joint ODM, the submitters decided to organize it as a composition of several metamodels. We show the architecture of the current Adopted Specification of the ODM in Fig. 8.1.

In order to support well-known Semantic Web ontology languages, the ODM has two separate metamodels, namely OWL and RDF. These languages are W3C standards which form a basis for the Semantic Web, thus they are the central part of the ODM. Other metamodels have two-way mappings to and from the RDFS/OWL metamodels. That means that they are also used as a mediator between other metamodels.

Since the ODM needs an expressive logic language that can be used on the Semantic Web to describe string-based expressions, the ODM contains the Common Language (CL) metamodel. Apart from W3C ontology languages, the ODM supports other ontology language standards (ISO standards)

D. Gašević et al., *Model Driven Engineering and Ontology Development*, 2nd edn.,
DOI 10.1007/978-3-642-00282-3_8, © Springer-Verlag Berlin Heidelberg 2009

by defining a Topic Maps (TM) metamodel. The central metamodel in the joint submission (the one from 2004) was a Description Logics (DL) metamodel, since most of the current ontology languages (e.g., OWL) are based upon some of the DL classes. The role of this metamodel was to mediate all metamodels defined in the ODM. However, the next submission (2005) moved this metamodel somewhat to the side, leaving it as a non-normative metamodel, while the central role in the ODM is now played by RDFS and OWL metamodels. Finally, to provide connection with many existing systems based on databases, the earlier revisions of ODM defined an Entity Relationship (ER) metamodel, but the current adopted specification leaves it out of the scope.

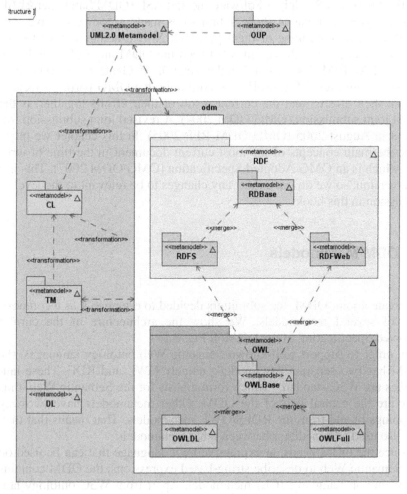

Fig. 8.1 The ODM Metamodels

Taking into account the importance of UML, the ODM developers want to create mappings between the standard UML metamodel and the RDFS and OWL metamodels, and hence establish a way to employ present UML models in ontology development. Furthermore, these developers define an Ontology UML Profile (OUP) using standard UML extension mechanisms. The purpose of the OUP is to enable the use of the standard UML graphical notation for developing ontologies.

8.2 A Few Objections to the ODM Specification

Before we start a more detailed explanation of the OMG's Ontology Definition Metamodel, we shall briefly discuss a few issues that might be interesting in relation to the new version of the MOF standard (OMG MOF2 2006) and usability. Some of the issues have been resolved in the current ODM specification, but it may be a good idea to be aware of them to better understand the specification and to be able to avoid confusion if any of these issues make it to the final version.

The current ODM specification was tailored with respect to the ECore metamodel, the heart of the Eclipse Modeling Framework (EMF). While ECore is similar to the MOF (particularly EMOF), there are differences. ECore is much simpler and is targeted toward implementation in CASE tools. Therefore, there might be some minor inconsistencies in the ODM with MOF 2. As the ODM is still a work in progress, some of the issues that are still here, if not all of them, are probably going to be resolved in the final version. In this section, we shall mention them briefly. Note that we have made some minor changes to the version of the ODM presented in this book regarding these issues, but those changes do not have any impact on the essence of the discussion. Many of these minor flaws that we are going to mention probably arise from the fact that there are many tools that operate with MOF standards, and the proposals have been constructed using CASE tools (EMF, for example), which all have their nonstandard way of handling some things.

There were many associations having the same name in the metamodel proposal that resided in the same package. An example of such a situation was that two different associations in the DL metamodel both have the same name—contains. However, the MOF specification clearly states that the name of any element within the same namespace must be unique. A solution could be found by renaming one of these associations, or by refactoring by extracting the class. The first solution seems less intrusive for this discussion, but the second is more elegant from the point of view of software engineering. The DL metamodel is left as a non-normative in the latest version, so that particular instance is not an issue. It also seems that the current version has been created with this suggestion in mind, so it shouldn't be a problem anymore; but the solution seems to be a little verbose and not particularly elegant: associations have names like "Domain-ForProperty," "NamespaceDefinitionForDocument," etc.

Many associations were left unnamed in the ODM joint submission. The MOF specification states that every Type must be named, and Association inherits Type, so this condition must be fulfilled. Also note that the UML2 Infrastructure specification allows unnamed Types but EMOF adds a constraint that every Type must be named. In this discussion, we have added names to associations, but this problem can be also solved with CASE tools, which can generate random names. However, random names are not convenient if a human has to work with them. Would it be pleasant to have to work with associations named "mnrt90490789" or "FF0AD3458B0BB"? This has also been resolved in the current adopted specification, the price being too verbose and inelegant association names. Associations model relationships between classes. If classes are subjects and objects, associations should represent verbs. Thus, their names should be verbs. A good rule would be that the ODM should name associations after the names of the properties that are their counterparts in RDF(S), even if they are not verbs. In our opinion, if an association does not have a direct RDFS counterpart, a verb should be used for its name. In the specification, most of the names of properties were used for naming association ends, not associations.

Another objection to the ODM adopted specification compared to some of the previous submissions is that the creators drove away from the notion that they are modeling in the MOF MS. They tried to simulate some features (e.g., anonymous resources and multiple inheritance) from the RDF(S) MS in places where they are not elegantly achievable, or not needed at all, as in cases of the metamodeling power of RDF(S). In trying to achieve that, they traded some simple and natural modeling artifacts for more complex alternatives. For example, many if not all attributes from the previous submissions are now promoted to classes. Such a process may or may not make some new features possible, but it makes the specification more complex and potentially less usable.

In the following descriptions of RDFS and OWL metamodels, we usually refer to an association end's name instead of an association name where the association end's name is a direct counterpart of an RDFS and OWL concept. For example, instead of the ClassGeneralization association, we often refer to an RDFStype, one of its ends.

The earlier technical objections that we mentioned have been more or less resolved since the previous edition of this book. What is left to be done is to polish them and make them elegant and as close as possible to the RDF and OWL specifications. In our opinion, the revised joint submission (OMG ODM 2005), despite some technical fallacies, was a bit more elegant and in accordance with the RDF(S) and OWL. Since the new version of the OWL specification is on the horizon (Bao et al. 2008), it would be wise to explore the possibility of synchronization in creating the ODM 2 and OWL 2.

8.3 The Resource Description Framework Schema (RDFS) Metamodel

Resource is one of the basic RDFS concepts; it represents all things described by RDF and OWL. It may represent anything on the Web: a Web site, a Web page, a part of a Web page, or some other object named by a URI. Compared with the concept of ontologies, it could be viewed as a root concept, the Thing. In the RDFS MS, rdfs:Resource is defined as an instance of rdfs:Class. Since we use the MOF as a meta-metamodeling language, this concept will be defined as an instance of MOF Class named RDFSResource. This is the root class of most of the other concepts from RDFS and OWL metamodels that will be described: RDFSClass, RDFSProperty, RDFStatement, etc. The hierarchy of concepts in the RDFS metamodel is shown as a class diagram in Fig. 8.2. Other class diagrams depict these concepts in more detail. Note that, since the RDFS is self-defined and rdfs:Class inherits rdfs:Resource, in the RDFS MS, rdfs:Resource is an instance of itself. However, in the MOF MS, RDFSResource is an instance of an MOF Class, not RDFS Resource, because the MOF is a meta-metamodel, not RDFS.

Among the concepts shown, the most important ones are:
- RDFSResource,
- RDFSClass,
- RDFProperty, and
- RDFStatement.

These are the basis for forming subject-predicate-object triples, such as "This section–describes–RDFS metamodel."

Figure 8.3 shows the basic characteristics of the RDFSResource and RDFSClass concepts.

Fig. 8.2   RDFS metamodel—hierarchy of concepts

RDFS defines a concept that is used for grouping similar resources—
rdfs:Class. In an MOF-based metamodel, it can be represented using the
MOF Class named RDFSClass, which, following the specification, inherits
RDFSResource. This is determined by RDFtype (rdf:type property from
RDFS MS). An RDFSResource can have many types, and multiple
RDFSResource instances can have the same type. RDFSsubClassOf models inheritance in the M1 layer, and ontological inheritance, among various
instances of RDFSClass. An RDFSClass instance can inherit many other
RDFSClass instances and can be inherited by many other RDFSClass instances, forming complex inheritance hierarchies. Do not confuse
RDFSsubClassOf with generalization between RDFSClass and RDFSResource. It is the same property in RDFS MS because RDFS is both metamodel and meta-metamodel, but in MOF MS, we use generalization associations to model inheritance in the M2 layer, not RDFSsubClassOf.

The next important concept in the RDFS metamodel that needs to be
explained is the RDFStatement, shown in Fig. 8.4. A statement is a subject-predicate-object triple that expresses some fact in a way similar to the
way facts are expressed in the English language. The fact that Bob Marley
was Jamaican, is expressed through a statement, whose subject is "Bob
Marley," whose predicate is "was," and whose object is "Jamaican." Following the definition of rdf:Statement definition from the RDFS MS, in
the MOF MS, a statement is modeled as an MOF Class RDFStatement.
The subject, predicate, and object of an RDFStatement are determined using the associations SubjectForStatement, ObjectForStatement and Predi-
cateForStatement (that have RDFsubject, RDFobject, and RDFpredicate
association ends), which are the counterparts in the MOF MS of the properties rdf:subject, rdf:object, and rdf:predicate.

Fig. 8.3   RDFSClass

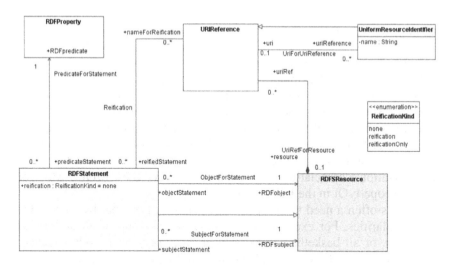

Fig. 8.4   RDFS statement

From the definition of RDFStatement, we can see that two associations, subject and object, link RDFStatement to RDFSResource, while predicate association links it to RDFProperty. This design protects the model from statements that do not have sense, for example "Bob Marley"-"Cuba"-"Jamaican." The predicate should be a resource that represents a verb, such as "be" or "memorize," or some characteristic of a resource, like "name." In the RDFS MS, such a resource is an rdf:Property, a concept that represents a type of relationship between resources.

In the M2 layer, RDFS defines two properties, rdfs:domain and rdfs:range, that connect an rdf:Property with an rdfs:Class, making it possible to distinguish various types of relations between various types of resources in the M1 layer. In the MOF MS, the RDFS metamodel represents a property using MOF Class named RDFProperty, a descendant of RDFSResource, as shown in Fig. 8.5.

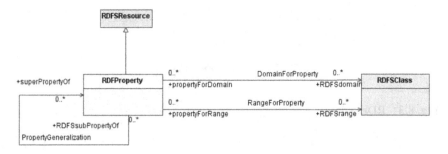

Fig. 8.5   RDFSProperty

DomainForProperty and RangeForProperty associations (and their ends, RDFSdomain and RDFSrange) represent corresponding rdfs:domain and rdfs:range relations in the RDFS MS. RDFSdomain determines which types of resources can be at the "source" end of a relation and RDFSrange determines the type of the "destination" end. Another difference between properties and their object-oriented counterparts is that properties can form complex hierarchies, just as classes do. This is modeled by the Property-Generalization association, a counterpart in the MOF MS of rdfs:subPropertyOf in the RDFS MS.

There is often a need to group resources not by type, but by some arbitrary similarities. For example, we could make a group of all authors of this paper, or all basketball teams that are members of the NBA league. For such cases, RDFS uses rdfs:Container. In the MOF MS, we model this as an MOF Class RDFSContainer, which inherits RDFSResource (Fig. 8.6). RDFSContainer also has a few descendants defined: RDFBag (a group of unordered resources), RDFAlt (for resources that are alternative to each other), and RDFSeq (a group of resources in which order is important). MemberOfResource association (RDFSmemberOf association end) models the containment of one RDFSResource in another RDFSResource.

Fig. 8.6 RDFS containers

RDF containers are open in the sense that the core RDF specifications define no mechanism to state that there are no more members. The RDF Collection vocabulary of classes and properties can describe a closed collection, i.e., one that can have no more members. A collection is represented as a list of items, a representation that will be familiar to those with experience of Lisp and similar programming languages. RDFList modeled in the MOF MS is shown in Fig. 8.7. An RDFfirst relation connects an RDFSList with its first element, which can be any RDFSResource. RDFSrest connects an RDFSList with a sublist containing other elements, recursively forming the order of all elements.

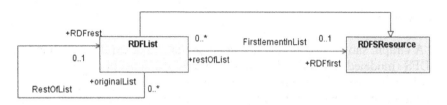

Fig. 8.7 RDFS collections

In Figs. 8.8 and 8.4 we can see a few details of RDFSResource.
RDFSResource has an association URIRefForResource to URIReference,
which is primarily intended to identify an instance of RDFSResource (and
all concepts that inherit it; Fig. 8.4).

The RDFS specification also defines that an rdfs:Resource can have
comments and labels attached. As these characteristics are described in
RDFS MS using rdf:Property instances, namely rdf:comment and rdf:label,
in MOF MS we model them using the MOF Association concept. On the
other end of these associations is PlainLiteral, a concept that is used to represent simple data, such as numbers, text, etc. Therefore, using these two
associations, we can add various textual, numeric, or other comments and
labels to our data. One special kind of RDFSLiteral is RDFXMLLiteral,
which represents XML textual data.

RDFSseeAlso points to another resource that could be useful to look at.
RDFSisDefinedBy points to another RDFSResource that defines the first
one.

Fig. 8.8   RDFS Resource

A Graph, shown in Fig. 8.9, is a concept that is not explicitly defined in
RDFS (modeled in RDFS MS). It is similar to the concept of a Package in
UML. It is used for grouping statements that belong to similar domains.
Containment is denoted by the StatementForGraph association, which
links one Graph to one or more RDFStatement.

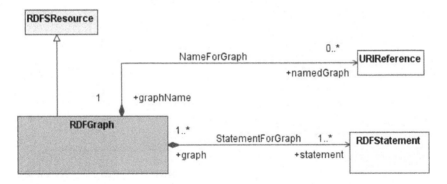

Fig. 8.9   The graph concept

Giving graphical diagrams here as an example of the use of an RDFS metamodel would not be easy, because RDF(S) does not have a standard graphic representation. A plain UML diagram given here would not represent concepts from an RDFS metamodel, but concepts from a UML metamodel, which are not the same thing. Fortunately, in the next section we shall define a UML profile for modeling RDFS concepts using a standard UML extension mechanism. In that section, we shall provide a few examples of RDFS and OWL ontologies.

8.4 The Web Ontology Language (OWL) Metamodel

The Web Ontology Language is built on top of RDF(S), using RDF(S) as both a meta-metamodel (M3) and a metamodel that is a base for extension (M2). In the MOF MS, the first dependency (the use of RDFS as a meta-metamodel) is replaced by using the MOF as a meta-metamodel. The second dependency means that the concepts of the OWL metamodel extend the concepts of the RDFS metamodel. Figure 8.10 shows the hierarchy of OWL concepts—we can see that most OWL concepts inherit the RDFS concepts RDFSResource, RDFProperty, and RDFClass. RDFSClass is a base concept of the OWL concepts that represent classes (OWLClass, OWLRestriction, and OWLDeprecatedClass); RDFProperty is inherited by many concepts that represent properties in OWL (OWLObjectProperty, OWLDatatypeProperty, and so on).

There are some concepts in the OWL metamodel that are not explicitly defined in the OWL language (RDFS MS), and their names are not prefixed with "OWL" in this metamodel.

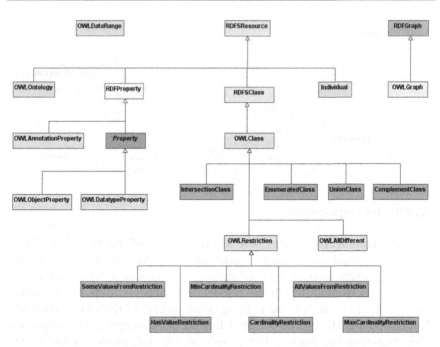

Fig. 8.10 The OWL hierarchy

Classes provide an abstraction mechanism for grouping resources with similar characteristics. Like RDF classes, every OWL class is associated with a set of individuals, called the class extension. As OWL in many cases refines the concept of a class, it needs to model it separately, for example to inherit RDFSClass together with a new concept, OWLClass. Fig. 8.11 shows how OWLClass is modeled.

Besides defining a class by name and connecting individuals using RDFtype, classes can be defined in OWL in several other ways. Enumeration is defined by exhaustively enumerating its instances so OWLoneOf is provided for building classes by enumeration. As a class can be constructed in OWL as a complement of another class or as a union or intersection of other classes, OWLcomplementOf, OWLunionOf, and OWLintersectionOf association ends of corresponding associations are provided. These associations and the multiplicities of their association ends are also shown in Fig. 8.11.

The OWL metamodel also defines two associations, which are counterparts of properties of the OWL language: OWLequivalentClass and OWLdisjointWith. OWLequivalentClass asserts that two classes have the same class extension, and OWLdisjointWith asserts that two class extensions do not have any common individual.

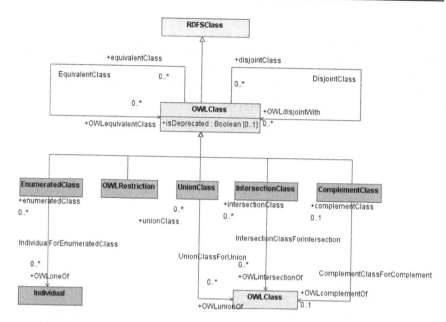

Fig. 8.11   OWLClass

OWLClass inherits RDFSClass. Because OWL Full fully supports RDFS, we can also use the RDFSClass concept if we model using OWL Full. However, it is more convenient to use the OWLClass concept, because it is valid in OWL Lite and OWL DL also.

OWLClass is a set of individuals, which are modeled in OWL with the owl:Thing concept. Thanks to the fact that OWLClass extends RDFSClass, it also extends the associations of RDFSClass from the RDFS metamodel. One of these associations is TypeForResource (RDFtype end), which enables various RDFSResources to state that some OWLClass is their type. Other associations in which RDFSClass takes part, among which Class-Generalization (RDFSsubTypeOf end) is one of the most important, are also inherited.

OWLRestriction is a special kind of OWLClass, and thus it inherits the OWLClass concept. It is not a "real" class, but a concept that enables constraints in OWL. Before we describe how restrictions are modeled, we should looook at the details of the concepts that model properties in OWL, because OWLRestiction is a concept tightly connected to properties.

OWL refines the concept of rdf:Property by distinguishing two basic kinds of properties, owl:ObjectProperty and owl:DatatypeProperty. Recall from our discussion of the RDFS metamodel that RDFProperty has a domain and range that could both be RDFSClass and that RDFSDatatype is a subclass of RDFSClass. This means that RDF does not distinguish relations between classes from relations between data types. The OWL metamodel, following the OWL language derived from the RDFS MS, introduces two distinct types of properties: OWLObjectProperty (a relationship between two OWLClasses) and OWLDatatypeProperty (a relationship between OWLClass and RDFSDatatype).

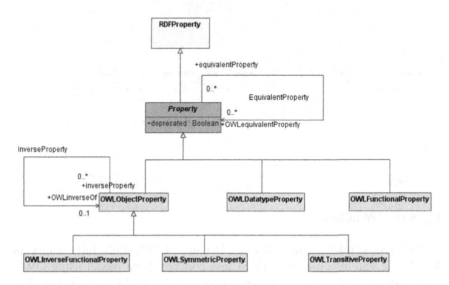

Fig. 8.12   OWL properties

The OWL metamodel in the OMG-adopted specification includes the abstract MOF Class Property (see Fig. 8.12), which is not included in the standard OWL language as a common superclass of OWLObjectProperty and OWLDatatypeProperty. This concept was introduced to solve the impedance mismatch between the RDFS and MOF concepts. In particular, the MOF Association is dependent on the classes that are at its ends, and a class has to "know" which association ends it hosts. However, adding EquivalentProperty association directly to RDFProperty, as it is defined in OWL's owl:equivalentProperty would imply a difference in the RDFS metamodel when it is used alone and when it is used as a base of the OWL metamodel.

Properties in OWL cannot have a Datatype as a domain, only as a range. That is why InverseProperty association is applicable only to OWLObjectProperty. OWL also defines several other refined kinds of properties, namely owl:FunctionalProperty for relationships that have functional characteristics, owl:TransitiveProperty for transitive relationships, owl:SymmetricProperty for symmetric relationships, and owl:InverseFunctionalProperty. These types of properties are represented in the MOF MS as subclasses of Property or OWLObjectProperty with names analogous to those in the RDFS MS.

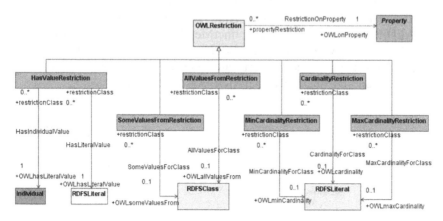

Fig. 8.13   OWLRestriction

OWLRestriction, shown in Fig. 8.13, is an anonymous class of all individuals that satisfy certain restrictions on their properties. Obviously, it is an MOF counterpart of the owl:Restriction concept from the RDFS MS. RestrictionOnProperty association connects OWLRestriction and a property on which that restriction is applied. There are two kinds of restrictions on properties: value constraints and cardinality constraints. A value constraint puts constraints on the range of the property when applied to this particular class description. Value constraints are modeled using HasIndividualValue, HasLiteralValue, SomeValuesForClass, and AllValuesForClass associations. A cardinality constraint puts constraints on the number of values a property can take, in the context of this particular class description. Cardinality constraints are modeled using MinCardinalityForClass, CardinalityForClass, and MaxCardinalityForClass associations.

We have mentioned that OWL makes a significant distinction between named individuals ("objects") and plain data values. In the OWL metamodel, individuals are modeled using the Individual concept, which is shown in Fig. 8.14. As Individual inherits RDFSResource, it also inherits all its associations with other concepts, of which one of the most important is TypeForResource, which connects RDFSResource with its type, RDFSClass. In the case of Individual, TypeForResource association has a constraint that the other end has to be an OWLClass. OWL also introduces properties that are used to state that some individuals are the same as (owl:sameAs) or different from (owl:differentFrom) others. In the OWL metamodel these properties are modeled as the associations SameIndividual and DifferentIndividual.

Connecting many instances of Individual to a number of individual owl:differentFrom (or DifferentIndividualin the MOF MS) connections would overcrowd the model. That is why OWL introduces the owl:AllDifferent class and owl:distinctMembers property to connect that class with all individuals that are different from each other. In the OWL metamodel, this class and property are modeled as the OWLAllDifferent MOF Class and DistinctIndividual MOF Association.

Fig. 8.14   Individuals

Fig. 8.15   OWLDataRange

A data range represents a range of data values. It can be either a datatype or a set of data values. Data ranges are used to specify a range of datatype properties. They are modeled as the OWLDataRange MOF Class (see Fig. 8.15), which is a descendant of RDFSDatatype, connected with RDFSLiteral via the ElementsOfDataRange association.

OWL groups similar concepts together in an ontology using the owl:Ontology concept. This concept does not extend any other concept explicitly, but as RDFS specifies that everything can be a resource, it is an owl:Ontology as well. ODM defines OWLOntology as a descendant of RDFSResource. You can see the details of OWLOntology and its associations in Fig. 8.16. It includes Imports association, which enables the use of data from other ontologies in an ontology that can import them. Other associations, BackwardCompatibleWith, IncompatibleWith, and PriorVersion are intended to support different versions of an ontology.

A VersionInfo statement generally has a string giving information about the version as its object, for example RCS/CVS keywords. A PriorVersion statement contains a reference to some other ontology. This identifies the specified ontology as a prior version of the containing ontology. A BackwardCompatibleWith statement also contains a reference to another ontology. This identifies the specified ontology as a prior version of the containing ontology, and indicates further that it is backward compatible with the containing ontology. In particular, this indicates that all identifiers from the previous version have the same intended interpretations in the new version. An IncompatibleWith statement contains a reference to another ontology. This indicates that the containing ontology is a later version of the referenced ontology, but is not backward compatible with it.

Figure 8.17 shows the OWL Utilities—concepts that are not part of the base of OWL but are intended for version control, deprecated concepts, etc. Deprecation is a feature commonly used in versioning software (for example, see the Java programming language) to indicate that a particular feature has been preserved for backward-compatibility purposes, but may be phased out in the future. Deprecating a term means that the term should not be used in new documents that commit to the ontology. This allows an ontology to maintain backward-compatibility while phasing out an old vocabulary. In the OWL language both classes and properties can be deprecated. OWL DL allows annotations on classes, properties, individuals, and ontology headers. That is why OWLAnnotationProperty is included in the OWL metamodel. An example of annotation property is the dc:creator property defined in the DC vocabulary (http://dublincore.org/), if one wants to use it to annotate who the creator of an OWL ontology concept is.

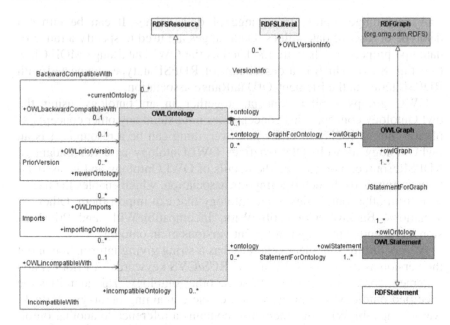

Fig. 8.16   OWLOntology

This support for annotations, ontology headers, importing, and version information in the OWL metamodel is the first comprehensive attempt to cover all those features in the OWL language. In previous similar solutions, only IBM's submission to the ODM RFP (ODM IBM 2003) had considered such features, and hence that submission was used as a basis for the present OWL metamodel.

Fig. 8.17   OWL Utilities

The OWL metamodel, together with the RDFS metamodel, forms the basis for ontology development in the Model Driven Architecture. The main advantage is that it is compatible with the Web Ontology Language, which is one of the key technologies of the Semantic Web.

9 The Ontology UML Profile

UML profile is a concept used for adapting the basic UML constructs to a specific purpose. Essentially, this means introducing new kinds of modeling elements by extending the basic ones, and adding the new elements to the modeler's repertoire of tools. Also, free-form information can be attached to the new modeling elements. The Ontology UML Profile extends UML in a standard way to enable ontology modeling in the widely used UML modeling tools.

The OMG adopted specification (OMG ODM 2007) contains a formal specification of UML profile for RDFS and OWL. The profile presented in this chapter is our proposal from 2003 (Djurić et al. 2005b), which is intended to be practical and easy to use, and still be highly compliant with the OWL and RDFS standards. We believe that we succeeded in this goal; that is, we are presenting it in this chapter in a narrative form through examples. It is a good source for learning because the standard is very similar, and after going through these examples you will be able to quickly adapt to any changes in future versions and revisions of standard OUP.

9.1 Classes and Individuals in Ontologies

The Class is one of the most fundamental concepts in the ODM and the Ontology UML Profile. As we noted in the discussion about the essential concepts of the ODM, there are some differences between the traditional UML Class or the concept of a Class in object-oriented programming languages and an ontology class as it is defined in OWL (owl:Class). Fortunately, we are not trying to adopt UML as a stand-alone ontology language, since that might require changes to the basic concepts of UML (Class and others). We only need to customize UML as a support to the ODM.

In the ODM, the concepts that represent classes, i.e., RDFSClass, OWLClass, OWLAllDifferent, and OWLRestriction are modeled using the MOF Class concept. These constructs in the Ontology UML Profile are inherited from the UML concept that is most similar to them, UML Class.

D. Gašević et al., *Model Driven Engineering and Ontology Development*, 2nd edn.,
DOI 10.1007/978-3-642-00282-3_9, © Springer-Verlag Berlin Heidelberg 2009

However, we must explicitly specify that they are not the same as UML Class, which we can do using UML stereotypes. An example of Classes modeled in the Ontology UML Profile is shown in Fig. 9.1.

RDFSClass and OWLClass, ontology classes identified by a class identifier, have the stereotype «RDFSClass» or «OWLClass», OWLAllDifferent has the stereotype «OWLAllDifferent»; and OWLRestriction has the stereotype «OWLRestriction».

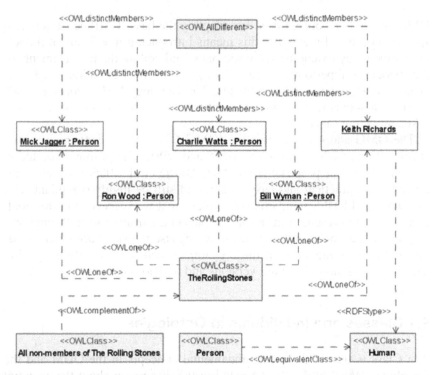

Fig. 9.1 Class diagram showing relations between ontology classes and individuals in the Ontology UML Profile

Figure 9.1 shows various types of ontology classes modeled in UML. The «OWLClass» Person is an example of an owl:Class class that is identified by a class identifier, while TheRollingStones is an enumeration. There is a class "All non-members of The Rolling Stones" that represents the complement of The Rolling Stones—all individuals whose type is not The Rolling Stones belong to this class. AllDifferent is an auxiliary class whose members are different individuals. Also shown are the «OWLClass» Human and the «equivalentClass» Dependency, which means that Person and Human are classes that have the same class description (i.e., all

Persons are Humans and vice versa). Note that in object-oriented modeling it would be highly unusual to model The Rolling Stones as a class rather than as an object of type RockNRollBand. However, ontology classes are not behavioral, but sets; and what would you call a set of all members of The Rolling Stones? Obviously—The Rolling Stones.

Fig. 9.2 Constructing union and intersection in an Ontology UML Profile

In the ODM, an instance of OWLClass is an OWLThing, an individual. An instance of RDFSClass is an RDFSResource, which means that it can be anything. In UML, an instance of a Class is an Object. OWLThing and UML Object have some differences, but they are similar enough; and so in the Ontology UML Profile, an OWLThing is modeled as a UML Object, which is shown in Figs. 9.1 and 9.2. The stereotype of an object must match the stereotype of its class («OWLClass» in this case). The «OWLThing» stereotype could be added as well. We can state that an individual has a type in three ways:

- By using an underlined name of an individual followed by ":" and its «OWLClass» name. For example, Mick Jagger:Person is an individual (OWLThing) whose type is Person. This is the usual UML method of stating an Object's type.

- By using a stereotype «RDFStype» between an individual and its «OWLClass». This method is also allowed in standard UML using the stereotype «instanceOf». For example, Keith Richards has «RDFStype» dependency link to Human, which is equivalent with Person («OWL-equivalentClass»). Thus, he is also a Human, just like other members of The Rolling Stones.
- Indirectly, through logical operators on «OWLClass». If an «OWLClass» is a union, intersection, or complement, it is a class of individuals that are not explicitly defined as instances of it. For example, in Fig. 9.2 Bob Dylan is not explicitly defined as a member of the Beatles and Wilburys union class, but he is its member since he is a member of Travelling Wilburys, which is connected with the Beatles and Wilburys through an «OWLunionOf» connection. A similar thing applies to Jeff Lynne and the Electric Light Wilbury Class. Since he is a member of the Travelling Wilburys and The Electric Light Orchestra, he is a member of Electric Light Wilbury, an «OWLintersectionOf».

Again, do not confuse an instance-of relationship between a UML Object and a UML Class or between an OWLThing and an OWLClass (all in the M1 layer) with the relationship between, for example, an instance of OWLClass (M1) and an OWLClass concept (M2). The latter is a linguistic instance-of relation, an instance-of relation between concepts from different layers (the definition of OWLClass and a concrete OWLClass, for instance: Tom Petty & the Heartbreakers). The ontological instance-of relation is an instance-of relation between concepts that are in the same linguistic layer, but in different ontological layers (for instance, «Ont-Class» Person and the object George Harrison are at different ontological layers since Human is the class [type] of George Harrison). For a more detailed discussion of ontological versus linguistic instance-of relations, see Atkinson and Kühne (2003).

9.2 Properties of Ontologies

The concept of Property is one of the most unsuitable concepts in ontologies for modeling with object-oriented languages and UML. The problem arises from a major difference between Property and the UML concepts similar to it, Association and Attribute. Since Property is an independent, stand-alone concept, it cannot be modeled directly with Association or Attribute, which cannot exist on their own. Some authors (Baclawski et al. 2002a) have suggested extending UML with new constructs to support a stand-alone Property, introducing aspect-oriented concepts into UML. In our view, this solution is rather extreme, since it demands nonstandard changes to UML.

Since Property is a stand-alone concept, it can be modeled using a stand-alone concept from UML. That concept could be the UML Class stereotype «RDFProperty», «OWLObjectProperty», or «OWLDatatypeProperty». However, Property must be able to represent relationships between Resources (Classes, Datatypes, etc., in the case of UML), which a UML Class alone is not able to do. If we look at the definition of a Property in the ODM more closely, we can see that it accomplishes representation of relations through its range and domain. We have found that in the Ontology UML Profile, the representation of relations in accordance with the ODM model should be modeled with the UML Association's or Attribute's stereotypes «domain» and «range». In order to increase the readability of diagrams, the «range» association is unidirectional (from a Property to a Class).

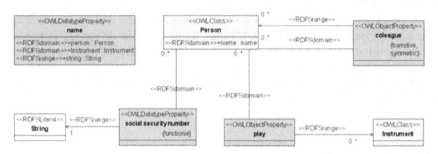

Fig. 9.3   Ontology properties shown in a UML Class diagram

OWL defines two types (subclasses) of Property—OWLObjectProperty and OWLDatatypeProperty. OWLObjectProperty, which can have only individuals in its range and domain, is represented in Ontology UML Profile as the Class stereotype «OWLObjectProperty». OWLDatatypeProperty is modeled with the Class stereotype «OWLDatatypeProperty».

An example of a Class Diagram that shows ontology properties modeled in UML is shown in Fig. 9.3. It contains four properties: two «OWLDatatypeProperty»s (name and socialSecurityNumber) and two «OWLObjectProperty»s (play and colleague) UML Classes. In cooperation with «RDFSdomain» and «RDFSrange» UML Associations, or «RDFSdomain» and «RDFSrange» UML Attributes, these properties are used to model relationships between «OWLClass» UML Classes. Tagged values describe additional characteristics; for example, the «OWLObjectProperty» colleague is symmetric (if one Person is a colleague of another

Person, the other Person is also a colleague of the first Person) and transitive (if the first Person is a colleague of the second Person, who is a colleague of the third Person, the first and the third Person are colleagues).

There is an important issue that must be clarified with respect to this diagram. In UML, relations are represented by Associations (represented graphically as lines) or Attributes, which looks nice and simple. Ontology UML Profile diagrams may look overcrowded, since each relationship requires a box and two lines to be properly represented. The solution employed here uses standard graphical symbols, but UML allows custom graphical symbols for a UML profile. For example, a custom graphical symbol for a Property could be a tiny circle with lines, which reduces the space required on a diagram. Additional custom settings, such as distinct colors for «OWLClass» (green), «OWLObjectProperty» (orange), and «OWLDatatypeProperty» (orange), can be used to increase the readability of diagrams. For the sake of readability, the UML profile that we have used allows two styles of presentation of the domain and range of an «OWLDatatypeProperty». An example of the first style (a UML Class with two UML Associations) is socialSecurityNumber; and an example of the second one (a Class with Attributes as its domain or range) is name. The second style is allowed only for an «OWLDatatypeProperty» whose range multiplicity is equal to or less than one. So, if an «OWLDatatypeProperty» has a range multiplicity of 0..1 or 1, the style using Attributes can be used to reduce the clutter.

9.3 Statements

OWLStatement is a concept that represents concrete links between ODM instances—individuals and data values. In UML, this is done through Link (an instance of an Association) or AttributeLink (an instance of an Attribute). A Statement is a kind of instance of a Property, which is represented by a UML Class stereotype («OWLObjectProperty» or «OWLDatatypeProperty»). Since an instance of a Class in UML is an Object, a Statement in the Ontology UML Profile is modeled with the Object's stereotype «OWLObjectProperty» or «OWLDatatypeProperty» (the stereotype of an Object in UML must match the stereotype for its Class' stereotype). UML Links are used to represent the subject and the object of a Statement. To indicate that a Link is the subject of a Statement, LinkEnd's stereotype «RDFsubject» is used, while the object of the Statement is indicated with LinkEnd's stereotype «RDFobject». LinkEnd's stereotypes are used because, in UML, Link cannot have a stereotype.

These Links are actually instances of Property's «RDFdomain» and «RDFrange». In brief, in the Ontology UML Profile a Statement is represented as an Object with two Links—the subject Link and the object Link, which is shown in Fig. 9.4. The Persons represented, Mick Jagger and Keith Richards, are colleagues. Keith Richard also plays an Instrument, guitar.

Fig. 9.4   Individuals and statements shown in a UML Object diagram

As with Properties of an ontology, the diagram's readability can be further increased by using distinct colors and custom graphical symbols. A tiny circle can be used instead of the standard box for representing a Statement in order to reduce clutter in a diagram.

9.4 Different Versions of the Ontology UML Profile

The ODM specification (and especially the part that deals with the Ontology UML Profile) is still under development, although it approaches the final specification. For that reason, the final version of the Ontology UML Profile will probably be different than the version we have described. However, the version described here should be very useful for getting a feeling for what it is like to create ontologies with UML. It is very easy to get accustomed to a similar profile once you have got a feel for working with one profile.

To show you what the differences could look like, we shall show you diagrams of an ontology similar to those which we have just talked about. There is another reason why we are showing these diagrams here. Some of the tools described and the discussion in this book refer to this older version of the Ontology UML Profile (Djurić et al. 2005b) which is called GOOD OLD AI Ontology UML Profile. This profile was later updated (but there is no point in updating tools until the official specification has been finished).

So, here is what classes look like (Fig. 9.5):

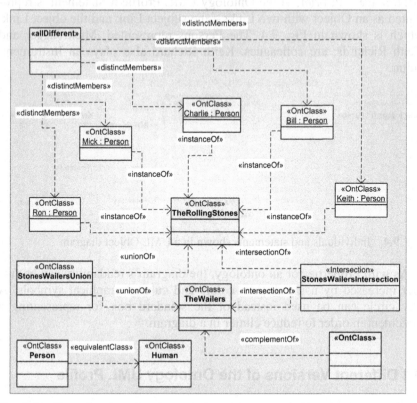

Fig. 9.5 Class diagram showing relations between ontology classes and individuals in the Ontology UML Profile

Properties (Fig. 9.6):

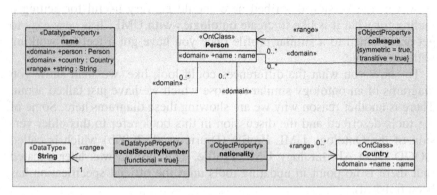

Fig. 9.6 Ontology properties shown in UML Class Diagram

Statements (Fig. 9.7):

Fig. 9.7   Individuals and statements shown in a UML Object diagram

Of course, when the specification has been completed, you should look at the specification document for the exact details. Some of these details, especially the most important ones, will probably be the same or almost the same as those we have described in this chapter. However, there might be many less important details that are a little different. Something that is important, however, is that you can start from the examples that we have shown you and very quickly catch up with the specification.

10 Mappings of MDA-Based Languages and Ontologies

The MOF-based ontology metamodels of ontology languages presented in this book, namely the ODM and the Ontology UML Profile (OUP), are defined in the context of the MDA's metamodeling architecture. However, such a definition is not sufficient; they need to interact with real-word ontologies, for example with OWL ontologies. It is obvious that we need to develop transformations to support conversions between MDA ontology languages and OWL. The current ODM specification itself provides a solution to this problem by defining the QVT transformations among the defined metamodels in the specification. In this chapter, we analyze the problem of transformations in terms of the modeling and technical spaces that we described earlier in the book (see Chap. 5). Accordingly, we first identify all modeling spaces related to this problem and depict their mutual relations. Using those relations, we recommend tools and techniques for implementing these transformations, and finally describe one such implementation.

10.1 Relations Between Modeling Spaces

Figure 10.1 shows all modeling spaces that we have recognized as important in order for the MDA standards and the present Semantic Web ontology languages (OWL and RDF(S), in the first place) to be used cooperatively. In the MOF modeling space, we have defined the ODM and the OUP. It is important to note that the ODM is defined in the M2 layer, while the OUP resides in both the M1 and M2 layers, according to Atkinson and Kühne (2002). In Fig. 10.1, we show them both in the M2 layer for the sake of clarity. Concrete real-world models are located in the M1 layer and consist of classes and their instances. According to Atkinson and Kühne (2003), we must have more than one ontological layer in the M1 layer, and in the case of UML we have two ontological layers: one for classes and one for class instances (i.e., objects). For all MDA layers, one can use XMI, an XML-compatible format for sharing metadata that we

D. Gašević et al., *Model Driven Engineering and Ontology Development*, 2nd edn.,
DOI 10.1007/978-3-642-00282-3_10, © Springer-Verlag Berlin Heidelberg 2009

have described in Chap. 4. In the bottommost layer (M0, not shown in the figure, but below M1), these are things from reality.

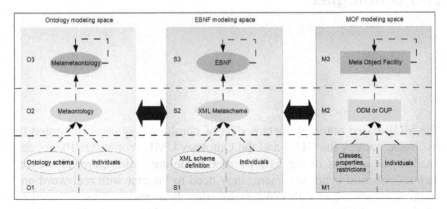

Fig. 10.1 M2-based mappings between the ontology modeling space and the MOF modeling space through the EBNF modeling space

The ontology modeling space includes the W3C recommendation for the Web Ontology Language (OWL). This ontology language is based on XML and RDF(S), and thus an XML format is being used for exchanging OWL ontologies. In this modeling space, we can identify various abstraction layers in order to find their relations to the MOF modeling space. The layer above bottommost is denoted as O1. In the O1 layer we build ontologies, i.e., we create classes, properties, relations, and restrictions. Ontological instances are located in the O1 layer in the ontology modeling space. We use an analogy between the topmost layer defined in the ontology modeling space and the results given in Decker et al. (2000). In that paper, an ontology language (Ontology Inference Layer, or OIL) was described using another ontology language (RDF[S]). In fact, Decker et al. created a metaontology. Finally, we can say that there is a metaontology that defines OWL and that this metaontology is in the O2 layer. We also refer to this modeling space, as well as the RDF(S) modeling space described in Chap. 5, relying on a similar assumption. Actually, we have generalized the treatment, in that the O3 layer is defined using RDF(S) as well. Note that such a layered organization of ontologies is already known in AI as Brachman's distinction of knowledge representation systems (Brachman 1979). However, this organization does not make a separation between ontological and linguistic relations (Atkinson and Kühne 2003), as the schema and instances of an ontology are defined in different layers, similarly to what the MDA modeling framework initially did (M1 for models and M0 for instances). Using definitions of ontological and linguistic relations as well as modeling spaces, we have recognized that we actually have the same situation in the ontology modeling space—two ontological layers in the O1 linguistic layer of the ontology modeling space. In the bottommost layer of the ontology modeling space (O0), there are things from reality.

We now make some important statements that one must take account of in order to provide transformations between these two modeling spaces:

1. The role of the MOF (M3) is epistemologically equivalent to the role of a meta-metaontology (O3).
2. The role of the O2 layer (metaontology) is equivalent to that of the metamodel layer (M2; e.g., the ODM and the OUP); that is to say, they both specify ontology languages in terms of different modeling spaces.
3. The O1 layer has a role equivalent to that of the model layer (M1) of the MOF modeling space. In fact, this conclusion comes from Atkinson and Kühne's ontological and linguistic layers (Atkinson and Kühne 2003), where one linguistic layer (in this case M1) can contain many ontological layers. Accordingly, the two ontological layers residing in the O1 linguistic layer (ontology schema and ontology instances) are equivalent to the classes and objects comprising the M1 layer in the MOF modeling space.

Formally, we can say that: $M3 \Leftrightarrow O3$, $M2 \Leftrightarrow O2$, and $M1 \Leftrightarrow O1$.

Since both the ontology and the MOF modeling spaces use XML for sharing their metadata, we can include a new modeling space in this discussion. Of course, this is the Extended Backus-Naur Form (EBNF) modeling space that defines XML. This modeling space also has a layered organization very similar to the organization of both the ontology and the MOF modeling spaces, but this organization is defined in terms of syntax, not semantics (Klein 2001). We can look at the EBNF modeling space in terms of the W3C XML Schema recommendation. The topmost level (S3) of the EBNF modeling space is a universal, well-known, and self-defined syntax, also called EBNF. When we analyze the context of the XML technical space formally defined in the EBNF modeling space, we find that the S2 layer comprises a schema for schemas (i.e., a metaschema). This metaschema defines the validity of XML Schema definition documents. Domain-specific XML vocabularies (i.e., schemas) and concrete XML documents are defined in the S1 layer. Accordingly, we can draw conclusions about equivalences between these two modeling spaces: $S3 \Leftrightarrow O3$, $S2 \Leftrightarrow O2$, and S1 ⇔ O1. Finally, note that there exist similar relations between the MOF and EBNF modeling spaces: S3 ⇔ M3, S2 ⇔ M2, and S1 ⇔ M1.

Avoiding elaborations of the most recent research issue of an M3-neutral infrastructure for bridging modeling spaces (Bézivin et al. 2005), we have used the above epistemological relations between these three modeling spaces to describe the transformations requested in the OMG ODM RFP. In fact, these transformations should be applicable to the model layer (M1, O1, and S1), but they are actually driven by their metamodels (i.e., metaontologies or metaschemas) (Bézivin et al. 2005).

10.2 Transformations Between Modeling Spaces

It is obvious from the descriptions above that we cannot provide direct mappings between the ontology modeling space and the MOF modeling space. In fact, this transformation can only be defined through the EBNF modeling space. It is important to define a *pair* of transformations in order to enable two-way mapping (one transformation for each direction) between all OWL ontologies and all ontologies represented in an MDA-based ontology language. The transformations can be based on "metadefinitions" of OWL (i.e., on its metaontology) and an MDA-compliant language (i.e., a metamodel). This transformation principle is compliant with Bézivin's principle of metamodel-based model transformation (Bézivin 2001). Practically, in terms of the EBNF modeling space, these transformations are based on the XML schemas of both OWL and XMI (i.e., the XML schema of the UML and ODM XMI formats). Figure 10.2 shows the OUP/OWL transformation of an OUP model (i.e., an OUP document in XMI format) to its equivalent OWL ontology (i.e., an OWL document in XML format). This transformation maps the M1 layer into its corresponding OWL layer (O1). The most suitable implementation for this transformation is in XSLT, since in this case an XML document is converted into another XML document. The opposite transformation (from OWL to the OUP) can also be implemented in XSLT. However, we do not recommend this kind of implementation, since we may use different XML representations (e.g., XML schemas) with different XML tag names to represent the semantics of an OWL ontology and its instances (for details, see Decker et al. 2000). For example, the concept *book* can be represented by several different tags (*book, bookInfo,* etc.), but the ontology specifies that all these tags represent the same ontology concept. In this case we suggest using a programming language to implement the transformation. For example, this transformation can be implemented in Java, but Java needs to be empowered with an OWL parser (e.g., Jena; McBride 2002). Note also that a concrete XSLT is a valid XML document. Accordingly, we can say that the XSLT language itself is defined using an XML schema that resides in the metaschema layer (S2), as the XML Schema language itself.

Fig. 10.2 An example of a transformation in the XML technical space: the transformation of the OUP into OWL

Figure 10.3 shows an example of some transformations within the MOF modeling space. This figure is organized according to the transformation schema proposed in Kurtev and van den Berg (2003) for transforming XML schemas to application models. In the MOF modeling space, we can only transform those ontology languages that have an MOF-compliant metamodel. Therefore, we illustrate the transformation between the OUP and the ODM. In terms of the MOF modeling space, the transformations between these languages should be implemented in one of the QVT languages (e.g., ATL [OMG QVT 2008]), and the chosen QVT language should have its own metamodel. Although the OUP metamodel can reside in both the M1 and M2 layer, we have placed it in the M2 layer (see Fig. 10.3) in order to avoid problems that can arise when transforming between different metamodeling layers. As a matter of fact, this can happen if we use a standard UML profile for ontology development without the user's extensions (see Atkinson and Kühne 2002 for details). Note that this transformation can also be implemented through the EBNF modeling space in terms of XML schemas and XML documents.

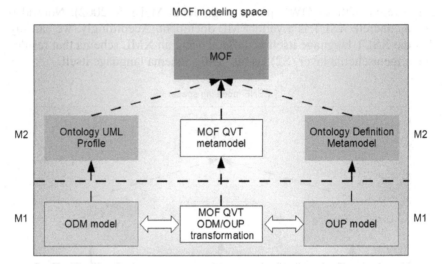

Fig. 10.3   Transformations in the MOF modeling space: transformations between OUP and ODM

Summarizing all these facts about transformations between the ontology and MOF modeling spaces, Fig. 10.4 gives some guidelines on how to perform transformations between every pair of the languages discussed above. In this figure, we indicate only the transformations between the languages considered that can be done by employing one transformation technique. At first sight, one might think that transformation between MDA-based languages (i.e., the ODM and the OUP) and OWL can be done within the MOF modeling space by simply using the QVT language. However, that is not possible, since OWL is not part of the MOF modeling space, and it is not a MOF-based language. This means that a MOF-based transformation technology (e.g., QVT) cannot be applied to that pair of transformations. QVT can only be applied to MOF-based languages. So we have to look for an intersection between those two languages. Since bridges exist between OWL and XML and between the MOF and XML, but not between OWL and the MOF, the transformation can only be defined in the EBNF modeling space, as shown in Fig. 10.4. In the rest of this section (Sect. 10.3), we explain in detail an experience from the development of a bridge between the OUP and OWL by using XSLT.

The above consideration has one consequence on the current version of the ODM. The ODM specification defines QVT-based mappings between the OWL/RDFS metamodels and the metamodels of languages such as the UML, Common Logics, Topic Maps, and Entity-Relationship model. However, all these transformations are defined in the M2 level (metamodels), and thus everything happens in the MOF modeling space. This means that, for example, there is a gap between the OWL concrete syntax (RDF/XML and OWL/XML [Bechhofer 2003; Hori et al. 2003]) and the OWL meta-model (i.e., an abstract syntax of OWL). While one may argue that this is a trivial task, the experience of the programming language area clearly shows that this is rather a challenging and nontrivial task (Klint et al. 2005). In the programming languages context, this assumes mapping between the concrete syntax of programming languages (typically defined in the EBNF) and abstract syntax (typically represented in the form of an abstract syntax tree). This mapping is usually implemented by the use of various parsing techniques. Similarly, we need to have effective techniques for mapping between the ODM metamodel(s) and the corresponding concrete syntax of the languages for which metamodels are defined in the ODM specification. There are a few options as to how one can approach this problem. In the rest of this section, we will discuss two of them.

Target language

		ODM		OUP			OWL	
Source language	ODM	–		EBNF	MOF	EBNF	MOF	
				XSLT	QVT	XSLT	TCS, Xtext	
	OUP	EBNF	MOF	–			EBNF	MOF
		XSLT	QVT				XSLT	TCS, Xtext
	OWL	EBNF	MOF	EBNF	MOF	–		
		Programmed[*], XSLT	TCS, xText	Programmed[*], XSLT	TCS, xText			

[*] preferred case (e.g. Java empowered with a library for parsing OWL)

Fig. 10.4 Overview of possible transformations between OWL, the ODM, and the OUP: modeling spaces in which the transformations can be done (EBNF and MOF modeling spaces) and implementation technologies for these transformations (XSLT, Query/View/Transformation (QVT), and programming languages)

First, if one regards the OMG's ongoing model-to-text initiative (OMG MOF-to-Text 2004) as a part of the MDA technical space, then transformations between the ODM and OWL's concrete syntax are possible in terms of the MDA technical space. The model-to-text initiative at the OMG is in its initial stages of development (i.e., there is just a request for proposals to the OMG [OMG MOF-to-Text 2004]). There have already been several well-known proposals to this request. Developed as a part of the ATL model transformation framework, Concrete Textual Syntax (TCS) is a bidirectional transformation language for defining bridges between the MOF/Ecore-based metamodels and EBNF grammars (Jouault et al. 2006). Xtext (2008) has a similar purpose, which was initially developed in the scope of the openArchitectureWare platform (OAW 2008). Xtext is currently a part of the Textual Modeling Framework (TMF) that is being developed in the scope of the Eclipse modeling project. In Chap. 11, we discuss how the ATL model transformation framework can be used to address this problem of mapping between different technical spaces relevant to the scope of the ODM specification.

Second, it is possible to address the problem of mapping between the concrete syntax of OWL and ODM by developing a parser. Such a parser would leverage an OWL API (e.g., Jena) in order to manage OWL ontologies (e.g., import into concrete syntax and export from the OWL graphs) in combination with a modeling framework such as the EMF. In Chap. 12, we analyze how IBM applied this approach in their EMF-based implementation of ODM (Pan et al. 2006).

With the evolution of the OMG's model-to-text initiative and frameworks such as the TMF, we can anticipate that the ODM specification will also need to standardize the mappings between its metamodels and the concrete syntax of the included languages. For tool developers, this is very important, as there is no need for every developer to create a new solution to the mappings of the standardized metamodels and their standardized concrete syntax. Thus, standardization of their mappings is a natural step.

10.3 Example of an Implementation: An XSLT-Based Approach

In the previous section, we explained the conceptual solutions for transforming between MOF-based ontology languages (i.e., the ODM and OUP) and OWL. In this section, we show an example of an implementation that transforms an OUP-based ontology to its equivalent OWL ontology (Gašević et al. 2004a, 2004b; Klein and Visser 2004). The transformation provides us with Semantic Web ontologies that can be used in real-world Semantic Web applications. It was developed to support the GOOD OLD AI Ontology UML Profile (OUP; Djurić et al. 2005b), since the official OMG UML Ontology UML Profile has not yet been adopted.

10.3.1 Implementation Details

The main idea of having a UML profile for ontology development is to use existing UML tools. In fact, current UML tools (e.g., IBM Rational Rose and Poseidon for UML) support mainly the XMI standard (OMG XMI 2002)—an MDA XML-based standard for meta-metamodel, metamodel, and model sharing. Since XMI is XML-based, one can employ XSLT to transform XMI documents into the target documents. These target documents can be written in an ontology language, for example OWL, which also has its own XML syntax. On the other hand, when we use an approach based on the XSLT principle, we do not need to modify a UML tool; instead, we just apply an XSLT to the output of the UML tool. Accordingly, we can use the well-defined XML/XSLT procedure shown in Fig. 10.5.

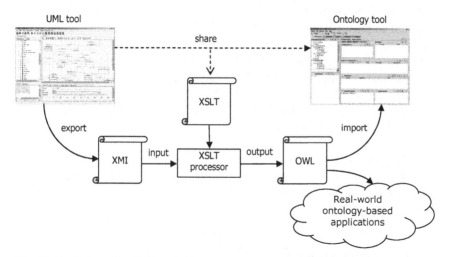

Fig. 10.5 Using the XSLT principle: extensions of present UML tools for ontology development

A UML tool can export an XMI document that an XSLT processor (e.g., Xalan; http://xml.apache.org) can use as input. An OWL document is produced as the output, and this format can be imported into a tool specialized for ontology development (e.g., Protégé 2005), where it can be further refined. On the other hand, since we obtain an OWL document, we do not need to use any ontology tool; the document obtained can be used as the final OWL ontology.

The XSLT that we have implemented for mapping OUP models to OWL ontologies contains a set of rules (i.e., XSLT templates) that match the UML XMI constructs of the OUP models and transform them into equivalent OWL primitives. In developing these rules, we faced some serious obstacles resulting from evident differences between the source and target formats. We note some of these obstacles below:

- The structure of a UML XMI document is fairly awkward, since it contains a full description of the UML model that it represents, for example classes, attributes, relations (associations, dependencies, and generalization), and stereotype descriptions.
- In some cases, the OUP uses more than one UML construct to model one OWL element. For example, to model the *someValuesFrom* restriction using OUP (see Fig. 10.7), we need three UML classes and three relations (i.e., one association and two dependencies). This is especially difficult, since each UML construct has a different stereotype.
- UML tools can only draw UML models, and they do not have an ability to check the completeness of an OUP ontology. Thus, the XSLT is required to perform this kind of checking of XMI documents. This is the only way to avoid the generation of erroneous OWL ontologies.
- The XSLT must make a distinction between classes that are defined in other classes (and cannot be referenced using their ID), and classes that can be referenced using their ID. Accordingly, we have included the *odm.anonymous* tagged value in the OUP, which helps us differentiate between these two cases.

Taking all this into account, it becomes obvious that the XSLT that we have developed is too large to be included in this book. However, this transformation is available on the book's Web page, together with supplementary materials.

10.3.2 Transformation Example

In order to illustrate the application of the above XSLT, we have built the well-known Wine ontology using the GOOD OLD AI Ontology UML Profile (Djurić et al. 2005b). We show a part of this ontology in Fig. 10.6. WineDescriptor is a class equivalent to the union of the classes WineTaste and WineColor, whereas the WineColor class is an enumeration of the instances of the WineColor class (i.e., individuals), White, Rose, and Red. Note that there are two anonymous classes (Union and Enumeration) in Fig. 10.6. These classes are defined through other classes (e.g., the anonymous Enumeration is defined in the class WineColor) and cannot be used outside of their definitions. Note also that we use the tag value *odm.anonymous* with a value *true* to denote anonymous classes. This helps us differentiate between anonymous and nonanonymous classes in the automatic transformation of OUP models.

An example of a class diagram that depicts ontology properties modeled in UML is shown in Fig. 10.7. In this example the `Wine` class has the «`ObjectProperty`» `locatedIn`, i.e., the `Wine` class is the domain of the property `locatedIn`. The range of the «`ObjectProperty`» `locatedIn` is the `Region` class. Since ontology languages (i.e., OWL and the ODM) may specify various features of object properties, we have introduced tagged values describing those characteristics: *symmetric, transitive, functional,* and *inverseFunctional.*

Figure 10.7 also depicts a restriction of a class on a property—the «`ObjectProperty`» of `Wine` `locatedIn` has a *someValuesFrom* restriction on the «`OntClass`» `Region`. That means that each instance of the `Wine` class must have at least one instance of the property `locatedIn` whose range is the `Region` class. An additional restriction is the multiplicity (i.e., how many property instances can be attached to a class), defined as the multiplicity of the association between the `Wine` class and the `locatedIn` property.

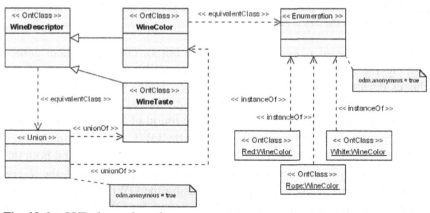

Fig. 10.6   OUP class-oriented stereotypes (an excerpt from the Wine ontology)

In the OUP, a `Statement` is represented as an `Object` with two `Links`, the subject `Link` and the object `Link`, shown in Fig. 10.8. Here we have a statement that says the `Region`'s instance `MendocinoRegion` is `locatedIn` the `SonomaRegion`, and its `adjacentRegion` is the `CaliforniaRegion`.

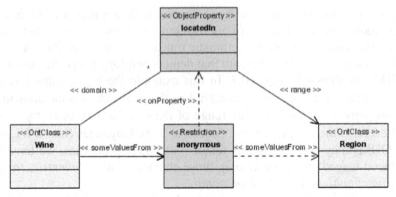

Fig. 10.7   An OUP class property and its restriction in the Wine ontology

Fig. 10.8   The OUP fully supports ontology instances through OUP statements: an example from the Wine ontology

Figure 10.9 depicts an excerpt from the output OWL document generated by the XSLT. Figure 10.9a shows the OWL representation of the classes defined in Fig. 10.6. Note how OUP classes with the tagged value *odm.anonymous* are mapped into OWL (e.g., `WineDescriptor` has an equivalent anonymous class, defined as the union of the `WineTaste` and `WineColor` classes). Figure 10.9b shows the OWL definition of the `locatedIn` property, which has the `Region` class as its range, and both the `Region` and the `Wine` classes as its domain. On the other hand, the `Wine` class additionally restricts this property, using the OWL *someValuesFrom* restriction. Since the OUP provides full support for OWL statements, we are able to transform these statements into equivalent OWL constructs (i.e., full individual descriptions). Figure 10.9c shows the OWL representation of the statements shown in Fig. 10.8.

This example clearly illustrates the power of our solution to generate both an ontology schema (classes, properties, etc.; Devedžić 2002) and ontology instances (bodies of knowledge; Chandrasekaran et al. 1999). This feature is not supported in other MDA-based proposals for ontology development.

In the next subsection, we outline our first practical experience with this solution.

10.3.3 Practical Experience

We have already noted that the transformation that we have developed enables us to create complete OWL ontologies using standard UML tools—specific ontology development tools are not a necessity for ontology development anymore. Specifically, to use the OUP and our XSLT in practice, we need to employ a suitable UML tool that supports the following:

- Attaching stereotypes to all of the UML concepts that we have in the OUP. For instance, the present UML tools rarely allow objects and link ends to have a stereotype (e.g., the objects in Fig. 10.6).
- A convenient way to use tagged values and attach them to any UML element (e.g., the *odm.anonymous* tagged value in Fig. 10.6).
- Creating relations between different UML primitives, such as those shown in Fig. 10.6. We emphasize especially the importance of relations (e.g., UML dependencies) between a UML class and a UML object. This kind of relation is valid in the UML syntax, and can be represented on class diagrams (also called static structure diagrams in the UML specification [OMG UML 2007a, 2007b]).
- The XMI standard for serialization of UML models, since our XSLT is based on the UML XMI format.

We have analyzed two UML tools: IBM Rational Rose[1] and Poseidon for UML.[2] Whereas Poseidon for UML satisfies all of the above mentioned requirements, IBM Rational Rose does not provide support for most of them (e.g., an object cannot have a stereotype, and a class and an object cannot be related using any UMLs relation). Additionally, Poseidon for UML uses the NetBeans MDR[3] repository for storing MOF-compliant metamodels and the definition of the MOF itself. This is an important feature, because by using model repositories we can benefit from all of the advantages of the MDA (Bock 2003). Furthermore, Poseidon for UML has already found its place in ontological engineering, since it is a UML tool recommended to be used with the Protégé UML backend for importing UML models (Protégé UML 2008).

---

[1] http://www.rational.com
[2] http://www.gentleware.com
[3] http://mdr.netbeans.org

```
<owl:Class rdf:ID="WineDescriptor">
    <owl:equivalentClass>
        <owl:Class>
            <owl:unionOf rdf:parseType="Collection">
                <owl:Class rdf:about="#WineTaste"/>
                <owl:Class rdf:about="#WineColor"/>
            </owl:unionOf>
        </owl:Class>
    </owl:equivalentClass>
</owl:Class>

<owl:Class rdf:ID="WineTaste">
    <rdfs:subClassOf rdf:resource="#WineDescriptor"/>
</owl:Class>

<owl:Class rdf:ID="WineColor">
    <rdfs:subClassOf rdf:resource="#WineDescriptor"/>
    <owl:equivalentClass>
        <owl:Class>
            <owl:oneOf rdf:parseType="Collection">
                <WineColor rdf:about="#Red"/>
                <WineColor rdf:about="#Rose"/>
                <WineColor rdf:about="#White"/>
            </owl:oneOf>
        </owl:Class>
    </owl:equivalentClass>
</owl:Class>
                        a)
```

```
<owl:ObjectProperty rdf:ID="locatedIn">
    <rdfs:range rdf:resource="#Region"/>
    <rdfs:domain rdf:resource="#Wine"/>
</owl:ObjectProperty>

<owl:Class rdf:ID="Wine">
    <!-- ... -->
    <rdfs:subClassOf rdf:resource="#PotableLiquid"/>
    <rdfs:subClassOf>
        <owl:Restriction>
            <owl:onProperty rdf:resource="#locatedIn"/>
            <owl:someValuesFrom
                rdf:resource="#Region"/>
        </owl:Restriction>
    </rdfs:subClassOf>
</owl:Class>
                        b)

<Region rdf:ID="SonomaRegion"/>
<Region rdf:ID="CaliforniaRegion"/>
<Region rdf:ID="MendocinoRegion">
    <locatedIn rdf:resource="#SonomaRegion"/>
    <adjacentRegion rdf:resource="#CaliforniaRegion"/>
</Region>
                        c)
```

Fig. 10.9 The resulting OWL description: (**a**) classes generated for the OUP shown in Fig. 10.6; (**b**) object property OWL descriptors for the model shown in Fig. 10.7; (**c**) OWL statements obtained from Fig. 10.8

The second important decision is how to generate the OWL equivalent of an OUP model, since the same OWL definition (e.g., an OWL class) can be generated in more than one way (e.g., an OWL class can be defined using an unnamed class as either an equivalent class or a subclass). We decided to generate OWL ontologies using a technique similar to that employed by the Protégé OWL plug-in.[4] Hence, we have managed to provide an additional way to import Poseidon's models into Protégé through OWL. Since Protégé has more advanced features for ontology development, it can be used to further improve and refine an OUP-defined ontology.

We have tested our solution using the Wine ontology (Noy et al. 2001). First, we represented this ontology in Poseidon using the OUP. Parts of this ontology were used in the previous subsection in order to illustrate the OUP (e.g., Figs. 10.6, 10.7, and 10.8). Then we exported this extended UML representation into XMI. After applying the XSLT, we obtained an OWL document. Finally, we imported this document into Protégé using the OWL plug-in. A screenshot that depicts a part of this imported OWL ontology is shown in Fig. 10.10.

---

[4] http://protege.stanford.edu/plugins/owl/

We must admit that we have found a certain difference between the OWL generated by the XSLT and the OWL produced by Protégé. The difference was detected in the representation of OWL individuals. To represent individuals, Protégé uses `owl:Thing` with an attribute `rdf:type` that refers to its type (i.e., its OWL class). For example, `Red` is an instance of the `WineColor` class, and is represented as follows:

```
<owl:Thing rdf:ID="Red" rdf:type="#WineColor"/>
```

In our solution, an individual is represented using a tag that has the same name as its OWL class. For example, the same instance of `Red` is represented as follows:

```
<WineColor rdf:ID="Red"/>
```

Fig. 10.10 An example of an OWL ontology generated from the OUP and imported into Protégé: the Wine ontology

We have found this difference unimportant, since these two representations of individuals have the same meaning in the OWL notation. Additionally, Protégé is able to recognize OWL instances defined in both ways since it uses Jena for parsing OWL ontologies.

The current XSLT version has a limitation in that it does not support packages (i.e., multiple OUP ontologies in one UML model). This means that it is unable to produce more than one OWL document (i.e., ontology). Actually, even though the OUP supports multiple ontologies within the same XMI project, the XSLT standard and XSLT processors introduce this limitation. Of course, this can be overcome using some nonstandard XSLT primitives (i.e., XSLT extensions) that provide for the production of multiple documents from one source XML document (e.g., the SAXON XSLT processor and its XSLT extensions).

In Chap. 13, we show additional examples of the practical usage of this XSLT in transformations of ontologies developed with OUP into the OWL language.

10.3.4 Discussion

One very important remark to be made is that the XSLT implemented is not a part of the OMG's ODM specification (OMG ODM 2007). Even the original OMG ODM RFP presumes transformations between the ODM and the OUP, as well as transformations between the ODM and OWL (see Fig. 10.11). This means that if one wants to transform an OUP-defined ontology into OWL, that ontology should first be transformed into the ODM, and subsequently from the ODM to OWL. However, as we have shown, it is also possible to implement everything using an XSLT because all ontology representations have an XML binding: the ODM, as a MOF-defined metamodel, uses XMI format; the OUP, as a UML profile, uses the UML XMI format; and OWL has an XML-based syntax. Our transformation from the OUP to OWL is a practical extension of the present UML tools that empowers them to be used for the development of ontologies expressed in a Semantic Web ontology language. It is a kind of bridge between ontological and software engineering, since the current MDA-compliant implementations (see Chap. 7) are at a very immature stage. Development of these ODM↔OUP and ODM↔OWL transformations is currently our primary activity.

Transformations from the OUP to the ODM and from the ODM to OWL offer the following advantages:

- When one wants to support a new ontology language (e.g., DAML+OIL) using the ODM-based principle, only one pair of transformations needs to be implemented: from the new language to the ODM, and from the ODM to the new language. If we want to support transformations between n different languages (such as the OUP and

OWL), then it is necessary to implement 2n transformations. If, instead, we implement transformations between every pair of ontology languages without using the ODM (e.g., between OWL and DAML+OIL), then we need n^2 transformations.

- When transforming ontologies through the ODM, we can validate them against a metamodel of an ontology language (i.e., the ODM). In this way, we can prevent transformation of an invalid ontology or issue a warning when an ontology is inconsistent. This feature is very important for OUP models, since existing UML tools are unable to check UML models that are based on a UML profile.

- Finally, one should note that the transformation mechanism for MOF-based ontologies is driven by ideas from Bézivin (2001), in which metamodel-based model transformations were proposed. In the case of MDA-based ontology languages, we have different metamodels (i.e., OWL and the OUP metamodel). However, the ODM serves as an integration point that decreases the number of transformations needed. Also, it is useful to have a central metamodel (in this case, the ODM) for each area.

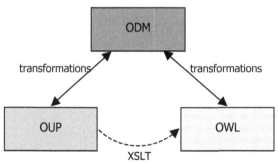

Fig. 10.11   Relations between the solution implemented and the transformations recommended in the OMG ODM RFP

Part III Applications

11 Modeling Tools and Ontology Development

In this chapter, we give a few tutorials on how to use some of the currently available UML tools to create ontologies using the Ontology UML Profile. We also provide a brief overview of the Atlas Transformation Language (ATL) and its tooling support. Here we will show how ATL can be used for transforming ODM, and thus continue our discussion about transformations provided in Chap. 10.

Before we start, you should be aware of some constraints that the tools that are available today have. The biggest and most important problem is that only a few tools can successfully exchange models with each other. The lack of a common model exchange standard when the first UML tools became widely popular at the end of the 1990s caused differences in the way they perform the serialization of models. Despite the fact that in the meantime UML XMI has been adopted as the standard for exchanging models, some of these tools still use proprietary non-XML formats (IBM Rational Rose, for example). Even when they perform serialization into UML XMI, one must be aware that the UML XMI formats used are different, and so you cannot usually open a model created in one tool in another tool without losses.

Today, most tools try to support UML 2 as some sort of add-in built on top of the facilities of the old UML. Even when UML 2 is fully supported, that does not solve the interoperability problem, because the underlying metamodeling infrastructure is usually different, often significantly. As a word of warning: you should be very careful when choosing your UML tool. Some are friendlier than others, especially those that are built on "standard" metadata repositories: NetBeans MDR (based on the OMG MOF 1.4 standard) and Eclipse EMF (based on Ecore, which is not standard but has wide support). The rule of thumb is that (currently) tools based on each of these repositories support some interoperability with other tools based on the same repository, but almost no interoperability with those based on a competing repository.

This information may seem too technical to you, but it is important at the current stage of the evolution of UML and MDA tools. Remember, you can draw diagrams using any tool, you can even use chalk and a blackboard,

D. Gašević et al., *Model Driven Engineering and Ontology Development*, 2nd edn., DOI 10.1007/978-3-642-00282-3_11, © Springer-Verlag Berlin Heidelberg 2009

but in the end you would like to be able to open your model in another tool, or to perform a transformation to another technology.

For example, your team could start from an ontology, transfer it to a UML platform-neutral domain model, and then generate a Java implementation. To do all these things, you need to be aware of which tools can "talk" to each other, and with current tools this is often a problem. This is the bad news.

The good news is that serious efforts are being made in the industry to enable interoperability. The OMG UML 2 and MOF 2 standards are the key specifications in that direction. Unfortunately, seeing how that effort resulted in the past, we will have to wait more than a few years until vendors implement them in their tools and achieve real interoperability. Luckily, the Semantic Web and ontologies are still under development, too, so when they are ready for the big scene and find their killer applications, proper MDA-based ontology tools will hopefully be available.

11.1 MagicDraw

One of the UML tools that can easily be used for ontology development is MagicDraw. This section gives a short tutorial on how to use it to create ontologies using the Ontology UML Profile.

The MagicDraw core is based on the NetBeans Metadata Repository, which means that it correctly supports serialization to UML XMI for version 1.4 of the UML standard. The current version (16.0) also supports UML 2, but not at the core level (the same applies to other tools today). Because some MDR-based tools that are needed for transformation from the UML profiles to OWL ontologies are not regularly updated to new versions of XMI, we are going to use MagicDraw 9.5, which is the last version that works with XMI 1.2 (later versions use XMI 2.1). Do not worry about that, since everything else that is of concern, including the user interface, is the same; so this guide is good for any version of MagicDraw to date and probably a few years in the future.

11.1.1 Starting with MagicDraw

Like almost all other popular UML tools, MagicDraw is written on the Java platform, so it can be run on any major operating system. Of course, you have to install the Java virtual machine if you have not done so yet. MagicDraw is available in several editions; some of them can be used free of charge.[1] To start, you could try the Community Edition, which is free and supports only class diagrams, which is what you need to work with the OUP anyway. Get it from http://www.magicdraw.com and follow the installation procedure.

After opening MagicDraw, you will see the usual structure of the user interface that almost all UML tools follow (Fig. 11.1), so it should not be hard to accustom yourself to it. On the upper left, there are various navigation trees, which enable you to have control over your model's elements. The lower left corner contains a few property windows, where you can set detailed properties of your elements and their graphic representations in diagrams. The central part is the working area, where you can draw diagrams of your ontologies.

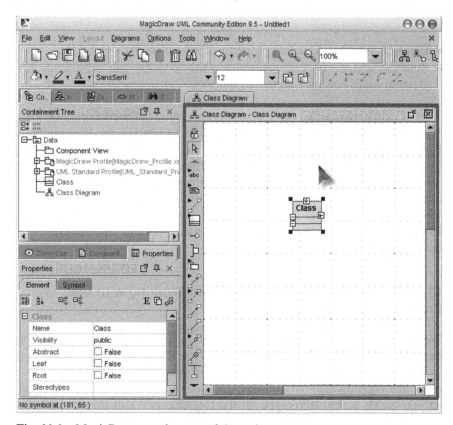

Fig. 11.1   MagicDraw—main parts of the main screen

---

[1] We are not affiliated with MagicDraw's creators in any way, so, please, if you have any question related to this tool, ask it at http://www.magicdraw.com.

When you start a new project, the most useful views on the left side are:

- The containment tree, where you can see the packages that your model contains. If you work with ontologies, those packages will represent various ontologies.
- The inheritance tree, which is useful if you want to see the inheritance of your model's elements.
- The diagrams tree, without which it would be very hard to browse in a project with many different diagrams. UML defines eight more kinds of diagram, but you will need only class diagrams to work with the OUP.

Below these views, you can find the Properties view, which contains two tabs:

- Element, where you can set properties for your model's elements.
- Symbol, where you can determine what a shape that represents this element looks like on a particular diagram.

UML tools, of course, offer many more views, but we have mentioned only a minimal set that you simply have to use when you are working with UML models. An additional piece of advice when you are looking for some particular functionality is to try selecting an element that you need to work with and invoke the context menu with a right click. The two options in the context menu most often used will probably be "Specification" and "Symbol(s) properties." The best way to get used to the tool you have chosen is to move around it and try as many options as you can on a simple model to see what can be done.

11.1.2 Things You Should Know when Working with UML Profiles

We have already given you an introduction to UML profiles, so you know the theory. Now we shall teach you how to use it with real UML tools.

Basically, it is pretty simple. You use profiles mostly by adding stereotypes and tagged values to ordinary UML model elements. Most tools will let you create a new stereotype on the fly, i.e., they will let you add any string you like as a stereotype of your element. This can lead to a mess in your model. Some other tools will at least try to make you more responsible, so that you must create a new stereotype first and then add it to the element. MagicDraw is such a tool. However, the best choice is to create a reusable profile that contains all necessary elements and then use it as a template for your projects. We provide such a profile which you can import into MagicDraw.

So if you have a reusable profile that you can import to your tool, you can start working on your models. If you do not have such a profile, you can create one by adding new elements whose type is the stereotype (by selecting *New element > stereotype*).

To make a profile available for use in your projects, place it into `<magicdraw install directory>/profiles`. In this case, you should place `Ontology UML Profile.xml.zip` in the profiles directory.

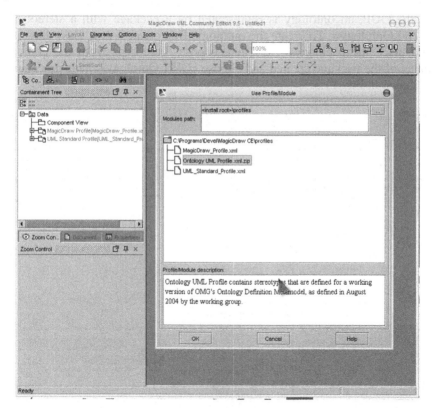

Fig. 11.2   Enabling the Ontology UML Profile in your project

Now, when you have made the profile available, the procedure should be simple (see Fig. 11.2):

- Select *File>New Project* from the main menu and create an ordinary UML project.

- Select *File>Use profile/module* from the main menu to select the Ontology UML Profile from the list of available profiles.
- MagicDraw uses a MagicDraw profile and a UML standard profile—you can remove them from your project if you like, to have a less bloated project.

Now, you are ready to work with ontologies using MagicDraw.

11.1.3 Creating a New Ontology

In the OUP, an ontology is represented by a package with a stereotype «OWLOntology». To create the ontology, first create a new class diagram and place the package in it. Then, choose Stereotype from the context menu of the package created and choose «OWLOntology». This procedure is shown in Fig. 11.3.

Fig. 11.3 Creating a new ontology

Now you can use the Specification dialog to set some properties of the Musician ontology (Fig. 11.4), or the Symbol(s) properties to customize the visual appearance of the ontology in the diagram (Fig. 11.5).

Fig. 11.4   Package specification diagram for the Musician ontology

Fig. 11.5   Symbol properties for the Musician ontology

Of course, one model element («OWLOntology») can be placed in multiple diagrams, each time with different details. You can also use diagrams to show the relations of this element to other ontologies using «owlImports», «owlPriorVersion», «owlBackwardCompatibleWith», and «owlIncompatibleWith». The easiest way to create such relationships is to drag the dependency between the selected packages and apply an appropriate stereotype to it (see Fig. 11.6).

Models (without diagrams) are intended to be read by machines, whereas diagrams are for you and your colleagues. Therefore, the symbol properties are not unimportant, and so you should choose carefully the colors and fonts and align the various elements in the diagrams.

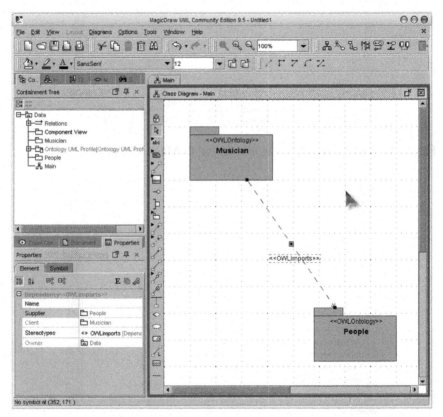

Fig. 11.6   Connecting ontologies—the Musician ontology imports the People ontology

The diagram given in Fig. 11.6 shows that elements in the Musician ontology use elements in the People ontology. These elements could be an ontology class or property in Musician that extends some class or property in People, or a class in Musician that is connected with a class in People, or two classes in Musician connected via some property in People. There are countless possibilities. Similar logic applies to imports into UML: if you need something from a package (ontology)—import it.

11.1.4 Working with Ontology Classes

When you are creating an ontology, you will usually start by identifying concepts (entities), i.e., ontology classes. As we have already seen, ontology classes in the OUP are modeled using UML classes with a stereotype «OWLClass».

When creating a class, you should put it in an ontology. It would be awkward if your classes just wandered around. So, you should select the Musician ontology and choose *New Element > Class* (Fig. 11.7). The new class will be created in the Musician package (ontology). Of course, you should add a stereotype once when your new class has been created to denote that it is not an ordinary UML class, but an ontology class.

Fig. 11.7   Creating a new ontology class inside an ontology

You will surely notice that the class created is not visible in any diagram. Why is that? As you will probably remember, UML is not just about pictures, it also defines objects as representations of reality. So the class that you have just created (let us say this is a class that represents a musician, which belongs to the Musician ontology) exists as an entity, but is not visually represented on any diagram. You do not have to represent it on a diagram at all, but you probably should show it on one or more diagrams, with more or fewer details (not all details have to be represented).

As we do not want to place all elements in a Main diagram, we need to create at least one diagram per ontology (package). So select the Musician package and create a new class diagram in it. For simple ontologies, one diagram should be enough. In the real world, you will probably need many diagrams per ontology, and many ontologies for the domain of your problem. To make the Musician class visible in a diagram, simply select it and use the drag-and-drop technique to place it on the diagram, as shown in Fig. 11.8. A box named "Musician" with a stereotype «OWLClass» will be created.

Fig. 11.8   Adding an existing element to a diagram

Almost all UML tools allow you to change details of the shape of boxes and lines. We recommend that you choose a different color for each of the main groups of elements. For example, all classes in our diagrams are light green,[2] to make them distinct from individuals (yellow), properties (light brown), and other concepts. Of course, you do not have to use this color scheme, but it is wise to stick to some rules of your choice to make your diagrams readable when your project grows.

If we add more element shapes to a diagram, the underlying elements will be created automatically. They will be nested in the package where the diagram is placed. For example, if we create the ontology classes Instrument, Album, Event, and Admirer by placing them in the Musician diagram, they will appear in the subtree of the Musician package (Fig. 11.9).

Fig. 11.9   Adding new classes to a diagram

---

[2] Figures in this book are printed in black and white, so you will see only different shades of gray.

11.1.5 Working with Ontology Properties

Now that we have placed the main classes on our Musician ontology diagram, we need to attach some properties to them. Without properties, they are just unrelated, isolated islands.

Owing to the significant difference between ontology properties and the UML elements most similar to them (i.e., attributes and associations), properties are represented by a stereotyped class and stereotyped associations that connect the property to its domains and ranges. When a property is simple (e.g., a musician's name), it can be represented as a stereotyped attribute.

You can create properties in the same way as you create classes, since they are represented in the same way—as stereotyped UML classes. Simple properties are represented as «OWLDatatypeProperty», while relationships between ontology classes are represented as «OWLObjectProperty». Figure 11.10 shows some properties from the Musician ontology placed in the Musician diagram.

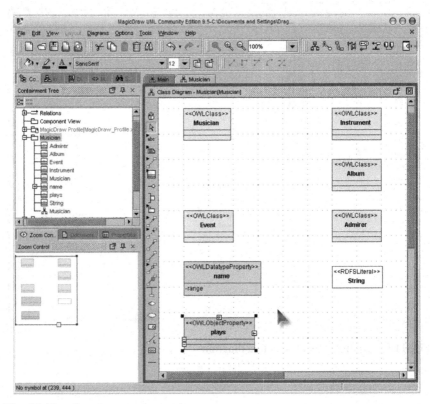

Fig. 11.10   Creating new properties

These properties are useful, but are not complete. Their main purpose is to connect entities, so we must add ranges and domains to them to make these connections.

If the property is a datatype property (a simple property in object-oriented terminology), we can specify a range as an attribute of an «OWLDatatypeProperty» stereotyped «RDFSrange». Figure 11.11 shows the dialog that appears upon opening the class specification of a name.

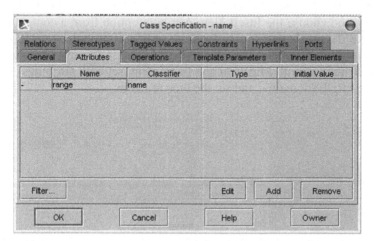

Fig. 11.11   Specification of «RDFSrange» of a name property

Fig. 11.12   Setting the range of a property

After the range has been created, a click on the Edit button will show the dialog with the attribute's details (Fig. 11.12). We need to select the type of the attribute, which in this case is String, an «RDFSLiteral». Of course, if this type has not been set, we should skip to the Stereotypes tab and select a stereotype of the attribute «RDFSrange».

We have now set the range of the property, but we still have not connected it with its domains, the classes that it describes. To attach a simple property (DatatypeProperty) to a class, select its representation on a diagram and choose the Insert New Attribute option from a context menu. To make the attribute different from an ordinary attribute, set «RDFSdomain» as the attribute's stereotype (Fig. 11.13). We now have added a name attribute to both Musician and Instrument, set both attributes' stereotypes to «RDFSdomain», and set the type to name.

Fig. 11.13 Setting the domain of a datatype property

So, in both cases, the name is the same property (represented by a stereotyped UML class) whose domain and range are represented by different corresponding stereotyped UML attributes.

The majority of the important relationships will, however, be object properties. The example that we shall consider is the "plays" relationship. This is represented by «OWLObjectProperty» too, but range and domain are represented using relationships, not attributes. These associations also have the stereotypes «RDFSdomain» and «RDFSrange».

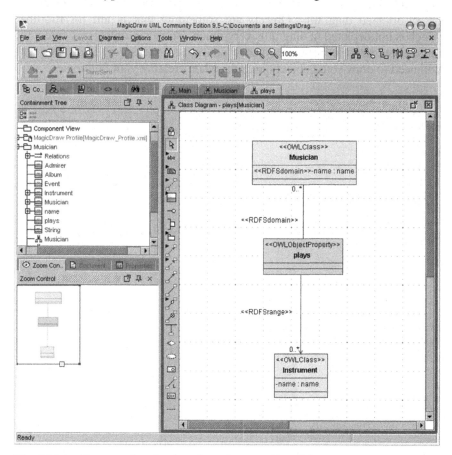

Fig. 11.14   Representing the domain and range of an object property

To avoid clutter in the existing diagram, we shall create a new class diagram for the purpose of representing the "plays" relationship (it is up to you how you arrange elements in your diagrams, of course). The new diagram is empty, so you should drag-and-drop the required existing elements from the containment tree (the folder-like view on the left side). Then associate Musician and "play" with one association and "plays" and Instrument with another. Add the appropriate stereotypes and multiplicities to these associations, and you have created a relationship (see Fig. 11.14).

11.1.6 Working with Individuals

One of the noticeable differences between ontology modeling and object-oriented modeling (i.e., UML) is that you will not see many objects in object-oriented diagrams. Objects are something that is left for runtime, which is not depicted in diagrams very much. However, ontologies care a lot more about specific instances of their concepts. So it is very likely that you will need to draw some object diagrams when creating your ontologies.

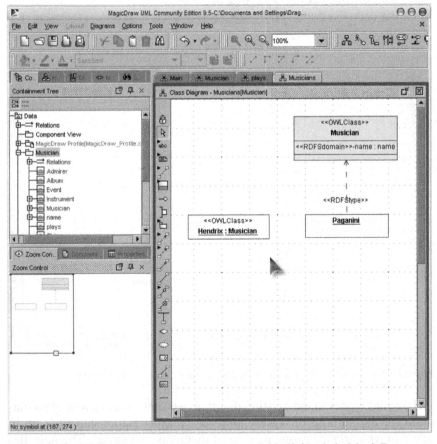

Fig. 11.15   Object diagram allowing one to model individuals in MagicDraw

Object diagrams are, in fact, class diagrams that contain objects. While the UML specification allows this, some tools still do not support placing objects in class diagrams. Fortunately, MagicDraw does.

Placing an object in a diagram is as simple as placing a class. The object is symbolized by a box. The difference from the symbol for a class is that the object's name is underlined and the box does not have compartments for attributes and operations (although these compartments can be omitted in class symbols, too). So we have created a new class diagram, named it "Artists," and placed a few objects in it (Fig. 11.15).

Fig. 11.16 Assigning a type to an individual

Most often, the type of an object is shown after its name (Hendrix:Musician) or through the «RDFtype» dependency (Paganini). To assign a classifier (type) to Hendrix in this diagram, go to its specification, choose the Assigned Classifiers tab and click on the Assign button. Then navigate the tree that pops up and select Musician (Fig. 11.16). Objects have the same stereotypes as their classes, so if a class has a stereotype, it will be shown in the object's symbol (e.g., we have added the «OWL-Class» stereotype to the Hendrix object).

To use the alternative approach of an «RDFStype» dependency, just drag-and-drop the desired class onto the same diagram where the object is and connect them with a dependency (shown by a dashed arrow symbol). Assign an «RDFStype» symbol to the dependency, and you have assigned a type to an individual.

11.1.7 Working with Statements

What instrument did Jimi Hendrix play? And Niccolo Paganini? Jimi Hendrix was a famous rock guitar player in the 1960s. His playing style was so distinctive and advanced, that he is often considered the greatest guitar player in the history of rock music. More than a century ago, Niccolo Paganini's virtuosity on the violin gained him the status of the greatest violinist of all time. His technique was so technically perfect that it looked impossible. Some thrilled listeners even claimed that the Devil himself guided Paganini's hands.

To describe what instruments they played, we must add new individuals, Electric Guitar and Violin, to the diagram. These are objects whose type is Instrument. Then we must create two statements: *Hendrix>plays>Electric Guitar* and *Paganini>plays>Violin*. A statement is represented by an object whose type is a class that represents property, which is associated with the subject and object of the statement. So we must create two statements of type *plays* and connect them to the appropriate individuals using links with «RDFsubject» and «RDFobject» stereotypes. The procedure for doing this in MagicDraw is similar to the procedure applied for creating individuals, and the result is shown in Fig. 11.17.

Hopefully, this short tutorial will help you when you are at the beginning of your work with the OUP and MagicDraw. As you discover this tool, you will find that most UML tools are similar, and that you can quickly familiarize yourself with other tools, as well with other UML profiles. If you have any in-depth questions about the advanced use of UML Profiles, you will probably find answers in the general literature, or in literature that deals with other UML profiles, or even in the literature about the tool you use. This is one case where we all can obtain benefits from the standards.

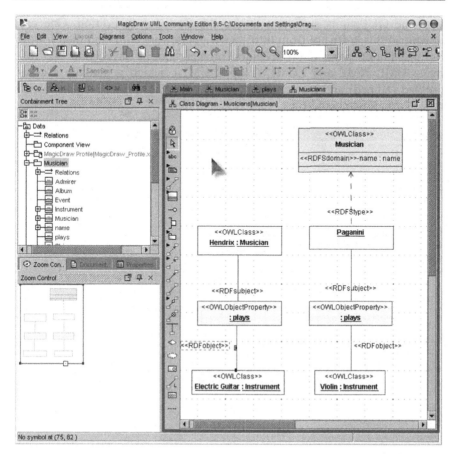

Fig. 11.17   Creating statements

11.2 Poseidon for UML

Another UML tool that can be easily adapted to ontology development is
Poseidon for UML. Since Poseidon for UML (Poseidon, for short) is quite
similar to MagicDraw with respect to the user interface, this section gives
just a short overview of the features that have been used to develop
ontologies using the GOOD OLD AI Ontology UML Profile. We assume
that the readers of this section have already read the section on
MagicDraw.

Similarly to MagicDraw, the Poseidon core is based on the NetBeans
Metadata Repository, which means that it correctly supports serialization
to UML XMI for version 1.4 of the UML standard. The considered version
here (4.0) also supports UML 2. For developing ontologies in Poseidon

with the OUP, it is sufficient to use the Community Edition. One can download this software from http://www.gentleware.com, and then follow the installation procedure.[3] Poseidon projects can be saved into two formats: UML XMI, and ZUML (Zipped UML), which is actually a compressed (zipped) archive containing the UML XMI project together with other Poseidon-specific files.

Fig. 11.18   The graphical user interface of Poseidon for UML

Poseidon is written on the Java platform, and so it can be run on any major operating system. Of course, you have to install the Java virtual machine if you have not done that yet. The organization of Poseidon's GUI is similar to that of most UML tools (see Fig. 11.18). In the upper left corner, there is a pane with a navigational tree that can provide various perspectives on the UML model under study: Class Centric, Diagram Centric, Inheritance Centric, Model Index, Package Centric, and State Centric. The default perspective is Package Centric, and in most cases this is the most suitable one for developing ontologies. A Poseidon UML project may contain many more packages, and each package may have a stereotype (e.g.,

---

[3] For any question related to this tool, please ask at http://www.gentleware.com.

the ontology stereotype). The lower left pane gives a bird's-eye perspective of the UML diagram shown in the work area.

The most important part of Poseidon's GUI is the upper right pane, which is actually the working area, where you can draw diagrams of your ontologies. The working area shows the current UML diagram. You can open more than one UML diagram at the same time, and all open diagrams are shown as separate tabs in the working area. Finally, the lower right pane has several tabs specifying features of a model element (e.g., a class, object, or association) selected in either the working area or the navigational tree, namely, Properties, Style, Documentation, Source Code, Constraints, and Tagged Values. The most important tab is Properties, which you use to specify various characteristics of model elements such as name, namespace, stereotype, and multiplicity.

The biggest difference between MagicDraw and Poseidon is that you cannot define a UML profile as a separate unit in Poseidon. In fact, you always have to create the necessary stereotypes in every new Poseidon model. In order to avoid such a rather annoying repetition of actions, we have developed an empty Poseidon project containing all OUP stereotypes, which is available on the Web page carrying the supplementary resources for this book (http://www.modelingspaces.org). After opening this project in Poseidon, you will have an empty package whose stereotype is "ontology," and also all of the stereotypes of the OUP.

11.2.1 Modeling Ontology Classes in Poseidon

To model ontology classes in Poseidon, you use UML class diagrams. You create diagrams in the navigational tree by selecting the target UML package (ontology) and then selecting the menu option *Create Diagram > Class Diagram*. Alternatively, you can create a class diagram through the context menu (which you open with a right click). Note that the same class can be shown in many UML class diagrams, since the diagrams are notational features, whereas classes, associations, and other elements are parts of UML models. At the top of the current UML class diagram, there is a toolbar containing all model elements that can be represented in a UML class diagram. Drawing on UML class diagrams is done in a way similar to that for MagicDraw. The difference is that we always use the property pane (lower left pane) to define characteristics of model elements. For example, to define a stereotype for modeling the ontology class (Ont-Class), you select the stereotype button, and then the stereotype dialog is shown (Fig. 11.19).

Fig. 11.19   Defining properties of UML model elements: the stereotype property

You should add one of the available stereotypes (left) to the list of selected stereotypes (right). You should use the same procedure to define stereotypes for the other model elements that you use for modeling ontologies (object, association, package, and dependency). All of the recommendations regarding the use of colors given in the section on MagicDraw are also applicable to Poseidon.

11.2.2 Modeling Ontology Individuals and Statements in Poseidon

To model individuals and statements in an ontology with Poseidon, you use UML object diagrams as you do in MagicDraw. The notation and rules for drawing individuals and statements are the same as those described for MagicDraw, so we shall not give details about Poseidon in this section. However, there is one important difference: you cannot draw UML objects in UML class diagrams in Poseidon, nor can you draw UML classes in UML object diagrams, even though it is allowed in the UML 2 specification. Since it is very important for modeling ontologies to represent relations between UML classes and UML objects (e.g., the definition of enumerations, as shown in Fig. 11.20), you should use UML deployment diagrams to represent this kind of relation.

11.3 Sharing Models Between UML Tools and Protégé

We have already described Protégé's UML backend, which allows the sharing of UML models between UML tools and Protégé by using the UML XMI format. In this section, we describe the practical steps that should be undertaken to exchange UML models and ontologies between UML tools and Protégé.[4]

Fig. 11.20 UML deployment diagrams for representing relations between UML objects and UML classes in Poseidon

To be able to use Protégé's UML backend, you need to install it first. This can be done by downloading the archive of the binary version of the backend on your local machine. This archive should just be uncompressed directly into the *plugins* folder of your Protégé installation. Please note that

---

[4]   UML   backend   users'   guide   at   http://protege.cim3.net/cgi-bin/ wiki.pl?UMLBackendUsersGuide.

even the full Protégé installation does not contain this plug-in, so you need to install it manually.

To be able to import a UML model developed in Poseidon, you should either save your project as an XMI file using the menu option *File > Export Project to XMI* or save your project as a ZUML file and then extract the XMI file using a zip archive extractor (e.g., WinZip). In Fig. 11.21, we show the Musician ontology in Poseidon, which we saved as an XMI file.

Fig. 11.21 The Musician ontology in Poseidon for UML, which we have imported into Protégé

Once you have created your UML model and saved it in the XMI format, you are able to start the importing process into Protégé. To do so, you take the following steps:

- Create an XMI file with your CASE tool (we give details of how to do this with selected tools below).
- Choose *Project > Build New Project* in Protégé.

- In the subsequent dialog, select *UML 1.4 Class Diagrams,*[5] check the option *Create from Existing Sources,* and click *Next.*
- In the subsequent dialog box, click on the + button near the *UML file* text box.
- Select the XMI file and click OK so that the name of the XMI file appears as the UML file name.
- Click OK to start the import process.

By applying the steps listed above, we have imported this UML model into Protégé, and the resulting Protégé ontology is shown in Fig. 11.22.

Fig. 11.22 The Musician ontology after importing the UML model shown in Fig. 11.21 into Protégé

However, in trying to perform this operation, you might face the problem that your XMI files generated in Poseidon cannot be imported into Protégé. When we analyzed this problem, we realized that only XMI files that do not contain UML diagrams can be imported into Protégé. This means that, before exporting Poseidon models into XMI, you should first delete all the diagrams.[6] In our experiments we used Protégé 3.3.1, since the UML backend was compiled for this version, even though the current Protégé version is 4.0. We have used versions 2.0 and 3.2.1 of Poseidon successfully in the previous example.

---

[5] Remember that we are loading UML models, not UML class diagrams. The wording used by Protégé is not correct.

[6] Be careful—delete only the UML diagrams (XML elements "UML:Diagram" and their content), not the UML model elements.

To import a UML model developed in MagicDraw, you can save your project as either an XMI.ZIP file, which needs to be unzipped, or as an XMI file. Note that the extension of the XMI file generated by MagicDraw is .XML. Such an XMI file can be imported into Protégé using the above procedure. Unlike the case for Poseidon, the UML models generated by MagicDraw can be imported into Protégé even if they contain UML diagrams. In our experiments, we used MagicDraw Community Edition version 9.5.

Finally, if you want to import a UML model developed in IBM Rational Rose, you should first save your UML model in XMI version 1.0 using the XMI add-in (option *Tools > UML 1.3 XMI Addin > Export*), and then import it into Poseidon to obtain a valid UML 1.4 model. Such a UML model can be imported into Protégé.

Once you have imported your UML model into Protégé, you can create an OWL ontology using the Protégé menu option *Project > Export to Format > OWL*.

In order to perform the opposite procedure of exporting a UML model from Protégé, you should take the following steps:

- Save your Protégé project in your usual format (e.g., OWL) before you begin the export.
- Choose the *File > Export to Format > UML 1.4* menu item in Protégé.
- Click OK to save the export into the specified XMI file.

In our experiments with Poseidon 2.0 and 3.2 and MagicDraw 9.5, we could import Protégé ontologies exported as XMI files. Note that the newly created UML classes may not be assigned to any UML class diagram in your target UML tool. In some tools such as Poseidon, apparently the only option for seeing the new UML classes after import is to drag the imported classes from the explorer panel into the target model. A similar procedure must be applied in other UML tools, which can be a time-consuming and very hard task, especially when you are dealing with a big ontology. However, in Poseidon, we faced another problem. Once you have imported the XMI file originally produced by Protégé, you get no diagram or perspective panel in Poseidon. The reason for this is in the missing UML:Diagram XML element that needs to be present in order for Poseidon to be able to display any UML model elements. One way to overcome this issue is to create a Poseidon project with only one class diagram and no other model elements. Then, from the XMI format of this new project, one needs to copy the UML:Diagram XML element along with its full content into the XMI file you originally exported from Protégé. After this preparation, you will be able to import your Protégé ontologies into Poseidon.

Finally, we advise you to look for further details about the Protégé backend at its Web site (Protégé UML 2008). Unfortunately, you must be prepared for many challenges when using this backend, as it is not being regularly maintained to keep up with new versions of Protégé and UML tools.

11.4 Atlas Transformation Language

ATL is a hybrid (i.e., declarative and imperative) and unidirectional transformation language (Jouault et al. 2008). ATL is based on the OMG OCL norm (OMG OCL2 2006) for both its data types and its declarative expressions. ATL and QVT share some common features, as they initially shared the same set of requirements defined in the QVT request for proposals (Jouault & Kurtev 2007). However, the actual ATL implementation is different from the OMG's QVT standard, although the QVT standard defines requirements primarily for tools, and not for languages.

11.4.1 Basics

The declarative part of ATL is based on *matched rules*. Such a rule consists of an input pattern that is connected to source models and an output pattern that is created in target models. ATL also supports *unique lazy* matched rules. They are *lazy,* since they are invoked explicitly from other rules. They are *unique,* since they only once create an element of the target model for a specific element of the source model, while all other executions of the same rule for that specific input element create references to the only target definition. That is, this type of rule is suitable for many-to-one transformations.

ATL has two imperative constructs: *called rule* and *action block.* A called rule is invoked as a procedure, whereas action blocks are sequences of imperative constructs that can be used in both matched and called rules. Along with these types of rules, the ATL language includes the notion of *helpers.* Reminiscent of Java's methods, helpers can, for example, be used to determine the bigger of two numbers. Helpers come from the OCL specification, where there are two types of helpers distinguished: *operation* and *attribute.* For further details about the ATL language, we refer to Jouault et al. (2008) and ATL UG (2006).

ATL can transform models whose modeling languages are defined in different metamodels (e.g., MOF and Ecore). This is enabled by the ATL architecture, whose model handler abstract layer abstracts away specificities of different model repositories (i.e., metamodeling languages) from the actual transformation execution.

11.4.2 ATL Integrated Development Environment

The ATL language is supported by a set of tools collected into one integrated development environment (IDE). In Fig. 11.23, we give a screenshot of the ATL IDE. The ATL IDE is built on top of the ATL transformation engine and comprises the *Editor, Builder,* and *Debug* tools.

Fig. 11.23   ATL Eclipse-based integrated development environment

The left hand side panel (Resource Navigator) displays projects in the workspace, directories, and files (e.g., models, metamodels, and transformations). The main panel (in the center) shows the currently open document with appropriate syntax highlighting, which depends on the document type. The right hand panel (Outline) shows information about the currently opened file. For example, if an ATL transformation is opened, it shows rules and helpers of that transformation. The bottom part is the Console window. It shows different ATL console messages, such as errors in ATL code at compile time.

11.4.3 Support for Technical Spaces

The ATL IDE has an advanced tooling support for technical spaces. Although mainly intended to deal with modeling languages, the ATL IDE also handles other kinds of models from different technical spaces (e.g., Java programs, XML documents, and databases). The ATL IDE provides tools for importing/exporting various XML and regular text-based formats into/from the ATL model repository. This is implemented in the form of the following tools:

- *XML injection:* takes an XML file as the input and produces its equivalent model that is conformant to the XML metamodel defined in the MOF or Ecore.
- *XML extraction:* produces an XML file from the model conformant to the metamodel defined in either the MOF or Ecore.
- *EBNF injection:* takes a textual file (written in a textual concrete syntax of a language) as the input and produces an equivalent model that is conformant to the language's metamodel defined in either the MOF or Ecore.
- *EBNF extraction:* produces a textual file (written in a textual concrete syntax of a language) from the model conformant to the language's metamodel defined in either Ecore or MOF.

In addition, the ATL IDE also includes the support for the Textual Concrete Syntax (TCS) language (Jouault et al. 2006). Being a bidirectional transformation language, TCS can be used to define rules for mapping between a text-based grammar and a metamodel, i.e., to enable for parsing text-to-model and for serializing model-to-text. Once created, such TCS rules are used to generate a lexer and parser of the language at hand. The produced lexer and parser are then leveraged by the EBNF Injector and EBNF Extractor. In Chap. 14, we show how TCS is used for mapping between OCL and Semantic Web rule languages. In the case of mappings between the ODM metamodels and UML,[7] we can leverage the ATL XML Injector/Extractor tools.

11.4.4 ATL for Transforming Between ODM and UML

In this section, we demonstrate how the ATL tools can be leveraged to support transformation between the OWL metamodel (from the ODM specification) and UML. To enable a transformation between these two languages, one needs to bear in mind the fact that each software language is defined by its abstract syntax and one or more concrete syntaxes. Thus, the bridge between two languages should be defined by the level of their abstract syntax (i.e., metamodels). This bridge requires that for either language at hand there is at least one bridge between its concrete and abstract syntax. In the concrete case of the transformation between UML and ODM, we need to provide the following:

1. transformation between the UML metamodel and ODM;
2. transformation between the UML metamodel and the UML textual concrete syntax, which is commonly used by the UML tools and/or standardized by an official body; and
3. transformation between the ontology language defined by ODM (e.g., OWL) and the language's textual concrete syntax, which is commonly used by the UML tools and/or standardized by an official body.

The above list indicates that the current ODM specification does not cover all these items. It actually only defines the first item, which is specified in the QVT language. The second transformation can also be considered solved, since the OMG's XMI specification provides an official norm for mapping between UML (and any other language defined by the MOF) and XMI. More importantly, most of today's MDE tools support XMI. However, the third item is not included in the ODM specification. Yet, to be able to import ontologies produced by tools implementing ODM, we need to have this transformation. The same applies in the opposite direction.

It is obvious that the full mapping between UML and ODM can only be done via a transformation chain consisting of the abovementioned three bidirectional transformations. Since the OMG's XMI specification provides a solution to one of these chained transformations (UML and UML

---

[7] This also applies to all other languages with the XML-based concrete syntax.

XMI), we only focus on the first and third transformations and their implementation in ATL.

The conceptual representation of the first transformation is given in Fig. 11.24. This transformation represents an ATL approach to the implementation of the transformation between the UML and ODM metamodels. Given that ATL is a unidirectional language, there is a need for two transformations for either direction (i.e., ODM2UML.atl and UML2ODM.atl).

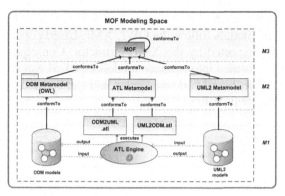

Fig. 11.24 ATL implementation of the bidirectional transformation between ODM and UML

The conceptual overview of ODM and the OWL XML-based concrete syntax is given in Fig. 11.25. The transformation process consists of two primary steps as follows:

1. XML injection from the XML modeling space into the MOF modeling space. This means that we have to represent OWL XML-based documents (Ontology.xml from Fig. 11.25) into a form compliant with the MOF. We use the XML injector that automatically transforms OWL XML-based documents into the models conforming to the MOF-based XML metamodel (step 1 in Fig. 11.25). This XML metamodel defines XML elements such as XML *Node, Element,* and *Attribute.* This means that the XML injector instantiates the MOF-based XML metamodel. Given that the XML metamodel is MOF-compliant, we can make use of XMI tools integrated into the ATL tooling and export XML models into the XML XMI format (steps 2 and 6 in Fig. 11.25).

2. This step is the core one for bridging between the concrete and abstract syntax of R2ML. It transforms XML models into ODM models. We transform the XML model (Onto_XML) created in step 1 into an ODM model (Onto_ODM) by using an ATL transformation named

XML2ODM.atl (step 3 in Fig. 11.25). This transformation is implemented as a sequence of ATL matched rules and other constructs and
executed on the ATL transformation engine. The output ODM model
(Onto_ODM) conforms to the ODM metamodel for OWL. Once converted into an instance of the ODM metamodel, we can export the
OWL ontology into the ODM XMI format (step 4 in Fig. 11.25). Thus,
we support the XMI-based concrete syntax of ODM, which is also in
accordance with the initial ODM RFP. Similarly, the ODM2XML.atl
transformation (step 5 in Fig. 11.25) enables the transformation of
ODM instance models into instance models of the XML metamodels.
These XML models follow the OWL XML-based concrete syntax and
they can be exported by the XML Extractor. Consequently, all UML
models transformed into instance models of ODM can be exported into
the OWL XML-based concrete syntax and can be used directly in tools
such as Protégé or Pellet.

Fig. 11.25   ATL transformation between the OWL XML-based concrete syntax
and the ODM metamodel

Finally, note that Guillaume Hillairet implemented the above
transformation between UML and ODM. His work is publically and freely
available at Hillairet (2007). The transformation is tested with the Eclipse
UML 2 tool[8] that aims to provide a complete implementation of the UML
2 metamodel. While Sects. 11.1 and 11.2 show how we can use the OUP
in the standard UML tools, Hillairet's transformations allow for using the
standard UML 2 (i.e., UML class models) for ontology development. This
in fact is very similar to Protégé's UML backend presented in Sect. 11.3,
but it is much more up-to-date. That is, it allows for the use of the most
recent versions of the UML 2 metamodel and their transformation
into/from ODM.

---

[8] http://www.eclipse.org/UML2

Moreover, Hillairet also developed the transformation between Ecore and ODM by using a similar ATL approach (Hillairet 2007). As explained in Chap. 4, whether something is a model, metamodel, or meta-metamodel is relative and is determined by the number of metasteps applied. Thus, this transformation allows us to have an OWL-based representation of UML models. As per work presented in Wimmer et al. (2006), Ecore/MOF-based metamodels represented in OWL can be analyzed by ontology mapping tools in order to automatically discover and generate QVT transformations between the metamodels at hand.

12 An MDA Based Ontology Platform: AIR

In the past few years, software engineering has witnessed two major shifts: model-driven engineering has entered the mainstream, and some leading development tools have become open and extensible.[1] AI has always been a spring of new ideas that have been adopted in software engineering, but most of its gems have stayed buried in laboratories, available only to a limited number of AI practitioners. Should AI tools be integrated into mainstream tools and could it be done? We think that it is feasible, and that both communities can benefit from this integration. In fact, some efforts in this direction have already been made, both by major industrial standardization bodies such as the OMG, and by academic laboratories. In this chapter, we present an example of such an idea that should inspire readers to think about the integration of their work with the tools that are already in the mainstream.

12.1 Motivation

The basic problem of the existing environments for the development of intelligent systems is their narrow specialization. Most of them have been implemented to support only the functionalities initially envisioned—most often knowledge representation and reasoning. This is perfectly right from the intelligent systems point of view. However, real-world applications and their development are rarely clearly bordered in their scope; that is why these environments are not enough. It is, therefore, necessary to integrate applications that are used for intelligent systems development into mainstream software platforms. This topic is going to gain more and more attention with the development of the Semantic Web (Berners-Lee et al. 2001) and with increased integration of intelligent techniques in common information systems.

In order to design and develop a reliable, robust, well-architectured, and easy-to-extend application or tool in any field, it is important to conform to

---

[1] Portions of this chapter have been reprinted with minor changes, with permission, from Djurić et al. (2007) ©2007 IEEE.

D. Gašević et al., *Model Driven Engineering and Ontology Development*, 2nd edn.,
DOI 10.1007/978-3-642-00282-3_12, © Springer-Verlag Berlin Heidelberg 2009

sound principles and rules of software engineering. Intelligent systems are no exception. It is especially important that AI development tools are designed closely following SE practices.

Keeping an eye on current developments and trends in software engineering can help design AI tools that will remain stable over a longer period of time. Some trends in software engineering are general, and span many if not all fields and application domains. Others are more specific, but can be relevant to AI. For example, a general trend in SE is the use of tailored versions of UML to alleviate design of system specifics, and a large portion of this book was about that approach. Another such trend is that of plug-in architectures, which allow easy and modular extension of tools and systems by use of features targeting specific groups of users. Probably the best known such platform is Eclipse (http://www.eclipse.org), a basis for top-quality Java and UML tools.

Another emerging SE trend that we have discussed, and which has intensive support from the OMG, is application development based on MDA (Miller and Mukerji 2003). MDA is a generally applicable idea, but is simultaneously of specific interest to AI developers since it has much in common with ontology modeling and development (Devedžić 2002).

This chapter presents AIR (Djurić et al. 2007), an integrated AI development environment based on MDA modeling concepts. Using the MDA philosophy in AIR makes it possible to employ mainstream software technologies that users are familiar with, and expand these technologies with new functionalities.

The development of AIR was motivated by the fact that although AI has always been a source of ideas that have been subsequently adopted in software engineering, most of these ideas have remained in laboratories. We believe that AI tools should be integrated with mainstream SE tools and thus become more widely known and used.

12.2 The Basic Idea

In order to integrate intelligent technologies with common information system technologies and take such systems out of the laboratory, we must develop appropriate tools. These tools must be easy to use and powerful enough to support the creation of demanding applications. The best solutions for such demands are tools that employ mainstream software technologies that users are familiar with, and expand them with new functionalities. This is the idea that is at the root of AIR. AIR is an integrated software environment for developing intelligent systems that:

- is based on open standards (OMG, W3C, etc.),
- uses existing mainstream software tools and architectures, and
- is extendable and adaptable.

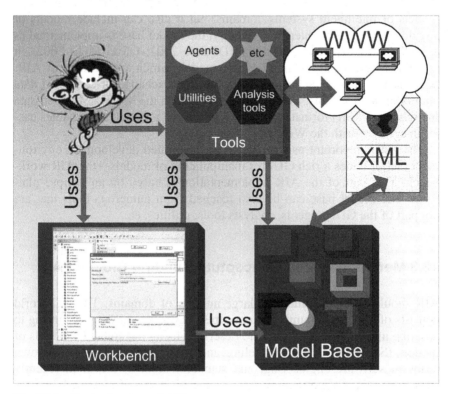

Fig. 12.1 Basic structure of AIR

We could itemize more characteristics, but these three are good examples of what AIR is intended to achieve. It is clear that today's tools must be built according to standards if they are to succeed, so compliance with OMG or W3C standards is a must whenever it is possible. In view of the fact that AIR is an academic project, it is illusory to expect that it can become a serious environment if it does not use existing solutions as its base. Such an approach would lead it away from its scope and route it toward reinventing the wheel. Therefore, AIR should use any existing solution that fits into its puzzle. As it is intended to support work with new technologies that are still extremely changeable, AIR must support easy and seamless addition of new functionalities and the replacement of existing parts with improved versions. Many of the technologies that it aims to support are still in an early phase, which means that they are frequently exposed to changes. AIR must be able to follow those changes.

The basic structure of AIR is depicted in the block diagram shown in Fig. 12.1. The central part of AIR is a model base. Primarily, this includes models of intelligent systems domains, but it also can include models of any domain that is of interest. Currently, the model base is implemented as a MOF-based metadata repository (Dirckze 2002; OMG MOF 2002). It contains MOF-based metamodels and models which are the core of AIR. AIR must have a mechanism that enables the exchange of contained data with other applications. This is achieved through the MOF XML Metadata Interchange (XMI) format, based on XML. Such a format also enables easier integration with the Web.

The other important part of AIR is an integrated development environment that provides a rich GUI for manipulation of models—the AIR workbench. This part of the AIR implementation is based on an Eclipse platform. The model base can be also reached from numerous tools that are not part of the GUI—agents, analysis tools, utilities, etc.

12.3 Metamodel—the Conceptual Building Block of AIR

AIR should be able to model a large number of domains. The real world consists of an infinite number of concepts and facts, which we are trying to describe using models. Models are described using metamodels, models of models (Seidewitz 2003). Modeling and metamodeling are well-known terms in software engineering, and standardization in this field recently started to gain more attention. AIR uses a MOF-based metamodeling architecture in accordance with the OMG's MDA standards. The basic metamodels that AIR uses and their place in this architecture are shown in Fig. 12.2.

In the center of this architecture is the MOF, a meta-metamodel used for the modeling of all metamodels. Besides the UML and CWM metamodels usual in such an architecture, the important metamodels are ODM and the Rule Definition Metamodel (RDM). For more specific purposes, such as Petri nets, fuzzy logic, or neural nets, specialized metamodels can also be included. Such metamodels should be added only if the existing models, the ODM for instance, lack support for some wanted features.

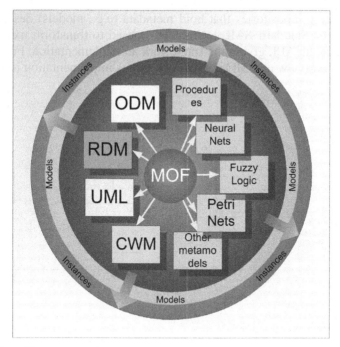

Fig. 12.2   AIR metamodels

The basic building block of AIR is a metamodel. A metamodel enables the domain of a problem to be described, i.e., it supports the creation of models that describe certain specific problems in that domain. The place of metamodels and their accompanying elements in the MDA architecture are shown in Fig. 12.3.

A metamodel is described by the MOF, and it is located in the M2 (metamodel) layer. To utilize the widespread support for UML tools, a corresponding UML profile can be added. This UML profile is an expansion of the UML metamodel in a standard way that enables UML to support new concepts. It is possible to add mappings to other UML profiles or metamodels, which enable several kinds of model to be used to model one problem, where each model is capable of capturing some specific details of the problem.

12.4 The AIR Metadata Repository

The heart of any well-designed application is its domain model. AIR stores its domain models in the model base, which is implemented as an MOF-based repository. The MOF specification also defines a framework for implementing repositories that hold metadata (e.g., models) described by metamodels. Standard XML technology is used to transform metamodels into a metadata API, giving the framework an implementation. Figure 12.4 shows an overview of a MOF repository and its implementation in Java.

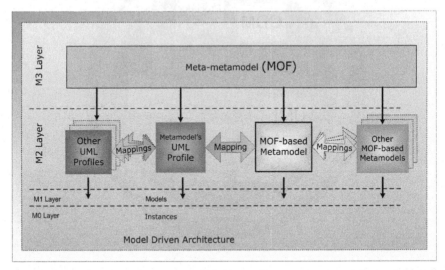

Fig. 12.3   A custom metamodel and UML profile

A conceptual view of a MOF-based repository is shown in the center of Fig. 12.4. This reflects the MDA four-layer MOF-based architecture (Miller and Mukerji 2003). The MOF metamodel is used as a meta-metamodel, which describes all other metamodels (including the MOF itself and UML). Custom metamodels can define mappings to UML, supported by UML profiles, which enable them to use support provided by UML tools.

The OMG has defined a standard format for platform-independent metadata interchange: XML Metadata Interchange (XMI). This serializes MOF-based metamodels and models into plain text (XML), which enables such data to be exchanged in a standard way, and to be read by any platform-specific implementation.

The Java implementation of the repository is based on the Java Metadata Interchange (JMI; Dirckze 2002), a Java metadata API. On the basis of any MOF-based metamodel (serialized to XMI), JMI-compliant metamodel-specific JMI interfaces can be generated. These interfaces can be used to access the Java metadata repository, which is implemented by Java classes. All data from the repository can be serialized into XMI and then exchanged with other repositories, regardless of their implementation. It is only required that they support MOF-based metadata (i.e., that they can "understand" the MOF XMI format).

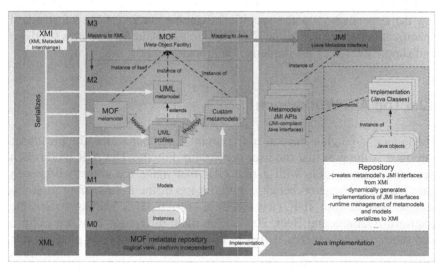

Fig. 12.4   Metadata repository structure (Java-based implementation)

The reference implementation for the JMI metadata repository is Unisys' CIM (http://www.unisys.com), but it seems that it has not been updated recently. The other implementation is NetBeans MDR (http://mdr.netbeans.org), a part of the open source NetBeans project. It is used by AIR as a metadata repository because of its generic implementation of JMI interfaces and frequent improvements and development. The NetBeans MDR implements JMI interfaces in a generic way, so any metamodel can be loaded from XMI and instantly implemented using Java reflection.

The JMI specification, which is based on version 1 of the MOF is, however, a little awkward to implement, so there is a competing solution that has lately became more popular—the EMF. The EMF (http://www.eclipse.org/emf) is based on Ecore—a meta-metamodel similar to the MOF (see Chap. 4 for details), which is simpler and more implementation-friendly. Ecore is not a standard specification, but its larger user base makes it an ad hoc standard.

This multistandard (JMI and Ecore) situation will hopefully be resolved with the specification of the Java representation of version 2 of the MOF standard. MOF2 takes into account the difficulties of implementing the old MOF, and so it defines two separate specifications: CMOF (Complete MOF) and EMOF (Essential MOF), which has the Ecore's simplicity. A part of AIR, the AIR Metadata Repository project (see http://www.e-nspire.com and http://air-mds.dev.java.net) is aimed at providing an EMOF-based repository for MOF2-based metamodels implemented using a lightweight Java approach. The lightweight approach is aimed at lowering the dependency on the specific hierarchies or interfaces of standard specifications (such as JMI or EMF) and to use plain Java objects (POJOs) and simple interfaces for implementing metamodels.

12.5 The AIR Workbench

Having a good architecture is an important thing, but a nice graphical user interface is the part that the user deals with directly. The AIR workbench provides various tools with a rich GUI that make the entire workbench user friendly. This workbench is built on top of the Eclipse plug-in architecture and Eclipse IDE (www.eclipse.org), today's leading extensible platform (Gamma and Beck 2004). The main difference between Eclipse and other extensible IDEs is that Eclipse consists entirely of plug-ins that work on a tiny platform runtime, whereas other IDEs are monolithic tools with some extensions. Thus, Eclipse core plug-ins are of equal importance as any other plug-in, including the AIR plug-ins.

Figure 12.5 depicts the Eclipse-based AIR plug-in architecture. Although only the Eclipse Core is mandatory here, there is no reason not to utilize the Eclipse UI (SWT, JFace, and Workbench), help and team support, so they are not discarded. Using the entire Eclipse IDE, AIR adds the plug-ins related to the MDR and intelligent systems—generic MDR support (AIR Framework, AIR NetBeans MDR, AIR MDR Core), support for specific metamodels (ODM, RDM, UML, CWM, etc.), and GUI-related support (AIR MDR Explorer). These plug-ins are inserted at extension points defined by plug-ins that are part of the Eclipse IDE. Being treated in exactly the same way as Eclipse native plug-ins, the AIR plug-ins also extend each other and allow future plug-ins to extend them.

A screenshot from the AIR Workbench is shown in Fig. 12.6. The Explorer shows MOF-based models and metamodels graphically, and serves as a starting point for model manipulation. By selecting an element, the user can reach menus specific to that element and perform various actions. These actions range from the usual ones (e.g., instantiating, deleting, and viewing properties) to more specific ones (e.g., opening various metamodel specific editors, and starting transformations). Owing to the underlying Eclipse architecture, these menus can be easily extended with new items that can initiate new actions.

Fig. 12.5   Eclipse-based AIR plug-in architecture

Fig. 12.6   An ontology in the AIR MDR Explorer

12.6 The Role of XML Technologies

The importance of XML technologies is well-known to the AI community, especially after the introduction of the Semantic Web (Decker et al. 2000). The Semantic Web architecture itself is based on XML. The standard Semantic Web knowledge model (RDF), as well as the language for specifying simple ontology vocabularies (RDFS) are defined on the top of XML. These two standards are the basis for the current W3C Web Ontology Language (OWL) recommendation. Of course, ontology languages are not an isolated example of applying XML in AI. For example, a language for sharing rules on the Semantic Web (RuleML) is based on XML as well. Moreover, there are several AI development tools that define their own XML formats for sharing their knowledge bases (e.g., the JessGUI tool (Jovanović et al. 2004) creates XML knowledge bases for Jess, a well-known expert system shell).

In the AIR framework, we use XMI for sharing metadata in MDA. In fact, XMI is not a specific XML format; it is rather a set of production rules that specify how one transforms a MOF-compliant model (i.e., metamodel and meta-metamodel) into a corresponding XML Schema and an XML document. Using this production principle, we have a standard way of sharing MDA metadata by XML. Of course, there are a few standard XML Schemas for MOF-compliant models, like the XMI schema for UML, as well as the XML schema for MOF. However, it is necessary to define XML schemas for every new custom model or metamodel.

Knowing that these two different communities (AI and MDA) both employ XML, we could bridge the gap between them using XML. Since they use different XML formats, we should define transformations between them. XSLT is becoming a natural solution to this problem. XSLT is a standard language for transforming XML documents into other documents, either XML or regular text. Chapter 11 illustrates how we support model sharing between a UML tool (Poseidon for UML that uses UML XMI) and an ontology editor (Protégé, i.e., its OWL plug-in). Applying this XSLT principle we do not have to change (i.e., reprogram and recompile) an existing tool; we just develop an auxiliary tool (i.e., an XSLT) that extends the existing functionalities. For further discussion on mappings between ontology and MDA-based languages we refer readers to Chap. 11. Similarly, the use of model transformation languages provides separation of the transformation logic and language specification from the core logic of the workbench or IDE we might be using.

12.7 Possibilities

Bringing AI and SE close together results in well-engineered AI systems with a firm SE backbone. There are a number of possibilities for achieving such a synergy. At one extreme there are disciplined approaches with low "coupling," such as developing and using an API for building AI systems (as in OKBC), or merely using UML-based CASE tools in the process of designing AI systems. At the other extreme, there are integrated AI development tools. In between, there are other opportunities to add more SE flavor to AI systems development. One can use a suite of tools instead of a complicated integrated tool, or extend the basic tool with a number of useful plug-ins, possibly with the idea of evolving the basic tool into a framework.

Using the MDA, UML, and MOF standards developed by the OMG is yet another possibility. True, it takes some time for AI developers to get used to them. In the long run, it does pay off as well. At its core are standard SE tools and XML technologies that many developers are familiar with. Due to MOF, it enables integration at the metamodeling level, which is related to ontological engineering. It also enables a smooth and gradual transition between the traditional and emerging modeling styles and paradigms.

Integrating AI and SE tools and approaches is something that both sides can benefit from. Yet academic tools are only a preview of what will be common in the future. Even the MDA has problems in attracting the majority of software developers and being well implemented by tools. Ontologies are also a new approach that is waiting for the spotlight of the mainstream community. One thing is sure: there are lots of similarities between AI (in this case, knowledge engineering) and SE (in this case, the MDA) approaches, and their lifecycle could be parallel. Building tools that benefit from the knowledge and experience of both communities is just a logical sequel.

13 Examples of Ontology

In the previous chapters we introduced the basic concepts of MOF-based languages for developing ontologies, such as the Ontology Definition Metamodel (ODM) and the Ontology UML Profile (OUP). We also discussed mappings between those languages and the OWL language. The purpose of this chapter is to illustrate the use of MOF-based languages for developing real-world ontologies. Here we discuss two different ontologies that we developed in different domains. The first example is a Petri net ontology that formalizes the representation of Petri nets, a well-known tool for modeling, simulation, and analysis of systems and processes. This Petri net ontology overcomes the syntactic constraints of the present XML-based standard for sharing Petri net models, namely Petri Net Markup Language. The second example covers issues in the e-learning domain. The case analyzed provides a foundation for ontologies for bridging between two very important fields in e-learning: learning objects and learning design. Whereas learning objects represent any kind of digital or non-digital content that can be used in technology-supported learning, learning design tries to describe the activities, methods, roles, objectives, and resources in a learning process. By describing both fields with ontologies, we enable the development of Semantic Web services such as searching for a suitable teaching method on basis of the specific content to be taught.

In both examples presented in this chapter we used the GOOD OLD AI Ontology UML Profile to develop the ontologies, because the XSLT that we described earlier, which is provided as supplementary material to this book, can transform such models into an OWL representation. Such OWL ontologies can be imported into the Protégé ontology editor and edited, as we have shown earlier when describing the XSLT.

13.1 Petri Net Ontology

Petri nets are formal tools for the modeling, simulation, and analysis of various kinds of systems (Petri 1962). These may be distributed systems,

D. Gašević et al., *Model Driven Engineering and Ontology Development*, 2nd edn.,
DOI 10.1007/978-3-642-00282-3_13, © Springer-Verlag Berlin Heidelberg 2009

communication protocols, multiprocessor systems, Web devices, agent systems, object-oriented systems, or adaptive hypermedia systems, to name but a few of the present uses of Petri nets. A Petri net graph consists of two types of nodes: places and transitions. Figure 13.1 shows an example of a Petri net model. In this figure, places are represented by circles, and transitions by rectangles. These two types of nodes are connected by directed arcs, in such a way that only nodes of different types can be connected (i.e., a place and a transition). Each Petri net place may have zero or more tokens (e.g., Buffer' has two in Fig. 13.1). Tokens support the dynamic nature of Petri nets; they are a feature used to simulate systems. The simulation involves the firing of transitions. A Petri net transition (e.g., Put in buffer) can be fired if each of its input places (e.g., ID:p1) has one or more tokens. After the transition has been fired, the tokens are removed from the input places (e.g., ID:p2 and Buffer) of the transition, and tokens are generated in the output places.

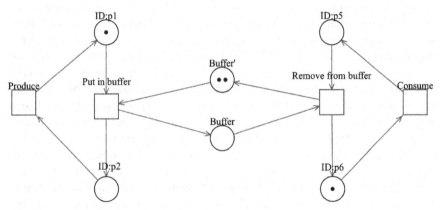

Fig. 13.1 An example of a Petri net model: the well-known synchronization problem of a consumer and producer

Note that Petri nets have evolved from their initial definition given in Petri (1962). One of the most important characteristics of Petri nets is that we have specific extensions for each type of application. Such extensions are called Petri net dialects, kinds, or types. Some examples of Petri net dialects are: time Petri nets, colored Petri nets, object-oriented Petri nets, and upgraded Petri nets. The basic type of Petri net is that of P/T nets, and they are the basic type for other Petri net dialects (Reisig 1985).

Currently, interoperability between Petri nets is possible at the level of the syntax for model sharing. Petri Net Markup Language (PNML) (Billington et al. 2003) is the result of a recent effort by the Petri net community aimed at providing XML-based model sharing. PNML is intended to be a part of the future ISO/IEC high-level Petri net standard (Petri Net Standards 2008). However, this initiative is also syntactically oriented, i.e., it introduces some constraints that enable the validation of documents against their definition (e.g., validating whether an arc connects two nodes of different types, i.e., a place and a transition). In order to overcome these issues, we have developed a Petri net ontology using the GOOD OLD AI Ontology UML Profile that was later transformed into OWL.

13.1.1 Organization of the Petri Net Ontology

We defined our Petri net ontology using experience from previous formal descriptions of Petri nets (metamodel, ontologies, and syntax) (Gašević and Devedžić 2004, 2007). These descriptions indicate very useful directions for selecting key concepts of Petri nets and specifying their mutual relations. PNML is of primary importance here—it is closely related to the Petri net ontology. We enhanced the usability of PNML by defining mappings to and from Semantic Web languages (RDF and OWL).

Having in mind the extensible nature of Petri nets and of many Petri net dialects, the Petri net ontology has been organized to have a common part that contains concepts common to all Petri net dialects. This common part may be specialized to a concrete Petri net dialect. In fact, this is the same principle that PNML is based on (Billington et al. 2003). In Fig. 13.2, we show the common part of the Petri net ontology, which we call the core Petri net ontology. The core Petri net ontology was extracted from the ontology sources that we analyzed.

We have introduced some concepts that do not really exist in Petri net models in order to obtain a more suitable concept hierarchy in the core ontology. We call these concepts "synthetic concepts." An overview of these concepts is given in Table 13.1. The meanings of some of the Petri net concepts referred to in the table (e.g., module and structural element) are clarified in Sect. 13.1.2. In that subsection, we also describe how the Petri net ontology has been defined using UML and the Protégé ontology development tool.

Net
- place (0..*)
- transition (0..*)
- page (0..*)
- place reference (0..*)
- transition reference (0..*)
- module instance (0..*)

Place
- name (1)
- marking (1)
- initial marking (1)
- position (1)

Transition
- name (1)
- position (1)

Arc
- from node (1)
- to node (1)
- position (0..*)
- mulitiplicity (1)

Page
- place (0..*)
- transition (0..*)
- page (0..*)
- place reference (0..*)
- transition reference (0..*)
- module instance (0..*)

Module
- name (1)
- place (0..*)
- transition (0..*)
- arc (0..*)
- page (0..*)
- place reference (0..*)
- transition reference (0..*)
- module instance (0..*)
- module interface (1)

Module instance
- name (1)
- place (0..*)
- transition (0..*)
- arc (0..*)
- page (0..*)
- place reference (0..*)
- transition reference (0..*)
- module instance (0..*)
- module interface (1)

Module interface
- input (0..*)
- output (0..*)

Place reference
- reference (1)
- name (1)
- position (1)

Transition reference
- reference (1)
- name (1)
- position (1)

Graphical information
- position (1)
- font style (1)
- color (1)
- ...

Marking
- token (0..*)
- graphical information (1)

Initial marking
- token (0..*)
- graphical information (1)

Name
- graphical information (1)

Token
- –

Multiplicity
- graphical information (1)

Fig. 13.2 Organization of the core Petri net ontology: key concepts, their mutual relations, and their cardinality

Table 13.1 Overview of the synthetic concepts in the core Petri net ontology, which are generalizations of the concepts in Fig. 13.2

Synthetic concept	Concepts generalized
Node reference	Place reference, transition reference
Node	Place, transition, node reference
Structural element	Page, module instance
Model element	Structural element, arc, node

For the development of the ontology we used the GOOD OLD AI Ontology UML Profile (OUP) given in Djurić et al. (2005b). Using this OUP, one can represent relations between the core concepts of the Petri net ontology and the specifics of a Petri net dialect. To do this, we suggest using the OUP's package mechanism. In the OUP, we attach <<ontology>> to a package. That means that the package is an ontology. Accordingly, we have put all core concepts of the Petri net ontology in an <<ontology>> package. If we wish to extend the Petri net ontology with concepts from a Petri net dialect, we only need to create a new <<ontology>>, related to the core <<ontology>> through the <<imports>> dependency. We illustrate this extension principle in Fig. 13.3.

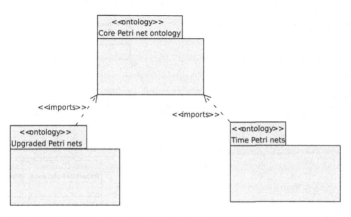

Fig. 13.3 Extension mechanism of the Petri net ontology: support for Petri net dialects

This example depicts how we can extend the core Petri net ontology (<<ontology>> *Petri net core*) with concepts from upgraded and time Petri nets (i.e., we attach new properties to the core classes to describe a Petri net dialect). An additional advantage of this approach is that we have the ability to merge concepts from a number of ontologies (i.e., <<ontology>> packages). As a result, we obtain one ontology definition, which can be expressed, for instance, in OWL (by applying an XSLT). Comparing our approach with the current PNML proposal for Petri Net Definition Types (Billington et al. 2003), one can see that our approach improves the maintainability of Petri net concepts, and better supports reusability of the concepts in the Petri net ontology. So far, we have defined extensions of the Petri net ontology for: P/T nets, time Petri nets, and upgraded Petri nets.

13.1.2 The Core Petri Net Ontology in the Ontology UML Profile

In the core Petri net ontology package, we have defined all of the concepts, properties, relations, and restrictions shown in Table 13.1 and Fig. 13.2. The core Petri net hierarchy is shown in Fig. 13.4. We have defined all relations among classes in the Petri net ontology using the <<ObjectProperty>> stereotype.

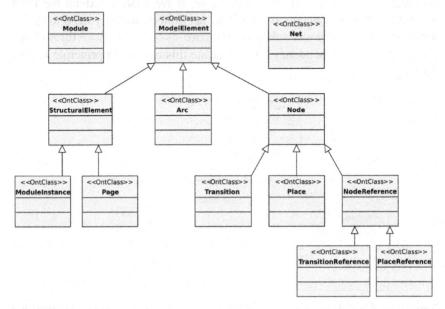

Fig. 13.4   Class hierarchy of the Petri net ontology, shown in the Ontology UML Profile

Figure 13.5 shows how the <<ObjectProperty>> *name* is defined as a graphical feature. In this case, the *name* property has as its range (through the <<range>> association) the *NameDescriptor* <<OntClass>>. However, this class is inherited from *GraphicalFeature. GraphicalFeature* was introduced to the Petri net ontology as the root class for all of the classes that constitute the range of a graphical feature. Similarly, we have defined other graphical features (e.g., marking). In addition, the *name* property has a domain *Net* and *Node*.

Figure 13.6 illustrates how we have related the *ModelElement* class to the *StructuralElement, Net,* and *Module* classes. In fact, we have defined the <<ObjectProperty>> stereotype *element,* whose range is the *ModelElement* class. On the other hand, the domain of this property is the following classes: *Module, StructuralElement,* and *Net.*

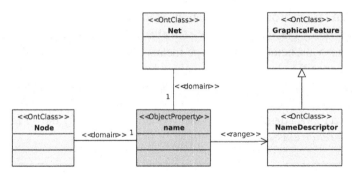

Fig. 13.5 An example of a graphical feature defined in the Ontology UML Profile: the *name* object property

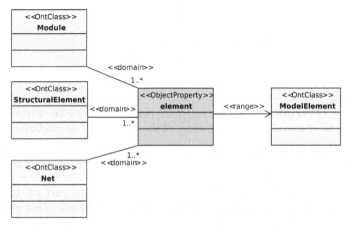

Fig. 13.6 The collections of elements of the Petri net model that contain the *StructuralElement, Module,* and *Net* classes, modeled by <<ObjectProperty>> stereotype *element*

Figure 13.4 shows that the *PlaceReference* and *TransitionReference* classes are inherited from the *NodeReference* class and inherit its *reference* object property. This property is defined to have its range in the *Node* and *NodeReference* classes. However, the *PlaceReference* and *Transition-Reference* classes have an additional restriction on the *reference* property. That is to say, it may only take values from the *Place* and *PlaceReference* classes when it is a property of the *PlaceReference* class. Similarly, it may only take values from the *Transition* and *TransitionReference* classes when it is a property of the *TransitionReference* class. In Fig. 13.7, we show how this restriction is defined for the *PlaceReference* class. Using the

<<allValuesFrom>> association stereotype, we have defined the *PlaceReference* class to have a <<Restriction>>. The <<allValuesFrom>> association stereotype means that a property with this restriction for a specific class must take values from a specific set. Using two dependency stereotypes, we have specified that this restriction is defined on the property *reference* (<<onProperty>> *reference*), and that it must take <<allValuesFrom>> the <<Union>> of the *Place* and *PlaceReference* classes.

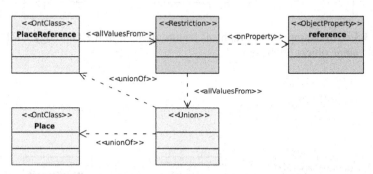

Fig. 13.7 The restriction that the *reference* property of the *PlaceReference* class must have all of its values from the union of the *Place* and *PlaceReference* classes

Figure 13.8 shows an excerpt from the Petri net ontology expressed in OWL. It was generated using an XSLT for transformation from the OUP ontology (i.e., XMI) to OWL. The figure illustrates part of the OWL *TransitionReference* restriction on the *reference* property. This restriction states that *TransitionReference*'s property *reference* must take all of its values from (*allValuesFrom*) the union of the classes *Transition* and *TransitionReference*.

```
<owl:Class rdf:ID="PlaceReference">
    <rdfs:subClassOf rdf:resource="#NodeReference"/>
    <rdfs:subClassOf>
        <owl:Restriction>
            <owl:onProperty rdf:resource="#reference"/>
            <owl:allValuesFrom>
                <owl:Class>
                    <owl:unionOf rdf:parseType="Collection">
                        <owl:Class rdf:about="#Place"/>
                        <owl:Class rdf:about="#PlaceReference"/>
                    </owl:unionOf>
                </owl:Class>
            </owl:allValuesFrom>
        </owl:Restriction>
    </rdfs:subClassOf>
</owl:Class>
```

Fig. 13.8 Part of the Petri net ontology in OWL: the *TransitionReference* class restriction

13.1.3 An Extension Example: Upgraded Petri Nets

Here we illustrate an ontology that describes upgraded Petri nets (a Petri net dialect for modeling hardware; Štrbac 2002) in order to show how the Petri net ontology can be extended. The same procedure can be applied to describe other Petri net dialects (e.g., time Petri nets and colored Petri nets). Figure 13.9 shows the concepts that need to be introduced into the ontology in order to support upgraded Petri nets. Most of these concepts are ontology properties: *attribute X* and *attribute Y* are graphical features of the *Place* class; *function, function firing level,* and *time function* are features of the *Transition* class; and *typeArc* is a feature of the *Arc* class. The extension of the ontology for upgraded Petri nets also requires a restriction on the *Arc* class: an arc can only connect a place and a transition.

Core ontology concepts	PLACE	TRANSITION	ARC
Upgraded Petri net extensions	▪ *attribute X*— graphical feature ▪ *attribute Y*— graphical feature	▪ *function*—property ▪ *function firing level*— property ▪ *time function*— property	▪ *an arc can only connect a place and a transition*— restriction ▪ *typeArc*—property

Fig. 13.9 The relation between the core Petri net concepts and their extensions for upgraded Petri nets

In terms of the OUP, this extension means that we have a new <<ontology>> package, which contains all concepts and restrictions specific to upgraded Petri nets. Figure 13.10 shows how we have attached the *typeArc* property to the *Arc* class. In fact, the domain of the *typeArc* property is *Arc,* whereas the enumeration *ArcType* is the range of the *typeArc*. The enumeration *ArcType* consists of four individuals: "normal," "inhibitor," "reset," and "read."

Having introduced all concepts and restrictions for upgraded Petri nets in the OUP model, we can generate its OWL equivalent using an XSLT. Figure 13.11 contains an excerpt from the OWL ontology generated for the *Arc* class. On the left side (Fig. 13.11a), we show the definition of the *Arc* class for the core Petri net ontology. On the right side (Fig. 13.11b), we show an excerpt form the corresponding definition in the ontology for upgraded Petri nets. It should be noted that Fig. 13.11b depicts only how the *typeArc* property is added in the OWL ontology. First, we added the *typeArc* property as a definition of a new object property, which has the *Arc* class as its domain and the *ArcType* class as its range. *ArcType* is an enumeration that consists of the individuals we have already mentioned.

The *Arc* class has only a cardinality restriction on the *typeArc* property. Note that the *Arc* class for upgraded Petri nets contains all of the definition of the *Arc* class in the core Petri net ontology (i.e., the definition shown in Fig. 13.11a). Then, following the same principle, the XSLT converter produces the other parts of the OWL ontology for upgraded Petri nets.

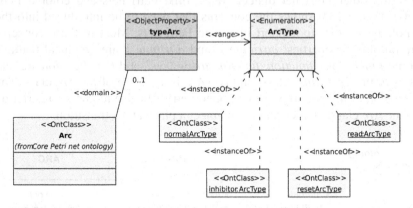

Fig. 13.10 An extension of the *Arc* class for upgraded Petri nets: the *typeArc* property with its range (the enumeration of the following values: "normal," "inhibitor," "reset," and "read")

```
<owl:Class rdf:ID="Arc">
    <rdfs:subClassOf rdf:resource="#ModelElement"/>
    <rdfs:subClassOf>
        <owl:Restriction>
            <owl:onProperty rdf:resource="#multiplicity"/>
            <owl:maxCardinality
            rdf:datatype="&xsd;#nonNegativeInteger">
            1</owl:maxCardinality>
        </owl:Restriction>
    </rdfs:subClassOf>
    <rdfs:subClassOf>
        <owl:Restriction>
            <owl:onProperty rdf:resource="#fromNode"/>
            <owl:cardinality
            rdf:datatype="&xsd;#nonNegativeInteger">
            1</owl:cardinality>
        </owl:Restriction>
    </rdfs:subClassOf>
    <rdfs:subClassOf>
        <owl:Restriction>
            <owl:onProperty rdf:resource="#toNode"/>
            <owl:cardinality rdf:datatype=
            "&xsd;#nonNegativeInteger">
            1</owl:cardinality>
        </owl:Restriction>
    </rdfs:subClassOf>
</owl:Class>
                    a)
```

```
<owl:ObjectProperty rdf:ID="typeArc">
    <rdfs:range rdf:resource="#ArcType"/>
    <rdfs:domain rdf:resource="#Arc"/>
</owl:ObjectProperty>
<owl:Class rdf:ID="ArcType">
    <owl:oneOf rdf:parseType="Collection">
        <ArcType rdf:about="#normal"/>
        <ArcType rdf:about="#inhibitor"/>
        <ArcType rdf:about="#reset"/>
        <ArcType rdf:about="#read"/>
    </owl:oneOf>
</owl:Class>
<ArcType rdf:ID="normal"/>
<ArcType rdf:ID="inhibitor"/>
<ArcType rdf:ID="reset"/>
<ArcType rdf:ID="read"/>
<owl:Class rdf:ID="Arc">
    <!-- This extended Arc class has the same content
    as the Arc class in the Core Petri net ontology plus
    the following content: -->
    <rdfs:subClassOf>
        <owl:Restriction>
            <owl:onProperty rdf:resource="#typeArc"/>
            <owl:maxCardinality
            rdf:datatype="&xsd;#nonNegativeInteger">
            1</owl:maxCardinality>
        </owl:Restriction>
    </rdfs:subClassOf>
    <!--Restriction that an arc can only connect a place
    and transition-->
</owl:Class>
                    b)
```

Fig. 13.11 OWL definition of the *Arc* class: (**a**) for the core Petri net ontology; (**b**) for the ontology of upgraded Petri nets

Figure 13.12 shows how we have extended the *Place* class. We have added the *attributeX* and *attributeY* properties, so that each instance of the *Place* class may have instances of those properties. The ranges of *attributeX* and *attributeY* are *AttributeXDescriptor* and *AttributeYDescriptor* classes, respectively. Using the same principle, we have introduced two other datatype properties, namely *firingLevel* (Integer) and *functionName* (String).

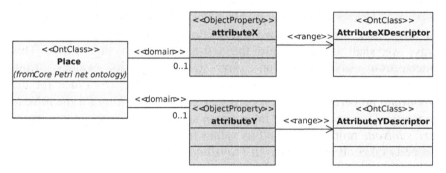

Fig. 13.12   Attaching the *attributeX* and *attributeY* properties to the *Place* class

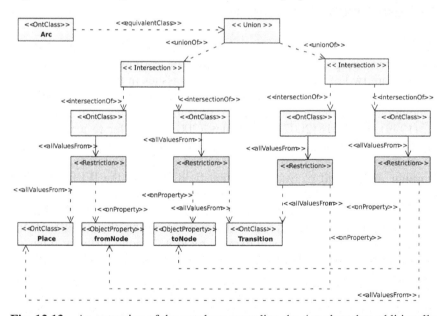

Fig. 13.13   An extension of the ontology regarding the *Arc* class that additionally restricts this class: an arc may connect only a transition and a place. This restriction is represented in the OUP that can be transformed to OWL using an XSLT

Figure 13.13 shows how we have put a restriction on a Petri net arc using the Ontology UML Profile. Note that this restriction is not part of the core Petri net ontology, since it is not a generally applicable rule for all Petri net dialects. However, most Petri net dialects have this restriction, and hence we have applied it here.

This restriction means that a Petri net arc (<<OntClass>> *Arc*) may connect only a *Place* and a *Transition*. This statement is expressed as a union (<<Union>>) of two intersections (<<Intersection>>). Our <<OntClass>> *Arc* is an equivalent class (<<equivalentClass>>) of this union. Since these two intersections are defined in a symmetric way, we shall describe only the left-hand one in Fig. 13.13. This intersection says that an *Arc* takes all its values from (<<allValuesFrom>> association) <<OntClass>> *Place* for the *fromNode* property and from <<OntClass>> *Transition* for the *toNode* property. The second (right) intersection specifies the opposite statement: *Arc*'s *toNode* property takes all its values from *Place,* and *Arc*'s *fromNode* property takes all its values from *Transition.*

13.2 Educational Ontologies[1]

Specifying reusable chunks of learning content and defining an abstract way of describing designs for various units of learning (e.g., courses and lessons) are two of the most current research issues in the e-learning community. One field of research in this area is that of learning objects. Among the many important definitions of learning objects such as Barrit et al. (1999), Richards (2002), and Wiley (2002), we refer to a very broad definition (Duval 2002): A learning object is any entity, digital or nondigital, that can be used, reused, or referenced during technology-supported learning. As a result of research in that field we have the IEEE Learning Object Metadata (LOM) standard, which is a standardized set of metadata fields (e.g., title, description, and category) that describe learning objects. However, in addition to this vague definition, learning objects suffer from a lack of ability to semantically express relations among different types of objects in the context of their use in an educational setting (Koper 2001). Accordingly, there is a second field of research referred to as learning design, which can be defined as the application of a pedagogical model to a specific learning objective, a specific target group, and a specific context or knowledge domain (Koper and Olivier 2004). As a response to these

---

[1] Portions reprinted with minor changes, with permission, from Knight et al. (2006).

activities, there has been an initiative by IMS to define learning design-related recommendations (IMS LD IM 2003).

Although the two aforementioned initiatives are interrelated, some questions still have to be answered, such as the following: How can we employ just some specific parts of a learning object, rather than the learning object as a whole in a specific learning design? How can we reuse the same learning design in different contexts with different learning objects? How can we personalize the content of the same learning object according to learners' models in the same learning design? How can we develop more extensive search and ranking services for learning objects and learning designs?

To address these problems, we have developed a set of ontologies to link learning designs and learning content.[2] The use cases that have driven our efforts involve enabling teachers to reuse learning designs not through complete automation of the process, but through better search services.

13.2.1 Conceptual Solution

We start from the premise that learning design offers tremendous potential for content repurposing. Starting with some educational content in the form of learning objects (including images, text, and animations) and some Web-based learning support services (chat, messaging, and multiple-choice tests), learning designs can choreograph the order in which the content will be presented, how it will be integrated into learning support services, how it will be sequenced, and how it will be assigned to learners in a lesson. Conceptually, this can be pictured as pulling learning objects from a repository and using the learning designs to integrate the learning objects into activities that involve the learners. In fact, one can regard a learning design as a kind of workflow chain definition specifying what activities learners will be involved in and what learning objects will be used in those activities. The IMS-LD specification (IMS LD IM 2003) provides a capability to reference external learning objects through URI property elements and keep a clear separation between the learning design and the content being referenced.

When learning objects are incorporated into a learning design, there may be many possible learning objects to choose from. A course author

will be able to automatically search through learning object repositories for

---

[2] We are very grateful to our colleagues Colin Knight and Griff Richards at Simon Fraser University, Canada; Jelena Jovanović at the University of Belgrade, Serbia and Montenegro; and Katrien Verbert at the Katholieke Universiteit Leuven, Belgium, for helping us write this section on educational ontologies.

suitable content. Ideally, the learning objects will contain metadata that will help the course author to identify the most suitable content for a specific purpose. However, this assumes that the learning object will have a single instructional context for which it can be useful. From the standpoint of learning object reuse, it would be advantageous for a learning object to have many different uses, so that expensive multimedia content elements could be reused in as many different learning objects as possible. For example, a learning object that contains pictures of the Acropolis could be used for both a grade 10 art course and a university-level history course.

The optimal way to facilitate the integration of learning objects into a learning design without compromising reusability is to treat the contexts for learning objects (learning object contexts, or LOCs) as distinct entities from the learning objects themselves, as shown in Fig. 13.14. The learning objects exist independently of any presupposed instructional context, meaning that they can be used in any situation in which a course author finds them useful. Within an extensive domain of many different instructional contexts, many different LOCs can be created and associated with learning objects in a many-to-many relationship. If a course author decides that a particular learning object is useful in a grade 7 biology course, a new context object is created associating that learning object with that specific context.

If we annotate the learning object with context information such as the prerequisites and competencies applicable to the learning object in a grade 7 biology course, we establish an implied ownership relation. In this case, the learning object can be owned by learning designs that target seventh-grade biology or an equivalent course. If we instead choose to include the information in the learning design, the learning design will be tied to a particular context, which reduces its reusability. Looking again at Fig. 13.14, we see the domain of instructional contexts. This shaded background represents all of the possible ways a given learning design could be used in practice. The learning objects remain outside this domain, so that they can be used by other learning designs in other contexts. In fact, a new LOC is created by associating any such learning object with a specific context.

An LOC would contain data that was specific to a single learning object in a particular instructional context. Learning objectives, competencies, and the evaluation would be stored in this object as opposed to the learning object, so that the learning object could be associated with multiple LOCs and various learning objectives, competencies, and evaluations. The LOC could also contain context-specific information about the subject domain ontology, since the specification of subject domain annotations will be dependent on the context.

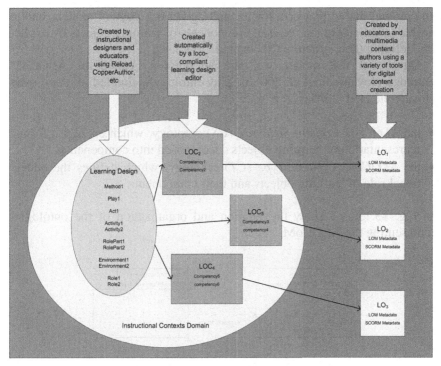

Fig. 13.14   Learning object contexts: a conceptual model

13.2.2 Mapping the Conceptual Model to Ontologies

In our efforts to provide an explicit specification (i.e., ontology) of the conceptual model depicted in Fig. 13.14, we have identified a need for the following three ontologies: (a) an ontology of learning object content, (b) an ontology of learning design, and (c) an ontology connecting those two ontologies. In the remainder of this section, we describe each of these ontologies in detail.

13.2.2.1 Learning Object Content Ontology

Having looked at several content models (e.g., Learnativity, the SCORM content aggregation model, CISCO RLO/RIO, and NETg), we decided to use the Abstract Learning Object Content Model (ALOCoM), the result of a recent EU ProLearn NoE project (Verbert et al. 2004), as a basis for an ontology that describes learning object content. The ALOCoM was designed to generalize all of the other content models mentioned, to provide an ontology-based platform for integrating various content models, and to enable (semi)automatic reuse of components of learning objects by explicitly defining their structure (Sheth et al. 2005).

On top of that model, we built an ontology called the ALOCoM ontology (Jovanović et al. 2005b). This ontology is divided into two parts (Jovanović et al. 2005a):

- the *ALOCoM Content Structure (CS)* ontology, which enables a formal representation of learning objects decomposed into components;
- the *ALOCoM Content Type (CT)* ontology, which defines the educational role of learning objects and their components.

In Fig. 13.15, we show the relation and organization of the ontologies representing the ALOCoM.

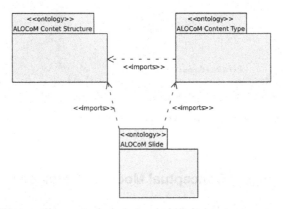

Fig. 13.15 Organization of the ALOCoM ontologies: the ALOCoM Content Structure ontology, the ALOCoM Content Type ontology, and an extension of these two ontologies (ALOCoM Slide)

The organization of the ALOCoM ontology was inspired by the IBM Darwin Information Typing Architecture (DITA), which contains a core part with general-purpose concepts (e.g., text, paragraph, list, ordered list, list item, and table) that can be extended depending on the specific needs of the author or user. Therefore, we organized the ALOCoM ontology as an extensible infrastructure consisting of a core part (containing the ALOCoM CS and ALOCoM CT packages, i.e., ontologies) with concepts common to all types of learning objects, and an unlimited number of extensions, each extension supporting one specific type of learning object (e.g., the ALOCoM Slide ontology, which defines concepts specific to slide presentations).

The ALOCoM Content Structure ontology distinguishes between *ContentFragment*s (CFs), *ContentObject*s (COs), and *LearningObject*s (LOs) (see Fig. 13.16). CFs are content units in their most basic form, such as text, audio, and video. These elements can be regarded as raw digital resources and cannot be further decomposed. Navigational elements enable the sequencing of content fragments in a content object. Besides CFs, COs can also include other COs. LOs aggregate COs around a learning objective. Finally, the ontology defines aggregational and navigational relationships between content units. Aggregation relationships are represented in the form of the *hasPart* property and its inverse *isPartOf*. Navigational relationships are specified by an *ordering* property that defines the order of components in a CO or LO in the form of an *rdf:List*.

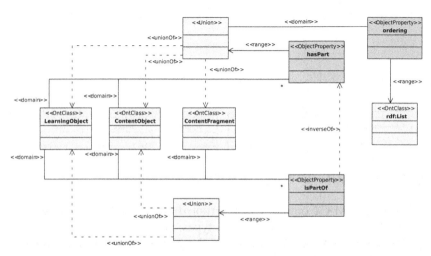

Fig. 13.16   A sketch of the major properties of the ALOCoM ontology

The ALOCoM ontology defines a number of CF types, divided into two main categories of continuous and discrete CFs (see Fig. 13.17). Accordingly, we extended the *ContentFragment* class of the ontology with the *ContinuousCF* and *DiscreteCF* classes, respectively representing these two main CF types. The *DiscreteCF* class is specialized further into *Text, Image,* and *Graphic* classes, while the *ContinuousCF* class is extended with *Audio, Video, Animation,* and *Simulation* classes.

In addition, we extended the *ContentObject* class of the core ontology with a number of classes representing various kinds of COs that can be part of almost any type of LO. We based those classes on elements of DITA. One ontology class has been introduced for each DITA element that we found appropriate for describing content units typical of the learning domain. Accordingly, many of the DITA building blocks, such as *section*, *paragraph*, and *list*, are included in the core ontology as either direct or indirect subclasses of the *ContentObject* class. We did not include those DITA elements that are related to presentation, such as the *searchtitle* element, which is used when transforming a DITA element to XHTML to create a title element at the top of the resulting HTML file.

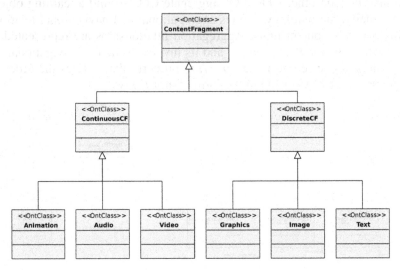

Fig. 13.17   The hierarchy of the *ContentFragment* class

The ALOCoM CT ontology is also rooted in the ALOCoM and has CF, CO, and LO as basic, abstract content types. However, these concepts are now regarded from the perspective of the educational/instructional roles they might have. Therefore, concepts such as *Definition, Example, Exercise,* and *Reference* have been introduced as subclasses of the *ContentObject* class (see Fig. 13.18), whereas concepts such as *Tutorial, Lesson,* and *Test* are some of the subclasses of the *LearningObject* class. The creation of this ontology was mostly inspired by a thorough examination of existing learning object content models (Verbert and Duval 2004) and of closely related work presented in Ullrich (2005). The concepts defined in this ontology are used as values for the Learning Resource Type element of the IEEE LOM standard.

In Fig. 13.19a, we show how we have extended the ALOCoM core concepts to support slide presentations, and Fig. 13.19b illustrates how we have extended the *hasPart* property in the *SlidePresentation* class, so that it may take only values that are instances of the Slide class.

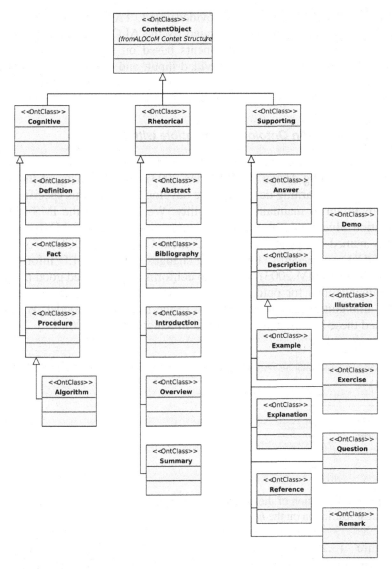

Fig. 13.18 Part of the ALOCoM Content Type ontology: the *ContentObject* class and its subclasses

The ALOCoM ontology is used in the development of two Semantic Web applications. The first one is TANGRAM (http://iis.fon.rs/ TANGRAM), a system for a personalized assembly of learning object components. The input of the TANGRAM personalization algorithm is a learner's study topic of interest defined in terms of the domain ontology (e.g., the SKOS vocabularies discussed in Sect. 3.2.8) and based on the learner's profile. Based on the provided input, TANGRAM searches for learning object components (annotated by the ALOCoM ontologies); aggregates the most suitable components based on matching between the ALOCoM annotations and the provided input; and returns the aggregated and personalized content to the learner. Further details about TANGRAM can be found in Jovanović et al. (2006a, 2006b).

13.2.2.2 LOCO—An Ontology Compatible with IMS-LD

The IMS-LD Information Model and its XML binding constitute a specification for learning design (IMS LD IM 2003). Because many of the tools and editors for learning design will be developed around this specification, it is important to maintain compatibility. We have used the IMS-LD Information Model as a blueprint for the creation of an IMS-LD–based ontology named the Learning Object Context Ontology (LOCO). To create the LOCO, we needed to make some changes to the IMS-LD Information Model (IMS LD IM 2003) in order to conform to established good practice recommendations for ontology design (Noy et al. 2001), and to resolve some ambiguities and inconsistencies in the information model. We have reported these inconsistencies in detail in Knight et al. (2006).

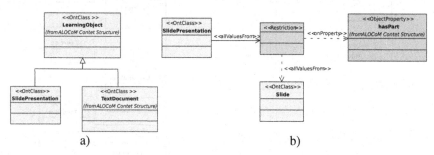

a)   b)

Fig. 13.19   Extension of the ALOCoM to support slide presentations (**a**), and the additional restriction on the *hasPart* property (**b**)

Figure 13.20 shows the LOCO's classes and their inheritance relationships, expressed in the GOOD OLD AI OUP. The main emphasis is on the *Learning_object* class, since our goal is to make a connection between learning content (e.g., represented in the ALOCoM ontology by the *LearningObject* class) and learning design (i.e., the LOCO). In the LOCO, the *Learning_object* class is a subclass of the *ResourceDescription* class. Accordingly, the *Learning_object* class inherits the following properties from the *ResourceDescription* class (see Fig. 13.21): *item, metadata, title,* and *hasResource.*

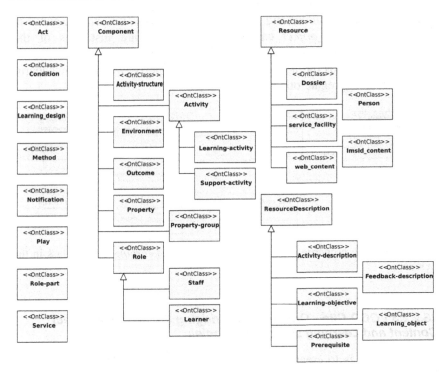

Fig. 13.20 Class organization of the LOCO

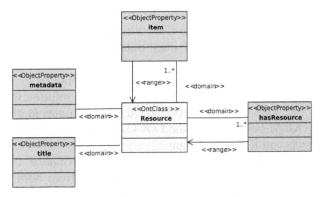

Fig. 13.21 The properties of the *Resource* class in the LOCO

Let us describe the *hasResource* property in order to illustrate one of the class properties of the LOCO (see Fig. 13.22). Initially, the range of the *hasResource* property is the *Resource* class. However, according to the IMS-LD specification, we have to restrict this range, so that the range is a union of the *web_content* and *Imsld_content* classes (i.e., *hasResource* in the class *Learning_object* can take values that are instances of the *web_content* and *Imsld_content* classes). Additionally, the *Learning_object* class has the *hasLearning_object* property, which allows learning objects to aggregate other learning objects.

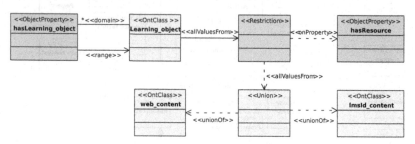

Fig. 13.22   The properties of and restriction on the *Learning_object* class in the LOCO

13.2.2.3 LOCO-Cite—Ontology for Bridging the Learning Object Content and Learning Design Ontologies

The final step is to create an ontology that serves as a bridge linking the LOCO and the ALOCoM ontology in accordance with the conceptual model of learning object contexts shown in Fig. 13.14. Because this makes an explicit reference to a specific learning object, we have named this ontology LOCO-Cite. The LOCO and the ALOCoM ontology must be related to each other through LOCO-Cite, which links properties and classes across the boundaries of the individual ontologies to create a larger, unified ontology. Considering the constraints of the current versions of Protégé, which are not designed to work with multiple ontologies in the same view, we found the use of the OUP to be a suitable solution to this problem. Figure 13.23 shows how we organized the ontologies in order to connect the ALOCoM ontology and the LOCO, and thus the representation of learning objects and learning designs.

Figure 13.24 indicates how the *LearningObjectContext* class in the LOCO-Cite ontology is linked to related concepts from both the LOCO (the *Learning_object class* in Figs. 13.20 and 13.22) and the ALOCoM Content Structure ontology (the *LearningObject* class in Fig. 13.16). First, we have defined a relation between the LOCO-Cite ontology and the ALOCoM ontology by saying that the *LearningObjectContext* class in LOCO-Cite is an *equivalentClass* to the *LearningObject* class in the ALOCoM ontology. Then, we have created a relation between the

LOCO-Cite ontology and the LOCO through the *hasLearningObject* property of LOCO-Cite's *Learning_object* class, whose range is the *LearningObject* class in the ALOCoM Content Structure ontology.

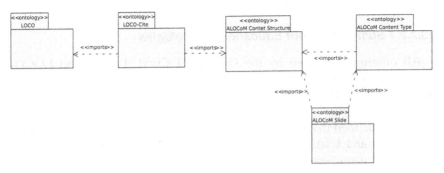

Fig. 13.23 Connecting the ALOCoM ontology and the LOCO through the LOCO-Cite ontology

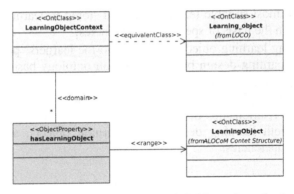

Fig. 13.24 Linking the LOCO and the ALOCoM ontology by introducing the *LearningObjectContext* class and the *hasLearningObject* into the LOCO-Cite ontology

The LOCO ontologies are in the development of the Semantic Web application LOCO-Analyst (http://iis.fon.rs/LOCO%2DAnalyst/). LOCO-Analyst is an educational tool aimed at providing teachers with feedback on the relevant aspects of the learning process taking place in a Web-based learning environment; it thus helps them improve the content and the structure of their Web-based courses. LOCO-Analyst provides teachers with feedback about all kinds of activities their students performed and/or took part in during the learning process; the usage and the comprehensibility of the learning content they had prepared and deployed in a learning content management system of interest (e.g., Moodle); and contextualized social interactions among students (i.e., social networking) in the virtual learning environment. Further details about LOCO-Analyst can be found in Jovanović et al. (2007a, 2007b).

13.2.2.4 Summary About Educational Ontologies

All ontologies defined by the OUP (ALOCOM, LOCO, and LOCO-Cite, in the present case) can be transformed into their OWL equivalents using the XSLT that we developed, as we have already illustrated for the Petri net ontology.

Having defined the above ontology-based framework for bridging learning objects and learning designs, we have provided an infrastructure for potential semantic services such as:

- employing descriptions of learning designs and learning objects by ontologies to search and reuse them, either as a whole or as disaggregated components;
- finding the most suitable teaching method stored in learning design repositories on the basis of specific competencies;
- personalizing learning objects according to the learners' profiles within a specific learning design by employing an ontology-based description of learning object content; and
- ranking learning designs returned by searches using various weight factors for the relationships defined in the proposed ontologies, users' reviews of both learning designs and learning objects, and ontology-defined competencies.

14 Beyond the Ontology Definition Metamodel: Applications

The previous chapters provided a detailed overview of the elements defined in the ODM specification, along with possible tool support and examples of the developed ontologies. In this chapter, we analyze the research results that go beyond the ODM specification and focus on several different applications of the ODM. We start with a description of the first implementation of ODM. Next, we analyze how the ODM-based metamodels can be used for model driven engineering of ontology reasoners. Finally, we show how the ODM is applied in collaboration with many other different languages. This includes UML, programming languages, Semantic Web ontology, and rule languages.

14.1 Integrated Ontology Development Toolkit

IBM's Integrated Ontology Development Toolkit (IODT) is the first official implementation of the ODM (Pan et al. 2006). This implementation is referenced in the final adopted ODM specification. In Fig. 14.1a, we give a high-level outline of the IODT conceptual solution. The core is the Ecore-based ODM (EODM), an implementation of the ODM. As per the original ODM RFP, IODT allows for transformation of various types of formats and models into OWL ontologies, as well as generation of Java from the OWL models.

In Fig. 14.1b, we give the architecture of IODT. Given that IODT is developed by using the EMF, the architecture makes use of the EMF-generated API from the EODM. This API is complemented by a series of utility methods needed for software developers. On top of the API and utility methods, IODT implements an OWL parser. This parser allows for parsing RDF-based graphs of the OWL ontologies and their mappings into the instance models of the ODM. The topmost layer includes an OWL reasoner, ODM editor, and a set of transformations into the other languages. In addition, IODT has a high-performance ontology repository, called SOR (it was called Minerva in the first versions of IODT). Querying of the

D. Gašević et al., *Model Driven Engineering and Ontology Development*, 2nd edn., DOI 10.1007/978-3-642-00282-3_14, © Springer-Verlag Berlin Heidelberg 2009

repository is done through the use of SPARQL, the W3C-adopted query language for RDF.

Fig. 14.1 Integrated ontology development toolkit: (**a**) conceptual solution; (**b**) software architecture

Being based on the EMF, IODT is also developed as a plug-in that can be used from the Eclipse workbench. This workbench follows development principles similar to those described in Chap. 12. In Fig. 14.2, a screenshot of the IODT workbench is shown. The figure highlights the graphical concrete syntax used for OWL ontologies. This graphical concrete syntax is also based on UML. Instead of using standard UML profile notation for stereotypes, IODT introduces its own icons of every ODM concept, which are attached to the UML elements.

For IODT, we can say that it is the most complete implementation of the ODM. However, as per the report of the developers of the tool, the current version does not support set operators (e.g., intersectionOf, unionOf and complementOf, instance editing capabilities, and work with multiple ontologies). The UML tools discussed in Chap. 12 fully support the OUP and generation of the OWL through our OUP to OWL translator. Yet IODT also supports the opposite direction—importing ontologies into their UML-based representations.

The graphical notation used in IODT requires certain improvements though. For example, as shown in Fig. 14.2, there is no explicit relationship established between a restriction and the restriction's set of values (e.g., the *AllValuesFrom* restriction on the *TransitionReference* class for the property *reference* to take values from the union of *Transition* and *TransitionReference*). Moreover, although the authors of IODT have also proposed conceptual mappings with different languages (Pan et al. 2006; see Fig. 14.1a), the toolkit available for download does not provide these.

Similarly, it is also not clear how IODT leverages the reasoner together with the ODM representation of ontologies and makes use of the SOR repository together with the ODM.

Fig. 14.2   User interface of the OWL modeling tool in IODT

Finally, IODT is publicly available for download,[1] but it is not an open source project. Its implementation appears to be robust and represents a good direction for development of the future ODM tools. However, important components are missing: know-how strategies for ontology and Semantic Web application development; collections of modeling patterns (Gangemi and Presutti 2009); relations with other Semantic Web and modeling standards (e.g., SWRL and OCL); and integrated tooling encompassing all these different development perspectives. The rest of this chapter presents the current state of the art in addressing some of these open research challenges.

---

[1] http://www.alphaworks.ibm.com/tech/semanticstk

14.2 TwoUse: UML and OWL Modeling

Recognizing the needs for the development of Semantic Web applications, Parreiras et al. (2007a) proposed a method for combining ontology and software modeling languages. Semantic Web applications by their nature require the use of ontologies in order to accomplish tasks of knowledge management in the open world of the Web. The key issue is that such systems need to manage ontology-based metadata about different resources in which everyone can say anything about anything. On the other hand, Semantic Web applications by their nature are still regular software systems whose implementation is done by commonly used software programming languages such as Java.

To design the above mentioned Semantic Web systems, developers can continue using proven software engineering approaches. These approaches are typically based on a closed world assumption such as UML. However, in this new context, developers also need to be aware of the fact that there is the open world of the networked knowledge of the Web. This implies that they need to integrate the use of ontology-based reasoning at both design time and runtime. At design time, developers first need to have an integrated perspective on both the internal software design and the external ontology. Yet they can verify software models by leveraging the ontology-based reasoning services such as consistency checking. At runtime, developers need to generate software systems that use Semantic Web tools (e.g., reasoners), which can impact and even drive the behavior of software systems.

Fig. 14.3   Conceptual solution of the TwoUse approach

To achieve the above goal, Parreiras et al. propose the TwoUse approach (2007a). It supports combined use of two languages—UML and OWL. This integration is done at the level of the metamodels of the two languages (Fig. 14.3). The figure shows that the ODM and the UML metamodels are integrated through a weaving TwoUse metamodel. While software modeling involves the use of ontologies and UML, the runtime software entities are generated in Java (i.e., EBNF modeling space). These Java-based programs make use of ontology reasoners and ontologies, which are located in the RDF(S) modeling space. At the same time, the TwoUse models can be translated to OWL ontologies in order to perform certain reasoning tasks at design time.

In Fig. 14.4, the details of the TwoUse weaving metamodel are shown. By following the mappings between OWL and UML from the ODM specification, TwoUse integrates the corresponding elements of the two metamodels (e.g., OWLClass with UML Class via TUClass). The key characteristic of this approach is to recognize that certain elements can only exist in an ontology, and that some other elements can only exist in the software model (i.e., UML). Those elements that need to be used in both types of models are contained in the TwoUse metamodel by their references to the original elements in both UML models and ontologies. Similarly, it is important to notice that TwoUse models and their instances are not completely translated to OWL. Rather, only those elements that need to interact with the open world via ontologies are translated. This is natural, as there is no need to translate an instance for each class or runtime object of Java. Many such elements are responsible only for internal tasks of the software system logic (e.g., keeping some temporary objects), but there is no interest in sharing them via ontologies.

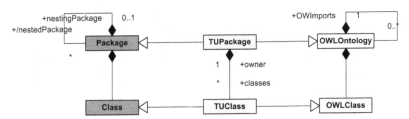

Fig. 14.4 TwoUse metamodel—weaving the UML metamodel and the ODM (Parreiras et al. 2007a); elements from the UML metamodel do not have any filling, elements from the ODM have dark gray filling, and those from the TwoUse metamodel have light gray filling

In addition to weaving, this approach also proposes an extension of OCL in order to allow the use of ontology reasoning services with standard

OCL constraints (Parreiras et al. 2007b). This extension is entitled OCL-DL and consists of the three key operations: (i) *owlIsInstanceOf,* that is used to check if an object can be classified as an instance of an OWL class; (ii) *owlAllTypes,* that is used to check all types whose logical requirements the context object satisfies; and iii) *owlAllInstances,* that is used to return all instances of the type of the context object.

The TwoUse design process makes use of the combined UML and OUP notations along with the OCL-DL constraints. In Fig. 14.5, we give an example of a software model represented in the TwoUse UML profile that comprises the standard UML and OUP notations. The only pure UML class is *Product,* while the classes *FreeTradeZone, Country, Customer,* and *PurchaseOrder* are presented in both UML and OWL (i.e., in TwoUse). The classes such as *DutyFreeOrder* along with the OWL classifiers obtained through the OWL restrictions (*CountriesFromEU, CustomersFromEUCountries,* and *OrdersFromEUCustomers*) are presented only in the OWL modeling space. This is natural, as those classifiers are typically used to classify objects dynamically (i.e., this is an ontology reasoning service), which would not be possible in UML and OCL. Once such models are completed, they are translated to Java code, along with the appropriate invocations of an OWL reasoner. For example, the method getChanges at the class PurchaseOrder will invoke the OWL reasoning service for dynamic classification for the OCL-DL constraint shown in Fig. 14.5.

Fig. 14.5 An example of a TwoUse model represented in its UML profile (Parreiras et al. 2007a)

The TwoUse approach demonstrates a very pragmatic combination of the UML and OWL languages, which follows the style of Semantic Web applications. Not only does it respect the closed-world nature of software designs and the open-world nature of ontologies, but it also promotes synergies between the two complementary modeling styles. Going further with this approach, the authors investigated how ontology-based reasoning can also be leveraged in the model transformation languages (Parreiras et al. 2008). This is done in a similar way as the OCL-DL extension of the OCL (e.g. to dynamically classify instances), which now integrates the domain knowledge into the model transformations done in ATL.

TwoUse also shows an important pattern for integration of ontologies with domain specific modeling languages in general. The major role of the ODM is to enable seamless weaving of the OWL language with the other software languages at the level of their metamodels. This is very important for tool developers, as they now have this integration solved at the level of language description rather than embedding it into their tools. Thus, they can exchange, consistently interpret, and manage such models. Moreover, the reasoning services of ontologies are leveraged to validate software models at design time and drive them at runtime.

Despite the obvious benefits, TwoUse still does not have a comprehensive integrated development framework. Some of its features are supported through the use of UML tools such as Papyrus UML.[2] Likewise, the implementation of OCL-DL does not seem to be fully completed in the current tools. For the OCL-DL implementation, one of the main challenges to be solved is related to the transformation of the context object (i.e., the UML object that represents the context of an OCL constraint) into OWL. Not all software objects need to be present in the OWL model. Next, the issue is to determine the smallest subset of the original UML model around the object at hand (i.e., the context), which needs to be translated into OWL, in order to obtain the correct ontology reasoning.

14.3 Model Driven Engineering of Ontology Reasoners

Description logics were introduced as a knowledge representation formalism in Chap. 1. Much of the reasoning in description logics (such as satisfiability) is based on the *tableau algorithm* (Horrocks 1997). The tableau algorithm tries to prove the satisfiability of a concept C, by demonstrating a model in which C can be satisfied, i.e., by showing if there exists an interpretation I that is a model for the concept C. Other DL reasoning tasks can also rely on satisfiability.

---

[2] http:/www.papyrusuml.org

A tableau is a graph which represents such a model (Fig. 14.6) with nodes corresponding to individuals and edges corresponding to relationships between the individuals. In some cases the tableau is a tree (Fig. 14.6). New nodes are created according to expansion rules. These rules are different in different description logics.

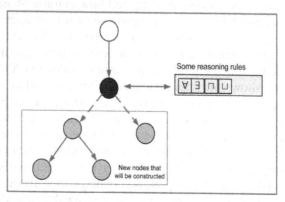

Fig. 14.6   A tree of a tableau

The OMG has developed a MOF-based (non-normative) metamodel of description logics (OMG ODM 2007). Based on this DL metamodel and on the tableau algorithm, Krdžavac et al. have developed a DL reasoner called LoRD (2006). The idea underlying LoRD's reasoning process is illustrated in Fig. 14.7. LoRD relies on a repository used for storing and retrieving the models that conform to both DLs and tableau metamodels.

LoRD's distinct characteristic is that its reasoning process is performed using the ATL transformation of the input DL model conformant with the OMG's DL metamodel to the equivalent output tableau model. During this process, the input model is first read using the ATL parser and loaded into the Java metadata repository, which is based on a JMI-compliant repository. The generated JMI interfaces for both metamodels can be integrated into the ATL language and help in the implementation of the reasoning rules. The interfaces support extension of the rules for very expressive description logics.

The transformations performed in the M1 level are supported by bridging the DL metamodel and the tableau metamodel in the M2 level (Fig. 14.7), using another ATL transformation. In the M1 level, the input DL model is transformed into the tableau model in two steps, according to the reasoning expansion rules (Horrocks 1997).

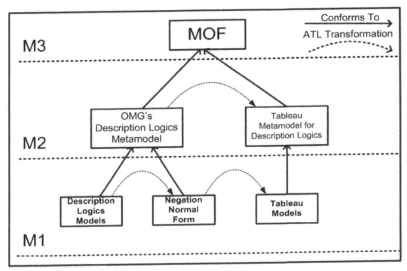

Fig. 14.7   Transformation processes underlying the LoRD reasoner

Without the MDE approach, this process does not lead to an optimal so-lution. A detailed analysis is presented in Krdžavac et al. (2006), but generally the problem is that there is a need to do several things manually. Using the MDE approach to implementing the reasoner improves this situation greatly with respect to the situation when classical object-oriented programming or LISP programming is used. There is a greater level of automation, from higher-level abstract models to object-oriented models, to a running system. MDR NetBenas Explorer enables generating JMI in-terfaces that allow for handling the models in the M1 level (Fig. 14.6). It cannot be done using the object-oriented methodology or LISP program-ming. Parsing of ontologies, common to several other reasoners imple-mented using the object-oriented methodology, is avoided in LoRD. Last but not the least, unlike existing publicly available reasoners like Racer and FaCT, LoRD is completely suitable for extensions and can be inte-grated into today's intelligent metamodeling frameworks as a plug-in. (Again, see Krdžavac et al. 2006 for details.)

As already mentioned in Sect. 3.6, popular reasoners like Racer and FaCT can only flag an OWL class as consistent or inconsistent, but they cannot explain their decision. This may be very restricting in practical ap-plications. Contrary to that, LoRD can use the tableau model and the trans-formations to it to find useful information about the input model.

For example, an improved version of LoRD has been successfully applied in an e-assessment system for analyzing students' answers and solutions to the problems the system puts to them (Radenković et al. 2008), as in Fig. 14.8. Here QTI stands for Question and Test Interoperability, a well-known specification in the area of e-assessment developed by the IMS Global Learning Consortium, Inc. (Lay and Pierre 2006). QTI has its own specific concepts, vocabulary, and a metaphor of assessment sessions and actors. A QTI assessment system is an e-assessment system based on the QTI specification.

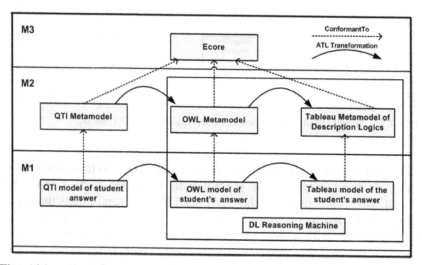

Fig. 14.8 Applying the LoRD reasoner in a QTI assessment system (after Radenković et al. 2008)

Each answer/solution that a student enters during a session with the assessment system shown in Fig. 14.8 is internally represented as a QTI model conformant to the QTI metamodel (developed not only for use in this system, but with all QTI-based systems). Since the version of LoRD applied in this system uses OWL models as its input, appropriate ATL (meta)model transformations from QTI to OWL representation needed to be developed as well. Likewise, transformations from OWL to tableau (meta)models have been developed to enable the reasoner to make inferences about the student's answers. During this transformation, the reasoner can save information about possible semantic mistakes in the answers, partially correct answers, and alternative answers. The information can then be formatted and displayed to the user. This is an important advantage over other DL reasoners that can only find out whether the student's answer is correct or not.

14.4 Model Driven Engineering and Semantic Web Rules

As shown in the previous chapters, there have been a lot of efforts to enable sharing UML models using ontology languages (OMG ODM 2007). This way, modeling tools can process ontologies by using the same generic frameworks for processing models (e.g., EMF and QVT). Consequently, ontologies can be taken into consideration in software design from the early stages of the software lifecycle just like other widely used software modeling languages, such as UML. However, there has been much less attention to the problem of sharing OCL constraints with rule languages used on the Semantic Web, such as Semantic Web Rule Language (SWRL; Horrocks et al. 2004) and F-Logic (Kifer et al. 1995). This has the consequence that one cannot translate OCL constraints defined over UML models into, for example, the corresponding constraints defined over OWL ontologies. Addressing this problem is very important if one wants to fully support model driven Semantic Web engineering, that is, the development of Semantic Web-based applications by following the MDE principles (Brambilla et al. 2007).

A promising solution to this problem is the W3C's effort called the Rule Interchange Format (RIF; Ginsberg 2006). RIF aims at being a standard rule interchange language agreed upon by rule language developers. A natural consequence is the reduced number of transformations needed to be implemented. Moreover, this reduces the problem of rule mappings to be defined by the language experts (i.e., the quality of mappings is improved), and yet increases the reusability of transformations.

While the RIF is still under development, the best known related research initiatives are the REWERSE Rule Markup Language (R2ML) (R2ML 2008) and RuleML (RuleML 2008). R2ML has been used to investigate how OCL can be translated into Semantic Web rule languages, that is, SWRL (Milanović et al. 2006, 2008). Being defined by using a MOF-based metamodel, R2ML distinguishes between four types of rules: integrity, derivation, production, and reaction. In addition, R2ML provides a set of modeling elements for defining vocabularies (similar to OWL and UML). Its MOF-based definition allows for the convenient use of model transformation languages. Thus, the transformation between OCL and SWRL is developed as a chain of ATL transformations. Besides the key transformation between the OCL metamodel and the SWRL metamodel (Brockmans et al. 2006), the transformation also makes use of the ATL XML Extractor/Injector for bridging between the SWRL RDF/XML concrete syntax and the metamodel; and ATL EBNF Extractor\Injector along with the TCS language for bridging between the OCL textual concrete syntax and the OCL metamodel. All these transformations are publicly available (Milanović 2007a, b).

In particular, these transformations are based on the investigation of the mapping between the OWL metamodel and the UML metamodel from the ODM specification. Given that SWRL is defined over OWL, a SWRL metamodel (i.e., Rule Definition Metamodel, RDM) can be defined over the ODM metamodel. To be able to define similar types of rules over UML models, one needs to use the OCL language. Therefore, the transformation between SWRL and OCL fully relies on the transformation between UML and OWL. Given that the R2ML language is used as a pivotal interchange format, there was a need first to provide mappings of R2ML with both languages under study (i.e., OCL and SWRL). In this process, both OCL constraints and SWRL rules are translated into R2ML integrity alethic rules (i.e., rules that must always hold). The definition of the R2ML integrity rules is shown in Fig. 14.9.

Fig. 14.9   The R2ML metamodel of integrity rules

The corresponding *LogicalFormula* must have no free variables (see Fig. 14.10), that is, all the variables from this formula must be quantified.

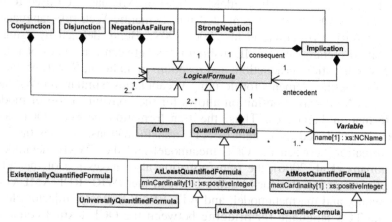

Fig. 14.10   The concept of a logical formula in R2ML

The general concept of *LogicalFormula* can include *Conjunction, Disjunction, NegationAsFailure, StrongNegation,* and *Implication*. The concept of a *QuantifiedFormula* is essential for R2ML integrity rules, and it subsumes existentially quantified formulas and universally quantified formulas. In addition, *LogicalFormula* can also be *AtLeastQuantifiedFormula, AtMostQuantifiedFormula,* and *AtLeastAndAtMostQuantifiedFormula* for defining cardinality constraints with R2ML rules. This expressiveness of the R2ML logical formulas can fully support the logical expressions of OCL and SWRL.

From the specific elements of OCL and SWRL, atoms are the major part that require special attention. In Tables 14.1, 14.2, and 14.3, we show mappings between SWRL atoms and OCL in detail. Since both OWL and OCL distinguish between data values and objects, we have divided the mappings in the tables accordingly. In all the mappings shown in the tables, *CD* represents a class description from Bechhofer et al. (2004), an expression *T* is a translation operator of a SWRL element to an OCL element, and *t* is a variable.

Table 14.1 Mappings of SWRL classification atoms to OCL constraints

SWRL expression	OCL expression
ClassAtom(classID, t)	t.oclIsKindOf(classID)
ClassAtom(UnionOf(CD1, CD2), t)	t.oclIsKindOf(CD1) or t.oclIsKindOf(CD2)
ClassAtom(IntersectionOf(CD1, CD2), t)	t.oclIsKindOf(CD1) and t.oclIsKindOf(CD2)
ClassAtom(ComplementOf(CD), t)	not t.oclIsKindOf(classID)
ClassAtom(OneOf({objID1,. ..,objIDn}), t)	t = objID1 or t = objID2 or . .. t = objIDn
ClassAtom(ObjectRestriction(objPropID, allValuesFrom(CD)), t)	t.allInstances()->forAll(t.objPropID = x) implies t.oclIsKindOf(CD)
ClassAtom(ObjectRestriction(objPropID, someValuesFrom(CD)), t)	t.allInstances()->exists(t.objPropID = x) implies t.oclIsKindOf(CD)
ClassAtom(ObjectRestriction(objPropID, hasValue(objID)), t)	t.objPropID = objID
ClassAtom(ObjectRestriction(objPropID, mincardinality(n)), t)	t.objPropID.size() >= n
ClassAtom(ObjectRestriction(objPropID, maxcardinality(n)), t)	t.objPropID.size() < = n
ClassAtom(ObjectRestriction(objPropID, mincardinality(m), maxcardinality(n)), t)	t.objPropID.size() >= n and t.objPropID.size() <= n
ClassAtom(ObjectRestriction(objPropID, cardinality(n)), t)	t.objPropID.size() = n

Let us now consider the use of the defined mappings in the example of the UML model and its associated OCL constraint from Fig. 4.17. The UML model represents relations between members of a family. For a given class *Person*, we can define a UML association with the *Person* class itself modeling that one person is a parent of another one. This is represented by the *hasFather* association end. In a similar way, we can represent the relation that a person has a brother by adding another association with the *hasBrother* association end to our model. However, if we want to represent that a person has an uncle (i.e., the *hasUncle* association end), there should be a constraint based on *hasFather* and *hasBrother* association ends. We want to say that if a person has a father, and the father has a brother, then the father's brother is an uncle of the person. This can be expressed by the UML class diagram and OCL text-based concrete syntax as it is shown in Fig. 4.17.

Table 14.2 Mappings of SWRL Datarange Atoms to OCL constraints

SWRL expression	OCL expression
DatarangeAtom(datatypeID, t)	t.oclIsKindOf(datatypeID)
DatarangeAtom(OneOf({objID1,. ..,objIDn}), t)	t = objID1 or t = objID2 or . .. t = objIDn
DatarangeAtom(DataRestriction(dataPropID, allValuesFrom(dataTypeID)), t)	t.allInstances()->forAll(t. dataPropID = x) implies t.oclIsKindOf(dataTypeID)
DatarangeAtom(DataRestriction(dataPropID, someValuesFrom(datatypeID), t)	t.allInstances()->exists(t. dataPropID = x) implies t.oclIsKindOf(dataTypeID)
DatarangeAtom(DataRestriction(dataPropID, allValuesFrom(OneOf({dataLiteral}))), t)	t.allInstances()->forAll(t. dataPropID = x) implies (t.oclIsKindOf(objID1) or t.oclIsKindOf(objID2) or . .. t.oclIsKindOf(objIDn))
DatarangeAtom(DataRestriction(dataPropID, someValuesFrom(OneOf({dataLiteral}))), t)	t.allInstances()->exists(t. dataPropID = x) implies (t.oclIsKindOf(objID1) or t.oclIsKindOf(objID2) or . .. t.oclIsKindOf(objIDn))
DatarangeAtom(DataRestriction(dataPropID, hasValue(dataLiteral), t)	t. dataPropID = dataLiteral
DatarangeAtom(DataRestriction(dataPropID, mincardinality(n)), t)	t.dataPropID.size() >= n
DatarangeAtom(DataRestriction(dataPropID, maxcardinality(n)), t)	t.dataPropID.size() < = n
DatarangeAtom(DataRestriction(dataPropID, mincardinality(m), maxcardinality(n)), t)	t.dataPropID.size() >= n and t.dataPropID.size() <= n

The same model can be represented as an OWL ontology consisting of the *Person* class and object properties *hasFather, hasBrother,* and *hasUncle* (see Fig. 14.11a). As in the UML model in which the OCL rule has been defined for the *hasUncle* association end, a SWRL rule has to be defined on the OWL ontology for inferring the value for the *hasUncle* object property. This SWRL rule is given in Fig. 14.11b.

Table 14.3 Mappings of the other SWRL Atoms to OCL

SWRL expression	OCL expression
IndividualvaluedPropertyAtom(objectID1, objectID2)	objectID1.individualvaluedPropertyID = objectID2
DatavaluedPropertyAtom(objectID, dataLiteral)	objectID.datavaluedPropertyID = dataLiteral
SameAs(objectID1, objectID2)	objectID1 = objectID2
DifferentFrom(objectID1, objectID2)	not (objectID1 = objectID2)
BuiltIn(builtinID, x, t)	x T(builtinID) t

The purpose of the previous paragraphs is just to introduce the basic information about the mappings between SWRL and OCL. This certainly cannot be considered a full reference, and we refer interested readers to Milanović et al. (2006, 2008) for further details. Likewise, for practical use of the discussed mappings, we refer readers to the ATL transformations presented in Milanović (2007a, b). Finally, let us mention that mapping from SWRL to OCL requires the full definition of the OWL ontology over which the SWRL rules are defined. Since for navigation of the UML models OCL fully depends on its features, its constraints can only be valid if their underlying UML models are fully specified. This is unlike SWRL and OWL, where properties are first class concepts. This means that there is no need to navigate the property names via their containing classes, as is the case with properties in UML.

Another issue that needs to be considered is the opposite transformation from OCL to SWRL. OCL comprises a very rich library of the collection operations that can be used in the OCL constraints. Although our research demonstrates that most of them can be translated to OCL, there is a small subset for which we cannot find equivalents in SWRL. One may argue that the inability to represent all OCL collection operations in another rule language may obsolete the whole process of mapping OCL constraints into SWRL rules. However, our goal is to support model driven development of Semantic Web applications. As OCL is more expressive than SWRL (as well as a few other Semantic Web rule languages we investigated—F-logic, KAoS, and Rei), the presented transformation of OCL to the rule languages can fully satisfy the development of Semantic Web applications. Moreover, the transformation of OCL to SWRL also enables analysis and verification of OCL constraints through the use of SWRL reasoning services. Consequently, either direction of the mappings can produce beneficial implications.

```xml
<rdf:RDF>
    <owl:Ontology rdf:about=""/>
    <owl:Class rdf:ID="Person"/>
    <owl:ObjectProperty rdf:ID="hasUncle">
        <rdfs:domain rdf:resource="#Person"/>
        <rdfs:range rdf:resource="#Person"/>
    </owl:ObjectProperty>
    <owl:ObjectProperty rdf:ID="hasFather">
        <rdfs:domain rdf:resource="#Person"/>
        <rdfs:range rdf:resource="#Person"/>
    </owl:ObjectProperty>
    <owl:ObjectProperty rdf:ID="hasBrother">
        <rdfs:domain rdf:resource="#Person"/>
        <rdfs:range rdf:resource="#Person"/>
    </owl:ObjectProperty>
</rdf:RDF>
```

a)

```xml
<ruleml:imp>
  <ruleml:_rlab ruleml:href="#example1"/>
  <ruleml:_body>
    <swrlx:individualPropertyAtom swrlx:property="hasParent">
      <ruleml:var>x1</ruleml:var>
      <ruleml:var>x2</ruleml:var>
    </swrlx:individualPropertyAtom>
    <swrlx:individualPropertyAtom swrlx:property="hasBrother">
      <ruleml:var>x2</ruleml:var>
      <ruleml:var>x3</ruleml:var>
    </swrlx:individualPropertyAtom>
  </ruleml:_body>
  <ruleml:_head>
    <swrlx:individualPropertyAtom swrlx:property="hasUncle">
      <ruleml:var>x1</ruleml:var>
      <ruleml:var>x3</ruleml:var>
    </swrlx:individualPropertyAtom>
  </ruleml:_head>
</ruleml:imp>
```

b)

Fig. 14.11 The UML model from Fig. 4.17 and its OCL rule translated into: (**a**) an OWL ontology, and (**b**) a SWRL rule

References

Adida, B. & Birbeck, M. (2008), *RDFa Primer* [Online]. Available: http://www.w3.org/TR/xhtml-rdfa-primer/ [Accessed: 2008, December 24].

Arnold, W.R. & Bowie, J.S. (1985), *Artificial Intelligence: A Personal Commonsense Journey*, Prentice Hall, Englewood Cliffs, NJ.

van Assem, M., Gangemi, A., & Schreiber, G. (eds.) (2006), *RDF/OWL Representation of WordNet* (W3C Working Draft, 19 June 2006) [Online]. Available: http://www.w3.org/TR/2006/WD-wordnet-rdf-20060619/ [Accessed: 2008, December 20].

Atkinson, C. & Kühne, T. (2002), "Profiles in a strict meta-modeling framework," *Science of Computer Programming*, Vol. 44, no. 1, pp. 5–22.

Atkinson, C. & Kühne, T. (2003), "Model-driven development: A metamodeling foundation," *IEEE Software*, Vol. 20, no. 5, pp. 36–41.

ATL UG (2006), *ATL: Atlas Transformation Language – User Manual, version 0.7* [Online]. Available: http://www.eclipse.org/m2m/atl/doc/ATL_User_Manual%5Bv0.7%5D.pdf [Accessed: 2008, December 15].

Baader, F., Calvanese, D., McGuinness, D., Nardi, D., & Patel-Schneider, P. (eds.) (2003), *The Description Logic Handbook*, Cambridge University Press, Cambridge, UK.

Baclawski, K., Kokar, M., Kogut, P., Hart, L., Smith, J.E., Letkowski, J., & Emery, P. (2002a), "Extending the unified modeling language for ontology development," *Software and Systems Modeling*, Vol. 1, no. 2, pp. 142–156.

Baclawski, K., Kokar, M., Smith, J.E., Wallace, E., Letkowski, J., Koethe, M.R., & Kogut, P. (2002b), *UOL: Unified Ontology Language: Assorted Papers Discussed at the DC Ontology SIG Meeting* [Online]. Available: http://www.omg.org/cgi-bin/doc?ontology/2002-11-02 [Accessed: 2008, December 14].

Bandwidth Market (2008), *Bandwidth Market, Glossary* [Online]. Available: http://www.bandwidthmarket.com/glossary/A7.html [Accessed: 2008, December 28].

Bao, J., Kendell, E., McGuinness, D., & Wallace, E. (2008), *OWL 2 Web Ontology Language Quick reference Guide* [Online]. Available: http://www.w3.org/2007/OWL/wiki/Quick_Reference_Guide [Accessed: 2008, December 11].

Barr, A. & Feigenbaum, E.A. (eds.) (1981), *The Handbook of Artificial Intelligence* (3 volumes), William Kaufmann, Los Altos, CA.

Barrit, C., Lewis, D., & Wieseler, W. (1999), *CISCO Systems Reusable Information Object Strategy Version 3.0* [Online]. Available:

http://www.cisco.com/warp/public/779/ibs/solutions/learning/whitepapers/el_cisco_rio.pdf [Accessed: 2008, December 28].

Bechhofer, S. (2003), *OWL Web Ontology Language Parsing OWL in RDF/XML* [Online]. Available: http://www.w3.org/TR/owl-parsing/ [Accessed: 2008, December 15].

Bechhofer, S., van Harmelen, F., Hendler, J., Horrocks, I., McGuinness, D.L., Patel-Schneider, P.F., & Stein, L.A. (2004), *OWL Web Ontology Language Reference* [Online]. Available: http://www.w3.org/TR/owl-ref/ [Accessed: 2008, December 28].

Berners-Lee, T. (1997–2004), *Design Issues: Architectural and Philosophical Points, W3C* [Online]. Available: http://www.w3.org/DesignIssues/ [Accessed: 2008, December 28].

Berners-Lee, T., Fischetti, M., & Dertouzos, T.M. (1999), *Weaving the Web: The Original Design and Ultimate Destiny of the World Wide Web by Its Inventor*, Harper, San Francisco.

Berners-Lee, T., Hendler, J., & Lassila, O. (2001), "The semantic web," *Scientific American*, Vol. 284, no. 5, pp. 34–43.

Bézivin, J. (2001), "From object composition to model transformation with the MDA," *Proceedings of the 39th International Conference and Exhibition on Technology of Object-Oriented Languages and Systems*, Santa Barbara, CA, pp. 350–355.

Bézivin, J. (2004), "In search of a basic principle for model driven engineering," *Upgrade*, Vol. 5, no. 2, pp. 21–24.

Bézivin, J. (2005), "On the unification power of models," *Software and System Modeling*, Vol. 4, no. 2, pp. 171–188.

Bézivin, J. & Lemesle, R. (1998), "Ontology-based layered semantics for precise OA&D modeling," *Proceedings of the Workshop on Object-Oriented Technology*, Jyväskylä, Finland, pp. 151–154.

Bézivin, J., Dupé, G., Jouault, F., Pitette, G., & Rougui, J.E. (2003), "First experiments with the ATL model transformation language: Transforming XSLT into XQuery," *Proceedings of the 2nd OOPSLA Workshop on Generative Techniques in the Context of Model Driven Architecture*, Anaheim, CA.

Bézivin, J., Djurić, D., Devedžić, V., Favreau, J., Gašević, D., & Jouault, F. (2005), "An M3-neutral infrastructure for bridging model engineering and ontology engineering," *Proceedings of the 1st International Conference on Interoperability of Enterprise Software and Applications*, Geneva, Switzerland.

Bézivin, J., Büttner, F., Gogolla, M., Jouault, F. Kurtev, I., & Lindow, A. (2006), "Model transformations? Transformation Models!," *Proceedings of the ACM/IEEE 9th International Conference on Model Driven Engineering Languages and Systems*, Genoa, Italy, pp. 440–453.

Billington, J., Christensen, S., van Hee, K., Kindler, E., Kummer, O., Petrucci, L., Post, R., Stehno, C., & Weber, M. (2003), "The Petri net markup language: Concepts, technology, and tools," *Proceedings of the 24th International Conference on Applications and Theory of Petri Nets*, Eindhoven, pp. 483–505.

Bock, C. (2003), "UML without pictures," *IEEE Software*, Vol. 20, no. 5, pp. 33–35.

Bojārs, U. & Breslin, J.G. (2008), *SIOC Core Ontology Specification* [Online]. Available: http://rdfs.org/sioc/spec/ [Accessed: 2008, December 21].

Boley, H., Tabet, S., & Wagner, G. (2001), "Design rationale of RuleML: A markup language for Semantic Web rules," *Proceedings of the 1st Semantic Web Working Symposium*, Stanford University, CA, pp. 381–401.

Booch, G., Rumbaugh, J., & Jacobson, I. (1998), *The Unified Modeling Language User Guide*, Addison-Wesley, Reading, MA.

Brachman, R.J. (1979), "On the epistemological status of semantic networks," in *Associative Networks: Representations and Use of Knowledge by Computers*, ed. N.V. Findler, Academic Press, Burlington, MA, pp. 3–50.

Brachman, R.J. & Schmoltze, J.G. (1985), "An overview of the KL-ONE knowledge representation system," *Cognitive Science*, Vol. 9, no. 2, pp. 171–216.

Brachman, R.J., McGuinness, D.L., Patel-Schneider, P.F., Resnick, L.A., & Borgida, A. (1991), "Living with CLASSIC: When and how to use a KL-ONE like language," in *Principles of Semantic Networks*, ed. J. Sowa, Morgan Kaufmann, San Francisco, CA, pp. 401–456.

Brambilla, M., Ceri, S., Facca, F.M., Celino, I., Cerizza, D., Valle, E.D. (2007), "Model-driven design and development of semantic Web service applications," *ACM Transactions on Internet Technology*, Vol. 8, no. 1, article number 3.

Brickley, D. & Guha, R.V. (2004), *RDF Vocabulary Description Language 1.0: RDF Schema, W3C Working Draft* [Online]. Available: http://www.w3.org/TR/PR-rdf-schema [Accessed: 2008, December 28].

Brickley, D. & Miller, L. (2007), *FOAF Vocabulary Specification 0.91* [Online]. Available: http://xmlns.com/foaf/spec/ [Accessed: 2008, December 21].

Brockmans, S., Volz, R., Eberhart, A., & Löffler, P. (2004), "Visual modeling of OWL DL ontologies using UML," *Proceedings of the 3rd International Semantic Web Conference*, Hiroshima, pp. 108–213.

Brockmans, S., Haase, P, Hitzler, P., & Studer, R. (2006), "A Metamodel and UML Profile for Rule-extended OWL DL Ontologies," *Proceedings of the 3rd European Semantic Web Conference*, Budva, Montenegro, pp. 303–316.

Brown, A., Conallen, J., & Tropeano, D. (2005), "Introduction: Models, modeling, and model-driven architecture (MDA)," in *Model-Driven Software Development*, eds. S. Beydeda, M. Book, V. Gruhn, Springer, Berlin, Heidelberg, pp. 1–16.

Budinsky, F., Steinberg, D., Merks, E., Ellersick, R., & Grose, T.J. (2009), *Eclipse Modeling Framework, 2nd edition*, Addison-Wesley, Reading, MA.

Carlson, D. (2001), *Modeling XML Applications with UML: Practical e-Business Applications*, Addison-Wesley, Reading, MA.

Ceccaroni, L. & Kendall, E. (2003), "A graphical environment for ontology development," *Proceedings of the 2nd International Joint Conference on Autonomous Agents and Multiagent Systems*, Melbourne, pp. 958–959.

Chandrasekaran, B., Josephson, J.R., & Benjamins, V.R. (1999), "What are ontologies, and why do we need them?" *IEEE Intelligent Systems*, Vol. 14, no. 1, pp. 20–26.

Chaudhri, V.K., Farquhar, A., Fikes, R., Karp, P.D., & Rice, J.P. (1998), *Open Knowledge Base Connectivity 2.0.3* [Online]. Available: http://www.ai.sri.com/~okbc/spec/okbc2/okbc2.html [Accessed: 2008, December 28].

Clark, A. (2001), *Mindware: An Introduction to the Philosophy of Cognitive Science*, Oxford University Press, New York.

Clark, P. & Porter, B. (2004), *KM – the Knowledge Machine 2.0: Users Manual* [Online]. Available: http://www.cs.utexas.edu/users/mfkb/km/userman.pdf [Accessed: 2008, December 28].

Community Transitions (2008), Neuropsychological Terms and Definitions [Online]. Available: http://www.brainrehab.org/NeuropsychTerms.html [Accessed: 2008, December 17].

Conallen, J. (2002), *Building Web Applications with UML*, 2nd edition, Addison-Wesley, Reading, MA.

Corcho, O., Fernández-López, M., & Gómez-Pérez, A. (2002), "Methodologies, tools and languages for building ontologies. Where is their meeting point?" *Data and Knowledge Engineering*, Vol. 46, no. 1, pp. 41–64.

Cranefield, S. (2001a), "Networked knowledge representation and exchange using UML and RDF," *Journal of Digital Information*, Vol. 1, no. 8, article no. 44, 2001-02-15.

Cranefield, S. (2001b), "UML and the Semantic Web," *Proceedings of the Semantic Web Working Symposium*, Stanford University, CA, pp. 113–130.

Czarnecki, K. & Helsen, S. (2006), "Feature-based survey of model transformation approaches," *IBM Systems Journal*, Vol. 45, no. 3, pp. 621–645.

DAML Ontology Library (2008), *DAML Ontology Library, DARPA* [Online]. Available: http://www.daml.org/ontologies/ [Accessed: 2008, December 28].

Davies, J., Fensel, D., et al. (eds.) (2002), *Towards the Semantic Web: Ontology-driven Knowledge Management*. John Wiley, New York.

Davis, I. (2006), *GRDDL Primer* [Online]. Available: http://www.w3.org/TR/2006/WD-grddl-primer-20061002/ [Accessed: 2008, December 23].

Davis, R., Shrobe, H., & Szolovits, P. (1993), "What is a knowledge representation?" *AI Magazine*, Vol. 14, no. 1, pp. 17–33.

DC Metadata Schema (2008), *Dublin Core Metadata Schema* [Online]. Available: http://dublincore.org/documents/dcmi-terms/ [Accessed: 2008, December 28].

Decker, S., Melnik, S., van Harmelen, F., Fensel, D., Klein, M., Broekstra, J., Erdmann, M., & Horrocks, I. (2000), "The Semantic Web: The roles of XML and RDF," *IEEE Internet Computing*, Vol. 4, no. 5, pp. 63–74.

Denny, M. (2002), *Ontology Building: A Survey of Editing Tools* [Online]. Available: http://www.xml.com/pub/a/2002/11/06/ontologies.html [Accessed: 2008, December 28].

Denny, M. (2004), *Ontology Tools Survey, Revisited* [Online]. Available: http://www.xml.com/pub/a/2004/07/14/onto.html [Accessed: 2008, December 28].

Devedžić, V. (1999), "Ontologies: Borrowing from software patterns," *ACM Intelligence*, Vol. 10, no. 3, pp. 14–24.

Devedžić, V. (2002), "Understanding ontological engineering," *Communications of the ACM*, Vol. 45, no. 4, pp. 136–144.

Devedžić, V. (2004a), "Education and the semantic web," *International Journal of Artificial Intelligence in Education*, Vol. 14, pp. 39–65.

Devedžić, V. (2004b), "Web intelligence and artificial intelligence in education," *Educational Technology & Society*, Vol. 7, no. 4, pp. 29–39.

deVos, A. & Rowbotham, C.T. (2001), "Knowledge representation for power system modelling," *Proceedings of the 22nd International Conference on Power Industry Computer Applications*, Sydney, pp. 50–56.

deVos, A., Widergren, S.E., & Zhu, J. (2001), "XML for CIM Model Exchange," *Proceedings of the 22nd International Conference on Power Industry Computer Applications*, Sydney, pp. 31–37.

Dirckze, R. (2002), *Java Metadata Interface (JMI) Specification Version 1.0* [Online]. Available: http://jcp.org/en/jsr/detail?id=40 [Accessed: 2008, November 14].

Djurić, D. (2004), "MDA-based ontology infrastructure," *Computer Science and Information Systems*, Vol. 1, no. 1, pp. 91–116.

Djurić, D., Gašević, D., & Devedžić, V. (2005a), "Ontology modeling and MDA," *Journal of Object Technology*, Vol. 4, no. 1, pp. 109–128.

Djurić, D., Gašević, D., Devedžić, V., & Damjanović, V. (2005b), "A UML profile for OWL ontologies," in *Model Driven Architecture (European MDA Workshops: Foundations and Applications, MDAFA 2003 and MDAFA 2004, Twente, The Netherlands, June 26–27, 2003 and Linköping, Sweden, June 10–11, 2004. Revised Selected Papers)*, eds. U. Aßmann, M. Aksit, & A. Rensink, Lecture Notes in Computer Science, No. 3599, Springer, Berlin, Heidelberg, pp. 204–219.

Djurić, D., Gašević, D., & Devedžić, V. (2005c), "MDA standards for ontology development" in *Ontologies in the Context of Information Systems*, eds. R. Sharman, R. Ramesh, & R. Kishore, Springer, Heidelberg.

Djurić, D., Gašević, D., & Devedžić, V. (2006), "The Tao of modeling spaces", *Journal of Object Technology*, Vol. 5, no.8, Nov-Dec 2006, pp. 125–147.

Djurić, D., Devedžić, V., & Gašević, D. (2007), "Adopting software engineering trends in AI", *IEEE Intelligent Systems*, Vol. 22, no.1, 2007, pp. 59–66.

DOM (2005), *Document Object Model (DOM), W3C* [Online]. Available: http://www.w3.org/DOM/ [Accessed: 2008, December 28].

Domingue, J., Dzbor, M., & Motta, E. (2004), "Semantic layering with Magpie," in *Handbook on Ontologies*, eds. S. Staab & R. Studer, Springer, Berlin, Heidelberg, pp. 533–553.

Duddy, K. (2002), "UML2 must enable a family of languages," *Communications of the ACM*, Vol. 45, no. 11, pp. 73–75.

DUET (2008), *DAML-UML Enhanced Tool (DUET) Documents* [Online]. Available: http://codip.grci.com/wwwlibrary/wwwlibrary/wwwlibrary/DUET_Docs/ [Accessed: 2008, December 2008].

Durkin, J. (1994), *Expert Systems: Design and Development*, Macmillan, New York.

Duval, E. (2002), *IEEE Standard for Learning Object Metadata, IEEE Learning Technology Standardization Committee* [Online]. Available: http://ltsc.ieee.org/wg12/files/LOM_1484_12_1_v1_Final_Draft.pdf [Accessed: 2008, December 28].

e-Learning Guru (2008), *e-Learning Guru, Glossary* [Online]. Available: http://e-learningguru.com/gloss.htm [Accessed: 2008, December 28].

Evans, R. & Gazdar, G. (1996), "DATR: A language for lexical knowledge representation," *Computational Linguistics*, Vol. 22, no. 2, pp. 167–216.

Falkovych, K., Sabou, M., & Stuckenschmidt, H. (2003), "UML for the Semantic Web: Transformation-based approaches," in *Knowledge Transformation for the Semantic Web*, eds. B. Omelayenko & M. Klein, Frontiers in Artificial Intelligence and Applications, Vol. 95, IOS, Amsterdam, pp. 92–106.

Favre, J.M. (2004a), "Foundations of Model (Driven) (Reverse) Engineering: Models – Episode I, Stories of the Fidus Papyrus and of the Solarus," *In Proceedings of Dagstuhl Seminar 04101 on Language Engineering for Model-Driven Software Development*, Dagsthul, Germany.

Favre, J.M. (2004b), "Foundations of the Meta-pyramids: Languages and Metamodels – Episode II, Story of Thotus the Baboon," *Proceedings of Dagstuhl Seminar 04101 on Language Engineering for Model-Driven Software Development*, Dagsthul, Germany.

Fensel, D. (2004), *Ontologies: A Silver Bullet for Knowledge Management and Electronic Commerce*, 2nd edition, Springer, Berlin, Heidelberg.

Fensel, D. & Musen, M.A. (2001), "The Semantic Web: A brain for humankind," *IEEE Intelligent Systems*, Vol. 16, no. 2, pp. 24–25.

Fensel, D., van Harmelen, F., Horrocks, I., McGuinness, D.L., & Patel-Schneider, P.F. (2001), "OIL: An ontology infrastructure for the Semantic Web," *IEEE Intelligent Systems*, Vol. 16, no. 2, pp. 38–45.

Fernández-López, M., Gómez-Pérez, A., Sierra, J.P., & Sierra, A.P. (1999), "Building a chemical ontology using Methontology and the Ontology Design Environment," *IEEE Intelligent Systems*, Vol. 14, no. 1, pp. 37–46.

Fikes, R. (1998), *Multi-use Ontologies, Stanford University* [Online]. Available: http://www.ksl.stanford.edu/people/fikes/cs222/1998/Ontologies/tsld001.htm [Accessed: 2008, December 28].

Fowler, M. (2003), *UML Distilled, A Brief Guide to the Standard Object Modeling Language*, 3rd edition, Addison-Wesley, Reading, MA.

Frankel, S.D. (2003), *Model Driven Architecture: Applying MDA to Enterprise Computing*, Wiley, New York.

Friedman-Hill, E. (2003), *Jess in Action*, Manning, Greenwich, UK.

Gaines, B.R. (1991), "An interactive visual language for term subsumption languages," *Proceedings of the 12th International Joint Conference on Artificial Intelligence*, Sydney, pp. 817–823.

Gamma, E. & Beck, K. (2004), *Contributing to Eclipse: Principles, Patterns, and Plug-Ins*, Addison-Wesley, Reading, MA.

Gamma, E., Helm, R., Johnson, R., & Vlissides, J. (1995), *Design Patterns: Elements of Reusable Object-Oriented Software*, Addison-Wesley, Reading, MA.

Gangemi, A. & Presutti, V. (2009), "Ontology Design Patterns," in *Handbook on Ontologies,* 2nd edition, eds. S. Staab & R. Studer, Springer, Berlin, Heidelberg, in press.

Gardner, T., Griffin, C., Koehler, J., & Hauser, R. (2003), "A review of OMG MOF 2.0 Query/Views/Transformations submissions and recommendations towards the final standard," *Proceedings of the 1st International Workshop on Metamodeling for MDA*, York, UK.

Gašević, D. & Devedžić, V. (2004), "Reusing Petri nets through the Semantic Web," *Proceedings of the 1st European Semantic Web Symposium*, Heraklion, Greece, pp. 284–298.

Gašević, D. & Devedžić, V. (2007), "Interoperable Petri net models via ontology," *International Journal of Web Engineering and Technology*, Vol. 3, no. 4, 2007, pp. 374–396.

Gašević, D. & Hatala, M. (2006), "Ontology mappings to improve learning resource search," *British Journal of Educational Technology*, Vol. 37, no. 3, pp. 375–389.

Gašević, D., Djurić, D., Devedzić, V., & Damjanović, V. (2004a), "Converting UML to OWL ontologies," *Proceedings of the 13th International World Wide Web Conference on Alternate Track Papers & Posters*, NY, pp. 488–489.

Gašević, D., Djurić, D., Devedžić, V., & Damjanović, V. (2004b), "UML for read-to-use OWL ontologies," *Proceedings of the 2nd IEEE International Conference on Intelligent Systems*, Vrana, Bulgaria, pp. 485–490.

Gašević, D., Djurić, D., & Devedžić, V. (2005), "Bridging MDA and OWL ontologies," *Journal of Web Engineering*, Vol. 4, no. 2, pp. 119–134.

Gašević, D., Kaviani, N., & Hatala, M. (2007), "On metamodeling in megamodels," *Proceedings of the ACM/IEEE 10th International Conference on Model Driven Engineering Languages and Systems*, Nashville, TN, pp. 91–105.

Genesereth, M.R. & Fikes, R.E. (1992), *Knowledge Interchange Format, Version 3.0, Reference Manual* [Online]. Available: http://www-ksl.stanford.edu/knowledge-sharing/papers/kif.ps [Accessed: 2008, December 28].

Ginsberg, A. (2006), *RIF Use Cases and Requirements*, W3C Working Draft [Online]. Available: http://www.w3.org/TR/rif-ucr/ [Accessed: 2008, December 21]

Gómez-Pérez, A. & Corcho, O. (2002), "Ontology languages for the Semantic Web," *IEEE Intelligent Systems*, Vol. 17, no. 1, pp. 54–60.

Graves, A. (2006), *An RDF Representation of WordNet* [Online]. Available: http://wordnet.princeton.edu/~agraves/index_archivos/Page381.htm [Accessed: 2008, December 26].

Grose, T., Doney, G., & Brodsky, S. (2002), *Mastering XMI: Java Programming with XMI, XML, and UML*, Wiley, New York.

Gruber, T.R. (1992), *Ontolingua: A Mechanism to Support Portable Ontologies*, Knowledge Systems Laboratory, Stanford University, CA.

Gruber, T.R. (1993), "A translation approach to portable ontology specifications," *Knowledge Acquisition*, Vol. 5, no. 2, pp. 199–220.

Gruber, T.R. (2005), *Ontology of Folksonomy: A Mash-up of Apples and Oranges* [Online]. Available: http://tomgruber.org/writing/ontology-of-folksonomy.htm [Accessed: 2008, December 26].

Guarino, N. (1995), "Formal ontology, conceptual analysis and knowledge representation," *International Journal of Human-Computer Studies*, Vol. 43, no. 5/6, pp. 625–640.

Haarslev, V. & Moller, R. (2001), "RACER system description," *Lecture Notes in Computer Science*, Vol. 2083, pp. 701–705.

Haase, P., Broekstra, J., Eberhart, A., & Volz, R. (2004), "A comparison of RDF query languages," *Proceedings of the 3rd International Semantic Web Conference*, Hiroshima, pp. 502–517.

Haase, P., Brockmans, S., Palma, R., Euzenat, J., & d'Aquin, M. (2007), *Updated Version of the Networked Ontology Model*, NeOn Project Deliverable D1.1.2 [Online]. Available: http://www.neon-project.org/web-content/index.php?view=weblink&catid=17%3Aproject-reports&id=86%3Ad112-networked-ontology-model-eval&option=com_weblinks [Accessed: 2008, December 14]

Hagget, P. & Chorley, R.J. (1967), "Models, paradigms and new geography," in *Models in Geography*, Methuen, London.

Halpin, H. & Shepard, H. (2006), *Evolving Ontologies from Folksonomies: Tagging as a Complex System* [Online]. Available: http://www.ibiblio.org/hhalpin/homepage/notes/taggingcss.html [Accessed: 2008, December 26].

Handschuh, S. & Staab, S. (2002), "Authoring and annotation of Web pages in CREAM," *Proceedings of the 11th International World Wide Web Conference*, Honolulu, pp. 462–473.

Handschuh, S. & Staab, S. (eds.) (2003a), *Annotation for the Semantic Web*, IOS, Amsterdam.

Handschuh, S. & Staab, S. (2003b), "CREAM – creating metadata for the Semantic Web," *Computer Networks*, Vol. 42, no. 5, pp. 579–598.

Handschuh, S., Staab, S., & Volz, R. (2003a), "On deep annotation," *Proceedings of the 12th International World Wide Web Conference*, Budapest, pp. 431–438.

Handschuh, S., Volz, R., & Staab, S. (2003b), "Annotation for the deep Web," *IEEE Intelligent Systems*, Vol. 18, no. 5, pp. 42–48.

Heflin, J. & Hendler, J. (2001), "A portrait of the Semantic Web in action," *IEEE Intelligent Systems*, Vol. 16, no. 2, pp. 54–59.

Hendler, J. (2001), "Agents and the semantic web," *IEEE Intelligent Systems*, Vol. 16, no. 2, pp. 30–37.

Hendler, J. (2007), "The dark side of the semantic web," *IEEE Intelligent Systems*, Vol. 22, no.1, pp. 2–4.

Hendler, J. & McGuinness, D. (2000), "The DARPA agent markup language," *IEEE Intelligent Systems*, Vol. 15, no. 6, pp. 72–73.

Hillairet, G. (2007), *ATL Use Case – ODM Implementation (Bridging UML and OWL)* [Online]. Available: http://www.eclipse.org/m2m/atl/usecases/ODMImplementation/ [Accessed: 2008, December 15].

Hofstadter, D. (1994), *Fluid Concepts and Creative Analysis – Computer Models of the Fundamental Mechanisms of Thought*, Basic Books/Harper Collins, New York.

Hori, M., Euzenat, J., & Patel-Schneider, F.P. (2003), *OWL Web Ontology Language XML Presentation Syntax* [Online]. Available: http://www.w3.org/TR/owl-xmlsyntax/[Accessed: 2008, December 15].

Horrocks, I. (1997), *Optimising Tableaux Decision Procedures for Description Logics*. PhD Thesis. University of Manchester.

Horrocks, I. (2004), *The FaCT System* [Online]. Available: http://www.cs.man.ac.uk/~horrocks/FaCT/ [Accessed: 2008, December 26].

Horrocks, I. & van Harmelen, F. (2002), *Reference Description of the DAML+OIL Ontology Markup Language* [Online]. Available: http://www.daml.org/2001/03/reference [Accessed: 2008, December 28].

Horrocks, I., Patel-Scheider, P.F., Boley, H., Tabet, S., Grosof, B., & Dean, M. (2004), SWRL: A Semantic Web Rule Language Combining OWL and RuleML, W3C Member Submission [Online]. Available: http://www.w3.org/Submission/SWRL/ [Accessed: 2008, December 21]

IMS LD IM (2003), *IMS Learning Design Information Model, Version 1.0 Final Specification, Revision 20* [Online]. Available: http://www.imsglobal.org/learningdesign/ldv1p0/imsld_infov1p0.html [Accessed: 2008, December 28].

Jouault, F. & Kurtev, I. (2007), "On the interoperability of model-to-model transformation languages," *Science of Computer Programming*, Vol. 68, no. 3, pp. 114–137.

Jouault, F., Bézivin, J., & Kurtev, I. (2006), "TCS: a DSL for the Specification of Textual Concrete Syntaxes in Model Engineering," *Proceedings of the 5th International Conference on Generative Programming and Component Engineering*, Portland, USA, 249–254.

Jouault, J., Allilairea, F., Bézivin, J., & Kurtev, I. (2008), "ATL: A model transformation tool," *Science of Computer Programming*, Vol. 72, nos. 1–2, pp. 31–39.

Jovanović, J. (2005), *Dynamic Generation of Educational Contents on the Semantic Web*. MSc Thesis. University of Belgrade, Serbia.

Jovanović, J., Gašević, D., & Devedžić, V. (2004), "A GUI for Jess," *Expert Systems with Applications*, Vol. 26, no. 4, pp. 625–637.

Jovanović, J., Gašević, D., & Devedžić, V. (2005a), "TANGRAM: An ontology-based learning environment for intelligent information systems," *Proceedings of the 10th World Conference on E-Learning in Corporate, Government, Healthcare, and Higher Education (E-Learn2005)*, Vancouver, pp. 2966–2971.

Jovanović, J., Gašević, D., Verbert, K., & Duval, D. (2005b), "Ontology of learning object content structure," *Proceedings of the 12th International Conference on Artificial Intelligence in Education*, Amsterdam, pp. 322–329.

Jovanović, J., Gašević, D., & Devedžić, V. (2006a), "Dynamic assembly of personalized learning content on the semantic web," *Proceedings of the 3rd European Semantic Web Conference*, Budva, Montenegro, pp. 544–558.

Jovanović, J., Gašević, D., & Devedžić, V. (2006b), "Ontology-based automatic annotation of learning content," *International Journal on Semantic Web and Information Systems*, Vol. 2, no. 2, pp. 91–119.

Jovanović, J., Gašević, Brooks, C., Devedžić, V., Hatala, M., Eap, T., Richards, G. (2007a), "Using semantic web technologies for the analysis of learning content," IEEE Internet Computing, Vol. 11, no. 5.

Jovanović, J., Knight, C., Gašević, D., Richards, G. (2007b), "Ontologies for effective use of context in e-Learning settings," *Educational Technology & Society*, Vol. 10, no. 3, pp. 47–59.

Juerjens, J. (2003), *Secure Systems Development with UML*, Springer, Berlin, Heidelberg.

Kalfoglou, Y. (2001), "Exploring ontologies," in *Handbook of Software Engineering and Knowledge Engineering*, Vol. 1, Fundamentals, ed. S.K. Chang, World Scientific, Singapore, pp. 863–887.

Karp, R., Chaudhri, V., & Thomere, J. (1999), *XOL: An XML-Based Ontology Exchange Language*, Technical Report, SRI International [Online]. Available: http://www.ai.sri.com/~pkarp/xol/xol.html [Accessed: 2008, December 28].

Kendall, E.F., Dutra, M.E., & McGuinness, D.L. (2002), "Towards a commercial ontology development environment," *Proceedings of the 1st International Semantic Web Conference* (Posters and Demos), Chia, Sardinia.

Kifer, M., Lausen, G., & Wu, J. (1995), "Logical foundations of object oriented and frame-based languages," *Journal of the ACM*, Vol. 42, no. 4, pp. 741–843.

Klein, M. (2001), "Tutorial: The semantic web – XML, RDF, and relatives," *IEEE Intelligent Systems*, Vol. 16, no. 2, pp. 26–28.

Klein, M. & Visser, U. (2004), "Guest editors' introduction: Semantic web challenge 2003," *IEEE Intelligent Systems*, Vol. 19, no. 3, pp. 31–33.

Kleppe, A., Warmer, J., & Bast, W. (2003), *MDA Explained: The Model Driven Architecture: Practice and promise*, Addison-Wesley, Reading, MA.

Klint, P., Lämmel, R., & Verhoef, C. (2005), "Toward an engineering discipline for grammarware," *ACM Transactions on Software Engineering and Methodology*, Vol. 14, no. 3, pp. 331–380.

Knight, C., Gašević, D., & Richards, G. (2006), "An ontology-based framework for bridging learning design and learning content," *Educational Technology & Society*, Vol. 9, no. 1, pp. 23–37.

Knublauch, H. (2004), "Ontology-driven software development in the context of the Semantic Web: An example scenario with Protégé/OWL," *Proceedings of the International Workshop on the Model-Driven Semantic Web* (at the 8th International Conference on Enterprise Distributed Object Computing), Monterey, CA.

Knublauch, H., Fergerson, R.W., Noy, N.F., & Musen, M.A. (2004), "The Protégé OWL plugin: An open development environment for Semantic Web applications," *Proceedings of the 3rd International Semantic Web Conference*, Hiroshima, pp. 229–243.

Kobryn, C. (2001), "The road to UML 2.0: Fast track or detour," *Software Development Magazine*, April 2001, pp. 73–75.

Kopena, J. & Regli, W.C. (2003), "DAMLJessKB: A tool for reasoning with the Semantic Web," *IEEE Intelligent Systems*, Vol. 18, no. 3, pp. 74–77.

Koper, R. (2001), *Modeling Units of Study from a Pedagogical perspective – The Pedagogical Metamodel Behind EML* [Online]. Available: http://hdl.handle.net/1820/36 [Accessed: 2008, December 28].

Koper, R. & Olivier, B. (2004), "Representing the learning design of units of learning," *Educational Technology & Society*, Vol. 7, no. 3, pp. 97–111.

Krdžavac, N., Djurić, D., & Devedžić, V. (2006), "MDA-based architecture of a description logics reasoner," *Proceedings of 3rd IFIP Conference on Artificial Intelligence and Innovations (AIAI-2006)*, June 7–9, 2006, Athens, Greece, pp. 98–105.

Kremer, R. (1998), "Visual languages for knowledge representation," *Proceedings of the 11th Workshop on Knowledge Acquisition, Modeling and Management*, Banff, Canada.

Kurtev, I. (2005), *Adaptability of Model Transformations*. PhD Thesis, University of Twente, The Netherlands.

Kurtev, I. & van den Berg, K. (2003), "Model Driven Architecture based XML processing," *Proceedings of the ACM Symposium on Document Engineering*, Grenoble, France, pp. 246–248.

Kurtev, I., Bézivin, J., & Aksit, M. (2002), "Technological spaces: An initial appraisal," *Proceedings of the Confederated International Conferences CoopIS, DOA, and ODBASE, Industrial Track*, Irvine, CA.

Kühne, T. (2005), "Matters of (Meta)- modeling," *Software and Systems Modeling*, Vol. 5, no. 4, pp. 369–385.

Kühne, T. (2006), "Clarifying matters of (meta-) modeling: an author's reply," *Software and Systems Modeling*, Vol. 5, no. 4, pp. 395–401.

Larman, C. (2001), *Applying UML and Patterns: An Introduction to Object-Oriented Analysis and Design*, 2nd edition, Prentice-Hall, Upper Saddle River, NJ.

Lassila, O. (1998), "Web metadata: A matter of semantics," *IEEE Internet Computing*, Vol. 2, no. 4, pp. 30–37.

Lay, S., Pierre, G. (2006), *IMS Question and Test Interoperability Assessment Test, Section, and Item Information Model* [Online]. Available: http://www.imsglobal.org/question/qtiv2p1pd2/imsqti_infov2p1pd2.html [Accessed: 2008, December 26].

Leigh, J. (2008), *Getting Started With Sesame 2.2* [Online]. Available: http://wiki.aduna-software.org/confluence/display/SESDOC/GettingStarted [Accessed: 2008, December 26].

Lenat, D.B. (1995), "CYC: A large-scale investment in knowledge infrastructure," *Communications of the ACM*, Vol. 38, no. 11, pp. 33–38.

Lenat, D.B. & Guha, R.V. (1990), *Building Large Knowledge-Based Systems: Representation and Inference in the Cyc Project*, Addison-Wesley, Reading, MA.

Li, Y.F. (2007), *A Formal Modeling Approach to Ontology Engineering – Modeling, Transformation & Verification*, PhD Thesis, National University of Singapore, Singapore.

Luke, S. & Heflin, J. (2000), *SHOE 1.01. Proposed Specification*, SHOE Project Technical Report, University of Maryland [Online]. Available: http://www.cs.umd.edu/projects/plus/SHOE/spec.html [Accessed: 2008, December 28].

MacGregor, R. (1991), "Inside the LOOM classifier," *SIGART Bulletin*, Vol. 2, no. 3, pp. 70–76.

Maedche, A. & Staab, S. (2001), "Ontology learning for the semantic web," *IEEE Intelligent Systems*, Vol. 16, no. 2, pp. 72–79.

Manola, F. & Miller, E. (2004), *RDF Primer, W3C Recommendation* [Online]. Available: http://www.w3.org/TR/REC-rdf-syntax/ [Accessed: 2008, December 28].

Martin, D., Burstein, M., Hobbs, J., Lassila, O., McDermott, D., McIlraith, S., Narayanan, S., Paolucci, M., Parsia, B., Payne, T., Sirin, E., Srinivasan, N., & Sycara, K. (2004), *OWL-S: Semantic Markup for Web Services* [Online]. Available: http://www.daml.org/services/owl-s/1.1/overview/ [Accessed: 2008, December 28].

McBride, B. (2002), "Jena: A Semantic Web toolkit," *IEEE Internet Computing*, Vol. 6, no. 6, pp. 55–59.

McCarthy, J. (1999), *Concepts of Logical AI* [Online]. Available: http://www-formal.stanford.edu/jmc/concepts-ai/concepts-ai.html [Accessed: 2008, December 28].

McCarthy, P. (2004), *Introduction to Jena* [Online]. Available: http://www.ibm.com/developerworks/xml/library/j-jena/ [Accessed: 2008, December 24].

McGuinness, D.L. (2002), "Ontologies come of age," in *Spinning the Semantic Web: Bringing the World Wide Web to Its Full Potential*, eds. D. Fensel, J. Hendler, H. Lieberman, & W. Wahlster, MIT Press, Boston, MA, pp. 1–18.

McIlraith, S.A., Son, T.C., & Zeng, H. (2001), "Semantic Web services," *IEEE Intelligent Systems*, Vol. 16, no. 2, pp. 46–53.

Mellor, S.J., Clark, A.N., & Futagami, T. (2003a), "Guest editors' introduction: Model-driven development," *IEEE Software*, Vol. 20, no. 5, pp. 14–18.

Mellor, S.J., Scott, K., Uhl, A., & Weise, D. (2003b), *MDA Distilled: Principles of Model-Driven Architecture*, Addison-Wesley, Reading, MA.

Mens, T. & van Gorp, P. (2006), "A Taxonomy of Model Transformation," *Electronic Notes in Theoretical Computer Science*, Vol. 152, pp. 125–142 .

Middleton, S.E., De Roure, D., & Shadbolt, N.R. (2004), "Ontology-based recommender systems," in *Handbook on Ontologies*, eds. S. Staab & R. Studer, Springer, Berlin, Heidelberg, pp. 477–498.

Milanović, M. (2007a), *ATL Use Case – Sharing Rules Between OCL/UML and SWRL/OWL* [Online]. Available: http://www.eclipse.org/m2m/atl/usecases/SharingRulesBetweenOCLUML_SWRLOWL/ [Accessed: 2008, December 22].

Milanović, M. (2007b), *Modeling rules on the Semantic Web*. MSc Thesis, University of Belgrade, Serbia.

Milanović, M., Gašević, D., Giurca, A., Wagner, G., & Devedžić, V. (2006), "Towards sharing rules between OWL/SWRL and UML/OCL," *Electronic Communications of the European Association of Software Science and Technology*, Vol. 5.

Milanović, M., Gašević, D., Giurca, A., Wagner, G., & Devedžić, V. (2008), "Sharing OCL constraints by using web rules," *Electronic Communications of the European Association of Software Science and Technology*, Vol. 9.

Miles, A., Brickley, D. (2005), *SKOS Core Guide, W3C Working Draft* [Online]. Available: http://www.w3.org/TR/2005/WD-swbp-skos-core-guide-20051102 [Accessed: 2008, December 25].

Miller, J. & Mukerji, J. (2003), *MDA Guide Version 1.0.1*, OMG Document omg/2003-06-01, [Online]. Available: http://www.omg.org/docs/omg/03-06-01.pdf [Accessed: 2008, December 14].

Miller, G.A., Fellbaum, C., Tengi, R., Wakefield, R., Langone, H., Haskell, B.R. (2006), *WordNet – A Lexical Database for the English Language* [Online]. Available: http://wordnet.princeton.edu/ [Accessed: 2008, December 28].

Minsky, M. (1985), *The Society of Mind,* Simon and Shuster, New York.

Mitchell, F. (1998), *An Introduction to Knowledge Acquisition,* Dept. of Computer Science, University of Aberdeen, UK.

Mizoguchi, R. & Kitamura, Y. (2001), "Knowledge systematization through ontology engineering – a key technology for successful intelligent systems," Invited paper, *Pacific-Asian Conference on Intelligent Systems,* Seoul.

Motik, B., Patel-Schneider, P.F., & Horrocks, I. (2007), *OWL 1.1 Web Ontology Language – Structural Specification and Functional-Style Syntax* [Online]. Available: http://www.webont.org/owl/1.1/owl_specification.html [Accessed: 2008, December 14].

Myers, B.A. (1990), "Taxonomies of visual programming and program visualization," *Journal of Visual Languages and Computing,* Vol. 1, no. 1, pp. 97–123.

Naiburg, E.J. & Maksimchuk, R.A. (2001), *UML for Database Design,* Addison-Wesley, Reading, MA.

Navigli, R., Velardi, P., & Gangemi, A. (2003), "Ontology learning and its application to automated terminology translation," *IEEE Intelligent Systems,* Vol. 19, no. 1, pp. 22–31.

Neches, R., Fikes, R.E., Finin, T., Gruber, T.R., Senator, T., & Swartout, W.R. (1991), "Enabling technology for knowledge sharing," *AI Magazine,* Vol. 12, no. 3, pp. 36–56.

Newell, A. (1982), "The knowledge level," *Artificial Intelligence,* Vol. 18, no. 1, pp. 82–127.

Niles, I. & Pease, A. (2001), "Towards a standard upper ontology," *Proceedings of the 2nd International Conference on Formal Ontology in Information Systems (FOIS-2001),* Ogunquit, ME, pp. 81–88.

Noy, N.F. & McGuinness, D.L. (2001), *Ontology Development 101: A Guide to Creating Your First Ontology,* Knowledge Systems Laboratory, Stanford University, CA.

Noy, N.F., Fergerson, R.W., & Musen, M.A. (2000), "The knowledge model of Protégé-2000: Combining interoperability and flexibility," *Proceedings of the 12th International Conference on Knowledge Engineering and Knowledge Management Methods, Models, and Tools,* Juan-les-Pins, France, pp. 17–32.

Noy, N.F., Sintek, M., Decker, S., Crubézy, M., Fergerson, R.W., & Musen, M.A. (2001), "Creating Semantic Web contents with Protégé-2000," *IEEE Intelligent Systems,* Vol. 16, no. 2, pp. 60–71.

NumberNut.Com (2008), *NumberNut.Com Glossary* [Online]. Available: http://www.numbernut.com/glossary/r.shtml [Accessed: 2008, December 27].

OAW (2008), *openArchitectureWare: a platform for model-driven software development* [Online]. Available: http://www.openarchitectureware.org/ [Accessed: 2008, December 15].

ODM DSTC (2003), *Ontology Definition Metamodel,* DSTC Initial Submission, OMG Document ad/2003-08-01 [Online]. Available: http://www.omg.org/cgi-bin/doc?ad/03-08-01 [Accessed: 2008, December 14].

ODM Gentleware (2003), *Ontology Definition Metamodel*, Gentleware Initial Submission, OMG Document ad/03-08-09 [Online]. Available: http://www.omg.org/cgi-bin/doc?ad/03-08-09 [Accessed: 2008, December 14].

ODM IBM (2003), *Ontology Definition Metamodel*, IBM Initial Submission ad/03-07-02, OMG Document ad/03-07-02 [Online]. Available: http://www.omg.org/cgi-bin/doc?ad/03-07-02 [Accessed: 2008, December 14].

ODM Sandpiper&KSL (2003), *Ontology Definition Metamodel*, Sandpiper Software Inc and KSL Initial Submission, OMG Document ad/03-08-06 [Online]. Available: http://www.omg.org/cgi-bin/doc?ad/03-08-06 [Accessed: 2008, December 14].

OMG BPDM (2008), *Business Process Definition Metamodel (BPDM), Version 1.0*, OMG Document formal/2008-11-05 [Online]. Available: http://www.omg.org/spec/BPDM/1.0/zip [Accessed: 2008, December 14].

OMG CORBA (2002), *UML Profile for CORBA, v 1.0*, OMG Document formal/02-04-01 [Online]. Available: http://www.omg.org/cgi-bin/doc?formal/02-04-01 [Accessed: 2008, December 28].

OMG DAF (2005), *Utility Management System Data Access Facility, v2.0.1*, OMG Document formal/05-06-01 [Online]. Available: http://www.omg.org/cgi-bin/doc?formal/2005-06-03 [Accessed: 2008, December 14].

OMG EAI (2004), *UML Profile for Enterprise Application Integration (EAI)*, OMG Document formal/04-03-26 [Online]. Available: http://www.omg.org/cgi-bin/doc?formal/2004-03-26 [Accessed: 2008, December 28].

OMG MOF (2002), *OMG Meta Object Facility (MOF) Specification v1.4*, OMG Document formal/02-04-03 [Online]. Available: http://www.omg.org/cgi-bin/apps/doc?formal/02-04-03.pdf [Accessed: 2008, December 14].

OMG MOF2 (2006), *Meta Object Facility (MOF) Core Specification OMG Available Specification Version 2.0*, OMG Document formal/06-01-01 [Online]. http://www.omg.org/docs/formal/06-01-01.pdf [Accessed: 2008, December 12].

OMG MOF-to-Text (2004), *OMG MOF Model to Text Transformation Language – Request for Proposal*, OMG Document ad/04-04-07 [Online]. Available: http://www.omg.org/docs/ad/04-04-07.pdf [Accessed: 2008, December 28].

OMG OCL2 (2006), *OMG Object Constraint Language, Version 2.0*, OMG Document formal/06-05-01, [Online]. Available: http://www.omg.org/spec/OCL/2.0/PDF [Accessed: 2008, December 14].

OMG ODM (2004), *Ontology Definition Metamodel – Preliminary Revised Submission to OMG RFP ad/2003-03-40, Vol. 1* [Online]. Available: http://codip.grci.com/odm/draft [Accessed: 2008, December 28].

OMG ODM (2007), *Ontology Definition Metamodel – OMG Adopted Specification*, OMG Document ptc/2007-09-09 [Online]. Available: http://www.omg.org/cgi-bin/apps/doc?ptc/07-09-09.pdf [Accessed: 2008, December 11].

OMG ODM RFP (2003), *OMG Ontology Definition Metamodel Request for Proposal*, OMG Document: ad/2003-03-40 [Online]. Available: http://www.omg.org/cgi-bin/doc?ad/2003-03-40 [Accessed: 2008, December 14].

OMG ODM RFP (2005), *Ontology Definition Metamodel – Third Revised Submission to OMG RFP ad/2003-03-40*, OMG Document ad/05-08-01

[Online]. Available: http://www.omg.org/cgi-bin/apps/doc?ad/05-08-01.pdf [Accessed: 2008, December 28].

OMG PRR (2007), *Production Rule Representation (PRR), Version 1.0 Beta 1*, OMG Document dtc/2007-11-04 [Online]. Available: http://www.omg.org/spec/PRR/1.0/Beta1/PDF [Accessed: 2008, December 14].

OMG QVT (2008), *OMG MOF QVT Final Adopted Specification*, OMG document 05-11-01 [Online]. Available: http://www.omg.org/docs/ptc/05-11-01.pdf [Accessed: 2008, December 11].

OMG SBVR (2008), *Semantics of Business Vocabulary and Business Rules (SBVR), Version 1.0*, OMG Document formal/08-01-02, [Online]. Available: http://www.omg.org/spec/SBVR/1.0/PDF [Accessed: 2008, December 14].

OMG UML (2007a), *OMG Unified Modeling Language (UML) Specification: Infrastructure, Version 2.1.2, Final Available Specification*, OMG Document formal/07-11-04 [Online]. Available: http://www.omg.org/spec/UML/2.1.2/Infrastructure/PDF/ [Accessed: 2008, December 11].

OMG UML (2007b), *OMG Unified Modeling Language: Superstructure, Version 2.1.2, Final Available Specification*, OMG Document formal/07-11-02 [Online]. Available:http://www.omg.org/spec/UML/2.1.2/Superstructure/PDF [Accessed: 2008, December 11].

OMG XMI (2002), *OMG XMI Specification, v1.2*, OMG Document formal/02-01-01 [Online]. Available: http://www.omg.org/cgi-bin/doc?formal/2002-01-01 [Accessed: 2008, December 28].

O'Reilly, T. (2005), *What Is Web 2.0?* [Online]. Available: http://www.oreillynet.com/pub/a/oreilly/tim/news/2005/09/30/what-is-web-20.html [Accessed: 2008, December 22].

OWL Ontology Library (2008), *OWL Ontology Library*, Stanford University [Online]. Available: http://protege.stanford.edu/plugins/owl/owl-library/ [Accessed: 2008, December 28].

Pan, Y., Xie, G.T., Ma, L., Yang, Y., Qiu, Z., & Lee, J. (2006), "Model-Driven Ontology Engineering," *Journal on Data Semantics*, Vol. 7, pp. 57–78.

Parreiras, F.S., Staab, S., & Winter, A. (2007a), "On marrying ontological and metamodeling technical spaces," *Proceedings of the 6th Joint Meeting of the European Software Engineering Conference and the ACM SIGSOFT International Symposium on Foundations of Software Engineering*, Dubrovnik, Croatia, pp. 484–497.

Parreiras, F.S., Staab, S., & Winter, A. (2007b), "TwoUse: Integrating UML Models and OWL Ontologies," *Fachbereich Informatik 2007*, Arbeitsberichte aus dem Fachbereich Informatik, University of Koblenz, Koblenz, Germany [Online]. Available: http://www.uni-koblenz.de/~aggrimm/arbeitsberichte/arbeitsberichte_16_2007.pdf [Accessed: 2008, December 19]

Parreiras, F.S., Staab, S., Schenk, S., & Winter, A. (2008), "Model Driven Specification of Ontology Translations," *Proceedings of the 27th International Conference on Conceptual Modeling*, Barcelona, Spain, pp. 439–448.

Paslaru Bontas, E. & Mochol, M. (2005), "Towards a reuse-oriented methodology for ontology engineering," *Proceedings of the 7th International Conference on Terminology and Knowledge Engineering*, Copenhagen, Denmark

[Online]. Available: http://page.mi.fu-berlin.de/mochol/papers/TKE2005.pdf [Accessed: 2008, December 22].

Patel-Schneider, P., Horrocks, I. (2007), *OWL 1.1 Web Ontology Language Overview, Editor's Draft of 23 May 2007* [Online]. Available: http://www.webont.org/owl/1.1/overview.html [Accessed: 2008, December 11].

Patel-Schneider, P.F., Hayes, P., Horrocks, I., & Harmelen, F. (2004), *A Proposal for a SWRL Extension to First-Order Logic* [Online]. Available: http://www.daml.org/2003/11/swrl/ [Accessed: 2008, December 14].

Payne, T. & Lassila, O. (2004), "Semantic Web services," *IEEE Intelligent Systems*, Vol. 19, no. 4, pp. 14–15.

Petri, C.A. (1962), *Kommunikation mit Automaten*, Schriften des IIM Nr. 3, Institut für Instrumentelle Mathematik, Bon.

Petri Net Standards (2008), *Petri Net Standards* [Online]. Available: http://www.informatik.uni-hamburg.de/TGI/PetriNets/standardisation/ [Accessed: 2008, December 28].

Phillweb (2008), *Theoretical Resources Off- and On-Line* [Online]. Available: http://www.phillwebb.net/Topics/Knowledge/KnowledgeDef.htm [Accessed: 2008, December 23].

Poole, J. (2002), *Common Warehouse Metamodel: An Introduction to the Standard for Data Warehouse Integration*, Wiley, New York.

Preece, A. & Decker, S. (2002), "Intelligent web services," *IEEE Intelligent Systems*, Vol. 17, no. 1, pp. 15–17.

Protégé (2008), *Protégé*, Stanford University [Online]. Available: http://protege.stanford.edu/ [Accessed: 2008, December 14].

Protégé Ontologies Library (2005), *ProtegeOntologiesLibrary* [Online]. Available: http://protege.cim3.net/cgi-bin/wiki.pl?ProtegeOntologiesLibrary [Accessed: 2008, December 28].

Protégé UML (2008), *Protégé UML Backend: Store Protégé Ontologies in UML* [Online]. Available: http://protege.cim3.net/cgi-bin/wiki.pl?UMLBackend [Accessed: 2008, December 14].

Protégé XMI (2008), *Protégé XMI Backend: Store Protégé Ontologies in MOF Metamodels* [Online]. Available: http://protege.cim3.net/cgi-bin/wiki.pl?XMIBackend [Accessed: 2008, December 14].

Prud'hommeaux, E. & Seaborne, A. (2008), *SPARQL Query Language for RDF*, W3C Recommendation 15 January 2008, [Online]. Available: http://www.w3.org/TR/rdf-sparql-query/ [Accessed: 2008, December 11].

Pulman, S.G. (1996), "Controlled language for knowledge representation," *Proceedings of the 1st International Workshop on Controlled Language Applications*, Katholieke Universiteit Leuven, Belgium, pp. 233–242.

R2ML (2008), *R2ML: REWERSE Rule Markup Language* [Online]. Available: http://oxygen.informatik.tu-cottbus.de/rewerse-i1/?q=node/6 [Accessed: 2008, December 21]

Radenković, S., Krdžavac, N., & Devedžić, V. (2008), "Towards more intelligent assessment systems." In: Technology Enhanced Learning – Best Practices, eds. M.D. Lytras, D. Gašević, P. Ordonez de Pablos, & W. Huang, IGI Publishing, New York, pp. 257–283.

Rapaport, W.J. (2000), "Cognitive science" in *Encyclopedia of Computer Science*, 4th edition, eds. A. Ralston, E.D. Reilly, & D. Hemmendinger, Grove's Dictionaries, New York, pp. 227–233.

Reisig, W. (1985), *Petri Nets: An Introduction*, Springer-Verlag, Berlin, Germany.

Richards, G. (2002), "Editorial: The challenges of the learning object paradigm," *Canadian Journal of Learning and Technology*, Vol. 28, no. 3, pp. 3–10.

RuleML (2008), *RuleML – The Rule Markup Initiative* [Online]. Available: http://www.ruleml.org/ [Accessed: 2008, December 21].

Rumbaugh, J., Jacobson, I., & Booch, G. (1998), *The Unified Modeling Language Reference Manual*, Addison-Wesley, Reading, MA.

Rumbaugh, J., Jacobson, I., & Booch, G. (2004), *The Unified Modeling Language Reference Manual*, 2nd edition, Addison-Wesley, Reading, MA.

Russell, S. & Norvig, P. (2002), *Artificial Intelligence: A Modern Approach*, 2nd edition, Prentice-Hall, Englewood Cliffs, NJ.

Schreiber, G., Wielinga, B., de Hoog, R., Akkermans, H., & van de Velde, W. (1994), "CommonKADS: A comprehensive methodology for KBS development," *IEEE Expert*, Vol. 9, no. 6, pp. 28–37.

Scott Cost, R., Finin, T., Joshi, A., Peng, Y., Nicholas, C., Soboroff, I., Chen, H., Kagal, L., Perich, F., Zou, Y., & Tolia, S. (2002), "ITtalks: A case study in the Semantic Web and DAML+OIL," *IEEE Intelligent Systems*, Vol. 17, no. 1, pp. 40–47.

Seaborne, A. (2004), *RDQL – A Query Language for RDF* [Online]. Available: http://www.w3.org/Submission/2004/SUBM-RDQL-20040109/ [Accessed: 2008, December 26].

Seidewitz, E. (2003), "What models mean," *IEEE Software*, Vol. 20, no. 5, pp. 26–32.

Selic, B. (2003), "The pragmatics of model-driven development," *IEEE Software*, Vol. 20, no. 5, pp. 19–25.

Sheth, A., Ramakrishnan, C., & Thomas, C. (2005), "Semantics for the Semantic Web: The implicit, the formal and the powerful," *International Journal on Semantic Web & Information Systems*, Vol. 1, no. 1, pp. 1–18.

Sigel, J. (2001), *Developing in OMG's Model-Driven Architecture, Revision 2.6*, Object Management Group White Paper [Online]. Available: http://www.omg.org/docs/omg/01-12-01.pdf [Accessed: 2008, December 28].

Sirin, E., Parsia, B., & Hendler, J. (2004), "Filtering and selecting Semantic Web services with interactive composition techniques," *IEEE Intelligent Systems*, Vol. 19, no. 4, pp. 42–49.

Sirin, E., Parsia, B., Grau, B.C., Kalyanpur, A., & Katz, Y (2007), "Pellet: A Practical OWL DL Reasoner," *Journal of Web Semantics*, Vol. 5, no. 2, pp. 51–53.

Smith, M.K., Welty, C., & McGuinness, D.L. (2004), *OWL Web Ontology Language Guide*, W3C [Online]. Available: http://www.w3.org/TR/owl-guide/ [Accessed: 2008, December 28].

Sowa, J.F. (2000), *Knowledge Representation: Logical, Philosophical, and Computational Foundations*, Brooks Cole, Pacific Grove, CA.

Staab, S. & Studer, R. (eds.) (2004), *Handbook on Ontologies*, Springer, Berlin, Heidelberg.

Stanford Encyclopedia of Philosophy (2008), *Stanford Encyclopedia of Philosophy* [Online]. Available: http://plato.stanford.edu/entries/cognitive-science/ [Accessed: 2008, December 28].

Štrbac, P. (2002), *An Approach to Modeling Communication Protocols by Using Upgraded Petri Nets*, PhD Thesis, Military Academy, Belgrade, Serbia.

Stuckenschmidt, H. & van Harmelen, F. (2005), *Information Sharing on the Semantic Web*, Springer, Berlin, Heidelberg.

SUO WG (2008), *Standard Upper Ontology Working Group (SUO WG), IEEE P1600.1* [Online]. Available: http://suo.ieee.org/index.html [Accessed: 2008, December 28].

SW Activity (2008), *Semantic Web Activity Statement*, W3C [Online]. Available: http://www.w3.org/2001/sw/Activity [Accessed: 2008, December 23].

Swartout, W.R. & Tate, A. (1999), "Guest editors' introduction: Ontologies," *IEEE Intelligent Systems*, Vol. 14, no. 1, pp. 18–19.

Tallis, M., Goldman, N.M., & Balzer, R.M. (2002), "The Briefing Associate: easing authors into the Semantic Web," *IEEE Intelligent Systems*, Vol. 17, no. 1, pp. 26–32.

Uhl, A. & Ambler, S.W. (2003), "Point/Counterpoint," *IEEE Software*, Vol. 20, no. 5, pp. 70–73.

Ullrich, C. (2005), "The learning-resource-type is dead, long live the learning-resource-type!" *Learning Objects and Learning Designs*, Vol. 1, no. 1, pp. 7–15.

van der Vet, P.E. & Mars, N.J.I. (1998), "Bottom-up construction of ontologies," *IEEE Transactions on Knowledge and Data Engineering*, Vol. 10, no. 4, pp. 513–526.

Verbert, K. & Duval, E. (2004), "Towards a global architecture for learning objects: A comparative analysis of learning object content models," *In Proceedings of the 16th World ED-MEDIA 2004 Conference*, Lugano, Switzerland, pp. 202–209.

Verbert, K., Klerkx, J., Meire, M., Najjar, J., & Duval, E. (2004), "Towards a global component architecture for learning objects: An ontology based approach," *Proceedings of OTM 2004 Workshop on Ontologies, Semantics and E-learning*, Agia Napa, Cyprus, pp. 713–722.

Vianu, V. (1997), "Rule-based languages," *Annals of Mathematics and Artificial Intelligence*, Vol. 19, no. 1–2, pp. 215–259.

Vinoski, S. (2002), "Web services interaction models, part 1: Current practice," *IEEE Internet Computing*, Vol. 6, no. 3, pp. 90–92.

VoCamp (2008), [Online]. *VoCamp Main Page*. Available: http://vocamp.org/wiki/Main_Page [Accessed: 2008, December 28].

Wagner, G., Tabet, S., & Boley, H. (2003), "MOF-RuleML: the abstract syntax of RuleML as a MOF model, Integrate 2003," *OMG Meeting, Boston* [Online]. Available: http://www.omg.org/docs/br/03-10-02.pdf [Accessed: 2008, December 28].

Wang, H.H., Dong, J.S., Sun, J., & Sun, J. (2006), "Reasoning support for semantic web ontology family languages using alloy," *Multiagent and Grid Systems*, Vol. 2, 2006, pp. 455–471.

Welty, C.A. (1996), *An Integrated Representation for Software Development and Discovery*, Rensselaer Polytechnic Institute, New York.

Wiley, D.A. (2002), "Connecting learning objects to instructional design theory: A definition, a metaphor, and a taxonomy," in *The Instructional Use of Learning Objects*, ed. D.A. Wiley, Agency for Instructional Technology and Association for Educational Communications of Technology, Bloomington, IN, pp. 1–35.

Wimmer, M., Reiter,T., Kargl, H., Kramler, G., Kapsammer, E., Retschitzegger, W., Schwinger, W., & Kappel, G. (2006), "Lifting metamodels to ontologies – a step to the semantic integration of modeling languages," *Proceedings of the ACM/IEEE 9th International Conference on Model Driven Engineering Languages and Systems*, Genoa, Italy, pp. 528–542.

WordNet (2008), *WordNet, Princeton University* [Online]. Available: http://wordnet.princeton.edu/ [Accessed: 2008, December 28].

Wuwongse, V., Anutariya, C., Akama, K., & Nantajeewarawat, E. (2002), "XML declarative description: A language for the Semantic Web," *IEEE Intelligent Systems*, Vol. 17, no. 1, pp. 54–65.

XML (2005), *Extensible Markup Language (XML) 1.0, W3C*, 3rd edition [Online]. Available: http://www.w3.org/TR/2004/REC-xml-20040204/ [Accessed: 2008, December 28].

XML Schema (2008), XML Schema, W3C [Online]. Available: http://www.w3.org/XML/Schema [Accessed: 2008, December 28].

XP et al. (2002), *The XPetal Tool* [Online]. Available: http://www. langdale.com.au/styler/xpetal/ [Accessed: 2008, December 14].

Xtext (2008), *Textual Modeling Framework: Xtext* [Online]. Available: http://wiki. eclipse.org/Xtext [Accessed: 2008, December 15].

Zahniser, R.A. (1993), "Design by walking around," *Communications of The ACM*, Vol. 36, no. 10, pp. 115–123.

Zhong, N., Liu, J., & Yao, Y. (eds.) (2003), *Web Intelligence*, Springer, Berlin, Heidelrberg.

Zhu, H. & Madnick, S. (2006), *A Lightweight Ontology Approach to Scalable Interoperability*. Massachusetts Institute of Technology, Working Paper CISL# 2006-06 [Online]. Available: http://web.mit.edu/smadnick/www/ wp/2006-06.pdf [Accessed: 2008, December 20].

Index